Asian Perspectives on International Investment Law

T0298940

With changes to the international investment law landscape and Asian countries now actively developing their network of bilateral investment treaties (BITs) and free trade agreements (FTAs), this volume studies issues relating to Asian perspectives on international investment law and forecasts the future of Asian contribution to its science and practice.

The book discusses the major factors that have been driving Asian countries to new directions in international investment rule-making and dispute settlement. It also looks at whether Asian countries are crafting a new model of international investment law to reflect their specific socio-cultural values. Finally, the book examines whether there are any 'Asian' styles of international investment rule-making and dispute settlement, or if individual Asian countries are seeking specific national 'models' based on economic structure and geopolitical interests.

This unique collection is exceptionally useful to students, scholars and practitioners of international investment law, international trade law and public international law.

Junji Nakagawa is Professor of International Economic Law at the Institute of Social Science, University of Tokyo, Tokyo, Japan. His publications include *Nationalization, Natural Resources and International Investment Law: Contractual Relationship as a Dynamic Bargaining Process* (Routledge, 2017); *WTO: Beyond Trade Liberalization* (Iwanami Shoten, 2013, in Japanese); *Transparency in International Trade and Investment Dispute Settlement* (Routledge, 2013); *Multilateralism and Regionalism in Global Economic Governance* (Routledge, 2011); *International Harmonization of Economic Regulation* (Oxford University Press, 2011); *Anti-Dumping Laws and Practices of the New Users* (Cameron May, 2007); and *Managing Development: Globalization, Economic Restructuring and Social Policy* (Routledge, 2006).

Routledge Research in International Economic Law

International Investment Law
A Chinese Perspective
Guiguo Wang

Culture and International Economic Law
Edited by Valentina Vadi and Bruno de Witte

Defences in International Investment Law
Francis Botchway

WTO Trade Remedies in International Law
Roberto Soprano

Cohesion and Legitimacy in International Investment Law
Public International Law and Global Administrative Law Perspectives
Chisomo Kapulula

International Challenges in Investment Law and Arbitration
Edited by Mesut Akbaba and Giancarlo Capurro

State Interest and the Sources of International Law
Doctrine, Morality, and Non-Treaty Law
Markus P. Beham

Trade Facilitation in the Multilateral Trading System
Genesis, Course and Accord
Hao Wu

Asian Perspectives on International Investment Law
Edited by Junji Nakagawa

For more information about this series, please visit www.routledge.com/
Routledge-Research-in-International-Economic-Law/book-series/INTECON
LAW

Asian Perspectives on International Investment Law

Edited by Junji Nakagawa

Routledge
Taylor & Francis Group

LONDON AND NEW YORK

First published 2019
by Routledge
2 Park Square, Milton Park, Abingdon, Oxon OX14 4RN

and by Routledge
52 Vanderbilt Avenue, New York, NY 10017

First issued in paperback 2020

Routledge is an imprint of the Taylor & Francis Group, an informa business

British Library Cataloguing-in-Publication Data
A catalogue record for this book is available from the British Library

Library of Congress Cataloging-in-Publication Data
Names: Asian International Economic Law Network. Conference
    (5th : 2017 : Xiamen da xue) | Nakagawa, Junji, 1955– editor.
Title: Asian perspectives on international investment law/edited by
    Junji Nakagawa.
Description: Abingdon, Oxon ; New York, NY : Routledge, 2019. |
    Series: Routledge research in international economic law | Includes
    bibliographical references and index.
Identifiers: LCCN 2018056218 | ISBN 9781138330535 (hardback) |
    ISBN 9780429447822 (ebook)
Subjects: LCSH: Investments, Foreign—Law and legislation—East
    Asia—Congresses.
Classification: LCC KNC747.A83 2017 | DDC 346.5/092—dc23
LC record available at https://lccn.loc.gov/2018056218

ISBN 13: 978-0-367-67111-2 (pbk)
ISBN 13: 978-1-138-33053-5 (hbk)

Typeset in Galliard
by Apex CoVantage, LLC

Contents

Figures

Tables

Contributors

Alejandro García Jiménez is a PhD Student at University of International Business and Economics (UIBE), Beijing, China.

Soo-Hyun Lee is Research Associate at The Asian Institute for Policy Studies, Seoul, Korea.

Céline Lévesque is Dean of the Faculty of Law – Civil Law Division, University of Ottawa.

Junji Nakagawa is Professor of International Economic Law at the Institute of Social Science, The University of Tokyo.

Fulvio Maria Palombino is Professor of International Trade Law at the University of Naples Federico II.

Relja Radović is Doctoral Researcher at the Faculty of Law, Economy and Finance, University of Luxembourg.

G. Matteo Vaccaro-Incisa is Assistant Professor of International Law at Institut d'Économie Scientifique et de Gestion (IESEG) School of Management, Paris, France.

Wei Yin is Lecturer at Southwest University of Political Science and Law and Research Fellow of China-ASEAN Legal Research Centre.

Giovanni Zarra is Adjunct Professor of Private International Law and International Litigation at the University of Naples Federico II.

Tianshu Zhang is Associate at Zhong Lung Law Firm, Beijing, China.

Zheng Lizhen is Associate Professor of International Law at the law school of Fujian Normal University.

Preface

The essays in this volume arouse out of the 5th biennial Conference of the Asian International Economic Law Network (AIELN), or AIELN V, held in Xiamen, China, on 16 and 17 July 2017. The conference featured the same theme of the title of this volume, presented by over 20 speakers and ensuing discussions. All of the contributors to this volume attended AIELN V and read his/her paper. The chapters are revised and updated versions of those papers.

I wish to acknowledge first the contribution of all the speakers and attendants at AIELN V for their enthusiasm and their role in ensuring the success of the conference. I also acknowledge the Chinese Society of International Economic Law (CSIEL) and the Institute of International Economic Law (IIEL), Xiamen University, for sponsoring and hosting the conference. Please let me mention the following members and staffs of the CSIEL and IIEL for their generous support: Professor Zeng Huaqun, Professor Chen Huiping, Professor Li Guoan, Professor Zhang Binxin, Professor Yang Fan, Professor Su Yu and Ms. Xiao Bin. Third, I wish to acknowledge the following members of the AIELN Steering Committee for their endorsement and support to the conference: Professor Heng Wang, Professor Bryan Mercurio and Professor Douglas Arner. Last, but not least, I wish to acknowledge our editors, Ms. Yongling Lam and Ms. Samantha Phua of Routledge, for their patience and encouragement, as always.

January 2019 in Tokyo
Junji Nakagawa

1 Introduction

Junji Nakagawa

International investment law has long been dominated by capital exporting countries in Western Europe and North America. The classic formulation of international minimum standard of the treatment of aliens and the right of diplomatic protection appeared in the late 19th century and the early 20th century in the context of protecting Western European and North American investments in Latin America through arbitral awards of claims commissions.[1] After WWII, Western Europe took the lead in concluding bilateral investment treaties (BITs) with capital importing countries. Later, the U.S. and Canada set the precedent of model investment treaties, based on the NAFTA investment chapter. This was also a precedent of including investment chapters in free trade agreements (FTAs). Western Europe and North America have also been active players in investor-state dispute settlement (ISDS).

In contrast, Asia has largely been rule-takers in international investment law. Although the first BIT was concluded by Pakistan, and the first BIT-based arbitration took place between a Hong Kong company and Sri Lanka,[2] many countries in Asia have not been active in concluding BITs and FTAs with investment chapters. Asian countries have also kept a low profile in ISDS, as both claimants and respondents.

The geography of international investment law has, however, started to change during the past decade, and Asian countries have come to actively develop their network of BITs and FTAs with investment chapters, with China, Republic of Korea (hereinafter "Korea") and India being the most active.[3] More recently, Asia has been actively engaged in the regional rule-making in international investment law. The ASEAN Comprehensive Investment Agreement, the China-Japan-Korea Trilateral Investment Agreement and the investment chapter of the Trans-Pacific Partnership (TPP) are notable examples. Finally, there is a sign that Asian countries will actively participate in ISDS. This is a logical outcome of the increasing economic importance of Asia in global investment market.[4]

The changing landscape of international investment law in Asia raises a number of questions to be seriously dealt with. What were the major factors that drove Asian countries to these new directions in international investment rule-making and dispute settlement? Are Asian countries merely taking rules from Western Europe and North America? Or, are they crafting a new model(s) of international investment law, reflecting their specific socio-cultural values? Are there any 'Asian' style of international investment rule-making and dispute settlement? Or, are individual Asian countries seeking their specific national 'models', depending on their economic structure and geopolitical interests?

The contributions in this volume tackle these and other questions on Asian perspectives on international investment law. Nine contributions in this volume may be categorized into the following three groups. The first group deals with the Asian approach to international investment law in general. The second group deals with specific provisions of international investment agreements concluded by Asian countries. And the third group deals with specific and institutional issues relating to investor-state dispute settlement in Asia.

Wei Yin's contribution reviews China's approach towards international investment agreements (IIAs). She starts with the assumption that Asian economies would like to embed their values into international investment law. She argues that China's dual identity as both a capital exporting and capital importing country is likely to affect China's stance toward IIAs. So as to verify the above assumption, Wei Yin tries to answer the following two questions on China's stance toward IIAs, namely, what is China's current stance toward IIAs? And what are the major factors to be considered in China's future investment policy?

Wei Yin traces the evolution of China's IIAs practice, which was initiated in 1982 with Sweden. Most IIAs signed in the 1980s and 1990s were characterized by a restrictive approach toward substantive protection and limited access to investor-state dispute settlement. On the other hand, recently concluded IIAs of China suggest that China intends to get its overseas investment protected while affording increased level of protection for foreign investors but nonetheless remaining sufficient regulatory space for public policy. However, Wei Yin argues, these recent IIAs of China do not fully reflect China's interests, in particular those under the One Belt One Road Initiative (BRI). It is, therefore, high time for China to negotiate new BITs with some BRI countries, with proper and sufficient treaty protection provisions. At the same time, China's outward foreign direct investment (FDI) is facing an unprecedented level of political backlash especially in developed countries. The most controversial issue is the political dimension associated with Chinese investors, state-owned enterprises (SOEs) in particular, and the state capitalism of China. This issue is likely to be dealt with in the BITs that China is negotiating with the U.S. and the EU. Wei Yin concludes that China will, in this process, walk a fine line between mitigating concerns of its investment and maintaining an open and non-discriminatory investment climate to Chinese investors and strike a balance between maintaining the legitimate right to regulate and offering protection for foreign investors.

In his contribution, Alenandro García Jiménez analyzes the trend of investment related dispute settlement between Far East Asia and Latin America. He starts with the analysis of the patterns of Far East Asian investments (China, Japan and Korea) in Latin America. Chinese investments into Latin America are largely directed towards mining, agriculture and electricity sectors, but Chinese investments in the field of infrastructure will increase substantially in the years to come.

Japanese investments in Latin America were also initially motivated by the acquisition of natural resources. However, nowadays, Japanese FDI is characterized by being diversified among manufacturing, extractive and services sectors. The majority of the investments from Korea in Latin America are directed towards the manufacturing industry.

Alejandro García Jiménez then analyzes the settlement of investment disputes between Far East Asia and Latin American countries. First, he traces the ratification of ICSID Convention by Japan, China and Korea, where Japan was the first to sign it in 23 September 1965 without any reservation to the application of the treaty. Korea followed in 18 April 1966, and China finally signed it on 9 February 1990. Of these three countries, China initially took a much restrictive approach, and it would only consider submitting to ICSID jurisdiction disputes over compensation resulting from expropriation and nationalization. However, China increases the scope of arbitrable disputes through a number of bilateral and regional treaties with different degrees of liberalization commitments. He then traces the case record of these three countries under the ICSID Convention and found that there is only one case that China has raised a claim against a Latin American country.[5]

Finally, Alejandro García Jiménez observes that the three Far Eastern Asian countries have developed mechanisms for the facilitation of investments and the avoidance of disputes. The origin for these non-litigation mechanisms could be found in the Confucian tradition, but in fact similar proposals have emerged in countries that do not share this cultural heritage, such as Brazil. Brazil is negotiating a peculiar kind of international agreement in the field of investments, the Agreement for Cooperation and Facilitation of Investments (ACFIs).

Relja Radović analyzes the reactions of Asian countries against investor-state dispute settlement mainly through the provisions of their BITs and investment chapters in their FTAs. He argues that, while the idea of sovereignty is often used in arguments against extensive international scrutiny, and while this idea is indeed embedded in the actions of several countries in Asia in their treaty practices, the advocated changes cannot properly affect the targeted arbitral practice.

He starts his analysis by tracing the treaty practices of Asian countries in investment and concludes that Asia is becoming a leading region in regard to the number of concluded BITs, primarily because of China, but also Korean and Indian practices. He then reviews the expansion of investor-state dispute settlement (ISDS) cases in Asia, where Indonesia faced some 10 arbitrations and India possibly more than 20. Countries which have faced challenges in their practice have developed animosities against ISDS being easily accessible to foreign investors, and some of them changed their BIT policy to reclaim the gateway issues back to the national level. He takes up three examples.

The first example is the mandatory requirements to resort to and/or exhaust domestic remedies in, for instance, the 2015 model BIT of India. The second example is the requirement of state consent that is prevalent in the treaty practice of Southeast Asian countries. For instance, Indonesia has been reported to aim to reassert the control over state consent to international arbitration with foreign investors and that it considered requiring special governmental consent to each arbitration in its future arrangements. The third example appears in the context of tackling the problem of parallel proceedings, and the preference for fork-in-the-road clauses can be noticed in intra-Asian treaties over those requiring investors to waive and/or withdraw claims from domestic proceedings.

Relja Radović argues that these changes indicate that sovereignism continues to instruct these Asian countries. And the state sovereignism appears highly reactionary, aiming to limit the possibilities for adjudicating investment claims, after experiencing the negative consequences of such claims under the current regime of investor protection. He then poses the question whether countries are indeed capable of thus limiting access to investment arbitration by virtue of the principle that it all starts and ends with state consent. He answers to this question negatively because they do not acknowledge the development of arbitrator-made jurisdictional rules which can tackle the hard conditions of access to investment arbitration.

In her contribution, Céline Lévesque explores the conditions that would entice Asian capital exporting countries, notably China, Japan, South Korea and Singapore, to embrace the idea of a Multilateral Investment Court, which has been promoted by the EU and Canada. In her analysis, she focuses on the political and practical feasibility of a new, stand-alone court. In order to assess feasibility, she focuses on the design of such court, looking into issues of representation and size, the selection criteria of judges and their status and terms, case-assignment and administrative support and cost sharing.

On representation, she argues, full representation (or one treaty party = one judge) is in all likeliness not workable. This arises the question of how much representativeness would be needed for a Multilateral Investment Court. She surveys other international courts, as they provide models in this regard, trying to balance merit choices with regional, legal and diversity representation. The expected caseload of the court should also have an impact on its size.

A key challenge for a Multilateral Investment Court is the need to limit the scope for the politicization of the nomination and selection process of judges. Céline Lévesque observes that general trend in this matter is that emphasis is being placed more on the goal of selecting independent and highly qualified judges than on the authority of states. She argues that more transparency and the use of screening and selection bodies can contribute to achieving independence and impartiality. Judges' tenure also has an impact on independence and impartiality. She suggests that longer, non-renewable terms would be in the interest of Asian capital exporting countries.

Céline Lévesque concludes her analysis by asking whether Asian capital exporting countries are willing to agree to a Multilateral Investment Court where they may not have a judge. Are we there yet?

The following three chapters deal with specific provisions of international investment agreements concluded by Asian countries. Zheng Lizhen analyzes provisions on protection of labour rights in international investment agreements that involve Asian countries. This chapter first surveys different types of labour standards in IIAs. The first type is the linkage mode adopted by IIAs of Japan, Austria and Belgium-Luxembourg Economic Union (BLEU). They are classified into the same group in that (1) they contain not-lowering requirements and (2) investor-state dispute settlement, state-to-state arbitration and economic sanction to disputes of labour standards are integrated with that of investment. The second type is the linkage mode adopted by New Zealand and European Free Trade Area (EFTA). The linkage practices exist under the framework of FTAs rather than BITs, and most of their labour provisions are applied to both trade and investment. They are unique because of their similar emphasis on effective enforcement of domestic labour laws, capacity building and consultations as the only resort of investment-relevant labour disputes. The third type is the linkage mode of the U.S. and Canada. They are unique because of more detailed obligation of effective domestic enforcement, unique complaint mechanism, state-to-state arbitration and economic sanction. The fourth type is the linkage mode of the EU, which is unique in (1) the high relevance of ILO instruments for effective domestic enforcement, (2) obligations of CSR (corporate social responsibility) promotion and (3) the supervision mechanism of joint social dialogue forum and state-to-state arbitration and the exclusion of economic sanction for non-compliance of the award.

Based on these classifications of linkage practices of IIAs, Zheng Lizhen then traces the evolution of linkage practices of Asian IIAs. She argues that the linkage practices of Asian IIAs have their roots in that of Multilateral Agreement on Investment (MAI) from 1995 to 1998. Four factors in current IIAs are borrowed directly from MAI, namely, (1) the aim of sustainable development in the preamble, (2) the reference to ILO instrument, (3) the not-lowering requirement and (4) the right of labour regulation. On the other hand, *Zheng Lizhen* observes, two factors of the MAI are missing during the evolution, namely, (1) the reaffirmation of ILO as the only competent authorities in developing investment-relevant labour standards and (2) the obligation of promoting investors to comply with the OECD Guidelines for Multinational Enterprises. At the same time, several new elements were added, including the obligation of effective enforcement of labour laws and arbitration for investment-relevant labour standard disputes. She concludes that legalization of investment labour standard linkage is much elevated in Asian IIAs compared with that of MAI.

Zheng Lizhen then anticipates the development of normative elements of linkage practices of Asian IIAs as part of the global linkage practices, but she also anticipates that the linkage practices of Asian IIAs will possibly show unique features in the process of evolution. One possible feature will be the tendency to strengthen labour standards in Asian IIAs, because of the relatively poor record of ratifying ILO instruments in Asia. The detailed obligations of the labour chapter of the TPP are a case in point. She anticipates that dilemma between sovereign right of labour regulation and cooperation for fair competition and protection of basic workers' right will be more obvious. Also, she anticipates that it is possible for developing Asian countries to exclude as much as possible public submission and joint social dialogue mechanism. Finally, she anticipates that the four existing types of linkage practices will continue to compete with each other in the negotiation of labour standard in Free Trade Area of the Asia Pacific (FTAAP).

In his contribution, Soo-Hyun Lee examines risks in the application of international investment law and ISDS in connection to newly industrialized countries with conglomerate-led economies in East Asia. Building off lessons from Korea and Japan, he takes up two prominent risk factors, corporate governance and state intervention, and examines how they can conflict with the standard of fair and equitable treatment (FET) in IIAs.

Soo-Hyun Lee addresses owner risk in South Korean conglomerates, focusing on nepotistic hiring and promotion. He then addresses the recent development in Korea where a conglomerate acted on behalf of the State for matters related to the public interest (national security) that resulted in material injury. Depending on the interpretation of full protection and security, he argues, one basis on which a foreign investor may seek compensation for a loss of assets can be a lack of due diligence on the part of the Korean government to protect foreign investors and their investments.

He then takes up the case of the attempted sale of the Toshiba Memory Corporation (TMC) and the subsequent legal dispute with Western Digital in Japan. The involvement of the Japanese government, he argues, through the state-backed consortium may be sufficient grounds to raise issues within the scope of international investment law, notably the standard of fair and equitable treatment.

Finally, Soo-hyun Lee discusses ways to mitigate these risk factors that he identified in his contribution. First of all, he argues, empowering civil society to ensure that public and private sector actors are accountable for their actions can be an effective measure in mitigating associated risks. Second, greater materiality should be placed on political risk and its potential impacts on treaty obligation related to investment. Specifically, he argues, Korea should set out clear guidelines in the instance of loss or damage to foreign assets resulting from any manner of North Korean provocation. Korea should also re-examine the text of its BITs to provide more specific guidelines on measuring for proportionality in exercising general regulatory measures for national security.

G. Matteo Vaccaro-Incisa analyzes the evolution of Chinese investment treaty policy and practice, focusing on the objective criteria and *ratione legis* (or legality requirement) condition in the definition of investment. After briefly tracing the development of the Chinese BIT program since its start in 1982, he then outlines the definition of investment in general in Chinese BIT program and found that the definition of investment remains an instance of overall uniformity through Chinese investment treaty practice.

He then focuses on the Chinese investment treaty practice on the objective criteria of investment. He observes that Chinese model investment treaties and almost all actual treaties do not list objective criteria to qualify the notion of investment. However, in connection with the process of updating its investment treaty network by renegotiating BITs, the definition of investment has progressively been articulated in greater detail, and its 2008 BIT with Columbia included the objective criteria of investment for the first time, followed by several BITs concluded thereafter. He explains this change comes from three factors, namely, (1) China's shift from a predominantly recipient country to a capital exporting country, (2) China modulates its growing economic power by emulating U.S. standards in the same field and (3) the presence of the objective criteria may contribute to settle jurisdictional debate on the definition of investment.

G. Matteo Vaccaro-Incisa then analyzes the *ratione legis* condition in Chinese investment treaty practice and found that the vast majority of Chinese investment treaties adopt this condition. By including the *ratione legis* requirement, he observes, states seems to establish a ground for an objection on admissibility of investment. Such a reading of the requirement is significant for China, as it still operates a systematic case-by-case admission screening on each foreign investment.

He observes that alterations to the Chinese template are taken in light of the concrete necessities of China, at home and abroad, without policy overturns. China's current BIT negotiations with the U.S. and the EU, if ever concluded, are expected to achieve a relatively uniform result on the definition of investment, which may in turn set the international standard in international investment law well beyond the two key issues analyzed.

In their coauthored contribution, Fulvio Maria Palombino and Giovanni Zarra analyze whether an Asian concept of due process has developed within the framework of the ASEAN member states' obligation to grant fair and equitable treatment (FET) to foreign investments. Their focus is on Article 11 of the ASEAN Comprehensive Investment Agreement (ACIA), which states that "each Member State shall accord to covered investments of investors of any other Member State fair and equitable treatment" (para.1), and, for greater certainty, pinpoints that this standard "requires each Member State not to deny justice in any legal or administrative proceedings in accordance with the principle of due process".

They find this provision quite innovative. First, it seems to entirely exclude that the FET may involve the violation of legitimate expectations or of proportionality. Second, it does not identify the content of the FET either by reference to the customary international law minimum standard or by relying on the generally accepted rules of international law. Then, they pose a question to what extent the ACIA's standard of due process may be considered as isolated from existing investment case law relating to the principle of due process.

They first argue for the relevance of arbitral case law on non-ASEAN tribunals in the interpretation of the ACIA, as its Article 40 sets forth the applicable rules of international law as among the applicable law of the investor-state arbitration. They argue that arbitral tribunals applying sources of general international law may not simply ignore the existing case law concerning such sources, and the standard of FET is no exception.

They argue that due process is a general principle of international law which arbitrators, including those acting in the ACIA framework, shall take into consideration. They then explore the content of due process. The first element of due process is denial of justice, or judicial misapplication of national law which proves manifestly unjust, and it should be distinguished from denial of law. The second element of due process is the procedural fairness in administrative proceedings. However, in light of the diversity of this element in host states, the arbitration case law provides that it must be established that (1) the host state's legal order is required to provide for the principle and (2) the denial of this principle must be able to cause a serious economic loss to the investment.

They conclude that the principle of due process has been shaped by arbitral tribunals according to the features typical of international investment law. Due process is contextual, and as such, its content depends on the normative field, rather than on national legal order where it is supposed to operate. Accordingly, they conclude that an Asian approach to due process may not exist nor is it desirable as a matter of principle.

In her contribution, Tianshu Zhang analyzes the role of a non-disputing contracting party (NDCP)'s expression of intention in investment arbitration. It is especially important in an investment dispute where the provision of that treaty appear ambiguous and other evidence fall short of clarifying the contracting parties' common intention. She takes up the case of *Sanum v. Laos*, where China, as the NDCP of the case, expressed its opinion on the territorial application of the PRC-Laos BIT through diplomatic letters and subsequent statements.

On 30 September 2016, the Singapore Court of Appeal (CA) reversed the judgement of the Singapore High Court (HC), upholding the Award on Jurisdiction delivered by an UNCITRAL tribunal on 13 December 2013 (the 2013 Award) that the PRC-Laos BIT applied to Macao. While the case was pending at Singapore courts, China and Laos exchanged letters (the 2014 Letters), stating that, in line with the "one country, two systems" policy and the Basic Law of Macao, the Chinese BITs do not automatically apply to Macao, unless the Chinese government decides so after consulting with the Macao Special Administrative Region. Tianshu Zhang analyzes the approaches taken by the tribunal and the two Singaporean courts on China's position of the PRC-Laos BIT's territorial application.

Lacking evidence indicating the contracting parties' intention, the tribunal found that the general rule of moving treaty frontiers (MTF) applied. However, with the 2014 Letters at hand, the HC concluded that the China's statements constitute a subsequent agreement between the contracting parties of the BIT, which confirmed the non-application of the BIT to Macao. On the other hand, the CA accepted that the BIT automatically extends to Macao and provided that the 2014 Letters contradicted the pre-existing position presented by other evidence and therefore cannot constitute a subsequent agreement with retroactive effect.

Tianshu Zhang concludes that, first, for a BIT being applied in a way not departing from the intention of the contracting parties at the time of concluding it, timing is crucial for an NDCP to react. She argues that even after the dispute has been decided by the tribunal, the opportunities are still open to the NDCP to respond to the findings of the award. Such reactions may not retroactively affect the concluded adjudications but will provide guidance for future cases. Second, the tribunal and the national courts should adopt the admissibility standard to allow all evidence that has been put forward should be assessed in consideration of all circumstances. Third, China learned a lesson from the Singaporean courts' judgements that it is important to take measures, such as clear statements, on important issues such as the territorial application of a BIT.

Notes

1 For the history of international investment law, see Dolzer and Schreuer (2012: 2–4). Also see Schill (2015).
2 See *Asian Agricultural Products Ltd. v. Republic of Sri Lanka*, ICSID Case No. ARB/87/3. Final Award, 27 June 1990.
3 As of August 2018, China has concluded 127 BITs and 22 treaties with investment provisions (TIPs). Korea has concluded 94 BITs and 20 TIPs. India has concluded 61 BITs and 13 TIPs. See UNCTAD, International Investment Agreements Navigator. [http://investmentpolicyhub.unctad.org/IIA] Also see the estimate of G. Matteo Vaccaro-Incisa in this book on China's IIAs. *Infra* p. 168.
4 See UNCTAD (2015: 5). (Note that "MNEs from developing Asia became the world's largest investing group, accounting to almost one third of the total".)
5 See *Tza Yap Shum v. The Republic of Peru*. ICSID No.ARB/07/6. Award 7 July 2011. Decision on Annulment 12 February 2015.

References

Dolzer, R. and Schreuer, Ch. (2012). *Principles of International Investment Law*, 2nd edn, Oxford: Oxford University Press.
Schill, S. W. (2015). Special Issue: Dawn of an Asian Century in International Investment Law? An Introduction. *The Journal of World Investment & Trade*, 16(5–6), 765–771.
UNCTAD (2015). *World Investment Report 2015: Reforming International Investment Governance*, Geneva: UNCTAD.

2 China's approach towards investment agreements and its interests involved in international investment rule making

Wei Yin

Introduction

During the past decade, the international investment law regime shaped by the 'North' experienced several changes along with the active engagement of the 'South', in the process of global investment policy making. Asian actors have increasingly become an important source of capital exporting. Various international investment agreements (IIAs) negotiated and/or concluded by Asian actors, and their increasing involvement in investment treaty arbitration, indicate a shift in the geography of international investment law, which is also reflected in China's evolving approach to IIAs. To protect their overseas investments and investors, to translate their economic importance into rule-making power, Asian economies would like to embed their values into the international investment law. It seems likely that the involvement of the Asia may reform the current IIAs regime or provide new investment law models, among which China is and will continue being an important player.

Since China has become a net capital exporter, its overseas investment, especially investment in relation to its 'Belt and Road' initiative (BRI), brings about opportunities and challenges worldwide. The dual identity of China, as both capital-exporting and importing country, is likely to affect China's stance toward IIAs. This chapter, thus, aims to explore two relevant questions, i.e. what is China's current stance towards IIAs? And what are the major factors to be considered in China's future investment treaty? To answer these questions, this chapter first discusses the role of China as an important emerging economy and the implications of Chinese overseas investment. Second, it examines its recently concluded treaties to illustrate its changing view towards investment protection. It then analyses the interests that China would like to reflect in its model IIAs, with a discussion on concerns from other major host countries, e.g. issues of state-owned enterprises (SOEs), market access and dispute resolution. Finally, it proposes suggestions regarding China's position in its on-going and future treaty negotiations.

1. The role of China's outward investment and relevant implications

With the growth of China's outward foreign investment,[1] China has emerged as a leading investor in many countries. In 2015, China even overtook Germany and became the net capital exporter. The country's foreign direct investment (FDI) outflows grew from very low during the 1990s to $7bn in 2001 (UNCTAD, 2003), and then to $123bn in 2014 and $128bn in 2015 (UNCTAD, 2016). As a result, China remains one of the largest investors worldwide. Previously, the lion's share of Chinese outward FDI was destined to Asia (Hong Kong was the most popular region that attracted large part of outward Chinese FDI), and North America was the second most popular destination for Chinese FDI outflows, the United States in particular (UNCTAD, 2003). In recent years, especially after the 2008 financial crisis, among developed countries, Europe has been the fastest growing destination rather than North America in attracting a large amount of Chinese investment (Ma and Overbeek, 2015: 442). According to the Ministry of Commerce of China (MOFCOM), in 2016, Chinese direct non-financial investment reached $170.11bn over 164 countries and regions (MOFCOM, 2017a). China has invested substantially in both developing and developed economies with diversified sectorial distribution. But it seems to be likely that natural resources, manufacturing and services sectors are the most attractive target industry for Chinese investment, especially made by Chinese state-owned investors while the mergers and acquisitions (M&As) began to stand out to support structural adjustment.[2]

The growth of China's FDI outflow can be attributed to a mix of internal economic incentives and external policy support. Although 'market seeking' is invariably a major motive, other motivations or incentives stand out in different industries and in different recipient economies. 'Resource seeking' can be regarded as an important motivation for Chinese firms, especially state-owned enterprises (SOEs),[3] since China has high demand for natural resources (Sauvant and Nolan, 2015: 894). Many multinational enterprises (MNEs), motivated by 'strategic asset seeking' through cross-border M&As, tend to increase their competitiveness, such as controlling or acquiring technological resources, advanced management and widely recognised brands (Zheng et al., 2016). Trade related FDI is also a common motivation, e.g. firms in service sectors investing abroad to facilitate export activities (Amighini et al., 2013: 324) or firms using investment as a means of accessing foreign markets to avoid trading restrictions (Gippner and Torney, 2017: 656). Apart from other motivations from the internal economic perspective, however, there are external policy incentives that support the outward Chinese FDI. These policies vary from financing subsidies to professional services and preferential regulatory treatment.[4] The BRI with China's early-launched 'go global' policy has generated a new round of Chinese outward FDI along BRI countries. Supported by the BRI, the establishment of Asian Infrastructure Investment Bank (AIIB) and Silk Road Fund help China to diversify its investment in emerging economies and developing countries instead of investing only in developed countries. The Chinese outward FDI in countries along the 'Belt and Road Initiative' accounts for $14.82bn in 2015, up 18.2% year on year (MOFCOM, 2016), and $14.53bn in 2016 (MOFCOM, 2017a). Spurred by these government policies, Chinese enterprises, large and small, private and state-owned, are embarking overseas expansion.

However, following a record spending spree in 2016, the pace of outbound investments slowed markedly after government agencies and the People's Bank of China (PBOC) warned in December 2016 that they would closely monitor 'irrational' overseas investments in foreign real estate, hotels, cinemas, entertainment and sports clubs. The curbs coincided with tighter capital controls, prompted by the fear of financial risks and the declining foreign exchanges reserves (i.e. the weakened currency). This move resulted in a 44.3% decline in non-financial investment in the first 7 months of 2017.[5] Despite the deep decline, Chinese investors invested in more than 4411 overseas companies in 148 countries in January–July 2017 (MOFCOM, 2017b).

China's official guidelines on outbound direct investments were jointly issued by Chinese authorities, including the National Development and Reform Commission (NDRC), MOFCOM and the PBOC and approved by the State Council, China. It not only reflects concerns about capital outflows and possible money laundering at the start of 2017, but also helps formalise and clarify the regulatory steps to seek approval for direct investments overseas. Under the guidelines, outbound investments are classified into three categories: prohibited, restricted and encouraged transactions, which could be regarded as a 'encourage pattern' with 'negative list' for overseas investment.[6] It suggests that Chinese government is trying to redirect capital into companies or industries that further national policy goals since the guidelines outlaw investment in irrational and unauthentic transactions but back and promote outbound investments alight with the BRI. The regulators are expected to establish investment blacklists to track and punish investors that violate the regulations. Nevertheless, it should be noticed that these curbs and regulations do not mean that China would set its overseas investment back but mean that Chinese authorities increasingly pay more attention to the quality of its overseas investment and encourage capital flows into sectors that can help boost long-term growth potential.

It should be emphasised that, apart from being the largest host country among developing countries, China is also an important home country of FDI among all emerging markets and a net outward investor. Profound changes are taking place in domestic and international market, which means that Chinese investors face not just relatively good opportunities but also various risks and challenges. One likely implication of this is that the government's interest in protecting its outward investment and facilitating market access for its investors would be further enhanced. The dual identity of China, in turn, most likely would determine or influence China's stance toward IIAs. It is instructive to consider China's interest as home country and host country of FDI when negotiating or concluding IIAs. Currently, China has signed more BITs than any other countries except Germany.[7] This large IIAs network (including BITs or treaties with investment provisions) is supposed to provide safeguards for Chinese overseas investment. However, a majority of existing IIAs are out of date, which were concluded to attract inward FDI but did not reflect the interest of China as a leading capital exporter. But most recently concluded IIAs suggest China's effort to strike a balance between the interests of investment protection and the right to regulate, reflecting China's willingness to actively integrate into global economy and to open up its market.[8] But concerns caused by the expansion and the nature of Chinese investment (which will be discussed in Section 3) still remain to be addressed in on-going and further treaty negotiations.

2. Emerging changes in China's newly concluded IIAs

2.1. *China's early IIAs practice*

China's IIAs practice, which was initiated in 1982 with Sweden,[9] has had a significant shift in focus during the past decade, and more recently, many free trade agreements (FTAs) contain investment chapters. Most BITs were signed before 21st century, especially in 1980s and 1990s, when China urgently intended to attract foreign investment, with a restrictive approach toward substantive protection and limited access to investor-state dispute settlement (ISDS). Even though China has several Model BITs, compared with those BIT models in other countries e.g. the US, in some cases, concluded treaties do not reflect the terms of its Model BIT. China adopts a pragmatic and flexible approach towards IIAs model preferred by the negotiation partner as to what terms would be incorporated in the BIT (Gallagher, 2016: 93). Model BIT, China does not look significantly different from those of many other countries, especially EU member countries. China's early IIAs are mainly 'European style' and adopt a more conservative stance, while a few recent IIAs suggest a gradual shift to 'American style' that is influenced by the Model BIT, US (e.g. China-Canada BIT).[10]

It is suggested that China has experienced three generation of IIAs, and the on-going treaty negotiation with major economies (e.g. the US and the EU) will be its new generation of IIAs,[11] although the current ones have not yet caught up with its treaty practice (e.g. the China-Canada BIT, the China-Korea FTA and the China-Australia FTA). The shift of China's treaty-making policy during different periods is mainly dominated by the demand of its domestic economic development and the role of China in global market. These shifts reflect China's willingness to grant stronger substantive and procedural protection for FDI and foreign investors. Before the conclusion of China's first BIT, China was reluctant in restricting its sovereignty over the entry of FDI to be impinged by international arbitration. With the gradual opening up of Chinese economy, China started to provide access to international arbitration and certain substantial protection, but several reservations remained. In most BITs entered during this period, China offered foreign investors limited access to arbitration by ad hoc tribunals under the UNCITRAL Arbitration Rules and to ICSID over the amount of compensation for expropriation and nationalisation (after China signed the ICSID Convention),[12] since

China was predominantly a capital-importing country. Starting with the BIT signed between China and Barbados in 1998,[13] China considerably broadened its consent to international arbitration for disputes with foreign investors under the rules of ICSID or UNCITRAL.[14] During this period, China embraced strong absolute and relative standards of investment treatment,[15] and comprehensive ISDS mechanism in its BITs.[16] Despite China's open attitude towards investment treaty arbitration, only few disputes arise under China's IIAs.[17] But being consistent with China's status as capital-exporting country, it is likely that China may fully embrace the ISDS arbitration (the revised one) in the future.

2.2. *The emerging features of China's IIAs practice*

Since China, as the world's second largest economic entity, has become an important capital exporter with its increasing outward investment and further promotion of BRI, so too has its resolve to protect Chinese interests overseas. The recently concluded IIAs suggest that China adopts a more liberal attitude towards IIAs and is trying to promote investment liberalisation and facilitation at international level. Moreover, China is taking a seemingly more positive and careful approach to treaty protection (ISDS and substantive protection). These newer treaties seem to reflect an increasingly important position advocated by many countries i.e. striking a balance between the interest of investor and host countries.[18] China intends to protect its overseas investment while affording increased levels of protection for foreign investors that nonetheless remains a sufficient regulatory space for public policy/interests. To ensure the right to regulate and to reduce the flexibility of tribunals to review the necessity of the measures in questions, the newer IIAs clarify the scope of treatment provision and the key concept and provide a slightly reformed dispute resolution clause.

These IIAs that China recently entered into provide a finite definition of 'investor' and asset-based definition of 'investment' by which China could effectively deny foreign investors and investments to the benefit of investment treaty protection when certain requirements are not satisfied[19]; the inclusion of the most-favoured nation (MFN) treatment to pre-establishment phase[20]; and exclusion of MFN applicable to dispute resolution procedures[21]; the introduction of a "national treatment, post-establishment" in like circumstances[22]; with statements to negotiate IIAs with specific countries on the basis of "national treatment, pre-establishment"[23]; the clarification that fair and equitable treatment (FET) is not additive to customary international law or generally accepted rules of international law[24]; the clarification of the concept of 'expropriation, indirect'[25]; the inclusion of an amicable consultation as a precondition for arbitration[26]; and a choice among local remedies, ICSID rules and UNCITRAL Rules toward dispute settlement[27]; and the reformed substantive requirements for ISDS arbitration, etc.[28] Another notable shift would be that China has begun to attach importance to the sustainable development in IIAs.[29]

These IIAs concluded by China are longer and include more details than China's earlier BITs. A brief review of recent treaties, especially the China-Canada

BIT and investment provisions in the China-Australia FTA, suggests that China is willing to negotiate and embrace IIAs with higher standards and more detailed and emerging dispute settlement provisions. It is likely that this trend will be reflected in the negotiation and future text of the China-EU BIT and China-US BIT. These treaty negotiations with the EU and the US are not only important for China but also very significant globally, as it is likely to set a symbol for global investment treaty making (Shan and Wang, 2015: 267). However, those newly signed treaties do not clearly address issues caused by the expansion of Chinese outward FDI, especially by state-backed investors, and have not embedded certain important China's interests, in particular under the BRI. It can be assumed that China would expect these issues to be addressed in the on-going and future treaty negotiations.

3. China's interests in IIAs and relevant controversial issues

It was suggested that China's new generation of IIAs should find a right balance between conflicting interests as a capital-exporting and capital-importing country, and between the interests of investment protection and the regulatory sovereignty, and China should also incorporate a reformed and improved dispute settlement mechanism.[30] However, on one hand, China's interests has not been fully reflected in current in force IIAs, and on the other hand, the stepped-up China's outward FDI is facing a 'unprecedented' level of political backlash, even regulatory concerns,[31] especially in developed countries, e.g. the US, Australia, Germany (Mitchell et al., 2017; Chazn, 2017; Miller, 2016; Bradsher and Mozur, 2016). Chinese investment in developing countries is usually accused of political motivations or even lack of corporate social responsibility considerations, e.g. environmental protection. The fear from advanced economies is partly attributed to the speed and scale of Chinese overseas expansion; the leading role of SOEs in outward FDI; the investment (particularly M&A) made in industries of political, economic and strategic importance in recipient countries.

The most controversial issue surrounds is the political dimension associated with Chinese investors, SOEs in particular, and many large multinational enterprises (MNEs). It is usually assumed that Chinese investors have close link with Chinese government thus serving non-commercial purposes or political objectives that substitute for the benefits to their shareholders, i.e. the Chinese government. The concern of political motivation derives from the low transparency of SOEs and the lack of modern corporate governance. Because of the opaqueness of SOEs investment, many US observers expect worst-case scenarios, for example, that SOEs may act to fulfil the foreign policy strategy of their governments.[32] In terms of the governance structure, the concern of political influence may result from the governmental officials' leading position in Chinese SOEs, e.g. seating in the board or acting as internal mangers (Backer, 2010). Another fear is that Chinese investors, especially in the case of SOEs, might receive financing subsidies or preferential treatment, thus leading to unfair competition that is detrimental to the level playing field (Backer, 2010: 62). And host countries concern that these investments might compromise national security interests while supporting China's global strategy, since SOEs usually prefer to invest in strategic assets and critical infrastructure, acquire know-how and control dwindling resources.[33]

For such concerns, although Chinese FDI is welcomed in some countries, a number of countries have strengthened their regulatory mechanisms to review incoming FDI or even minority equity investment by SOEs (and also by sovereign wealth funds), to ensure that such transactions meet their national interest considerations. However, over-reaction may lead to discriminatory or arbitrary regulatory or administrative treatment motivated by political considerations (e.g. nationality or state ownership) rather than real concerns (e.g. the nature of investment).[34] As the home country of Chinese SOEs, China would like to protect them via IIAs and thus ensure a fair and non-discriminatory treatment for SOEs and receive deserved rights, i.e. the access to investment treaty protection. However, an overview of its recently concluded treaties suggests that China has not addressed the issues of SOEs and its interests concerning protection of SOEs in IIAs.[35] This may require further clarification by China as to whether Chinese SOEs have access to investment treaty protection in its IIAs and whether Chinese SOEs constitute governmental instruments (which might be achieved via domestic SOEs reform).

Nevertheless, so far, the international discussions have focused only on the competitive neutrality concerning SOEs. This issue has also entered into the negotiations of recent regional agreement (e.g. Trans-Pacific Partnership (TPP)),[36] and is expected to do so in other on-going and further negotiations (e.g. the Transatlantic Trade and Investment Partnership (TTIP), the China-EU BIT and the China-US BIT).[37] Furthermore, the suspicion of Chinese SOEs is not merely blamed for unfair competition between Chinese SOEs and private enterprise in host countries, but also unfair competition and unequal market access in Chinese market, with a view that by snapping up foreign companies in critical industries of host countries while blocking other foreign investors from doing the same in China. Developed countries, especially some EU member states and the US, call for a level playing field for foreign investors and 'reciprocity' with China.[38] For developed economies, like the EU and the US, the treaty negotiations with China provide them a chance to address the concern of market access in China (Ewert, 2016: 2–3; Gloundeman and Salidjanova, 2016). China agreed in negotiating BITs with the EU and the US on the basis of a pre-establishment national treatment plus negative list approach.[39] The scope of the negative list is important for both China and its negotiators, as it affects all market entrants. Nevertheless, it is worthwhile for China to insist on the legitimate protection of its national interests in treaty negotiation, which will be complemented by its domestic reforms.

Providing sufficient protection for its investors is an urgent and necessary demand for China with further promoting BRI. Among regions and countries along BRI, as of 2016, China has signed BITs with most of them, but a large number of BITs were out of date (e.g. the lack of national treatment provision, restrictive procedural protection, limited 'transfer of capital'). These BITs cannot meet the desire of China as capital-exporting country and cannot provide sufficient protection for Chinese investment, especially in case of the ever-increasing Chinese outward investment under the BRI. Since the legal systems of some BRI countries (developing and less-developed areas) are relatively backward, Chinese investors might face various legal and regulatory risks.[40] In relation to dispute resolution, some IIAs signed with developing countries only contain rough provisions concerning international investment arbitration, limited scope of covered investment and include the requirement of 'exhaustion of local remedies' and the fork-in-the-road clause. Under this circumstance, it is the high time for China to negotiate new BITs with some BRI countries, with proper and sufficient treaty protection provisions. But, the question, as to what kinds of arbitration provisions should be included in future IIAs, remains to be addressed by China, i.e. adopting the NAFTA model of the US or the Investment Court System of the EU or proposing/providing a Chinese model.

4. Finding a proper way in on-going and future treaty negotiation

4.1. Implication of on-going regional IIAs

China recently has concluded a growing number of FTAs with its Asia-Pacific economies and a BIT with Canada. It should be noticed that the on-going negotiation of Regional Comprehensive Economic Partnership (RCEP) and the BIT negotiation with the EU and the US, once concluded, will have the potential to change the exiting global investment rules, and lay down a new form of IIAs standards. Although the final outcome of the TPP and the progress of the TTIP take times to see partly owing to Trump Administration and the Brexit, the draft text of these agreements will also influence China's on-going treaty negotiations (Du, 2015: 429). Compared with RCEP, the China-EU BIT and China-US BITs contain much higher standards, and the key points would be the issues of SOEs, market access, ISDS and even sustainable development (Kong, 2016; Frisbie, 2014). The text of the TPP provides a set of SOEs disciplines, including but not limited to definitions, commercial considerations, non-discrimination and dispute settlement, which intend to ensure that SOEs do not received unfair financing subsidies or other benefits from governments.[41] However, few BITs have expressly addressed the issues of SOEs that makes the result of Sino-EU and Sino-US BITs important for China and globally concerning SOEs. And the disciplines or restrictions on SOEs also have impact on market access in China.

4.2. The progress of China's on-going reform

As for China, its interest in these on-going treaty negotiations is not only to get involved in shaping the global investment policy, but also to accelerate its long-needed domestic economic and political reforms. The progress of these reforms, in turn, will impact China's future position toward IIAs and influence the political reactions to Chinese investment.[42] The on-going market-oriented reforms happening in China, which matters to the IIAs, include SOE reform[43] and the liberalisation of foreign investment. The new round of SOE reform focuses on 'mixed ownership' in which both public sector economy and non-public sector economy are important components, and both public and private capitals are encouraged in reforming SOEs. The detailed measures of SOE reforms aim to reduce the governmental interference into decision-making process, ensure SOEs' commercial orientation, reduce unfair financial and regulatory benefits for SOEs and upgrade modern corporate governance of SOEs.[44]

As for measures to open up domestic market and relax foreign investment policy, a significant move is the establishment of the Pilot Free Trade Zone (FTZ). The negative list, and reformed filling obligation for foreign investor in place of approval process, have been tested or refined in FTZ, Shanghai and also other FTZs (Xinhua, 2016; Morris, 2016). A related progress is that China has started to negotiate BITs with the EU and the US on the basis of pre-establishment national treatment with a negative list approach (Kaja et al., 2016). All these reforms suggest that China is increasingly willing to embrace liberalising commitments. But for developed countries, this level of reform is still not enough and not adequate since they suppose that Chinese investors still enjoy more liberal market in its territories. It is, however, particularly crucial for China to develop a sound regulatory framework that on one hand attracts high-quality FDI flows to boost domestic market and, on the other hand, protects fundamental national interests and its critical industries.

4.3. The choice of ISDS models

The question as to the inclusion of ISDS is another important issue for the on-going BIT negotiations and also for future BITs to be renewed with countries along BRI. This refers to which kind of investment arbitration models China would like to adopt, i.e. the US model, the EU model or others.[45] The US model can be regarded as the reformed ISDS or reformed NAFTA model, which is reflected in the TPP.[46] This model is adopted in the China-Canada BIT and the China-Australia FTA, but the ISDS in the TPP is also criticised for providing a privileged and powerful mechanism for foreign investors to challenges the right to regulate.[47] While the EU model – a permanent investment court system – dominated by contracting parties, is reflected in the EU-Canada FTA and the EU-Vietnam FTA (European Commission, 2016). Under the EU model, the determination of arbitrators and the qualification of arbitrators are highly restricted, but it is concerned for its practicability. And the EU model is also criticised for investment court's superior to domestic courts (Bronckers, 2015) or dissociating the Court from democratic control (Sornarajah, 2016). However, a recent opinion of the European Court of Justice (CJEU) on the EU-Singapore FTA questions the EU's competence to enter into agreements including ISDS clauses. CJEU clarifies that the ISDS is the area of shared EU and member state competence.[48] But on the other hand, this may serve as a further incentive for the EU to purse a multilateral convention on ISDS that suits the EU's proposal on multilateral investment court.[49] This opinion even makes the arbitration provision in the China-EU BIT negotiation more uncertain as the EU cannot have exclusive competence on this matter.

It should be noticed that, among BRI countries, 23 of them have signed IIAs with the US,[50] 13 of them are EU member states,[51] and 10 of them are ASEAN member countries. It can be predicted that the negotiation of RCEP, the Sino-EU and Sino-US BITs will influence their level of acceptance toward ISDS provisions, and these countries might be able to adopt highly standardised IIAs. The dual identity of China determines that China should strike a balance when concluding IIAs. But with developing countries along BRI, the interest as the home country of Chinese FDI should take precedence over the interest as a host country. It thus calls for a sufficient treaty protection for Chinese investors and the avoidance of FDI protectionism.[52]

Compared with the US model for ISDS,[53] the transparency requirement in the EU model is much higher, with higher operating cost concerning the permanent investment court, which cannot meet the practical demand of China. While the US model seems more suitable for China to be applied in the future negotiation with BRI countries. However, this should be combined with China's interests and take into account the actual conditions of China. When considering the dispute resolution provision, China could set the China-Canada BIT and the China-Australia FTA as samples and introduce necessary reform pursuant to specific situations. In terms of negotiations with less-developed countries, China could choose to exclude 'exhaustion of local remedies' clause and fork-in-the-road clause since it seems better for Chinese investors to recourse the protection provided by international arbitration. It can be learnt from the China-Australia FTA that China and its negotiators could provide a fixed list of arbitrators, the code conduct of arbitrator. As for the transparency of arbitration, it is likely to identify which kinds of arbitral documents will be available to the public. An appellate mechanism to review arbitral awards would also be a possible and desirable choice. It is reasonably arguable that highly standardised treaty protection included in IIAs is important for China's involvement in emerging trend of international investment law but it should be based on its own interests.

5. Conclusion

China is one of the major economic powers worldwide and has expanded its FDI globally. It is also actively engaging in the international rule-making process by significantly reforming its investment treaty regime, presumably serving its growing FDI, the BRI initiative and its political and economic needs. A review of its recently concluded IIAs suggests that China has gradually adopted a relative liberal perspective toward IIAs and is taking an increasingly positive stance toward ISDS and substantive protection. It is trying to promote investment liberalisation and facilitation at international level via the active involvement in global policy making and in deepening domestic reforms. Since a number of bilateral and regional-multilateral negotiations are underway between and among important economies (despite the rise of populism, unilateralism and protectionism), it must be expected that the success of these negotiations will shape the existing international investment law and policy regime, as well as support the multilateral system. It remains to be seen whether the position of China in its interaction with other major economies will result in a further adoption of recent treaty protection standards and its new generation of IIAs. However, this process brings about both opportunities and challenges for China.

The active performance of Chinese investors overseas, especially SOEs, cannot avoid creating anxieties from those countries where China seeks to invest, owing to the fear of non-commercial motivations (e.g. significantly reliance on SOEs and investment made in critical industries). The backlash in host countries also results from the barriers of market access in China. It can be assumed that the outcome of Sino-EU and Sino-US BIT negotiations would provide an answer to both questions and also set an example for dealing with the 'state capitalism' of China, even around the world. In this process, China appears to take effort to best protect its interests, i.e. the intention to make sure that its investors, whether SOEs or private entities, and corresponding investments, and receive adequate treaty protection and non-discriminatory treatment in a changing economic and regulatory landscape. For the EU and the US, a reliable and transparent rules and a level playing field in China for their investors are required as the most important cooperation basis.

Since China is a major backer and player of infrastructure investment, closely associated with sustainable development, China will become more actively to promote sustainable infrastructure and act as a sustainable and responsible investor in the foreseeable future. It is also very relevant when comes to the BRI, as the notion of 'sustainable development' has become a mainstream in trade area and is increasingly becoming important in investment, which is also an obligation as the home country of outward FDI. Under the circumstance of further promoting the BRI, investment treaty protection plays a fundamental and significant role for Chinese investors and investments. It provides China a chance to renew or negotiate IIAs with countries along the BRI on modern treaty protection (substantive and procedural) provisions and an opportunity for China to practice and gain more experiences from international investment arbitration. The dual role of China, as a crucial capital importing and capital-exporting country, is decisive to China's stance toward IIAs. In line with this, China will need to play an active role in moving this forward, on behalf of its own interest and in the interest of improving existing investment policy. China will, in this process, walk a fine line between mitigating concerns of its investment and maintaining an open and non-discriminatory investment climate to Chinese investors and strike a balance between maintaining the legitimate right to regulate and offering protection for foreign investors.

Notes

1 Several reasons suggest that Chinese outward foreign investment would continue to grow and influence China's investment policy making (Berger, 2008).

2 In 2016, overseas M&A projects account for 742 with a value of $107.2bn over 73 countries and regions (MOFCOM, 2017a).

3 It is not only relevant to investment in natural resource sector (e.g. energy sector) but also in the manufacturing and service sectors where Chinese manufacturing and service firms intend to provide facilities or services (Amighini et al., 2013: 324).

4 Although a number of government institutions provide specific instruments to promote or facilitate outward FDI, the principal ones are the Ministry of Commerce (MOFCOM) and the National Development and Reform Commission (NDRC) (the body charged with approving outbound investments) guided by the instruction of the State Council. And the State-owned Assets Supervision and Administration Commission of the State Council (SASAC) plays an important role in guiding the investment conduct of central SOEs. Sauvant and Chen (2013) provided a detailed discussion about the specific instruments used to encourage FDI outflows.

5 But compared to the overall of outbound non-financial investments, investments made in countries along the BRI in the first 7 months have not severely influenced by these curbs, declined only 2.8% year on year (MOFCOM, 2017c).

6 According to the *Notice of the State Council Forwarding the on Guiding Opinions of the National Development and Reform Commission, the Ministry of Commerce and the Peoples' Bank of China on Further Guide and Standardize Overseas Investment Direction* [2017/74], the government encourages those investments that help to promote BRI projects and infrastructure investment and to enhance China's technical standards, cooperation with high-tech and advanced manufacturing enterprises, exploration of energy recourses, agriculture cooperation, and overseas investments in service sectors. The restrictions cover deals in real estate, hotel, cinema, entertainment and sports club; deals in sensitive countries and regions; establishment of equity investment fund or investment platform but without specific industrial projects; using backward production equipment to carry out overseas investment; and activities that conflict with environmental standards. Prohibitions apply to deals involving core military technology, gambling, sex-related businesses and investment 'contrary to national security'.

7 According to the international investment agreements navigator of UNCTAD, as of December 2016, Germany has concluded 135 (131 in force) BITs and China has concluded 129 (110 in force) BITs.

8 China treats IIAs as a key strategy that underpins its economic development and its engagement in global market. China also intends to use IIAs to further open up its market and speed up its domestic reforms.

9 China-Sweden BIT only had very short and brief provision, and there was no option of investor-state dispute resolution. See *Agreement on the Mutual Protection of Investment between the Government of the Kingdom of Sweden and the Government of the People's Republic of China* (China-Sweden BIT).

10 Chi (2017) discussed the different styles of IIAs and the shift of China's treaty-making strategy.

11 There are different suggestions on the classification of the three generations of China's BIT or IIAs. According to Sauvant and Nolan (2015), the first generation is treaties concluded between 1992 and 1998, the second generation (1998–2008) and the third generation is after 2008. According to Berger (2008), Chinese BIT policy can be divided into three stages: the first state (1949–1981), the second state (1982–1998) and the third stage begin in 1998. Schill (2007) also discussed China's generation of treaty-making policy.

12 One possible explanation for China's acceptance of ICSID is that, previously China was the host state of foreign investment hence China intended to control over possible dispute and thus guarantee its sovereignty, while currently China is also the home state of its overseas investment and thus begin to consider protecting its investors overseas (Qi, 2012).

13 This agreement was the first BIT signed by China to offer unrestricted access for foreign investors to international arbitration under the rules of ICSID Arbitration Rules and UNCITRAL Arbitration Rules, with the only remaining restriction, namely the 'exhaustion of local administrative review procedure' before the international arbitration. See *Agreement between the Government of Barbados and the Government of the People's Republic of China* (signed in 1993, in force in 1999), Article 9 (3).

14 Although China offers unrestricted access to ICSID, there are only two cases against China registered at ICSID and five cases registered at ICSID that were filed by Chinese investors as of July 2017.

15 For example, the China-Brunei BIT (signed in 2000 but not in force) was the first BIT that includes up to date absolute standards of treatment for foreign investors. It covers general principle of the fair and equitable treatment, non-discrimination and full protection and security. See Agreement Between the Government of the People's Republic of China and the Government of His Majesty the Sultan and Yang Di-Pertuan of Brunei Darussalam Concerning the Encouragement and Reciprocal Protection of Investment (17/11/2000), Article 3 (1)&(2). The Article 3 (3) of the China-Netherlands BIT (2001) introduced the unrestricted national treatment, which was also adopted in the China-Germany BIT (2003) and the China-Finland BIT (2004).

16 For example, the Article 7 of the China-France BIT (2007) provides the choice of local court, ad hoc arbitration under UNCITRAL rules and ICSID, but before invoking international arbitrations, investors should exhaust the local remedies.

17 The reasons might be that China does not have any domestic legal mechanisms that allow enforcement of awards against state-owned assets; China's position on the unenforceability of non-ICSID arbitration awards; China's strict adherence to absolute sovereign immunity from jurisdiction and from execution (Sauvant and Nolan, 2015: 922–923).

18 There is an increasing scepticism and criticism towards ISDS among both developing and developed countries. The broader and vague language or wording in treaty provisions increases the possibility of inconsistent arbitral awards. The flexibility of arbitrator and the abuse of ISDS by investors have challenged the sovereign power over public policies and even lead to 'regulatory chill'. Many countries start to reform the ISDS and the EU also intends to replace the ISDS by the Investment Court System. The 'Guiding Principles for Global investment Policymaking' endorsed by G20 in 2016 also emphasises the host countries' right to regulate. Many scholars (Gaukrodger, 2017; Quick, 2015; Titi, 2014; Henckels, 2012) analysed and criticised the ISDS, as well as discussed the ISDS reform.

19 For example, the Article 9.6 of China-Australia FTA (2015) denies the benefits of treaty protection if the investor has no substantive business operations. The Article 15 (denial of benefits) of China-ASEAN Investment Agreement also requires the 'substantive business operation'. See also China-Japan-Korea trilateral investment agreement (signed in 2012, in force in 2014), Article 22.2; see China-Korea FTA (2015), Article 12.15.2.

20 For example, China-Canada BIT (2012), Article 5.1 and 5.2; China-ASEAN Investment Agreement (signed in 2009, in force in 2010), Article 5.1; China-Japan-Korea trilateral investment agreement (signed in 2012, in force in 2014), Article 4.1; China-Korea FTA (2015), Article 12.4.1; China-Australia FTA (2015), Article 9.4.1.

21 See China-ASEAN Investment Agreement (signed in 2009, in force in 2010), Article 5.4; see China-Canada BIT (2012), Article 5.3; see China-Australia FTA (2015), Article 9.4.2; see China-Korea FTA (2015), Article 12.4.3.

22 For example, China-Australia FTA (2015), Article 9.3.2 and 9.3.4; see China-Korea FTA (2015), Article 12.3.1; see China-Japan-Korea trilateral investment agreement (signed in 2012, in force in 2014), Article 3.1; see China-ASEAN Investment Agreement (signed in 2009, in force in 2010), Article 4; China-Canada BIT (2012), Article 6.

23 After China signed an FTA with Korea and Australia in 2015, Chinese government has even stated that to further enhance investment liberalisation and facilitation China will negotiate with Korea and Australia on the basis of pre-establishment national treatment with the negative list approach. China is also negotiating China-EU and China-US BITs with this approach.

24 See China-Korea FTA (2015), Article 12.5.1; see China-Japan-Korea trilateral investment agreement (signed in 2012, in force in 2014), Article 5; see China-Canada BIT (2012), Article 4.2.

25 'Indirect expropriation results from a measure of series of measures of a Contracting Party that has an effect equivalent to direct expropriation without formal transfer of title or outright seizure'. See China-Canada BIT (2012), Annex B.10.

26 See China-Australia FTA, Article 9.11; China-Canada BIT, Article 18; China-Korea FTA, Article 12.12.2; China-Korea-Japan trilateral investment treaty, Article 15.2; China-ASEAN Investment Agreement, Article 14.3.

27 Some treaties require compulsory consolidation, for example, China-Canada BIT (2012), Article 26, and China-Australia FTA (2015), Article 9.21. Most of these newly concluded treaties require the 'exhaustion of local remedies' or 'domestic administrative review procedures'. See China-Korea FTA, Article 12.12.7 and China-Japan-Korea trilateral investment treaty, Article 15.7. Before the China-Australia FTA, all existing IIAs concluded by China have introduced the 'exhaustion of local remedies' clause while in the China-Australia FTA, China no longer insists on the exhaustion of local administrative remedies clause.

28 The China-Canada BIT and the China-Australia FTA contain substantive requirements for transparency of ISDS arbitration, which require that awards and decision shall be publicly available, but disclosure of other certain matters still depends on the determination of Contracting Parties. See China-Canada BIT (2012), Article 28, and China-Australia FTA (2015), Article 9.17. In addition, the China-Australia FTA also provides the roster of arbitrator system (a list of individuals), the code of conduct for arbitrator and an appellate mechanism to review awards. See China-Australia FTA (2015), Annex 9-A and Article 9.23.

29 For example, the China-Korea FTA (2015), the China-Canada BIT (2012) and the China-Switzerland FTA (2013) provide sustainable development in the preamble. In addition, the China-Korea FTA and the China-Japan-Korea trilateral investment treaty also contain 'environmental measures' provision. See China-Korea FTA (2015), Article 12.16 and China-Japan-Korea trilateral investment treaty, Article 23.

30 Li (2014) discussed factors that need to be considered in China's future IIAs.

31 For example, in response to recent Chinese investment in infrastructure assets, the Australian government has made certain changes to tighten its foreign investment review mechanism on national security grounds (Laurenceson and Bretherton, 2016; Pearlman, 2016; Drysdale et al., 2015).

32 Any host countries would object to such behaviour, since SOE investments could undermine the national security (Miner and Hufbauer, 2015: 20). The transparency of sovereign wealth funds (SWFs), as another investment instrument of Chinese government, is also blamed by developed countries. According to the

Linburg-Maduell Transparency Index, most Chinese SWFs are below the recommended rating of 8 and thus do not have adequate transparency. This index is developed at the Sovereign Wealth Fund Institute by Carl Linaburg and Michael Maduell. It is a method of rating transparency in respect to sovereign wealth funds.

33 In order to address the concern of national security, many developed countries have established the national security review mechanism or have adopted legislative reforms, for example, FINSA and CFIUS in the US, foreign investment review with 'national interest test' in Australia and investment law with 'net benefit' principles in Canada (Dobson, 2014; Bath 2012; Georgiev, 2008).

34 The effects of state ownership can be neutralised through sound institutional governance that can isolate government-controlled entities from the 'regulatory, political and policy-making functions' of home states (Wolfe and Evans, 2011).

35 Although China has not expressly included state-owned entities in the scope of covered investors, in recent Chinese IIAs, 'governmentally owned or controlled' investors are protected (such as the China-ASEAN FTA, the China-Japan-Korea TIT, the China-New Zealand FTA). But it is legitimate to wonder whether investment treaty protection should be extended to or denied to SOEs thereunder, especially the access to ISDS, since China's outward investment undertake heavily through SOEs.

36 Glantz (2014) provided a discussion on the SOE issues in TPP negotiations.

37 Hufbauer and Cimino-Isaacs (2015) also analysed the issue of SOEs in treaty negotiations, in particular the TPP and the TTIP.

38 The growing gap in two-way investment flows between the EU and China is fuelling the EU's perceptions of a fundamental lack of 'reciprocity'. And Germany, France and Italy had called on the EU to grant them a right of veto over Chinese takeovers. This is not only because of Chinese investments made in most sensitive industries, but also because of a number of hurdles EU companies' investments in China faced with. Clegg and Voss (2016) discuss the market access issue between the EU and China, while Dollar (2017) analysed the market access issue between the US and China.

39 One year after China released its 2017 version of Negative List, the NDRC and MOFCOM jointly release the new negative list for foreign investment, named 'Special Administrative Measures on Access to Foreign Investment', on 28 June 2018, and a new negative list for foreign investment in the pilot free trade zones on 30 June 2018. It suggests an important move of China to implement policy for opening-up strategy and relaxing market access, which were emphasised in the report of 19th National Congress of the Communist Party of China.

40 These legal and regulatory risks may include fairness of judicial process, enforceability of contracts, speediness of judicial process, discrimination against foreign companies, confiscation/expropriation, unfair competitive practices, protection of intellectual property rights, protection of private property, integrity of accounting practices and price controls (Economist Intelligence Unit, 2015).

41 Competitive neutrality is one of core principles that set forth the obligation for states to ensure that SOEs act in line with commercial considerations. Fleury and Marcoux (2016) also discussed SOE disciplines in the TPP.

42 At present, Chinese investments face backlash in Europe. But the most important determinant of the reaction of Europe would be for China to make real progress on reforms that increase the role of markets and the level playing field for foreign investors in China (Martina, 2016).

43 The recent extensive market-oriented reform, which was announced at the Third Plenary Session of the 18th Central Committee of the Chinese Communist Party (CPP), is regarded as proactive responses to the TPP (Salidjanova and Koch-Weser, 2013).

44 According to the *Decision of the Central Committee of the Communist Party of China on Some Major Issues Concerning Comprehensively Deepening the Reform* (2014), these measures include, but are not limited to, organisation of state-owned capital investment and operation companies, disclosure of SOE finances, increase of dividend pay-out ratio for SOEs and improvement of bankruptcy system.
45 However, the ISDS provision in both the TTP and the TTIP face various criticisms. The reform of ISDS provision is still a controversial issue.
46 Trans-Pacific Partnership Agreement, Article 9.9, 9.22 and 9.23.
47 Johnson and Sachs (2015) provided a discussion on the ISDS provision in the TPP.
48 This opinion clarifies that the FTA areas of shared EU and member state competence are limited to non-direct investment, investor-state dispute settlement and related issues (Killick et al., 2017).
49 The EU has sought to champion its proposal of investment court system, while there has been significant resistance from member states to any mechanisms that circumvent the existing domestic legal system (Ankersmit, 2017; Chan and Poulton, 2017).
50 These countries include Albania, Armenia, Azerbaijan, Bangladesh, Bulgaria, Croatia, Czech Republic, Egypt, Estonia, Georgia, Jordan, Kazakhstan, Kyrgyzstan, Latvia, Lithuania, Republic of Moldova, Mongolia, Poland, Romania, Slovakia, Sri Lanka, Turkey and Ukraine.
51 Bulgaria, Cyprus, Croatia, Czech Republic, Estonia, Hungary, Latvia, Lithuania, Malta, Poland, Romania, Slovakia and Slovenia.
52 China's stance towards investment policy making was also reflected in 2016 G20 meeting. Under the Chinese G20 Presidency, the G20 Ministers agreed on the *G20 Guiding Principles for Global Investment Policymaking* and then endorsed it at the G20 Hangzhou Summit. Nine non-binding Guiding Principles provided aims to foster an open, transparent and conducive global policy environment; promote coherence in national and international investment policy making; and promote inclusive economic growth and sustainable development (OECD, 2016). China is increasingly interested in international investment and is concerned about protecting its outward foreign direct investment. This reflects the role of FDI in the development of China and especially its recent rise as a capital exporter (Sauvant, 2017).
53 The US model herein is the one previously adopted by the US in its BITs and FTAs, but not the current unilateralism under Trump's administration.

References

Amighini, A. et al. (2013). China's Outward FDI: An Industry-Level Analysis of Host-Country Determinants. *Frontiers of Economics in China*, 8, 324.
Ankersmit, L. (2017). Opinion 2/15 and the Future of Mixity and ISDS. *European Law Blog*, 18 May, http://europeanlawblog.eu/2017/05/18/opinion-215-and-the-future-of-mixity-and-isds/
Backer, L. (2010). Sovereign Investing in Time of Crisis: Global Regulation of Sovereign Wealth Funds, State-Owned Enterprises, and the Chinese Experience. *Transnational Law & Contemporary Problems*, 19.
Bath, V. (2012). Foreign Investment, the National Interest and National Security – Foreign Direct Investment in Australia and China. *Sydney Law Review*, 34.
Berger, A. (2008). China and the Global Governance of Foreign Direct Investment: The Emerging Liberal Bilateral Investment Treaty Approach. *German Development Institute Discussion Paper*, 10, 14 & 20–21.

Bradsher, K. and Mozur, P. (2016). Political Backlash Grows in Washington to Chinese Takeovers. *New York Times*, 18 February, www.nytimes.com/2016/02/18/business/dealbook/china-fairchild-semiconductor-bid-rejected.html?_r=0

Bronckers, M. (2015). Is Investor-State Dispute Settlement (ISDS) Superior to Litigation Before Domestic Courts?: An EU View on Bilateral Trade Agreements. *Journal of International Economic Law*, 18, 655.

Chan, L. and Poulton, E. (2017). EU Court Thwarts Prompt Ratification of EU-Singapore Free Trade Agreement. *Baker McKenzie*, 22 May, www.bakermckenzie.com/en/insight/publications/2017/05/eu-court-thwarts-prompt-ratification/

Chazn, G. (2017). EU Capitals Seek Strong Right of Veto on Chinese Takeovers. *Financial Times*, 14 February, www.ft.com/content/8c4a2f70-f2d1-11e6-95ee-f14e55513608

Chi, M. (2017). From Europeanization toward Americanization: The Shift of China's Dichotomic Investment Treaty-Making Strategy. *Canadian Foreign Policy Journal*, 23.

Clegg, J. and Voss, H. (2016). The New Two-Way Street of Chinese Direct Investment in the European Union. *China-EU Law Journal*, 5.

Dobson, W. (2014). China's State-Owned Enterprises and Canada's FDI Policy. SPP Research Paper No. 7–10.

Dollar, D. (2017). United States-China Two-Way Direct Investment: Opportunities and Challenges. *Journal of Asian Economics*, 50.

Drysdale, P. et al. (2015). Chinese ODI and the Need to Reform Australia's Foreign Investment Regime. EABER Working Paper Series No. 117.

Du, M. (2015). Explaining China's Tripartite Strategy Toward the Trans-Pacific Partnership Agreement. *Journal of International Economic Law*, 18, 429.

Economist Intelligence Unit (2015). Prospects and Challenges on China's "One Belt, One Road": A Risk Assessment Report. https://static1.squarespace.com/static/529fcf02e4b0aa09f5b7ff67/t/554c49cee4b06fc215162cb4/1431062990726/One+Belt%2C+One+Road.pdf

European Commission (2016). The Multilateral Investment Court. 22 December, http://trade.ec.europa.eu/doclib/press/index.cfm?id=1608

Ewert, I. (2016). The EU-China Bilateral Investment Agreement: Between High Hopes and Real Challenges, EGMONT Institute Security Policy Brief No. 68, pp. 2–3.

Fleury, J. and Marcoux, J. (2016). The US Shaping of State-Owned Enterprises Disciplines in the Trans-Pacific Partnership. *Journal of International Economic Law*, 19, 455.

Frisbie, J. (2014). Why an Investment Treaty with China Matters. *China Business Review*, 31 March, www.chinabusinessreview.com/why-an-investment-treaty-with-china-matters/

Gallagher, N. (2016). Role of China in Investment: BITs, SOEs, Private Enterprises, and Evolution of Policy. *ICSID Review-Foreign Investment Law Journal*, 31, 93.

Gaukrodger, D. (2017). The Balance between Investor Protection and the Right to Regulate in Investment Treaties, OECD Working Papers on International Investment 2017/02, www.oecd-ilibrary.org/docserver/download/82786801-en.pdf?expires=1495550398&id=id&accname=guest&checksum=7D081F17951C8525300819B258F090C1

Georgiev, G. (2008). The Reformed CFIUS Regulatory Framework: Mediating Between Continues Openness to Foreign Investment and National Security, *Yale Journal on Regulation*, 25.

Gippner, O. and Torney, D. (2017). Shifting Policy Priorities in EU-China Energy Relations: Implications for Chinese Energy Investments in Europe. *Energy Policy*, 101, 656.

Glantz, D. (2014). The United States and the Trans-Pacific Partnership. In Andrea Bjorklund, ed., *Yearbook on International Investment Law and Policy*, New York: Oxford University Press.

Gloundeman, L. and Salidjanova, N. (2016). Policy Considerations for Negotiating a U.S.-China Bilateral Investment Treaty, U.S.-China Economic and Security Review Commission Staff Research Report.

Henckels, C. (2012). Indirect Expropriation and the Right to Regulate: Revisiting Proportionality Analysis and the Standard of Review in Investor-State Arbitration. *Journal of International Economic Law*, 15.

Hufbauer, G. and Cimino-Isaacs, C. (2015). How Will TPP and TTIP Change the WTO System? *Journal of International Economic Law*, 18.

Johnson, L. and Sachs, L. (2015). The TPP's Investment Chapter: Entrenching, Rather Than Reforming, a Flawed System. CCSI Policy Paper.

Kaja, A. et al. (2016). China Moves Forward with Negative List for (Domestic and Foreign) Market Access. *Global Policy Watch*, 21 April, www.globalpolicywatch.com/2016/04/china-moves-forward-with-negative-list-for-domestic-and-foreign-market-access/

Killick, J. et al. (2017). EU Court Confirms EU Competence on Wide Range of Trade Areas in Opinion on EU-Singapore FTA. *White & Case*, 17 May, www.whitecase.com/publications/alert/eu-court-confirms-eu-competence-wide-range-trade-areas-opinion-eu-singapore-fta

Kong, Q. (2016). The "state-led-economy" Issue in the BIT Negotiation and Its Policy Implications for China. *China-EU Law Journal*, 5.

Laurenceson, J. and Bretherton, H. (2016). Chinese Investment and National Security: What Australians Think. *Australia-China Relations Institute*, 19 May, www.australiachinarelations.org/content/chinese-investment-and-national-security-what-australians-think

Li, Y. (2014). Factors to Be Considered for China's Future Investment Treaty. In W. Shan and J. Su, eds., *China and International Investment Law Treaty Years of ICSID Membership*, Leiden; Boston: Brill Nijhoff, pp. 171–179.

Ma, Y. and Overbeek, H. (2015). Chinese Foreign Direct Investment in the European Union: Explaining Changing Patterns, *Global Affairs*, 1, 442.

Martina, M. (2016). EU Business Lobby Warns of Protectionist Backlash If China Doesn't Open Market. *Reuters*, 31 August, http://uk.reuters.com/article/uk-china-eu-business-idUKKCN1173EF

Miller, R. (2016). Chinese Takeovers Trigger Global Backlash Ahead of G-20 Summit. *Bloomberg*, 25 August, www.bloomberg.com/news/articles/2016-08-25/chinese-takeovers-trigger-global-backlash-ahead-of-g-20-summit

Miner, S. and Hufbauer, G. (2015). State-Owned Enterprises and Competition Policy: The US Perspective. In *PIIE Briefing Toward a US-China Investment Treaty*, PIIE, p. 20.

Mitchell, T. et al. (2017). Chinese Investment in EU Dwarfs Flow the Other Way. *Financial Times*, 10 January, www.ft.com/content/79e3a2b2-d6f7-11e6-944b-e7eb37a6aa8e

MOFCOM (2016). Official of Outward Investment and Economic Cooperation of the Ministry of Commerce Comments on China's Outward Investment and Cooperation in 2015. 18 January, http://english.mofcom.gov.cn/article/newsrelease/policyreleasing/201602/20160201251488.shtml

MOFCOM (2017a). MOFCOM Department Official of Outward Investment and Economic Cooperation Comments on China's Outward Investment and Cooperation in 2016. 18 January, http://english.mofcom.gov.cn/article/newsrelease/policyreleasing/201701/20170102503092.shtml

MOFCOM (2017b). Brief Statistics on China's Non-Financial Direct Investment Overseas in January–July 2017. 24 August, http://fec.mofcom.gov.cn/article/tjsj/ydjm/jwtz/201708/20170802632318.shtml

MOFCOM (2017c). Investment and Cooperation Statistics about Countries along Belt and Road in January–July 2017. 24 August, http://fec.mofcom.gov.cn/article/fwydyl/tjsj/201708/20170802632321.shtml

Morris, D. (2016). China Issues Several Implementing Rules to Reform Its Foreign Investment Administrative System. *Lexology*, 14 October, www.lexology.com/library/detail.aspx?g=6ab9ea0b-2fd8-419f-83ab-9c0f52ccb573

OECD (2016). G20 Agrees Guiding Principles for Global Investment Policymaking, www.oecd.org/investment/g20-agrees-principles-for-global-investment-policymaking.htm

Pearlman, J. (2016). Australia Blocks Electricity Deal with China for "National Security" Reasons. *Telegraph*, 11 August, www.telegraph.co.uk/news/2016/08/11/australia-blocks-electricity-deal-with-china-for-national-securi/

Qi, T. (2012). How Exactly Does China Consent to Investor-State Arbitration: On the First ICSID Case Against China. *Contemporary Asia Arbitration Journal*, 5.

Quick, R. (2015). Why TTIP Should Have an Investment Chapter Including ISDS. *Journal of World Trade*, 49.

Salidjanova, N. and Koch-Weser, I. (2013). Third Plenum Economic Reform Proposals: A Scorecard, US-China Economic and Security Review Commission Staff Research Backgrounder. 19 November, www.uscc.gov/sites/default/files/Research/Backgrounder_Third%20Plenum%20Economic%20Reform%20Proposals–A%20Scorecard%20%282%29.pdf

Sauvant, K. (2017). China Moves the G20 Toward an International Investment Framework and Investment Facilitation. In Julien Chaisse, ed., *China's Three-Prong Investment Strategy: Bilateral, Regional, and Global Tracks*, London: Cambridge University Press, Forthcoming.

Sauvant, K. and Chen, V. (2013). China's Regulatory Framework for Outward Foreign Direct Investment. *China Economic Journal*, 7.

Sauvant, K. and Nolan, M. (2015). China's Outward Foreign Direct Investment and International Investment Law. *Journal of International Economic Law*, 18, 894 & 919–925.

Schill, S. (2007). Tearing Down the Great Wall: The New Generation Investment Treaties of the People's Republic of China. *Cardozo Journal of International and Comparative Law*, 15.

Shan, W. and Wang, L. (2015). The China-EU BIT and the Emerging "Global BIT 2.0". *ICSID Review-Foreign Investment Law Journal*, 30, 267.

Sornarajah, M. (2016). An International Investment Court: Panacea or Purgatory? Columbia FDI Perspectives No. 180.

Titi, C. (2014). *The Right to Regulate in International Investment Law*, Oxford: Hart Publishing.

UNCTAD (2003). E-brief: China: An Emerging FDI Outward Investor, http://unctad.org/sections/dite_fdistat/docs/china_ebrief_en.pdf

UNCTAD (2016). World Investment Report 2016 – Investor Nationality: Policy Challenges, http://unctad.org/en/pages/PublicationWebflyer.aspx?publicationid=1555

Wolfe, W. and Evans, A. (2011). China's Energy Investments and the Corporate Social Responsibility Imperative. *Journal of International Law and International Relations*, 6.

Xinhua (2016). China Tests "negative list" Approach in Four Regions. 9 April, http://english.gov.cn/state_council/ministries/2016/04/09/content_281475323760671.htm

Zheng, N. et al. (2016). In Search of Strategic Assets through Cross-Border Mergers and Acquisitions: Evidence from Chinese Multinational Enterprises in Developed Economies. *International Business Review*, 25.

3 Investment dispute-settlement trends between Far-East and Ibero-America

Alejandro García Jiménez[1]

1. East-Asian countries investment trends towards Ibero-America[2]

It is widely believed that Asia's contribution to innovation in global economic governance is not decisive; however, this continent is likely to continue leading global economic growth in the years to come and shaping the geography of global investment law (Schill, 2015: 766–768). The role of Asia as a capital-exporting region has clearly increased in recent years. According to the United Nations Conference on Trade and Development (UNCTAD) World Investment Report 2017, the People's Republic of China (PRC or China), Japan, Hong Kong Special Administrative Region (HK SAR), the Republic of Korea (South Korea or simply Korea), the Republic of Singapore (or simply Singapore) and Taiwan Province of China (Taiwan, Republic of China or ROC) were among the top 20 countries or regions in terms of Foreign Direct Investment (FDI) outflows in year 2016 (UNCTAD, 2017: 14).

However, if we consider the FDI stock, only Japan is among the top ten investors in Ibero-America, ranking 9th, whereas the United States of America and the Kingdom of Spain keep the first and second position respectively (UNCTAD, 2017: 57). The current advantage of Japan can be explained by the fact that the country of the rising sun started being a net capital exporter as early as the 1980s (Hamamoto and Nottage, 2013: 347), whereas Korea remained a net capital-importer until the mid-1990s (Shin, 2013: 393) and China has become an increasingly relevant capital exporter and a very fast-growing one in recent years. The proliferation of inter-regional Free Trade Agreements (FTAs) – most of which have investment chapters – between Asia and Latin America has been observed for years now (Wignaraja et al., 2013: 397–399).

The construction of contemporary Singapore after its recent independence in 1965 relied heavily in foreign capital. Nevertheless, this Asian country has become a large capital exporter with considerable economic exchange with Ibero-America and interests in the region. Singaporean direct investments stock in Ibero-American and Caribbean countries has been constantly growing in recent years (Singapore Government, International Enterprise Singapore, 2017: 1). However, Singapore is not within our geographical scope. Furthermore, it is difficult to track the capital flows from this country, which is a financial and operational hub that serves as a basis both for Asian Countries to go abroad and for Ibero-American Companies to operate in Asia. Singapore has concluded bilateral treaties with provisions related to investments with Panama, Peru, Mexico and Costa Rica and has signed an investments treaty with Colombia in 2013, although it has not yet entered into force. Singaporean Bilateral Investment Treaties (BITs) receive the name of Investment Guarantee Agreements (IGAs) (Ho, 2013: 623). Singaporean economic policy has a determined trans-Pacific vocation, having already concluded agreements such as the so-called P4 together with Brunei, New Zealand and Chile.

Thailand is also not within our geographical scope, but it has an ambitious BIT programme leaded by urban entrepreneurs with the objective of not lagging behind its neighbours and avoiding to become isolated in a context of regionalisation and stagnation of the multilateral global economic governance. Although the search of economic interest must not be fully disregarded, liberalisation commitments in Thai investment treaties are rather weak, to the extent that it has been suggested that they mostly seek to upgrade Thailand's diplomatic status as well as to gain experience and increase its negotiation capacity (Hoadley, 2007: 310–317). Thai investment treaties are geographically diversified (not to say scattered). With respect to the Ibero-American region, Thailand has concluded treaties in the field of investments with Peru, Argentina and Chile.

Malaysia's economic diplomacy has been clearly oriented towards the East and within the ASEAN, although bilateral negotiations with countries from other regions have recently started. The Malaysian FTA with Chile is in force since 2012 and its BITs with Argentina, Chile, Cuba, Peru and Uruguay since 1996, 1995, 1999, 1995 and 2002 respectively. Similarly to Thailand, Malaysia does not possess great economic interest in Ibero-America but rather uses economic diplomacy as a way to progressively upgrade its international status and acquire experience with countries that are not perceived as threatening for the Malaysian economy (Hoadley, 2007: 320–322), as well as to benefit from some of the advantages derived from freer trade and investment flows.

India does have considerable economic potential and certain political interest in the Ibero-American region. Indian interests focus on the field of energy and commodities but also see the region as a potential consumption market for Indian goods and services. The framework agreement between India and the Mercosur entered into force in 2009, and another one was signed with Chile in 2005 but never entered into force. The BITs of India with Mexico and Colombia entered into force in 2008 and 2012 respectively. The BIT with Argentina was terminated, but another one was signed in 2008, which has not yet entered into force.

Initiatives such as the Trans-Pacific Partnership (TPP) would have also enhanced trans-regional trade and investment flows between the Asian region (Japan, Singapore, Malaysia, Vietnam and Brunei) and Ibero-American countries (Chile, Mexico and Peru). According to estimations from the International Monetary Fund, Asian members of the TPP would have benefited most from the original TPP agreement. In the Ibero-American region Mexico would clearly benefit more than Chile and Peru. Other non-TPP signatories, such as Colombia or Guatemala could have largely benefited from joining the agreement (Cerdeiro, 2016: 4). The TPP in its original form would have entered into force after ratification by all the parties that signed the agreement of the 4th February 2016 or, after 2 years, by ratification of at least six States corresponding to 85% of the GDP of the signatories. Since there is no political interest from the US to ratify the agreement, the other signatories are negotiating a new version of the agreement under the name of "Comprehensive and progressive agreement for trans-pacific partnership". Other Asia-Pacific initiatives, such as the Regional Comprehensive Economic Partnership (RCEP), do not count on any Ibero-American members among its negotiators.

Korea, Japan and China are clear competitors in many fields, but they also act as cooperators. One of the many ways in which they compete in Ibero-America is through the conclusion of international treaties in the field of investments that grant better market-access for their companies and protect their investments in Ibero-America. The China-Japan-Korea Trilateral Investment Agreement is a clear example of cooperation among them in the field of investments (Zhu, 2015: 81). Another example of cooperation may be that the strong Chinese demand of raw goods actually fostered Japanese investments in South America in this sector in order to provide raw materials in the Asian markets (The Inter-American Dialogue, 2016: 4–5).

This chapter first analyses the patterns of Far-East Asian investments (China, Japan and the Republic of Korea) in Ibero-America. Second, we analyse the settlement of disputes between China, Japan and Korea and Ibero-American countries. We then look at the legal protection of FDI flows coming from the Far-East Asian nations into Ibero-America, with focus on the recent cooperative approaches to investments protection. We will also deal with some new proposals for international investment governance that have emerged during the last decade in Ibero-American countries such as the UNASUR Dispute Resolution Centre and the Brazilian ACFIs, which also include certain cooperative aspects.

1.1. Chinese investments in Ibero-America

Chinese investments in Latin America find their origins in the need for huge amounts of energy, minerals and other raw materials in times of very high Chinese growth rates (Yang, 2014: 2). Natural resources are secured in various ways, such as acquiring stakes in natural resource companies, extending loans to mining and petroleum investors and writing long-term procurement contracts for oil and minerals (Kotschwar, 2012: 4). The guarantees of these loans are frequently "revenues from future sales to Chinese companies" (Kotschwar, 2012: 3). Using this technique, China obtains oil from Brazil, Ecuador and Venezuela, soy, wheat and gas from Argentina, etc.

The Chinese economic model is trying to move into the so-called "new normal": a new economic scenario with lower but "better" growth, less dependent on basic manufactures and more value-added economic activities. If China succeeds in carrying out this transformation, it is expected that consumption would drive economic growth, instead of investments (Estevadeordal et al., 2014: 6), which would increase the income of Chinese consumers, who would demand higher quality products, including better food, and Latin America has a comparative advantage in the production of livestock and agricultural products (Estevadeordal et al., 2014: 18; ECLAC, 2015: 44).

Probably the main field for further cooperation with Ibero-America is that of infrastructure finance. China is encouraging the construction of infrastructure abroad as one of the main tools of its economic diplomacy in various forums, such as the Asian Infrastructure Investment Bank (AIIB), One Belt One Road (OBOR) or the Shanghai Cooperation Organization. The LAC-China Infrastructure Fund is the result of the cooperation between China and the Inter-American Development Bank.

China's policy at the beginning of the "Reform and Opening-up to the Outside World", approximately from 1979 to 2000, was based on attracting inward FDI and maintaining high levels of exportations (Yang, 2014: 5). Due to the increasingly large amounts of foreign reserves, the Fourteenth Communist Party of China (CPC) Congress in 1992 announced a policy to increase Chinese Outward Foreign Direct Investment (OFDI). But it was not until the 10th Five-Year Plan, released in 2001, that the "Going Out" strategy was officially formulated. In 2004, the National Development and Reform Commission (NDRC) determined the enhanced OFDI categories, namely, investments to obtain energy and natural resources, to export labour and machinery, to obtain technology and management skills and to "help China to participate in the restructuring of global production" (Yang, 2014: 5).

The subsequent Five-Year Plans have kept the emphasis on boosting Chinese OFDI (National Development and Reform Commission, 2012). Chinese OFDI has been encouraged through various mechanisms, including the progressive facilitation of approvals, access to financing support and access to risk security mechanisms (Yang, 2014: 6). The application procedure for granting OFDI licences has been progressively simplified and accelerated.

The aforementioned administrative measures and incentives, together with other economic factors, led to an almost tenfold increase of Chinese OFDI to the whole world from 2005 to 2014. The average volume of Chinese investments into Latin American countries was approximately USD 10 billion per year since 2010 (ECLAC, 2015: 34). Brazil, Venezuela and Argentina are the major recipients of Chinese OFDI in Ibero-America according to MOFCOM data (Ministry of Commerce of the People's Republic of China, 2014: 127) (Ministry of Commerce of the People's Republic of China, 2015: 135).

For most countries, the main field of Chinese investments is either energy or mining (The Heritage Foundation, 2016). Other economic fields that receive Chinese investments are agriculture (Argentina, Brazil and Peru); chemicals (Argentina); finance (Argentina and Brazil); transport (Argentina, Brazil and Venezuela); technology (Brazil); and real estate (Brazil). This data is coherent with the information from the IDB, according to which Chinese investments into Latin America are clearly directed towards mining, agriculture and electricity sectors (Estevadeordal et al., 2014: 5), at least up to now. There is a big chance that the share of Chinese investments in the field of infrastructure will increase substantially in the years to come. Precisely, some of the most sensitive sectors for the occurrence of investment disputes according to the empirical evidence collected by UNCTAD include "mining and petroleum extraction projects", "concession agreements for public services" and "build-operate-transfer (BOT) contracts" (UNCTAD, 2010: 74).

Chinese investments into Latin America are frequently carried out in the form of loans. Not every loan is an investment in legal terms. One must analyse them on a case-by-case basis, paying attention to the host State regulations and, most importantly, the definition of "investment" used in the applicable BITs or other International Investment Agreements (IIAs). Whether loans are protected or not under international treaties in the field of investments will depend on the definition of investment within the treaty itself.

Chinese policy banks, namely the China Development Bank (CDB) and China Export-Import Bank, support the strategic goals of the Chinese State. CDB frequently subsidises Chinese loans abroad and mainly supports enterprises investing in energy and natural resources, infrastructure, agriculture and forestry projects. Not only SOEs receive support from policy banks, but also successful private enterprises such as Huawei or ZTE (Yang, 2014: 14).

Frequently, China invests in countries with difficulties to obtain finance in the global capital markets. Some critics understand this as a confirmation of the political nature of Chinese investments. The Chinese explanation to this phenomenon is that actually, there are profitable opportunities in these countries that are not filled by Western nations for political differences (Yang, 2014: 17).

"Chinese companies usually channel most of their investments through third countries" according to the report of the First Forum of China and the CELAC (ECLAC, 2015: 34). A large proportion of Chinese OFDI is also carried out through Hong Kong Special Administrative Region, which is a member of the World Trade Organisation. Once in Hong Kong, Chinese capital benefits from the "one country, two systems" principle and enjoys more liberal laws and regulations. Mainland China investments are also carried out through other countries and territories, such as Luxembourg, the Cayman Islands, the Virgin Islands, Bahamas, Panama etc. Investing through Luxembourg, the Cayman Islands or the Virgin Islands grant Chinese enterprises tax advantages. Investing through the Netherlands make Chinese investors able to benefit from the legal protection that the BITs of this country generally offer. Some places, such as Bahamas, Panama and other Caribbean countries, are also used as free ports to avoid too much physical presence in dangerous places where China has important investments, such as Venezuela. Some places may grant Chinese investors several of these advantages simultaneously.

1.2. Japanese investments in Ibero-America

Japanese investments in Latin America were also initially motivated by the acquisition of natural resources for the flourishing Japanese industry after the Second World War by industrial conglomerates and trading companies such as Mitsubishi, Mitsui or Sumitomo (Kahn, 2016: 11). The first investments, carried out during the 1950s and the 1960s, focused in acquisitions in the Chilean and the Brazilian mining industries.

However, nowadays, Japanese FDI is characterised by being diversified among the three productive sectors; only 22% of Japanese direct investment stock to Ibero-American and Caribbean countries in 2015 was directed to the extractive sector, whereas 34% went to the services sector. More than half of the investments directed to the tertiary sector went to finance, insurance and transportation (Kahn, 2016: 29). Japanese manufacturing investments in areas such as naval construction, textile plants, steel and vehicles production are of great importance to the Latin American economy. Toyota arrived to Brazil as early as 1955, followed by Ishikawajima Harima shipyards, motorbike manufacturers (Yamaha and Honda) and electronics manufacturers (Sony). Nissan started manufacturing in Mexico in 1961 (Myers and Kuwayama, 2016: 3, 7). Manufacturing in Latin American countries has been a strategy for Japanese enterprises to avoid trade barriers and access other markets. Mexico, for instance, grants access to the whole North American market through NAFTA.

Cooperation between Japan and the Ibero-American region dates back to the beginning of the 20th century, when Brazil and other countries in the region accepted to receive Japanese immigrants. Since the creation of the Japan International Cooperation Agency (JICA) in 1974, Ibero-American countries have largely benefited from Japanese Official Aid to Development. Japan helped Brazil to create the Brazilian Agricultural Research Corporation (*Empresa Brasileira de Agropecuária*, EMBRAPA) and develop crops that were not found naturally in Brazil. Similarly, JICA helped Chile to develop its competitive salmon industry (Kahn, 2016: 20–22).

The construction of Japanese infrastructure consolidated during the 1970s by carrying out major projects in the areas of logistics and energy (Myers and Kuwayama, 2016: 1). Japanese infrastructure projects in Latin America are often carried out through the official aid.

1.3. Investments from the Republic of Korea in Ibero-America

Countries belonging to the Community of Latin-American and Caribbean States (CELAC) have received 5% of South Korean total FDI between 2001 and 2006, 7% during the period 2007–2012, and Korean economic interests in the region keep growing. Between 2007 and 2012, Brazil and Mexico received two-thirds of Korean FDI to the region, due to their interest as consumer markets. Furthermore, Mexico grants access to the North American market. Peru, Colombia, Chile and Panama also receive significant FDI from Korea. As for the sectors of the economy, the majority of Korean FDI is directed towards the manufacturing industry. In Brazil, most of Korean FDI was received by the industry, whereas in Central America investments go to the textile sector (ECLAC, 2016: 5, 13).

Ibero-America receives Korean Official Development Assistance through the Korean International Cooperation Agency (KOICA), which receives orders from the Ministry of Foreign Affairs for the development of projects related to the reduction of social inequalities, the improvement of the administration, transparency and sustainable development. The Ministry of Strategy and Finance also participates in the Korean cooperation to development in two ways. First, by supporting the construction of infrastructure through soft loans of the Economic Development Cooperation Fund (EDCF) granted by the Export-Import Bank of Korea (EximBank). And, second, by implementing the Knowledge Sharing Programme (KSP) of which Brazil, Colombia, Costa Rica, the Dominican Republic, Ecuador, El Salvador, Honduras, Mexico, Panama, Peru, Bolivia and Uruguay have already benefited (ECLAC, 2016: 14–15, 41–42).

Korean investments abroad are regulated in the Foreign Exchange Transactions Act (FETA) of 1998. Under this piece of legislation, it is considered "Overseas Direct Investment": (1) the acquisition by a Korean resident of at least 10% of a foreign company's equity interest, (2) overseas construction contracts, (3) long-term loans granted by Korean residents to foreign companies and (4) remittance of funds from a Korean resident company to its branches or offices overseas (Shin, 2013: 394).

2. The settlement of investment disputes between Far-East Asia and Ibero-American countries

No economic activity is completely immune to the emergence of disputes, and international investment transactions are not an exception. Conflicts often arise, even among best friends, as a result of the divergence of interests and there is a wide range of legal and non-legal means to solve them. According to the level of enforceability of the outcome of the process, we find consultations, conciliation, mediation and litigation. Different combinations of these methods are possible in order to settle an investment dispute.

It is often argued that the Confucian tradition has a powerful influence in the way that Asian countries handle their disputes. Seeking harmony is a Confucian value, which is also highly praised in other Asian philosophies and schools of thought. In other words, harmony is precious. This approach is supposed to favour non-litigation dispute-resolution methods, especially in civil and commercial cases. In fact, arbitration does not exclude the utilisation of other non-litigation dispute-resolution methods. The achievement of a harmonious society can be achieved through different dispute-resolution methods and even combinations of them.

Diplomatic means are always available to any country for the resolution of investment disputes in the Public International Law. The main disadvantage of diplomatic means for the resolution of investment disputes is that they are not the right of the investor, but rather a political action based on opportunity criteria (Lowenfeld, 2003: 387 *et seq.*). Some kinds of litigation, such as State-to-State arbitration, cannot be initiated by the investor whose rights have been violated.

On the contrary, the litigation in the courts of the receiving State, as well as investor-to-State arbitration endow an investor the right to initiate proceedings to seek remedy of its rights as an investor. As a general rule, the jurisdiction complies with the principle of territoriality, which means that disputes related to an investment are under the jurisdiction of the receiving State, thus will be resolved on the basis of its own procedural rules in the absence of any other agreement or instrument. Nevertheless, the territorial State can cede jurisdiction, for instance, to an international tribunal. Concerns about the lengthy proceedings and the mistrust of local Courts have made investor-to-State arbitration become the main system to settle investment disputes in our times. Investor-to-State arbitration is frequently divided into contract-based and treaty-based (Sornarajah, 2010: 276 *et seq.*). Consent in contract-based arbitration is expressed through a clause in a foreign-investment agreement. In treaty-based investment arbitration, "consent of the State is said to be given to all present and potential investors whose investment is protected by the treaty in advance of the dispute" (Sornarajah, 2010: 306).

The ICSID Convention is the most far-reaching multilateral investment treaty. An ICSID arbitrator or arbitral tribunal shall base their jurisdiction on ICSID Convention, Article 25(1), which requires three elements: the first one is a qualified foreign investor, the second one is the existence of an investment dispute and the third one is consent of the parties. A qualified investor who is a natural person must satisfy a double requirement concerning its nationality, namely, having the nationality of a contracting State and not having the nationality of the host State (article 25 (1)(a)). A qualified investor who is a juridical person must either have a nationality different to the host State or have the nationality of the host State but be under foreign control.

Among the Far-East Asian countries, Japan was the first to sign it on the 23rd September 1965, and entered into force on the 16th September 1967, without having notified any exception to the application of the treaty. Korea signed the ICSID Convention right after, on the 18th April 1966, and was the first in which the Convention entered into force among these three countries, on the 23rd March 1967. China signed the Washington Convention on the 9th February 1990, ratified it on the 7th January 1993 and entered into force on the 6th February 1993.

Article 25 (4) of the Washington Convention allows Contracting States to notify "the class or classes of disputes which it would or would not consider submitting to the jurisdiction of the Centre". China used this procedure to declare at the time of ratification that it would only consider submitting to ICSID jurisdiction "disputes over compensation resulting from expropriation and nationalization". Although there was a debate for some time, it is now widely recognised that specific consent to ICSID arbitration prevails over previous and more general notifications of intent (Willems, 2011: 27). Neither Japan nor Korea have made such reservations to the Washington Convention.

China has been respondent in three ICSID cases. Disputes related to Equity Joint Ventures are frequently administered by the China International Economic and Trade Arbitration Commission (CIETAC), but these disputes, as a general rule, are not related to the violation of international protection standards granted to investors. Zhang Yuqing explains that the origin of the use of CIETAC arbitration for foreign-investment disputes in China finds its roots in the Model ... Ventures, China recommended by the former Ministry of Foreign Economic Cooperation and Trade (MOFTEC), China the current Ministry of Commerce (MOFCOM), China (Zhang, 2005: 168, 171). Korea has also acted as a respondent in three ICSID cases, whereas Japan has never been successfully denounced in an ICSID case.

Within the ICSID system, Korean investors have acted as claimants in three cases, and Japanese investors have done so in only two occasions, but none of them has ever denounced a Latin American country. Chinese investors have raised five claims under the auspices of the ICSID Convention, one of which was against a Latin American nation, in *Tza Yap Shum v. Peru* case. We must bear in mind that arbitration proceedings may be confidential – especially if they are contract-based – depending on the governing law and the arbitration rules, but to our knowledge, the only investment dispute settlement case between a Far-East Asian investor and an Ibero-American country: the *Tza Yap Shum Case*.

A Chinese national and Hong Kong resident, Mr. Tza Yap Shum, invested through Hong Kong in Peru's fishmeal sector. Mr. Tza owned 90% of the Peruvian enterprise TSG Perú S.A.C. The Peruvian tax authorities audited the enterprise in January 2005 and ordered to freeze TSG's accounts in various financial institutions, leaving TSG no other option but to seek bankruptcy protection. Mr. Tza raised a claim against Peru on the basis of the China-Peru BIT and the ICSID Tribunal recognised that the measures carried out by Peru led to expropriation and were arbitrary.

In this case, both the Peruvian and the Chinese Governments agreed that Tza Yap Shum arbitral tribunal shall have no jurisdiction over the claim (Irwin, 2014: 19). The scope of arbitration in the 1994 China-Peru BIT was interpreted in an extensive way under a MFN clause. A detailed analysis of the jurisdiction of the ICSID tribunal in the *Tza Yap Shum Case* has been made by Jane Willems (Willems, 2011: 37). The argument used by Tza Yap Shum that Hong Kong treaties in the field of investments aims at protecting investors from all over the world, given its nature of economic hub. Tza Yap Shum's award was later annulled by the Decision of 12th February 2015.

3. The protection of Far-East Asian investments in Ibero-America

The political and geostrategic position of Japan and Korea during the Cold War and their strong bonds to the US and Western Europe, explain the much earlier development of an international legal system for investment protection in these two countries compared to the People's Republic of China. Japanese economic diplomacy traditionally focused on multilateral liberalisation, especially within the World Trade Organisation. China's interest in global economic governance structures is more recent, however; it rapidly developed a much wider net of investment treaties.

The different approach in terms of the negotiation and conclusion of international treaties in the field of investment protection is especially clear between Japan and China, as professor Nakagawa has analysed. Whereas Japan seeks to negotiate comprehensive FTAs with a few countries in which it has greater interests, China negotiates FTAs with many countries (Nakagawa and Liang, 2011: 2).

3.1. *The legal protection of Chinese investments*

Probably following the Confucian tradition, China has numerous internal mechanisms for solving investment disputes with foreign investors (Wang and He, 2013: 231) not only administrative reconsideration and litigation, as most countries provide, but also "complaint centres, mediation panels, and working panels . . . at different administrative levels" (Ministry of Commerce of the People's Republic of China, 2006). It is also often argued that litigation is discouraged in some Chinese BITs by providing a 3 months' advance notice to be able to initiate arbitration proceedings (Wang and He, 2013: 231). Some authors defend that mediation fits better the settlement of investment disputes involving Chinese parties than arbitration (Wang and He, 2013: 236).

Other authors defend that arbitration, unlike litigation in State courts, is "an indispensable part of China's legal culture" (Zhang, 2005: 180). As early as 2005, Chinese authors started pointing out a growing trend to use investment arbitration clauses both in international contracts involving Chinese parties and in investment-related treaties to which China is a party.

BITs are bilateral treaties that grant protection standards to foreign investors and provide a dispute-resolution mechanism for foreign investors to seek relief in case the aforementioned standards are violated. The dispute resolution-mechanisms contained in BITs usually include at least one kind of arbitration or a combination of two or more alternative kinds of arbitration, such as ICSID Arbitration Rules, ICSID Additional Facility Rules, United Nations Commission on International Trade Law (UNCITRAL) Arbitration Rules, ad hoc arbitration and institutional arbitration (such as ICC Court of Arbitration) (Rooney, 2007: 692).

In 1982, China signed its first China-Sweden BIT, and since then, it has become one of the countries with the biggest number of investment treaties. In terms of BITs signed, China ranks second, after Germany. In terms of BITs in force, China ranks third, after Germany and Switzerland.

Although various classifications of the Chinese BIT programme have been made, Chinese BITs are most often classified into first, second and third generation (Gallagher and Shan, 2009: 35). Some authors consider FTAs concluded by

China since 2006 as a fourth generation of the Chinese BIT programme (Vaccaro-Incisa, 2014: 11). First generation agreements were mainly signed between 1982 and 1989 (Gallagher and Shan, 2009: 35). Second generation agreements were mostly concluded between 1990 and 1997 (Gallagher and Shan, 2009: 38). The emergence of second generation BITs largely coincides with the signature on the 9th February 1990 of the ICSID Convention by China, which became binding on the Middle Kingdom on the 6th February 1993. Nevertheless, from 1993 to early 2000 both first and second generation, as well as mixed, BITs were signed. The third generation of Chinese BIT started being used in 1998 and is the current model (Shan et al., 2013: 143).

First generation Chinese BITs include the following substantive protections to investments: expropriation standards, fair and equitable treatment, national treatment and repatriation of investments and returns (Rooney, 2007: 702). As for the scope of disputes that could be arbitrated under Chinese BITs, it is limited to the amount of compensation for expropriation once the competent Chinese authority has determined the existence of a violation of the material protection standards (Rooney, 2007: 703).

Dispute-resolution clauses contained in first generation Chinese BITs have a strong influence of Soviet BITs (Irwin, 2014: 3). These clauses usually establish a period of 6 months for amicable negotiations. They also allowed submitting any dispute to the competent judicial or administrative institution of the host State. Some of the kinds of arbitration mentioned in first generation BITs were: (1) an ad hoc tribunal established according to the BIT, (2) an ad hoc tribunal established according to a later agreement among the parties (3) an ad hoc tribunal under UNCITRAL Arbitration Rules, (4) a sole arbitrator or (5) a tribunal established according to the Washington Convention (Rooney, 2007: 704). One must note, however, that very incipient BITs, such as China-Sweden BIT in 1982, do not contain any investor-State dispute arbitration clause (Willems, 2011: 21).

Second generation Chinese BITs grant more material and procedural protections than first generation ones. They generally add to the protections of first generation treaties other provisions such as full protection and security and MFN treatment. The scope of disputes arbitrable under second generation BITs is much broader than the one contained in first generation BITs, since it comprises any dispute concerning investments between an investor of one contracting party and the other contracting party (Rooney, 2007: 705). Consent clauses in newer Chinese BITs are similar to the European BITs (Willems, 2011: 25).

Dispute-resolution clauses in second generation BITs refer to a negotiations period of 6 months, after which disputes would be submitted to arbitration under the Washington Convention, unless both parties agree to submit their dispute to an *ad hoc* tribunal following the UNCITRAL Arbitration Rules or another set of rules.

The third generation BIT model was first used in the China-Barbados BIT in July 1998 (Gallagher and Shan, 2009: 40). This BIT first provided that all disputes may be submitted to ICSID for settlement. Unlike in second generation BITs, there was no longer limitation on the scope of disputes that could be submitted to ICSID for settlement. Later, China signed some BITs with the Netherlands (2001), Germany (2003), Finland (2004) and some other countries.

Almost all Ibero-American and Caribbean countries have at least one agreement in the field of investments in force with either the Government of the People's Republic of China or with the Government of the Republic of China, except for Brazil, Puerto Rico and Venezuela. The People's Republic of China has BITs in force with Argentina, Bolivia, Chile, Colombia, Cuba, Ecuador, Mexico, Peru and Uruguay. Furthermore, FTAs have entered into force between the PRC and Peru, Chile and Costa Rica.

As a result of the "one country, two systems" principles, it is possible for one country to sign treaties with the People's Republic of China and/or Hong Kong SAR and/or Macao SAR. No Latin American or Caribbean Country has signed a treaty in the field of investments with Macao and the only Latin American country that has actually signed one with Hong Kong SAR so far is Chile. The Chile-Hong Kong FTA entered into force on the 9th October 2014. On the 18th November 2016, a BIT was concluded with Chile, but it has not yet entered into force. Other countries are interested to sign an investment agreement with Hong Kong, such as Mexico.

Some Ibero-American countries maintain diplomatic relations with the Government of the Republic of China, with capital in Taipei. Most of these countries have signed some kind of treaty in the field of investments with the ROC, such as the Dominican Republic, El Salvador, Guatemala, Nicaragua and Paraguay. Honduras signed a BIT with Taiwan in 1996 but it was never ratified. The dispute-resolution mechanisms contemplated in international treaties to which the Republic of China is a party are not analysed in this study, since the biggest Latin American economies have diplomatic relations with the PRC.

The BIT between the Republic of China and Costa Rica entered into force on the 8th October 2004 and is still applicable despite the recognition by Costa Rica of the Government in Beijing in 2007. More recently, on the 13th June 2016, the PRC and the Republic of Panama established diplomatic relations. The ROC-Panama BIT on the 14th July 1992 is still applicable as well. This is consistent with the One-China principle, given Taiwan's status as a territory within the WTO, capable of carrying out its own agreements in economic matters.

3.2. The legal protection of Japanese investments

Japan has clearly adopted the position of a net capital exporter as early as the 1980s. Japanese economic growth from the end of the World War II was achieved thanks to its high savings rate, but also to the important amounts of FDI that the country of the rising sun received.

Until the beginning of the 21st Century, Japan gave preference to multilateral trade negotiations within the World Trade Organisation. Since then, its policy converged with the global tendency of negotiating FTAs. Japan sought to restore the competitiveness of its enterprises operating abroad, since other capital-exporting countries had started to conclude treaties that granted their own enterprises a competitive advantage. Such was the case of the Japan-Mexico Economic Partnership Agreement (EPA), which was a reaction to the NAFTA and the Mexico-EU FTA. The generalisation of the policies' based on bilateral agreements is also the result of the difficult negotiations within the WTO system. The bilateral negotiations of treaties with investments provisions, notably with South-East Asian nations, also largely depend on its security alliance with the US and therefore fostering the Asian regional integration and well as "maintaining balance between competition and cooperation with China" (Nakagawa and Liang, 2011: 4, 15). With the bilateralisation of the Japanese investment policy, Japan perceived the convenience of drafting a model BIT that could save transaction costs from negotiating each new treaty from scratch (Hamamoto and Nottage, 2013: 390).

The Japanese agricultural lobby was clearly against the liberalisation of agricultural trade, which became a major challenge while negotiating the EPA with Mexico and other major agricultural producers. A model of compromise was achieved by excluding certain agricultural products from the general liberalisation commitment. Japan chose to conclude EPAs with his major trade partners and investment targets as far as balance could be achieved between pursuing Japanese business interests abroad and the harm that Japanese agriculture may suffer. As for BITs, the main criteria adopted for choosing with whom to conclude them is the search for the promotion and protection of Japanese investments abroad. Based on the BIT policy released by Ministry of Foreign Affairs (MOFA), Japan in 2008, priority would be given to negotiating BITs with (a) countries in which Japan has carried out or may carry out substantial investments, (b) countries with difficult business environment or (c) providers of energy and natural resources (Nakagawa and Liang, 2011: 5, 7, 14, 15).

Japanese position as a capital exporter consolidated thanks to the large increase in outward FDI during the 1980s (Hamamoto and Nottage, 2013: 347). In the field of investments, Japanese bilateral treaties are characterised by the strong liberalisation of investments as well as the strong legal protections conferred to them, especially in the so-called "new-generation BITs", which in the case of Japan refer to those concluded after the beginning of the 21st Century. The strong protection of investments is achieved through clauses such as those granting national treatment before the investment has been carried out and, at post-investment stage, by using umbrella clauses. The high level of investments liberalisation is achieved through the prohibition of performance requirements or the prohibition to make an investment conditional to other activities such as hiring local employees or transferring technology (Nakagawa and Liang, 2011: 9–11).

Being coherent with the conciliatory approach to dispute settlement, Japanese BITs and EPAs adopt a two-tiered process. Adequate opportunity for consultations shall be granted before referring a matter to arbitration, which can be used only if the matter cannot be "satisfactorily adjusted by diplomacy". The elements of the arbitration proceedings often defined in the dispute-resolution clauses are rather standard: three arbitrators, the President of the International Court of Justice acting as appointing authority if parties or co-arbitrators fail to nominate, each party bears the costs of the arbitrator appointed by them and division of other costs incurred as a result of the arbitration.

Japanese BITs and investment chapters in EPAs also refer to investor-State dispute settlement. Priority is always given to amicable settlement. It is usually established a cooling-off period that ranges from 3 to 6 months after lodging the request for arbitration or the notice of intent. Both flexible and strict "fork-in-the road" clauses are found in Japanese investment treaties. The Japan-Mexico EPA adopts a flexible approach, since it allows to withdraw a claim previously submitted to a different jurisdiction. The Japan-Chile EPA adopts a strict approach, since if an investor choses to submit a dispute to a national court, the choice is definitive. The jurisdictional options that most often appear in Japanese arbitration clauses are: (1) litigation in State courts or administrative tribunals, (2) ICSID arbitration, (3) ICSID additional facility arbitration or (4) arbitration under UNCITRAL arbitration rules or (5) anther sort of arbitration agreed by the parties. ICSID conciliation is also sometimes found within Japanese investor-State dispute-resolution clauses (Hamamoto and Nottage, 2013: 373–388).

The first time that the question of investor-State clauses within Japanese investment treaties was raised at the Japanese Diet was in May 2011. The arguments that have been used in Japan for and against arbitration between States and investors are not different from the ones used in the rest of the World. Hamamoto highlights the fact that criticism was closely linked to the negotiations of the TPP, in which the US has been present for many years (Hamamoto, 2015: 933). Mexico and Chile are OECD members and Brazil may soon become one. These countries fulfil certain high-standard economic criteria; nevertheless, they are not perceived as threatening for the Japanese industry and therefore, the settlement of investment disputes with them is not subject to strict scrutiny from the Japanese public opinion and political forces.

The Japanese EPAs strategy initially gave priority to negotiations with Asian nations with the aim of enhancing political and economic stability in the region similar to what the NAFTA had achieved in North America or the free flow of capitals among EU Member States (González-Vigil and Shimizu, 2012: 23–25). Concerning the Ibero-American region, Japan has concluded an EPA with Peru and EPAs with Chile and Mexico, which entered into force in 2012, 2007 and 2005[3] respectively. Japan has also BITs in force with Peru and Colombia since 2009 and 2015 respectively. The country of the rising sun also signed a BIT with Uruguay, but it has not yet entered into force.

The investment chapter of the EPA with Mexico – in its 2004 version – was perceived from the Mexican side as an instrument in the line of the NAFTA and Mexican Agreements for Reciprocal Protection and Promotion of Investments, Mexico, "a clear mirror of a Mexican policy on international economic negotiations" that reduces the perceived levels of non-commercial risk, constraints the receiving State from carrying out actions distortive of international investments and sets forth legal protections that may have an important impact on foreign investments arriving to Mexico. The explicit permit for investment agencies – the Overseas Private Investment Corporation (OPIC) in the Mexican side and the Japan External Trade Organisation (JETRO) in the Japanese side – to provide support to investment projects (such as "equity investment, investment guarantees and insurance or reinsurance") is very much in the line of enhancing cooperative means to foster investments (Faya-Rodríguez, 2005: 145–146, 154–157).

The EPA with Peru sought to reinvigorate the bilateral trade and investment position between Japan and Peru, that had been deteriorating from the mid-1970s until the end of Alberto Fujimori's presidency in 2.000. According to JETRO, the main reasons that deteriorated Japanese investment flows into Peru were: (1) the insecurity created by terrorist groups, which targeted Japanese cooperation experts in 1991 as well as the hostages crisis following the assault to the residence of the Japanese Ambassador that started in December 1996, (2) Peruvian economic instability during the 1980s, (3) the "political mistrust with the U.S.A." and (4) Peru's trade policies during this period, namely the low quality of the infrastructure related to logistics. These factors may have led to deterioration in global investment flows to Peru, but Japanese ones diminished in great proportion (González-Vigil and Shimizu, 2012: 3).

Peru radically changed its approach to international economic governance since the beginning of the 21st Century, which crystallised in the Peru-US FTA of 2004 and the leading role within the APEC since 2008. Precisely during the XVI APEC leaders' summit that took place in Lima that year, Japan and Peru started formal consultations to eventually negotiate an EPA. From a Japanese pint of view, the EPA with Peru basically follows the lines previously drafted in the EPAs with Mexico and Chile (González-Vigil and Shimizu, 2012: 21, 25).

New-generation Japanese BITs and EPAs include "social clauses". The most frequent kind of social clauses are the ones referring to environmental protection, which refer to the prohibition of encouraging investments by relaxing environmental protection (Hamamoto and Nottage, 2013: 370–371). Some treaties, such as the Japan-Peru BIT, include reference to health, safety and labour standards (Art. 26).

All the new-generation BITs and FTAs, and even some old-generation ones, establish a joint committee composed of representatives from both countries who meet regularly with the function of monitoring the implementation of the treaty. Sub-committees for the improvement of the business environment are created in FTAs and even in the Japan-Peru BIT. In these sub-committees, not only government representatives, but also the private sector from both countries is represented (Hamamoto and Nottage, 2013: 371–373).

Japan's New-Generation BITs also include institutional arrangements for the improvement of the business environment. This is very much in line with the often-alleged Asian approach to dispute-settlement. Most of these BITs create bilateral joint committees composed by representatives of both countries' investors and their Public Administration. These committees aim at helping to implementing the agreements by trying to improve the business environment and issue advisory opinions on how to solve problems that may be submitted to them. Some of the New-Generation BITs also create contact points or liaison offices, whose role is to convey to the competent Administration the complaints that investors may submit to them using this rather discreet and informal channel (Nakagawa and Liang, 2011: 11).

Unlike other proposals for the improvement of the business environment, the Japanese one is fully operative and rather transparent: there are offices of JETRO in Lima, Mexico DF and Santiago de Chile, and the telephone number to contact them is easily available on the internet.

The BIT with Peru and the EPAs with Chile and Mexico include other innovative clauses. The BIT with Peru explicitly establishes a period of expiration of the right to raise claims after the investor knew or should have known about the damage or loss caused by the host State. The EPAs with Chile and Mexico refer to the possibility to consolidate ICSID claims, the public disclosure of documents in the arbitration *inter alia*.

3.3. The legal protection of Korean investments

The reconstruction of South Korea was carried out during the second half of the 20th Century with foreign capital: first with foreign aid, mostly coming from the US and later by attracting foreign private capital. Korea sought to attract FDI after the end of the War in 1953 in two ways. First, by improving the treatment legally given to foreign capital through the enactment of the Foreign Capital Inducement Promotion Law of 1960, Korea (Shin and Chung, 2015: 955). And, most importantly, by concluding international treaties in the field of investments that gave further international legal protection to foreign capital entering Korea.

Korea has progressively evolved into a relevant capital exporter, especially after its accession to the Organisation for Economic Cooperation and Development (OECD) in 1996. Nowadays, South Korea still adopts the role of a capital-importing country in its relations with Japan, the European Union and the United States, but it adopts a capital-exporter role with the rest of the world. The active BITs and FTAs programme carried out by Korea at the beginning of the 21st Century reflects its growing relevance as a capital exporter (Shin, 2013: 393).

Korea signed its first BIT with Germany as early as 1964; however, investor-State dispute settlement only appeared in the BIT with the Netherlands in 1975. The Republic of Korea has been consistently developing a portentous network of investment treaties (second in number of the Asian Continent, only surpassed by China) that serves both to make its investment environment attractive for foreign investors and to protect Korean investors abroad. During the 1970s, emphasis was given to BITs with capital-exporting European States. Korea started to sign BITs with developing countries during the 1980s, seeking to impose similar treaties to the ones that it had previously accepted to conclude with developed countries. In the 1990s, Korea concluded investment treaties with countries at various stages of development and started to show certain flexibility in negotiating the specific terms of the agreements according to its counterpart's demands. It was only in 2003 that Korea started to conclude FTAs. The investment chapters negotiated within FTAs are substantially similar to the ones in the North Atlantic Free Trade Agreement (NAFTA) (Shin and Chung, 2015: 955–957). Most Korean international treaties in the field of investments currently in force contain provisions allowing and regulating some kind of investor-State dispute settlement mechanism.

The Korean Government internally uses a model BIT and released a document in 2001 called "Our Country's Model BIT", frequently called the Model BIT, Korea, 2001, which is based on BITs that Korea has signed with European countries. Further amendments made to this model BIT for internal use have not been publicly disclosed (Shin and Chung, 2015: 957). The 2001 Korean BIT does not oblige the parties to liberalise investments. As for negotiating its FTAs, Korea seems to follow the Korea-US FTA, which does contain strong liberalisation commitments, similarly to the Model BIT, US, 2004 (Shin, 2013: 198).

The 2001 Korean Model BIT provides for a multi-layered dispute-resolution clause, which establishes in first place, that disputes should be first handled through consultations. If an agreement is not reached within 6 months, either contracting party may start *ad hoc* arbitration proceedings. Once the request for arbitration is received, the parties have 2 months to nominate one arbitrator each. The two nominated arbitrators shall select a national of a third State as the Chairman of the tribunal. If any of the appointments is not made within the deadline, either Contracting Party may ask the President of the International Court of Justice to do so.

Korea has BITs in force with various Ibero-American countries, namely Argentina, Bolivia, Chile, Costa Rica, Dominican Republic, El Salvador, Guatemala, Honduras, Mexico, Nicaragua, Panama, Paraguay and Uruguay. The first BIT signed between Korea and an Ibero-American country was the one with Peru (on the 3rd June 1993), but it has been terminated. The BITs with Brazil and Colombia were signed in 1995 and 2010 respectively, but never entered into force. Korea has also concluded FTAs with investment provisions with Chile, Peru and Colombia, which have entered into force in 2004, 2011 and 2016 respectively. Costa Rica, El Salvador, Guatemala, Honduras, Nicaragua and Panama have been holding negotiations since June 2015 in order to conclude a Central-American joint FTA with Korea (ECLAC, 2016: 11).

Like in Japan, one of the main obstacles while negotiating international economic treaties between Korea and Ibero-American countries is the opposition of the agricultural lobby. Also similar to Japan, the public opinion may become and obstacle in order to conclude investment treaties. When the FTA with the United States of America (KORUS FTA) was being negotiated, around the year 2006, investor-State dispute-settlement mechanisms become a major concern (Shin and Chung, 2015: 961–968).

After the KORUS FTA, Korea became rather sensitive about dispute settlement in the field of investments and developed its own positions in various aspects. First, since 2006, the definition of "investment", "investor" and "denial of benefits" has become narrower in Korean treaties. Second, the application of too broad concepts of "fair and equitable treatment" was avoided either by fully defining it within the treaty or by simply referring to the "minimum standard of treatment under customary international law" (Korea-Uruguay BIT, Art. 2(2), (3)). Third, to include an annex containing what their common understanding of "indirect expropriation" is in order to avoid unexpected results to come up. Fourth, the arbitration proceedings are regulated in much more detail. Whereas the 2001 Model BIT simply addressed a few essential elements of the proceedings and only refers to ICSID arbitration, the KORUS FTA devotes various articles to carefully regulate various options of arbitration available to investors (Shin and Chung, 2015: 968–978).

As part of its policy to attract FDI and the achievement of the *segyehwa* or globalisation, especially after the APEC summit of 1994, Korea also became a forerunner of the mechanisms for the facilitation of investments. As early as 1998, the Korea Trade-Investment Promotion Agency (KOTRA) created the Korea Investment Service Centre (KISC) that aimed at providing support administrative and advisory support to investors before, during and after the investment is carried out. In 2003, the KISC was transformed into Invest Korea. In 1999, the Foreign Investment Ombudsman (FIO), Korea was created with the function of handling specific grievances from foreign investors. After reforms in 2010, the Office of the Foreign Investment Ombudsman (OFIO) was given considerable powers that improve its effectiveness, such as chairing the Regulatory Reform Committee (RCC), Korea or sitting at the Presidential Council on National Competitiveness (PCNC), Korea, which grants wide access to high-level governmental authorities when handling foreign-investors' grievances (Nicolas et al., 2013: 23–25).

4. Ibero-American trends towards dispute resolution in the field of investments

Some of the newest trends in international economic governance come from Ibero-American countries, as well as some of the traditional doctrines related to the treatment of foreign investments. The Calvo Doctrine, proposed by Argentinian diplomat Carlos Calvo, originally consisted on giving exclusive jurisdiction to national courts over disputes with foreigners, under the argument that foreigners shall enjoy no more rights than nationals of a State. Some treaties in the field of investments concluded by Ibero-American countries, as well as pieces of legislation, and even Constitutions and regional agreements, included clauses inspired by this doctrine (Cremades, 2004: 2). The Drago Doctrine also finds its origins in Ibero-America, being announced by Argentinian Foreign Affairs Minister José María Drago at the very beginning of the 20th Century; this doctrine forbade the use of force to recover debts (Sornarajah, 2010: 279). In times of economic and social turmoil, these protectionist trends seem to recover political momentum (Cremades, 2004: 1).

Most Ibero-American countries have ratified the Washington Convention. The convention is fully in force in Argentina, Chile, Colombia, Costa Rica, El

Salvador, Guatemala, Honduras, Nicaragua, Panama, Paraguay, Peru and Uruguay. Some Latin American countries chose to withdraw from the Washington Convention, namely Bolivia, Ecuador and Venezuela. Meanwhile, Ecuador has been revising and denouncing some of its bilateral treaties in the field of investments; nevertheless, even after being denounced, BITs might still be applicable to a certain extent by virtue of the so-called "survival provisions".

We have already referred to the change of Peru's approach to dispute-settlement in the field of investments. In a similar line, Colombia has adopted a policy clearly based in the attraction of foreign capital by granting both national and international protections to investments, which include – but are not limited to – the resource to investor-State dispute-settlement mechanisms. Colombia even has an official Model BIT (Rivas, 2013: 183–187).

Some of the current proposals for economic governance coming from Ibero-America include the creation of a UNASUR Dispute Resolution Centre and the Brazilian model of Agreement for Cooperation and Facilitation of Investments (ACFI). The proposal originally came from Ecuador and aimed at creating an alternative to ICSID arbitration. The UNASUR Working Group on Dispute-Settlement in the field of Investments was created on the 23rd May 2008 in Brasilia with the aim of drafting an agreement for the creation of the Centre. Among the innovations that this initiative includes, the most interesting one may be the proposal for the creation of a legal counselling centre in the area of investment disputes for Member States, similar to the one that already exists in the context of the World Trade Organisation for the least developed countries (García Jiménez, 2017: 48–51).

Brazil has traditionally based its successful strategy to receive foreign investments in granting internal – not international – legal protections (García Jiménez, 2017: 51–54). Brazil is currently negotiating a peculiar kind of international agreement in the field of investments, the Agreements for Cooperation and Facilitation of Investments (ACFIs). In 2015, ACFIs were signed with Mozambique, Angola, Mexico, Malawi, Colombia and Chile, and in 2016, another one was signed with Peru. More recently, a regional investments agreement called the Protocol for Cooperation and Facilitation of Investments (PCFI) was signed among Mercosur original Member States. The PCFI was negotiated on the basis of the model ACFI. The main difference between a traditional investment treaty and an ACFI is the fact that the latter focuses on the prevention of disputes and the promotion of investments rather than on the legal mechanisms for dispute-settlement. ACFIs do not regulate investor-to-State arbitration. Another characteristic of ACFIs is that protection against indirect expropriation is not granted.

Like in Japanese EPAs, two institutions are created through ACFIs in order to allow the exchange of information, the prevention of conflicts and the non-litigation resolution of conflicts that might arise. The first kind of institution are the joint committees, composed by representatives of both signatories' governments and whose main function is to "administer the agreement" by following its implementation, to share opportunities for reciprocal investments, coordinate cooperation, to conduct consultations with the private sector and the civil society, to carry out the amicable settlement of disputes and to implement the dispute-resolution mechanisms contained in the ACFI (Brazil-Mexico ACFI, Art. 14).

The second kind of institution is the "focal point", whose main function is to support the investors of the other contracting party. Focal points also receive the name of "ombudsmen", which seems quite misleading to us. Ombudsman, Defensor del Pueblo, Médiateur de la République and similar institutions are always institutions created through domestic law, not through international treaties. Focal points contained in ACFIs were inspired by the South Korean Office of the Foreign Investment Ombudsman (OFIO), Korea (Rocha, 2015: 183). Nevertheless, OFIO is a national Korean institution established and regulated through domestic law, not through an international treaty. OFIO is a complementary mechanism to about 99 BITs and 20 other IIAs signed by the Republic of Korea.

ACFIs include exceptions to many of the material protections that it recognises (Rocha, 2015: 126). A literal interpretation of various clauses within the agreement would lead to very little legal consequence of signing such an international treaty in the field investments. The procedural legal consequences of the signature of an ACFI are also limited compared to other kinds of international treaties in the field of investments, such as BITs or FTAs, since ACFIS do not provide for an investor-State arbitration system, but rather a State-State dispute-settlement mechanism.

5. Conclusion

The economic and political interest of Asian countries in the Ibero-American region has been incessantly growing in recent years. The investments of China, Japan and Korea in the region have also become more relevant; Chinese investments are growing faster, but the stock of Japanese investments is still much bigger. Chinese investments in Ibero-America are still focused in securing energy and raw materials for their industry, although there is room for diversification in areas such as agricultural products and infrastructure. With very similar origins, Japanese investments are highly diversified nowadays, with a clear focus in services. Korean investments in Ibero-America are rather diversified with predominance of manufactures.

China is moving towards more liberal mechanisms for the settlement of investment disputes in order to grant legal protections to its investments abroad, as its role as a capital exporter consolidates. Japan and Korea also received huge amounts of foreign capital from abroad, but they became net capital exporters in the 1980s and the 1990s respectively. China made a general ICSID Convention, reservation to the Washington Convention, but it increases the scope of arbitrable disputes through a huge amount of bilateral and regional treaties with very different degrees of liberalisation compromises. Korea and Japan made no reservation to the Washington Convention and include modern jurisdictional means for the settlement of disputes in their bilateral treaties in the field of investments. The net of Japanese BITs is small but solid and is characterised by carefully choosing its counterparts and building strong and durable partnerships.

The three nations or Far-East Asia have developed mechanisms for the facilitation of investments and the avoidance of disputes. The origin for these non-litigation mechanisms in the field of investments could be found in the Confucian tradition, but in fact similar proposals have emerged in countries that do not share this cultural heritage, such as Brazil. Unlike in Ibero-America, where political tensions coexist among supporters and detractors of solving disputes in international jurisdictional forums, among Far-East Asian countries there is no hesitation about the need of international jurisdictional mechanisms for dispute settlement as a means of last resort and the cooperation and facilitation methods are complementary – although of great importance – to jurisdictional ones. The current political trend in Ibero-America seems to be generally favourable to the protection of foreign investments with exceptions such as Venezuela, but even in a cyclical conjuncture of political turmoil, contract-based arbitration is still possible. The inclusion of survival provisions in bilateral treaties may also enable the use of treaty-based arbitration even after the eventual denunciation of international treaties in the field of investments.

So far, there is no arbitration chamber clearly specialised in the administration of investment disputes between Asia and Latin America. Arbitration institutions such as HKIAC aim at administering these disputes. An arbitration chamber located in a third country with good relations with both regions, such as Spain, could be an additional guarantee of neutrality.

Notes

1 Ph.D. student at the University of International Business and Economics (UIBE, Beijing). This research has received the support of La Caixa Banking Foundation as part of the project LCF/BQ/AP14/1033001.
2 Meaning Spanish-speaking and Portuguese-speaking Latin America. The notion of Latin America is different, since it also includes French-speaking America, such as Québec.
3 The Japan-Mexico EPA was revised in 2012.

References

Cerdeiro, D. A. (2016). Estimating the Effects of the Trans-Pacific Partnership (TPP) on Latin America and the Caribbean (LAC). *IMF Working Paper*, 16(101), 1–30.
Chen, T. and Pérez Ludeña, M. (2014). *Chinese Foreign Direct Investment in Latin America and the Caribbean*, Santiago de Chile: Economic Commission for Latin America and the Caribbean (ECLAC).
Cremades, B. M. (2004). Disputes Arising Out of Foreign Direct Investment in Latin America: A New Look at the Calvo Doctrine and Other Jurisdictional Issues. *Dispute Resolution Journal*, 59(2).
Economic Commission for Latin America and the Caribbean (ECLAC) (2015). *First Forum of China and the Community of Latin American and Caribbean States (CELAC): Exploring Opportunities for Cooperation on Trade and Investment*, Santiago de Chile: Economic Commission for Latin America and the Caribbean (ECLAC).

Economic Commission for Latin America and the Caribbean (ECLAC) (2016). *Exploring Cooperation Between the Republic of Korea and the Community of Latin American and Caribbean States (CELAC) in the Areas of Innovation and SME Internationalisation Strategies*, Santiago de Chile: Economic Commission for Latin America and the Caribbean (ECLAC).

Estevadeordal, A., Mesquita Moreira, M. and Kahn, T. (2014). *Latin America and the Caribbean Investments in China: A New Chapter of the Relations Between Latin America and the Caribbean and China*, Washington, DC: Inter-American Development Bank.

Faya-Rodríguez, A. (2005). Reaching the Asian Tiger: A New Mexico-Japan International Framework for Investment. *Journal of World Investment & Trade*, 6, 145–157.

Fiezzoni, S. K. (2012). UNASUR Arbitration Centre: The Present Situation and the Principal Characteristics of Ecuador's Proposal. *Investment Treaty News*, 2(2), 6–7.

Gallagher, N. and Shan, W. (2009). *Chinese Investment Treaties: Policies and Practice*, Oxford: Oxford International Arbitration Series.

García Jiménez, A. (2017). On the Settlement of Investment Disputes Between China and Latin America. *China Legal Science*, 5(2), 34–62.

González-Vigil, F. and Shimizu, T. (2012). The Japan-Peru FTA: Antecedents, Significance and Main Features. *Institute of Developing Economies of the Japan External Trade Organisation Discussion Papers*, 335, 1–31.

Hamamoto, S. (2015). Recent Anti-ISDS Discourse in the Japanese Diet: A Dressed-Up But Glaring Hypocrisy. *The Journal of World Investment and Trade*, 16, 931–951.

Hamamoto, S. and Nottage, L. (2013). Japan. In C. Brown, ed., *Commentaries on Selected Model Investment Treaties*, Oxford: Oxford University Press, pp. 347 *et seq.*

Harris, D. J. (2004). *Cases and Materials on International Law*, London: Sweet & Maxwell.

The Heritage Foundation (2016). *China's Global Reach: China Global Investment Tracker*, Washington, DC: The Heritage Foundation.

Ho, J. (2013). Singapore. In C. Brown, ed., *Commentaries on Selected Model Investment Treaties*, Oxford: Oxford University Press, pp. 623 *et seq.*

Hoadley, S. (2007). Southeast Asian Cross-Regional FTAs: Origins, Motives and Aims. *Pacific Affairs*, 80(2), 303–325.

International Centre for the Settlement of Investment Disputes (ICSID) (2016). *ICSID Database: Cases in Which China Has Acted as a Respondent Under ICSID*, Washington, DC: International Centre for the Settlement of Investment Disputes (ICSID).

Irwin, A. (2014). Crossing the Ocean by Feeling for the BITs: Investor-State Arbitration in China's Bilateral Investment Treaties. *Boston University Global Economic Governance Initiative (GEGI) Working Papers Series*, 3, 1–32.

Kahn, T. (2016). *A Virtuous Cycle of Integration: The Past, the Present, and Future of Japan-Latin America and the Caribbean Relations*, Washington, DC: Inter-American Development Bank.

Kotschwar, B., Moran, T. H. and Muir, J. (2012). Chinese Investment in Latin American Resources: The Good, the Bad, and the Ugly. *Working Paper Series of the Peterson Institute for International Economics*, 12(3).

Lowenfeld, A. F. (2003). *International Economic Law*, Oxford: Oxford University Press.

Ministry of Commerce of the People's Republic of China (MOFCOM) (2006). Provisional Measures of the Ministry of Commerce on Handling Complaints Lodged by Foreign-Invested Enterprises. *MOFCOM Decree N°*, 2/2006 of October 1.

Ministry of Commerce of the People's Republic of China (MOFCOM), National Bureau of Statistics of China and State Administration of Foreign Exchange (SAFE) (2014). *2013 Statistical Bulletin of China's Outward Foreign Direct Investment*, Beijing: National Bureau of Statistics of China.

Ministry of Commerce of the People's Republic of China (MOFCOM), National Bureau of Statistics of China and State Administration of Foreign Exchange (SAFE) (2015). *2014 Statistical Bulletin of China's Outward Foreign Direct Investment*, Beijing: National Bureau of Statistics of China.

Myers, M. and Kuwayama, M. (2016). *A New Stage in the Relations Between Japan and Latin America and the Caribbean*, Washington, DC: The Inter-American Dialogue.

Nakagawa, J. and Liang, W. (2011). A Comparison of the FTA Strategies of Japan and China and Their Implications for Multilateralism. *Indiana University Research Centre for Chinese Politics and Business Working Paper*, 11, 1–35.

National Development and Reform Commission of the People's Republic of China (2012). *Plan for the Utilization of Foreign Capital and Overseas Investment in the 12th Five-Year Plan Period*, Beijing: National Development and Reform Commission (NDRC).

National Secretariat of Development and Planning (*Secretaría Nacional de Planificación y Desarrollo*) (SENPLADES) (2012?). *Bilateral Investment Treaties' Audit Goes on (Continúa Auditoría a los Tratados Bilaterales de Inversión)*, Quito: Secretaría Nacional de Planificación y Desarrollo (National Secretariat of Development and Planning).

Nicolas, F., Thomsen, S. and Bang, M. (2013). Lessons from Investment Policy Reform in Korea. *OECD Working Papers on International Investment*, 2013(02), 5–43.

Perrone, N. M. and César, G. R. (2015). Brazil's Bilateral Investment Treaties: More Than a New Investment Treaty Model? *Columbia University Academic Commons*, 159.

Qi, T. (2012). How Exactly Does China Consent to Investor-State Arbitration: On the First ICSID Case Against China. *Contemporary Asia Arbitration Journal*, 5(2), 265–291.

Rivas, J. A. (2013). Colombia. In C. Brown, ed., *Commentaries on Selected Model Investment Treaties*, Oxford: Oxford University Press, pp. 183 *et seq.*

Rocha, V. D. (2015). *The Legal Protection of Brazilian Investments Abroad*, Sao Paulo: University of Sao Paulo Law School Repository.

Rooney, K. M. (2007). ICSID and BIT Arbitrations and China. *Journal of International Arbitration*, 24(6), 689–712.

Schill, S. W. (2015). Special Issue: Dawn of an Asian Century on International Investment Law? An Introduction. *The Journal of World Investment & Trade*, 16, 765–771.

Shan, W., Gallagher, N. and Brown, C. (2013). *Commentaries on Selected Model Investment Treaties*, Oxford: Oxford Commentaries on International Law.

Shin, H. T. (2013). Republic of Korea. In C. Brown, ed., *Commentaries on Selected Model Investment Treaties*, Oxford: Oxford University Press, pp. 393 *et seq.*

Shin, H. T. and Chung, L. K. H. (2015). Korea's Experience with International Investment Agreements and Investor-State Dispute Settlement. *The Journal of World Investment & Trade*, 16, 952–980.

Singapore Government, International Enterprise Singapore (2017). *Singapore Investments in Latin America & the Caribbean Continue to Grow, with New Opportunities in Tech and Education*, Media Release 041/17.

Sornarajah, M. (2010). *The International Law on Foreign Investments*, 3rd edn, Cambridge: Cambridge University Press.

United Nations Conference on Trade and Development (UNCTAD) (2010). *Investor-State Disputes: Prevention and Alternatives to Arbitration*, 1st edn, New York and Geneva: UNCTAD Series on International Investment Policies for Development.

United Nations Conference on Trade and Development (UNCTAD) (2017). *World Investment Report of 2017: Investment and the Digital Economy*. United Nations Publication.

Vaccaro-Incisa, G. M. (2014). The Evolution of China's Policy and Treaty Practice in International Investment Law: An Outline. *Bocconi Legal Papers*, 4, 89–116.

Wang, G. and He, X. (2013). Mediation and International Investment: A Chinese Perspective. *Maine Law Review*, 65(1), 216–236.

Wignaraja, G., Ramizo, D. and Burmeister, L. (2013). Assessing Liberalization and Deep Integration in FTAs: A Study of Asia-Latin American FTAs. *Journal of East Asian Economic Integration*, 17(4), 385–415.

Willems, J. Y. (2011). The Settlement of Investor State Disputes and China New Developments on ICSID Jurisdiction. *South Carolina Journal of International Law and Business*, 8, 1–62.

Yang, J. (2014). Red Trojan Horses? A New Look at Chinese SOEs' Outward Investments. *Journal of China and International Relations*, 2(1).

Zhang, Y. (2005). Arbitration of Foreign Investment Disputes in China. In A. J. Van Den Berg, ed., *New Horizons in International Commercial Arbitration and Beyond*, The Hague: Kluwer Law International, pp. 180 *et seq*.

Zhu, D. Z. (2015). International Investment Agreements Among China, Japan and Korea: From "Bilateral" to "Trilateral": The Way Towards a Better Protection for Foreign Investors. *Manchester Journal of International Economic Law*, 12(1), 80–107.

4 Defending the undefendable

Asia's sovereignist battles against easy access to investment treaty arbitration

Relja Radović

1. Introduction

It could be said that modern international investment law was born in Asia.[1] However, when it comes to recent trends in this field, usually the other parts of the world emerge at the forefront. The backlash against investor-state arbitration, as well as attempts at reasserting state control over this dispute settlement mechanism, usually emphasise some radical challenges,[2] or more general restructuring proposals.[3] Quite noticeably, states from the Asian region are not among the loudest proponents of such changes.

Where does Asia stand when it comes to such global trends? In this respect, it is very dangerous to make such a broad generalisation as the term 'Asia' proposes, bearing in mind that it stands for by far the biggest continent, both geographically and politically. Nevertheless, a few reasons suggest that a special look should be taken at this region in the context of state reaction to the developments in investment arbitration practice. First, Asian approaches to international law have been often distinguished in legal scholarship, for different doctrinal reasons.[4] The states of the region are regularly singled out, be it in the context of an emerging Eastphalian international order, or for the expressions of quite Westphalian protective attitudes towards their sovereignty (see Ginsburg, 2011: 859, 870–873).[5] Second, there is an emerging focus on Asia in the particular context of international investment law and arbitration (see Schill, 2015). Finally, while the leading examples of state reactions to the growing investment caseload are often radical, this is not characteristic for Asia. But that does not mean that Asian states have remained passive, and the actions taken by them often share some common features. Nevertheless, the mention of 'Asia' in this context should not be understood as an attempt to attribute one particular trend to all the states on the continent, but rather as a limitation of the present examination.[6]

The topic I wish to address in this chapter relates to attempts to strengthen state control over access to investment arbitration in Asia, from a technical legal perspective. Namely, I seek to identify detailed legal actions taken by the states in this region aimed at addressing the growing arbitral caseload providing for easy access to arbitration to foreign investors. While identifying such actions, I aim to investigate their causes and their prospective outcomes. Does easy access to arbitration collide with an abstract idea of sovereignty, and therefrom derive understanding of the role of international adjudication? Could actions taken by states in Asia actually affect arbitral development of the law, and what could be their results? Generally, what is the contribution of the reactions from the Asian region to the arbitral development of the law governing access to investment arbitration, on the one hand, and to a broader movement towards strengthening the position of the state, on the other?

I argue that, while the idea of sovereignty is often used in arguments against extensive international scrutiny, and while this idea is indeed embedded in the actions of several states in Asia in their treaty practices, the advocated changes cannot properly affect the targeted arbitral practice. This is so because the practice has moved towards developing a sort of arbitral jurisdictional regulation, which is capable of producing new jurisdictional rules tackling the obstacles in the arbitral task of resolving internationalised and depoliticised investment disputes. In such circumstances, imposing stricter treaty requirements, which only delays the internationalisation of disputes between investors and states, cannot do much help. To this end, Section 2 discusses the emergence of investment arbitration in Asia, paying special attention to the reflections by the states in the region. Section 3 then turns to state reactions to the arbitral practice allowing easy access to investment arbitration, while Section 4 discusses the ability of such reactions to affect arbitral practice. Section 5 concludes.

2. The emergence and effects of investment arbitration in Asia

Asian states engaged in the conclusion of investment treaties from the very early years of such practice. However, they still required some time to fully accept such treaties with extensive (including procedural) investor protections, as preferred in the West, and it seems that they went through an adjustment process.[7]

A number of events signified that process. China liberalised its investment treaties starting from the late 1990s, primarily in terms of expanding the scope of disputes that could be arbitrated: from disputes relating to the amount of compensation for expropriation only, to all disputes.[8] This development took place after a period of reluctance to provide (stronger) foreign investor protection in BITs, because of its protectionist attitude towards state sovereignty (Schill, 2007: 77–83). At the time of writing, however, China had more than 120 signed BITs.[9] Chesterman (2016: 960) notes that Asia is becoming a leading region in regard to the number of concluded BITs, primarily because of Chinese, but also Korean and Indian practices. More importantly, new Chinese BITs contain quite open investor-state arbitration provisions.[10]

China was not alone in the liberalisation process towards international investor protection treaties during the 1990s.[11] India changed its policy during this decade and signed its first BIT in 1994 (Shetty and Weeramantry, 2016: 189–190).[12] A clear majority of the BITs signed by the member states of the ASEAN dates between 1990 and 2010, culminating in 1994 with over 30 BITs (see Crockett,

2015: 441, Fig. 1). Although slowed down afterwards, the proliferation of invest-ment treaties did not cease, and 2009 was a particularly productive year for the ASEAN states, when they concluded both a new intra-ASEAN investment agree-ment,[13] and few agreements with investment chapters between that organisation and other states in the region.[14] For illustration, at the time of writing South Korea had more than 90 BITs (in force or signed); India (after terminating many), Iran, Malaysia and Vietnam, 60; Indonesia (also in a termination process), Kazakhstan, Mongolia, Pakistan and Singapore, 40.[15] Others, such as Japan, have signed other types of international treaties with investment protection provisions,[16] and most such other agreements equally provided for investor-state arbitration (Salomon and Friedrich, 2015: 814). The picture of existing investment treaties is not clear though, because many bilateral and multilateral treaties overlap.[17]

The number of treaties thus concluded had to eventually result in an expand-ing arbitral practice. By 2016, Indonesia faced some 10 arbitrations or more (Yeo and Menon, 2016: 126), and India possibly more than 20 (Shetty and Weera-mantry, 2016: 190–191).[18] That an easy access to arbitration was a problem for some states was visible from their defences. Some argued that the dispute settle-ment clause in a BIT did not provide an offer of state consent to arbitrate,[19] while others argued that despite the possibility of recourse to arbitration in the dispute settlement clause, the only available forum to investors were domestic courts.[20] It is not surprising, therefore, that the states which have faced challenges in their practice have developed animosities against investment arbitration being easily accessible to foreign investors.[21]

Indonesia is the first of such countries which are seen as developing animosities towards the system (see Yeo and Menon, 2016; Price, 2017: 136–139). India and Thailand have also built negative attitudes towards investment treaties based on practical experiences.[22] The ASEAN sub-region was said to express 'consider-able hostility' towards such treaties (Sornarajah, 2015: 356). Another example of emerging reactions is China: when a Chinese BIT was used for the very first time to institute arbitration (notably against the other contracting state),[23] that case attracted much academic attention in China, criticising the arbitrators' lib-eral approaches in ruling on the Tribunal's jurisdiction.[24] This must be seen in the context of the so-called 'China disequilibrium': the fact that China has many BITs, but limited involvement in investment arbitration (Shen, 2011: 55–57).[25] Overall, although states in Asia have not reached as extensive caseload as states in other regions have,[26] they could have used this experience to build animosities and negative attitudes towards the system of investment arbitration.

The causes of such animosities and negative attitudes might be traced to arbi-tral practice providing for easy access to investment treaty arbitration. The emer-gence of that adjudicatory mechanism as 'arbitration without privity' has been labelled the 'original sin' committed in *AAPL v. Sri Lanka*, with the prospect of 'adventurism' in establishing arbitral jurisdiction (Sornarajah, 2015: 139–143). If that was indeed so, the 'original sin' was partly Asian, because the respond-ent state did not challenge jurisdiction in the case that created precedent. Still, investment tribunals have continued with the practices that many would call 'adventuristic'. Narrowly drafted dispute settlement clauses have been broadened.[27] Treaty clauses have been interpreted so as to empower tribunals to resolve contractual disputes as well,[28] and contract-based tribunals assumed jurisdiction over non-contractual claims.[29] What constituted an 'investment'[30] and who had standing to bring claims[31] has also been subject to broad interpretations, while some limiting factors advanced by states have been dismissed.[32] Once offered, consent to arbitration could not be easily withdrawn.[33] Territorial boundaries of application of BITs and thereby offered consents have been left uncertain.[34] The procedural aspects of access to investment arbitration have been loosened as well.[35] It would be probably an exaggeration to call all such developments 'radical',[36] but they certainly did prompt and continue to influence state dissatisfaction with the system.

To be fair, some tribunals have tried to advance state-friendly practices. Some tribunals have been sceptical about their jurisdiction to hear contractual claims.[37] Certain limits of the notion of 'investment' have been observed, both in terms of the qualifying assets[38] and the approval requirements.[39] Investors' abusive actions in corporate restructuring have been sanctioned.[40] To what extent such developments have affected states' attitudes towards investment treaty arbitration is not clear, but it seems that that extent is much smaller than the one of 'adventuristic' practices.

The animosities and negative attitudes developed in the region towards investment treaty arbitration as a system are best reflected in Indian and Indonesian decisions to replace their BITs with new ones, which should represent (in their view) more 'balanced' arrangements.[41] What came as a reaction to arbitral practices, and what was suggested by the states in the region to 'balance' the investment arbitration regime, is analysed in the following section.

3. The reactions in Asia: reasserting the gateway

While the alterations in different treaties as manifestations of state reaction to arbitral practice could be discussed endlessly, I focus here on three examples which aim to reclaim the gateway issues back to the national level.[42] These are the requirements to resort to and/or exhaust domestic remedies (Section 3.1), special governmental consent to investment arbitration (Section 3.2) and other means of prioritising domestic judiciary over international arbitration (Section 3.3). I will end by discussing their common rationales (Section 3.4).

3.1. *Mandatory resort to domestic remedies*

In 2015, India finalised its new Model BIT, India, 2015.[43] Besides many other innovations,[44] one of its main features is the introduction of the exhaustion of local remedies requirement.[45] In fact, investors are required to litigate for at least 5 years before Indian domestic courts or to demonstrate that the futility exception applies, if 'there are no available domestic legal remedies capable of reasonably providing any relief in respect of the same measure or similar factual matters for which a breach of this Treaty is claimed by the investor'.[46] Notably, only after using this 'Carlos Calvo's grandchild'[47] for at least 5 years, an investor can give notice of the dispute to the host state, thus triggering the dispute resolution mechanism under the treaty.[48] Thereafter the procedure includes an attempt at amicable settlement, a number of additional preconditions to arbitration, including some serious time limitations and the final institution of arbitration.[49] The internationalisation of the dispute has been drastically delayed, as the dispute resolution under the treaty can be triggered only 5 years after the dispute has already arisen. In an ideal scenario an investor has 6 months between the end of the consultations period and the expiry of the statute of limitations to initiate arbitration, which also includes a mandatory notification of the intention to arbitrate filed at least 90 days in advance.[50]

The requirement to make prior reference of the case to domestic judicial or administrative organs is not new in Asia. For example, newer Chinese BITs usually require foreign investors to exhaust the Administrative Review Procedure, with the aim of checking the compliance of the domestic administrative organs with Chinese domestic law.[51] Arguments that unsuitable proceedings, causes of action and reliefs available domestically render such requirements inapplicable might be attractive here.[52] The Indian Model BIT aims to prevent them, by providing that 'the investor shall not assert that the obligation to exhaust local remedies does not apply or has been met on the basis that the claim under this Treaty is by a different party or in respect of a different cause of action'.[53] This suggests that investors are required to litigate treaty claims before domestic courts from the beginning.[54] Arguably, the ASEAN Investment Agreement also introduced a hard requirement of the exhaustion of local remedies, by attaching the fair and equitable treatment standard to denial of justice (Sornarajah, 2015: 353).[55] In such instances the requirement to exhaust local remedies is of a different nature: it is a substantive requirement pertaining to the concept of denial of justice, and it cannot be regarded as limiting access to arbitration as such.[56] Factually, though, such a limitation of a substantive standard of protection at the same time limits the possibilities for internationalisation of certain aspects of investors' treatment.

Recognising that not all existing treaties can be terminated, India identified 25 BITs whose initial validity period has not expired (at the time of assessment, which was in 2016) and suggested conclusion of joint interpretive statements with each state co-party to such treaties.[57] Although the suggested statement does not aim to add new clauses to treaties, it is obvious that some measures are meant to prioritise national judiciaries. For example, the suggested interpretation of umbrella clauses refers investors to contractually agreed or regular domestic fora, although it is not clear whether that reference is made only for contractual or also for treaty claims.[58] As for dispute settlement clauses in particular, the proposed interpretation introduces the standard of ripeness, requiring investors to demonstrate that their claims are 'ripe for adjudication', which essentially amounts to the same standard as the substantive requirement of exhaustion of local remedies.[59]

A particular problem appearing with such hard requirements is whether they are properly justified. Indeed, certain benefits of local litigation requirements have been recognised, but they must be subject to some limitations controlling their potential to unreasonably restrict the access to international fora.[60] Investment tribunals have been trying to find a proper limitation, mostly being inspired by the futility test drawing an analogy to the exhaustion of local remedies requirement for diplomatic protection.[61] As seen earlier in this section, the Indian Model BIT limits the futility exception to situations when there is no remedy 'capable of reasonably providing *any relief* in respect of the same measure or similar factual matters'.[62] The narrow definition of this exception is obvious in comparison to general international law (emphasising *effective*, as opposed to *any* remedy),[63] but also to what investment tribunals have held as the appropriate standard(s).[64] Bearing in mind that the exhaustion of local remedies requirement is seen as a thing of the past in investment law (Schreuer, 2005: 1–3) and that conditions of local litigation found elsewhere require doing so for significantly shorter periods of time,[65] imposing such a fortified requirement, as the Indian Model BIT, India, 2015 does, could impose a significant burden on foreign investors in India and elsewhere.

3.2. International arbitration as an exception

A more categorical state reaction targets access to international arbitration as such. Southeast Asian states already, to a large extent, retain the power to decide whether an investor can be protected under investment treaties at all.[66] States in the region have successfully relied on that power in their defences against investment claims.[67] Nevertheless, some might go further. Indonesia has been reported to aim to reassert the control over state consent to international arbitration with foreign investors and that it considered requiring special governmental consent to each arbitration in its future arrangements (Losari and Ewing-Chow, 2015: 1010; Yeo and Menon, 2016: 128). In opposition, Crockett (2017) argues that Indonesia has not given up the investment arbitration mechanism and that it understands the benefits the availability of this mechanism brings. Which one of the two positions is correct is yet to be seen, as this state is still in the process of terminating old BITs, awaiting further developments.[68]

Insisting on case-by-case consent would not be surprising. This would follow the failure of the argument with the same effect in respect of the existing Indonesian BITs. In *Churchill Mining v. Indonesia*, Indonesia unsuccessfully argued that the jurisdictional clause contained in the UK-Indonesia BIT, providing that the respondent state 'shall assent' to arbitration, required subsequent consent to arbitral jurisdiction by the respondent government, which, it went on, had the right to withhold such consent.[69] However, in *Planet Mining v. Indonesia*, faced with the same jurisdictional objection, the Tribunal concluded that a similar jurisdictional clause did not provide a standing offer to arbitrate, but was still able to find special state consent elsewhere.[70] To advance its arguments Indonesia had to take advantage of specific wording clearly originating from the other party to the

BIT.[71] Bearing in mind the role played by arbitrators in determining the meaning of such clauses,[72] Indonesia now could seek to make sure that its desired interpretation will be given effect in the future. Its domestic law on foreign investment already contains the requirement of special agreement to arbitrate, which is probably understandable for disputes arising at the domestic level.[73] Now even disputes which are meant to be international from scratch (arising under an investment treaty) could be precluded from internationalising, unless one of the parties to such a dispute decides otherwise.

On the other hand, the Philippines has already implemented its unwillingness to commit to international arbitration. Its 2006 Philippines-Japan EPA made the condition of special consent as a transitional solution pending the final agreement on the investor-state dispute settlement mechanism.[74] That approach is somehow moderate, as it acknowledges the international nature of disputes that needs to be accommodated in the international sphere. It has been reported that the Philippine government resisted including the investor-state arbitration mechanism in that agreement due to being faced with investment claims.[75] Since then, that country has continued with (immoderate) resistance towards investor-state international arbitration. Surveying investment treaties concluded since 2009 by ASEAN, one can find the requirement of a special agreement between an investor and the state should they wish to commence ICSID arbitration, applicable in respect of the Philippines exclusively.[76] This follows the fact that the Philippines is not actively concluding new BITs[77] and can also be seen in light of its traditional care for the contents of investment treaties.[78] A similar approach was taken by few states from the region in the context of the Comprehensive and Progressive Agreement for Trans-Pacific Partnership (CPTPP), requiring special consent by virtue of bilateral side agreements.[79]

Such approaches rebut what was the main idea behind the investor-state dispute settlement mechanism in the first place. The availability of international fora for the settlement of disputes arising out of violations of international rights of investors, and the loss of state control over the gateway to such fora, has been regarded as the crucial feature of international investor protection.[80] Conversely, permanent governmental control over the gateway to international arbitration denies, or at least delays, the internationalisation of such disputes: in the event of governmental denial of consent, the investor has no other choice but to turn back to the traditional rules of diplomatic protection, which first brings him to the municipal courts.

3.3. Prioritising domestic procedures in competition with international arbitration

The third example of state attempts to reclaim the gateway to international arbitration appears in the context of tackling the problem of parallel proceedings. It appears that Western countries are willing to accept that the same case might change fora, advancing from the domestic to the international level. States in Asia seem reluctant to accept such scenarios. Accordingly, the preference for fork-in-the-road clauses can be noticed in intra-Asian treaties, over those requiring investors to waive and/or withdraw claims from domestic proceedings.[81] Investment treaties concluded by ASEAN usually include fork-in-the-road clauses (applicable generally or in respect of particular states).[82] For comparison, the US Model BIT,[83] the CPTPP,[84] CETA,[85] and the EU-Singapore FTA[86] all contain only waiver requirements. Some states, like Vietnam, have expressed firm preference for fork-in-the-road clauses in their mega-regionals,[87] and others have included such a clause in their revised model BITs in an attempt to strengthen the position of the host state.[88] States in Asia have also included in their investment agreements other types of clauses giving preference to domestic courts, should they be first seized of the dispute.[89]

While all these clauses aim to achieve the same effect – preventing parallel proceedings – fork-in-the-road clauses make the choice final, thus precluding the investor from bringing the case to arbitration after seizing domestic courts. It can be debated which clause dealing with parallel processes is more or less 'investor-friendly', but what matters here is the coordination between the domestic and international levels. It is not quite the same to offer investors an opportunity to switch levels, under the condition of withdrawing claims from local courts, and to preclude arbitrating disputes that were first submitted to national courts. The point of differentiation is clear: the former allows, and the latter precludes, the internationalisation of investment disputes.

Of course, there are other instances of state reactions to the developments in investment law in Asia. China has excluded the application of MFN clauses to dispute resolution clauses,[90] which can also be found in some newer Japanese[91] and ASEAN agreements,[92] in India's plans for the future,[93] and which can also be characterised as a global trend.[94] These developments limit investors' prospects of facilitating access to international fora by avoiding some conditions precedent such as to litigate domestically[95] or forks-in-the-road.[96] More substantially, the prospect of applying MFN clauses to dispute resolution provisions remains a danger for China in particular, because a substantial number of its old BITs containing narrow dispute settlement clauses remain in force, which investors might seek to extend (Eliasson, 2012: 98–100, 107). Furthermore, some states in Asia are still not parties to the ICSID Convention, keeping this forum unavailable for their investors.[97] All these elements more or less affect the ability of foreign investors to access international arbitration to settle disputes with their host states. However, when the most important elements – those expressing some kind of state reaction – are isolated (which seem to be still occasional and unsystematic), the question arises whether they share something in common.

3.4. Sovereignist rationales

States in Asia have reacted differently depending on their experiences.[98] But could it be said that there is a common rationale behind these reactions? It has been noted that some states in this region tend to commit to stricter obligations in the sphere of international economic law only when it comes to their relations with third states (compered to their interrelations).[99] This might be an indication that there are some common concerns or beliefs that these states might share, whose protection they might seek when sketching their positions for prospective treaty arrangements (unilateral reaction), and more easily achieve in the agreements among themselves (bilateral and plurilateral reaction).

One such belief might be the classical presumption that disputes between states and foreign nationals, and their relations generally, form domestic matters.[100] The history of international law reveals that this was not only regarded as a presumption, but some even saw it as an exclusivity of domestic affairs. The Calvo Doctrine argued that state relations with foreigners were to be governed by domestic law of the host state and subjected to the jurisdiction of the courts of that state exclusively (Garibaldi, 2006: 2, 7). The sovereignism behind that doctrine shares the same motives with some of the contemporary concerns about investment treaty arbitration: the fear of limiting states' adjudicative power.[101] Carlos Calvo's rationales assisted in the formation of the 'New International Economic Order' initiative (Garibaldi, 2006: 28–29; Shan, 2008: 254), which was actively supported by a substantial number of the states from Asia.[102] The subsequent massive conclusion of investment treaties marginalised the Calvo Doctrine for some time, but that doctrine has not been forgotten.[103] Its re-emergence can be observed in some state defences in investment cases, particularly when it comes to the questions of arbitral jurisdiction (Garibaldi, 2006: 38–40; Schill, 2006: 4–6). Calvo could restore further, however in a different form due to new demands of international economic relations (Shan, 2008: 302–304).[104] At the same time this means that sovereignism is not dead either, continuing to instruct state action (see Shan, 2008: 311–312). Just as the regulation of and the exercise of authority over foreign investment found their place in the Charter of Economic Rights and Duties of States as an expression of state sovereignism,[105] the same persisting rationale might be leading today's attempts to limit access to international arbitration to foreign investors.

In line with this reasoning, some international arrangements in Asia emphasised the primacy of national laws in providing investment protection.[106] The impressions of harmed state sovereignty have influenced attitudes towards investment arbitration, both in the past (when assessing its prospective repercussions for states)[107] and more recently (when analysing investment tribunals' activities).[108] Even when the criticisms of investor-state dispute settlement appeared purely declaratory and were not meant to result in an actual backlash, the concerns about the erosion of state sovereignty emerged at the top of such criticisms.[109]

That sovereignty concerns are at stake here is implied in the analysed changes themselves: when states limit access to arbitration, they do so from the importing state perspective, i.e. aiming to preserve their domestic competences as far as possible, at the expense of the rights of their own nationals investing abroad.[110] The understanding that the domestic government should deal with foreign investment is crucial for such changes, as every limitation of that power, which comes through the internationalisation of disputes with foreign investors, equals an erosion of state sovereignty.

To what extent such sovereignty concerns will actually be expressed seems to be determined by historical experiences and modern circumstances. Asia's ambivalence about international law in general has been argued to be dependent on negative historical experiences (see generally Chesterman, 2016). For example, Chi and Wang (2015: 874) note that China's protectionist approach to its sovereignty regarding investment treaties has been influenced by victimised narratives.[111] The liberalisation of that country's arbitration provisions in BITs has been noted along with the increase of Chinese investment abroad, when it had to move away from its old-generation BITs designed from the importing country perspective (Heymann, 2008: 516, 526; Chi and Wang, 2015: 874). Of course, the limitation of the state adjudicative space due to the inclusion of wider jurisdictional clauses in Chinese BITs was not spared of criticism,[112] and some even argued that China should also turn to special agreements to arbitrate.[113] Such suggestions, however, are sobered by the fact that China is today more of an exporter than an importer (Chi and Wang, 2015: 890–891). This example shows that concerns towards investment arbitration can generally be built on historical sentiments, but that their actual expression can be limited if the modern circumstances require so.

The question arises what prompts sovereignist concerns to revive and be given effect. It has been shown that the change in attitudes towards investment treaties appears as a consequence of 'hitting' claims (Poulsen and Aisbett, 2013; Haftel and Thompson, 2018).[114] For example, after Thailand was sued for the first time in a treaty-based arbitration in 2005, it was commented that perhaps such a possibility was simply overlooked in the state structure (Mangklatanakul, 2011: 82). The Philippines stopped concluding BITs after the famous *SGS v. The Philippines* case, which was initiated in 2002.[115] Western European and North American investors, whose countries of origin are traditionally seen as stronger economies, dominate in the number of claims against Asian states.[116] Hence, the existence of only one claim can indeed suffice to frighten capital-importing states that such claims will regularly repeat in the future. Now, when claims have hit, states might resort to attempts to introduce some elements in their new investment treaties, which would to some extent safeguard their sovereignty at the expense of the investors' right to initiate arbitration. Indeed, consenting to arbitration on a case-by-case basis, the exhaustion of local remedies, and the application of local laws to investment disputes were named three out of 'four great safeguards' for the developing, capital-importing countries, threatened by Western preferences.[117] State sovereignism, therefore, in this regard appears highly reactionary, aiming to limit the possibilities for adjudicating investment claims, after experiencing the reality of such claims under the current regime of investor protection.

This conclusion should not be endangered by the evidence that Asian states are willing to submit other types of economic law disputes to international resolution, such as trade disputes (see Chesterman, 2016: 959–960). The fact remains that these states are still reluctant to fully accept international adjudication, if compared to others (Koh, 2011; Chesterman, 2016: 961–962).[118] More importantly, investment disputes raise quite peculiar concerns. Certainly, it is easier to accept international law as the proper forum for adjudicating state-to-state disputes, being international per their definition, than those arising between a state and a foreign investor as one of its subjects, which become internationalised thanks to state consent to that effect.[119] The question that arises is whether states are indeed capable of thus limiting access to investment arbitration by virtue of the principle that it all starts and ends with state consent.

4. Defending the undefendable

Formally, access to investment arbitration is provided for in various treaties and subject to different conditions. States, as treaty-makers, should have absolute power to change whatever they wish when concluding new treaties, including their conditions. That is the theory. But the reality is much more complex. Three issues are central – at least for the present discussion – in that complexity: the internationalised and depoliticised quality of investment disputes (Section 4.1), the development of arbitral regulation of jurisdictional questions (Section 4.2) and the practical needs and possibilities of states to enforce their wishes in the conclusion of new investment treaties (Section 4.3).

4.1. *The internationalisation and depoliticisation of investment disputes*

International law has never provided a clear border between the domestic juris-diction of the state and the international one.[120] But whenever there is a question of interpretation and/or application of a treaty, that suffices to qualify the mat-ter as international.[121] The conferral of protective rights to foreign investors in investment treaties has the purpose of internationalising the regulation of state behaviour towards them. This purpose is equally reflected in the field of dispute resolution, where the internationalisation of investment disputes, and their reso-lution by international adjudicators, has been regarded as the main advantage offered to foreign investors by virtue of investment treaties.[122] There is another aspect to this phenomenon: at the same time, investment disputes have become depoliticised. As Professor Lowenfeld specified, 'the essence' of investment arbi-tration arrangements is 'that controversies between foreign investors and host states are insulated from political and diplomatic relations between states'.[123] On the one hand,

> the host state is assured that the state of the investor's nationality (as defined) will not espouse the investor's claim or otherwise intervene in the contro-versy between an investor and a host state [. . . while on the other hand] the state of the investor's nationality is relieved of the pressure of having its rela-tions with the host state disturbed or distorted by a controversy between its national and the host state.[124]

These two processes – the internationalisation and depoliticisation of invest-ment disputes – have largely shaped the investors' access to investment treaty arbitration. An investment dispute arises by virtue of a disagreement between an investor and his host state, as expressed in clearly conflicting legal views.[125] The investor then has a personal right to access international arbitration by accepting the offer to arbitrate in the relevant investment treaty.[126] Both the dispute and the arbitration are between the investor and his host state, and the investor's home state has no role to play by counterweighting different costs and concerns in establishing consent. These are some basic ideas which are borne in mind in any discussion on the rules governing access to investment treaty arbitration.

Against this background, taking a state-centric and deferential approach to the basic jurisdictional issues in investment disputes, as the International Court of Justice does in the inter-state context,[127] was not a pragmatic solution: faced with an exploding caseload, tribunals had to depart from a broad understanding that consent primarily protects state sovereignty and started regarding consent only as a means of jurisdictional regulation. A clear reflection of this is the offer-acceptance theory of consent.[128] Furthermore, states that are now considering consenting to arbitration on a case-by-case basis have seen that even when their treaties did not provide a standing offer to arbitrate, their consent could be found elsewhere.[129] What is crucial in that respect is the loss of state control over the gateway issues, i.e. it is up to the arbitrators to determine whether an investor was able to institute arbitration of an investment dispute.[130] The formality of an agreement to arbitrate does not allow disregarding the inquiry whether the state has consented to arbitration, but that inquiry is strongly influenced by the phenomenon of internationalisation of investment disputes.[131]

In other words, state consent is not seen any more as the guardian of state sovereignty, but only as the means of internationalising disputes and regulating arbitral jurisdiction. Of course, should states include in their treaties specific wording stressing the need for special consent in each particular case, that wording must be followed by investment tribunals. But at the same time, states must bear in mind that their concerns are not central in investment disputes; that consent is not merely a letter of the treaty, but a concept pertaining to the expression of will of the disputing parties; and that that concept does not operate in isolation from the idea of internationalising and depoliticising the resolution of investment disputes.

4.2. Arbitral jurisdictional regulation and conditions of access

In the environment of internationalised and depoliticised investment disputes and differently seen notion of consent, introducing harder conditions of access to arbitration probably cannot produce any drastic effects on arbitral practice. Investment arbitral practice has demonstrated that investment treaties cannot normally answer all questions of how such conditions of access should be applied in concrete cases.[132] Arbitral activity is therefore needed to supplement the gaps in a given jurisdictional framework. For example, despite naming the new requirement 'exhaustion of domestic remedies' in the Indian Model BIT, its true nature will be assessed by tribunals, quite possibly concluding that it is not a strict one. Tribunals have developed an entire toolkit for bypassing domestic litigation requirements, using MFN clauses and futility exceptions or even relying on more general considerations of efficiency.[133] There is nothing to guarantee to states that their view on such requirements will be followed and that one of the tools developed in the practice will not be used.

When applying such tools, tribunals can approach domestic judicial alternatives differently. In *Urbaser v. Argentina*, the Tribunal dedicated an extensive discussion to the requirement of local litigation and actual options available to the investor at the domestic level, finding that none of the options were suitable to fulfil the purpose of such requirement.[134] A different approach is to stress a clear expectation from the domestic judiciary. One tribunal, facing a clear exhaustion of domestic remedies requirement, determined the 'primary or direct remedy' for the issue at hand and, because such a remedy was not available before domestic courts, concluded that there was no effective domestic remedy to be exhausted.[135] In both instances, the domestic litigation/exhaustion of remedies requirements proved circumventable. The only question is against what standard the availability of domestic remedies will be assessed. Arbitral practice has also shown that fork-in-the-road clauses do not necessarily prevent submission of a dispute to international arbitration after seizing domestic courts.[136] Again, the question is not what the letter of the treaty says, but what issues will arise in practice and what view tribunals will take in the application of such clauses.[137] It cannot be simply assumed that local litigation will be seen favourably, as a panacea for all the issues usually arbitrated at the international level.

Such a developed arbitral practice forms sort of new jurisdictional rules governing investment treaty arbitration which must be observed. While states might have very strict requirements in mind when drafting treaty provisions, they can be seen quite differently by the actual appliers of the law – arbitrators. This follows the fact that arbitrators' agendas are set by investors, whose position and interests must be taken into account when resolving concrete jurisdictional questions. Therefore, imposing strict conditions of consent, or reasserting state control over the gateway to arbitration, will probably not bring any significant changes to investment arbitral practice, once the questions about their practical application are raised. While such changes are often motivated by the belief that 'tougher' state consent better safeguards its sovereignty, arbitral practice has left that page a long time ago.

4.3. *Political struggles and Pyrrhic victories*

Even if the reactions of some Asian states, which were discussed in Section 3, could indeed alter arbitral practice, it is questionable to what extent such reactions could be embodied into future investment treaties. The reactions from the region are not as radical as elsewhere, so as to, for example, argue in favour of switching to inter-state investment dispute settlement mechanisms.[138] From this perspective, the advocated changes might seem quite negotiable. But practically that is hardly the case, and it all depends on whom the advocates of the changes are talking to. For example, the former Trans-Pacific Partnership (TPP), which reflected the US approach to investment treaties regarding investor-state arbitration,[139] was said not to be endangered by prospective lack of ratifications on the side of Asian states, simply because of the cost-benefit weighting (Nottage, 2016: 33–36). This suggestion has proved true by the mere existence of the CPTPP. When India tried to impose its new Model BIT, India, 2015, containing the domestic litigation (or, as India likes to call it, 'exhaustion of domestic remedies') requirement, in its new India-Canada BIT, that attempt was unsuccessful, and the Indian government had to 'exceptionally' give up its wish to prioritise domestic dispute settlement procedures.[140] Therefore, when negotiating with economically strong countries, the proponents of changes should not be overly optimistic, although of course they may face varying experiences. Some states have firm negative attitudes towards investor-state arbitration,[141] while others are said to be passive players, appearing quite flexible towards their treaty partners.[142]

On the other hand, when such attempts at introducing changes into new BITs succeed, they appear as Pyrrhic victories. For example, the first BIT based on the new Indian Model BIT was announced in 2016 with Cambodia.[143] It has also been reported that India has agreed an interpretive note with Bangladesh concerning their existing BIT, based on the Indian proposal (Hepburn, 2017b). Similar developments followed later in the relations with Colombia, Belarus and Taiwan (Hepburn, 2019). India has been particularly noted for taking a capital-importing state perspective only, as by imposing harder requirements, it forgets its own investors abroad (Shetty and Weeramantry, 2016: 193).[144] Support for Indian investors abroad is indeed questionable: a state appointed committee observed that disputes between Indian investors and third states should be monitored

> to ensure that treaty interpretations espoused by Indian investors do not run contrary to the position adopted by the Indian government itself, keeping in mind the impact of such interpretations on future disputes brought by foreign investors against the Indian government.[145]

Questionable policy choices boomeranging to those wishing to limit access to investor-state arbitration can already be seen today in Asia. For example, Chinese investors who now wish to sue other countries for violations of the old-generation Chinese BITs are being precluded by the limits contained in their jurisdictional provisions.[146] Those whose claims find a way towards merits must thank the arbitral techniques that some would call 'adventuristic'.[147] Future developments will probably continue in the same direction. Already today there is a significant proportion of intra-Asian investment claims, while the proportion of Asian claims towards other states is rising (Salomon and Friedrich, 2015: 837–841). Building on the experience of international commercial arbitration, Kim (2012) suggested that investors from Asia will become more prominent users of the investment arbitration mechanism. Therefore, it is doubtful whose interests states from Asia protect when advocating for limiting access to international arbitration in their treaties.

When it comes to India and Indonesia – the two most active countries discussed here – it has to be noted that their actions are new, but not original. Terminating BITs is, one can say, popular recently, be it for similar reasons and in a similar manner as argued by these two states,[148] or for some completely different rationales.[149] But the actual possibilities for implementation are much more complex. Arguments against investor-state dispute settlement can be advanced for mere sentimental or political purposes.[150] Without any justified needs and actual possibilities for their implementation, sovereignist arguments for limiting access to investor-state arbitration may remain useful only in such sentimental respects.

5. Conclusion

The aim of this chapter was not to find 'an Asian approach' to investment law and arbitration. But the most notable examples of state action to reassert control over that system, which I discussed in Section 3, do appear to share some common features. First, as Asian states fully accepted investment arbitration step-by-step, their response was equally gradual. Their reactions are not as radical as the suggestions for the abandonment or reform of the entire system are. And second, those states in Asia which decided to act did so at the level of detailed treaty rules, aimed to prevent or delay the internationalisation of investment disputes and guided by the thought that the relations with foreign investors fall under the sovereign domain. That action runs contrary to Chesterman's (2016: 967) note that 'the distinction between domestic and international is likely to erode further', since the acting states rely precisely on that distinction. It also goes against the proposition that states' submission to international scrutiny in the field of foreign investment could have been advanced in the past decade (Nakagawa, 2007: 867). Nevertheless, the changes pursued by the acting states are unlikely to effect as desired, because they do not acknowledge the development of arbitrator-made jurisdictional rules which can tackle the hard conditions of access to investment arbitration. The future of investment arbitration in Asia, therefore, depends of the abilities to reconcile with the global developments in this field.

Notes

1 The very first bilateral investment treaty (BIT) was signed in 1959 between Pakistan and Germany, while the first BIT-based arbitration took place three decades later between a Hong Kong company and Sri Lanka: *Asian Agricultural Products Ltd v. Republic of Sri Lanka*, ICSID Case No. ARB/87/3, Final Award (27 June 1990).
2 Some states have turned to inter-state dispute settlement mechanisms. The Mercosur member states have recently signed a protocol for protection of foreign investment providing for state-to-state arbitration only: Protocolo de cooperación y facilitación de inversiones intra-Mercosur, Buenos Aires, 7 April 2017, not yet in force. Similar development took place within the Southern African Development Community (Peterson, 2017a).
3 Like the proposal of an Investment Court: European Commission, 'Commission proposes new Investment Court System for TTIP and other EU trade and

investment negotiations', 16 September 2015, http://europa.eu/rapid/press-release_IP-15-5651_en.htm, accessed 25 July 2018.

4 See, for example, Owada (2011); Tomuschat (2011); Chesterman (2016).

5 The concept of 'Eastphalia', however, should not be seen as pertaining only to and isolating Asian countries (Kim, 2018: 103). See also, for the Chinese example in particular, Coleman and Maogoto (2013).

6 Given the size of the continent, the emphasis in this contribution will be on East, Southeast and South Asia. References to other sub-regions will be made for comparison purposes.

7 For an overview of policy developments towards investor-state dispute settlement in East Asia and the Pacific, see Nottage (2016: 13–18).

8 This is said to be one of the main features of the new generation of Chinese BITs (Schill, 2007: 89–94; Chi and Wang, 2015).

9 More than 100 were in force. Data from UNCTAD, Investment Policy Hub, http://investmentpolicyhub.unctad.org/IIA, accessed 25 July 2018.

10 For example, Switzerland-ROC BIT, Art. 11, Bern, 27 January 2009, in force 13 April 2010.

11 As elsewhere, the 1990s brought a rapid growth in the number of BITs concluded by the states in the region (Salomon and Friedrich, 2015: 805–806; Nottage, 2016: 9).

12 In comparison, Indonesia, Malaysia, South Korea and Thailand started signing BITs already in the 1960s; Japan, the Philippines and Singapore in the 1970s; China and Laos in the 1980s; Cambodia, Hong Kong, Mongolia, Myanmar, North Korea, Taiwan and Vietnam only in the 1990s (Salomon and Friedrich, 2015: 804–806). Sri Lanka began signing investment treaties after opening its economic policy in the 1970s (Pathirana, 2017: 289–290), but never reached a large number of BITs.

13 ASEAN Comprehensive Investment Agreement, Cha-Am, 26 February 2009, in force 29 March 2012.

14 Agreement Establishing the ASEAN-Australia-New Zealand Free Trade Area, Cha-Am, 27 February 2009, in force 10 January 2010; ASEAN-China Investment Agreement, Bangkok, 15 August 2009, in force 1 January 2010; and ASEAN-Republic of Korea Investment Agreement, Jeju-do, 2 June 2009, in force 1 September 2009.

15 Data from UNCTAD, Investment Policy Hub, http://investmentpolicyhub.unctad.org/IIA, accessed 15 July 2018.

16 Other notable examples being China, Singapore, South Korea and Malaysia (Salomon and Friedrich, 2015: 812). Japan has concluded so-called economic partnership agreements (EPAs), which have some distinguishing elements from regular free trade agreements (FTA) (Hamamoto, 2015a: 198). It has mostly concluded such agreements with other Asian countries, being its region of priority (Hamamoto, 2015a: 191–198).

17 For example, between China, Japan and South Korea (Kang, 2017). Another example is ASEAN, whose member states have BITs both between themselves and with third states, which have also concluded investment agreements with ASEAN.

18 Other notable respondents are Mongolia, the Philippines and Vietnam in East Asia (see Salomon and Friedrich, 2015: 836), Kazakhstan, Kyrgyzstan and Turkmenistan in Central Asia, Pakistan in South Asia etc.

19 *Churchill Mining Plc v. Republic of Indonesia,* ICSID Case No. ARB/12/14, Decision on Jurisdiction (24 February 2014) at paras. 100–115; *Planet Mining Pty Ltd v. Republic of Indonesia,* ICSID Case No. 12/40, Decision on Jurisdiction (24 February 2014) at paras. 100–115.

20 *Sanum Investments Limited v. The Government of the Lao People's Democratic Republic,* PCA Case No. 2013–13, Award on Jurisdiction (13 December 2013) at para. 325.
21 See also Sornarajah (2012: 248–251). Of course, it cannot be said that this was a general, continental trend. Some states preserve *status quo* regarding their treaties, such as Turkey and Uzbekistan, because of their different experiences with the regime (Sattorova, 2017: 57–62), or Sri Lanka, for no obvious reasons (Pathirana, 2017: 298–299, 310–311).
22 Following the *White Industries Australia Limited v. India* and *Walter Bau Ag (In Liquidation) v. Thailand* cases, respectively (Sornarajah, 2015: 5, fn. 17). As for Thailand, see also Nottage (2016: 15).
23 *Señor Tza Yap Shum v. The Republic of Peru,* ICSID Case No. ARB/07/6, Decision on Jurisdiction and Competence (19 June 2009).
24 For example, Chen (2009); Shen (2011); Wang (2014: 349–353).
25 There has been one award rendered against China, which dismissed the claims for being 'manifestly without legal merit' under ICSID Arbitration Rules, Art. 41(5): *Ansung Housing Co. Ltd v. People's Republic of China,* ICSID Case No. ARB/14/25, Award (9 March 2017). At the time of writing, China was facing another pending arbitration: see *Hela Schwarz GmbH v. People's Republic of China,* ICSID Case No. ARB/17/19, Procedural Order No. 1 (9 March 2018).
26 See generally Sornarajah (2012: 245–246), and for East Asia and the Pacific, Salomon and Friedrich (2015: 834–837). Nottage and Weeramantry (2012) sought possible explanations for this phenomenon in the five theories on Japanese restraint towards litigation: cultural, institutional barriers, elite management, economic rationalist and hybrid theories.
27 *Sanum v. Laos* at paras. 329–342 (finding jurisdiction over the question of the occurrence of expropriation).
28 *SGS Société Générale de Surveillance S.A. v. Republic of the Philippines,* ICSID Case No. ARB/02/6, Decision of the Tribunal on Objections to Jurisdiction (29 January 2004) at paras. 113–129 (as for the umbrella clause) and 130–135 (as for the scope of consent).
29 *Cambodia Power Company v. Kingdom of Cambodia and Electricité du Cambodge,* ICSID Case No. ARB/09/18, Decision on Jurisdiction (22 March 2011) at paras. 327–338 (allowing claims under customary international law in a contract-based arbitration).
30 *Saipem S.p.A. v. People's Republic of Bangladesh,* ICSID Case No. ARB/05/7, Decision on Jurisdiction and Recommendation on Provisional Measures (21 March 2007) at paras. 119–128; and *White Industries Australia Limited v. The Republic of India,* ad hoc UNCITRAL arbitration, Final Award (30 November 2011) at paras. 7.6.1–7.6.10 (arbitral award as part of contractual investment).
31 *Sergei Paushok et al. v. The Government of Mongolia,* ad hoc UNCITRAL arbitration, Award on Jurisdiction and Liability (28 April 2011) at para. 202 (shareholders as claimants for the damage done to the company's assets).
32 *Malaysian Historical Salvors, SDN, BHD v. The Government of Malaysia,* ICSID Case No. ARB/05/10, Decision on the Application for Annulment (16 April 2009) at paras. 56–80 (dismissing the limitation of an 'investment' by the notion of the contribution to the economic development of the host state).
33 *Rumeli Telekom A.S. and Telsim Mobil Telekomunikasyon Hizmetleri A.S. v. Republic of Kazakhstan,* ICSID Case No. ARB/05/16, Award (29 July 2008) at para. 335.
34 *Tza Yap Shum v. Peru* at paras. 67–77 (finding that the China-Peru BIT covered a Chinese national residing in the Hong Kong SAR and that that conclusion was

not disturbed by the fact that Hong Kong could conclude its own BITs); *Sanum v. Laos* at paras. 205–300 (finding that the PRC-Laos BIT was applicable to the Macao SAR).

35 *Bayindir Insaat Turizm Ticaret Ve Sanayi A.S. v. Islamic Republic of Pakistan,* ICSID Case No. ARB/03/29, Decision on Jurisdiction (14 November 2005) at paras. 88–103 (dismissing a 'formalistic' approach to the conditions precedent to give notice of claims and negotiate).

36 For example, the International Court of Justice has also been willing to establish its jurisdiction over certain issues by implication: *Corfu Channel (United Kingdom of Great Britain and Northern Ireland v. Albania)* (Merits) (Judgment) (1949) ICJ Reports 4, pp. 23–26.

37 *SGS Société Générale de Surveillance S.A. v. Islamic Republic of Pakistan,* ICSID Case No. ARB/01/13, Decision of the Tribunal on Objections to Jurisdiction (6 August 2003) at paras. 156–162 (as for the scope of consent) and 163–174 (as for the umbrella clause).

38 *Mihaly International Corporation v. Democratic Socialist Republic of Sri Lanka,* ICSID Case No. ARB/00/2, Award (15 March 2002) at para. 59 (as for certain contingent and non-binding instruments).

39 *Yaung Chi Oo Trading Pte. Ltd. v. Government of the Union of Myanmar,* ASEAN Case No. ARB/01/1, Award (31 March 2003) at paras. 53–62 (as for the specific state approval of an investment).

40 *Fraport AG Frankfurt Airport Services Worldwide v. Republic of the Philippines,* ICSID Case No. ARB/11/12, Award (10 December 2014) at paras. 388–468 (as for the legality of an investment); *Philip Morris Asia Limited v. The Commonwealth of Australia,* PCA Case No. 2012–12, Award on Jurisdiction and Admissibility (17 December 2015) at paras. 535–588 (as for the abuse of process doctrine).

41 For India: Ahuja (2016: 138); Shetty and Weeramantry (2016: 192–193). In 2016, India sent notices of termination to its 58 BIT partners (Hepburn, 2017a). For Indonesia: Crockett (2015: 437); Price (2017: 134–135, 150).

42 I use the term 'gateway' for the conditions of the internationalisation of investment disputes, i.e. whose fulfilment makes an investment dispute arbitrable at the international level. But note that the same term is used in US domestic practice for the jurisdictional issues which must be decided by courts (Paulsson, 2013: 56–57).

43 Government of India, Indian Model BIT of December 2015, http://investment-policyhub.unctad.org/Download/TreatyFile/3560, accessed 25 July 2018.

44 See, for a commentary, Hanessian and Duggal (2017) and Ranjan and Anand (2017).

45 Model BIT, India, 2015, Art. 15.1.

46 Arts. 15.1–15.2 of the Indian Model BIT.

47 As baptised by Schreuer (2005: 3–5). It has been argued that local litigation requirements share origins with the exhaustion of domestic remedies (Pérez Aznar, 2016: 539–541).

48 Art. 15.2 of the Indian Model BIT.

49 Arts. 15.4–15.5 of the Indian Model BIT. For the complexity of the procedure, see Hanessian and Duggal (2017: 223, Fig. 1).

50 The Model BIT limits the possibility of initiating arbitration to 6 years from acquiring knowledge of the measure and damage/loss, or 12 months from the end of domestic proceedings.

51 Schill (2007: 92–93) argues that this requirement is different from the exhaustion of local remedies (essentially thus not being a gateway condition as defined here).

52 See, in that respect, *Urbaser SA and CABB v. The Argentine Republic,* ICSID Case No. ARB/07/26, Decision on Jurisdiction (19 December 2012) at paras. 164–182.

53 Art. 15.1 of the Indian Model BIT.
54 However, it has also been argued that this provision confuses local litigation with fork-in-the-road clauses and has no meaningful role in the context of local litigation requirements (Hepburn and Kabra, 2017: 105).
55 See Art. 11(2)(a) of the ASEAN Comprehensive Investment Agreement.
56 *Saipem v. Bangladesh* at para. 151. See further Crawford and Grant (2012: 903–904).
57 Government of India, Office Memorandum of 8 February 2016, http://indiainbusiness.nic.in/newdesign/upload/Consolidated_Interpretive-Statement.pdf, accessed 25 July 2018.
58 Office Memorandum at para. 8.3.
59 Office Memorandum at para. 12.1(c).
60 For benefits see Pérez Aznar (2016: 550–552). See also *Urbaser v. Argentina* at para. 136 (arguing that without proper opportunities to settle the dispute before domestic courts,

> [i]n addition to the mere result of having to wait another 18 months, Claimants would also have to suffer unequal and unfair treatment, as they would be required to present their case, while Respondent would be free from having to disclose its legal and factual defences to the claim, and simultaneously allowed to gather evidence supporting the investor's case in preparation of the prospective and likely arbitration').

61 See *Ambiente Ufficio S.p.A. et al. v. The Argentine Republic,* ICSID Case No. ARB/08/9, Decision on Jurisdiction and Admissibility (8 February 2013) at paras. 597–611. Other approaches ranging from the reliance on most-favoured-nation (MFN) clauses, to policy considerations, to the principle of effectiveness in treaty interpretation (D'Agnone, 2013; Pérez Aznar, 2016: 556–560).
62 Art. 15.1 of the Indian Model BIT (emphasis added).
63 Art. 15 of the ILC, 'Draft Articles on Diplomatic Protection' (2006) Official Records of the General Assembly, Sixty-first Session, Supplement No. 10 (A/61/10) ('there are no reasonably available local remedies to provide *effective redress*, or the local remedies provide *no reasonable possibility of such redress*' [emphasis added]).
64 As regards the futility standards in particular, see Pérez Aznar (2016: 556–557).
65 Time limitations of local litigation requirements usually vary from few months to 2 years (Schreuer, 2005: 3; Pérez Aznar, 2016: 540–541).
66 Through approval mechanisms (Sornarajah, 2012: 246–247, 2015: 352–353).
67 See, for example, *Yaung Chi Oo v. Myanmar* and *Rafat Ali Rizvi v. The Republic of Indonesia,* ICSID Case No. ARB/11/13, Award on Jurisdiction (16 July 2013).
68 Indonesia signed its last BIT in 2011 with Serbia, which is still not in force. Note that this BIT does contain state consent to arbitration: Serbia-Indonesia BIT, Art. 11, Belgrade, 6 September 2011, not in force.
69 *Churchill Mining v. Indonesia* at paras. 100–115, 148–231.
70 *Planet Mining v. Indonesia* at paras. 146–218. The jurisdictional clause provided that the respondent state 'shall consent in writing to the submission of the dispute to [ICSID] within forty-five days of receiving such a request from the investor'. However, all the claims by these two claimants were declared inadmissible because a fraudulent scheme was found to have permeated the investment, and now the claimants are seeking annulment; available at www.italaw.com/cases/1479, accessed 25 July 2018.
71 *Planet Mining v. Indonesia* at paras. 188–195. It has been noted that Indonesia was aware of the prospect of investors' bringing claims to international arbitration when signing BITs (Crockett, 2017: 846–852).

72 Notably, a number of Japanese BITs contain similar wording in their arbitration clauses to those in *Churchill Mining* and *Planet Mining*, however there have been no cases based on any of them to offer an interpretation. For example, Japan-Vietnam BIT, Art. 14(4), Tokyo, 14 November 2003, in force 19 December 2004 ('shall give its consent').

73 Art. 32(4) of the Law of the Republic of Indonesia No. 25/2007 Concerning Investment, http://investmentpolicyhub.unctad.org/InvestmentLaws/laws/93, accessed 25 July 2018. Note, however, that possible supplements including an offer of international arbitration could be adopted (Crockett, 2017: 844–845). Other examples of domestic laws requiring special agreement to international arbitration include Cambodia (Weeramantry, 2017: 946–947); Laos (Weeramantry and Mohan, 2017: 1007); and Myanmar (Bonnitcha, 2017: 984). Vietnamese Investment Law of 2014 restricted the submission of disputes between foreign investors and regulatory bodies to Vietnamese courts or arbitrations (international arbitration remains available only through investment treaties) (Nguyen and Nguyen, 2017: 925).

74 Japan-Philippines EPA, Art. 107(2), Helsinki, 9 September 2006, in force 11 December 2008.

75 'NGOs claim the Philippine-Japan free trade agreement is unconstitutional', *Investment Treaty News*, 8 June 2009, www.iisd.org/itn/2009/06/05/ngos-claim-the-philippine-japan-free-trade-agreement-is-unconstitutional/, accessed 25 July 2018.

76 Art. 33(1)(b), fn. 14 of the ASEAN Comprehensive Investment Agreement; Ch. 11, Art. 21(1)(b), fn. 14 of the ASEAN-Australia-New Zealand FTA; Art. 14(4)(b), fn. 8 of the ASEAN-China Investment Agreement; Art. 18(5)(a), fn. 20 of the ASEAN-Korea Investment Agreement; and ASEAN-India BIT, Art. 20(7)(b), Nay Pyi Taw, 12 November 2014, not in force.

77 The Philippines stopped concluding BITs in 2002, with the exception of the BIT with Syria signed in 2009 (Salomon and Friedrich, 2015: 808–809).

78 Reyes (2017: 1046–1048) thus argues that the Philippines has used BITs to advance its policy of economic nationalism.

79 See 'side instruments' signed between New Zealand and Brunei, Malaysia and Vietnam, available at www.mfat.govt.nz/en/trade/free-trade-agreements/free-trade-agreements-concluded-but-not-in-force/cptpp/comprehensive-and-progressive-agreement-for-trans-pacific-partnership-text/, accessed 23 July 2018.

80 See Section 4.1 below.

81 Cf. Art. 11(4) of the China-Switzerland BIT, with Art. 12(3) of the Agreement between the Government of the People's Republic of China and the Government of the Republic of Uzbekistan on the Promotion and Protection of Investments, Beijing, 19 April 2011, in force 1 September 2011; and China-Japan-Korea trilateral Investment Agreement, Art. 15(5), Beijing, 13 May 2012, in force 17 May 2014.

82 Art. 33(1) of the ASEAN Comprehensive Investment Agreement; Art. 14(5) of the ASEAN-China Investment Agreement (waiver requirement with the fork-in-the-road in respect of Indonesia, Philippines, Thailand and Vietnam); Art. 18 (6) of the ASEAN-Korea Investment Agreement; Art. 20(7) of the ASEAN-India Investment Agreement; Ch. 11, Art. 21(1) of the ASEAN-Australia-New Zealand FTA (domestic courts offered only in respect of Philippines and Vietnam; fork-in-the-road if the word 'or' is interpreted as such, as some tribunals have done: *Beijing Urban Construction Group Co. Ltd. v. Republic of Yemen*, ICSID Case No. ARB/14/30, Decision on Jurisdiction (31 May 2017) at para. 71).

83 Art. 26(2)(b) of the US Model BIT (2012), http://investmentpolicyhub.unctad.org/Download/TreatyFile/2870, accessed 29 July 2018. The 1994 US Model

BIT contained in Art. IX(3)(a) a fork-in-the-road-like provision, allowing access to international arbitration only if an investor has not resorted to domestic courts. That provision was replaced by the waiver requirement in the 2004 US Model BIT, which was seen as an encouragement of the use of domestic courts (Vandevelde, 2009: 312). The standardisation of the waiver requirement (as opposed to the fork-in-the-road) in both Canadian and US model BITs follows the NAFTA practice (Caplan and Sharpe, 2013: 829–830; Lévesque and Newcombe, 2013: 109–110).

84 Ch. 9, Art. 9.21(2)(b) of the Comprehensive and Progressive Agreement for Trans-Pacific Partnership, Santiago, 8 March 2018, in force 30 December 2018 (CPTPP).

85 Ch. 8, Art. 8.22(1)(f)-(g) of the Comprehensive Economic and Trade Agreement between Canada and the European Union, Brussels, 30 October 2016, not in force (CETA).

86 Ch. 3, Art. 3.7(1)(f) of the EU-Singapore Investment Protection Agreement (authentic text as of April 2018), http://trade.ec.europa.eu/doclib/press/index.cfm?id=961, accessed 23 July 2018. Singapore traditionally supports broad procedural investment protections (Nottage, 2016: 13).

87 Annex 12 of the EU-Vietnam Investment Protection Agreement (authentic text as of August 2018), http://trade.ec.europa.eu/doclib/press/index.cfm?id=1437, accessed 4 January 2019; Ch. 9, Annex 9-J of the CPTPP. Other states preferring fork-in-the-road clauses in regional investment protection arrangements include Indonesia, Philippines and Thailand. See note 82 above.

88 As did Thailand in its 2013 revised Model BIT (Nottage and Thanitcul, 2017: 817).

89 For example, Art. 14(6) of the Japan-Vietnam BIT:

> So long as an investor of either Contracting Party is seeking judicial or administrative settlement in the Area of the other Contracting Party or arbitral decision in accordance with any applicable previously agreed dispute-settlement procedures, concerning an investment dispute, or in the event that a final judicial settlement on such dispute has been made, such dispute shall not be submitted to arbitration referred to in the provisions of this Article.

Art. 17(4) of the Agreement between Japan and the Lao People's Democratic Republic for the Liberalisation, Promotion and Protection of Investment, Tokyo, 16 January 2008, in force 3 August 2008:

> if the disputing investor has not submitted the investment dispute for resolution under courts of justice or administrative tribunals or agencies, the disputing investor may submit the investment dispute to one of the following international conciliations or arbitrations.

90 For example, Ch. 10, Art. 131(2), fn. 13 of the Free Trade Agreement between China and Peru, Beijing, 28 April 2009, in force 1 March 2010.

91 For example, Japan-Switzerland EPA, Ch. 9, Tokyo, 19 February 2009, in force 1 September 2009.

92 Art. 6, fn. 4(a) of the ASEAN Comprehensive Investment Agreement.

93 The Indian Model BIT does not contain an MFN clause. Indian proposal of joint interpretive statements excludes the application of MFN clauses to dispute resolution issues: Office Memorandum of 8 February 2016 at para. 9.2(b).

94 Ch. 8, Art. 8.7(4) of the CETA; Ch. 9, Art. 9.5(3) of the CPTPP.

95 Cf. *Emilio Agustín Maffezini v. The Kingdom of Spain*, ICSID Case No. ARB/97/7, Decision of the Tribunal on Objections to Jurisdiction (25 January 2000) at paras. 38–64.

96 To my knowledge, no tribunal has so far allowed a fork-in-the-road clause to be bypassed using an MFN clause, however that possibility remains open, especially because some scholars have not seen an obstacle to such a conjunction (Schill, 2009: 191).

97 India, Myanmar, Laos and Vietnam (neither signed nor ratified); Thailand (signed but not ratified), available at https://icsid.worldbank.org/en/Pages/icsiddocs/List-of-Member-States.aspx, accessed 24 July 2018.

98 For example, Indian reaction was radical, which is said to be caused by its unsystematic approach to the conclusion of investment treaties, compared to other states like China (Kidane, 2017: 474). Thailand had a negative experience with contract-based arbitrations, which led to a reaction in that sector: requiring a special approval for public contracts with arbitration clauses (Nottage and Thanitcul, 2017: 828). On the other hand, Malaysia has not shown any negative reaction towards investment arbitration, because the system has been equally used by its own investors to protect their rights abroad (Jusoh et al., 2017). Japan continues to support the investor-state dispute settlement system in its current form because it has not encountered negative experiences, and it is very confident that it will not in the future (Fukunaga, 2018).

99 As for the ASEAN states: Chesterman (2016: 959). It is interesting to note that Myanmar has concluded BITs only with the states in the region (and Israel). See, for commentary, Malintoppi and Tan (2017: 232–243).

100 Faced with a request for injunction from starting or continuing arbitration, one domestic court has recently held that its state 'constitute[d] the natural forum for the litigation of the defendants' claim against the plaintiff' (*Union of India v. Vodafone Group plc United Kingdom & ANR* [2017] Delhi HC, CS(OS) 383/2017, p. 6). This view is in accordance with the presumption of territorial jurisdiction (see generally Ryngaert, 2015: 49). The domestic nature is particularly emphasised in non-inter-state legal relationships: see *Serbian Loans (France v. The Kingdom of the Serbs, Croats and Slovenes)* (Judgment) (1929) PCIJ Series A – No. 20, p. 41.

101 That fear is caused by the rivalry between powerful and weak states, at the expense of the latter (Garibaldi, 2006: 11). The Calvo Doctrine also played a role in the delayed accession of the Latin American states to the ICSID Convention (Garibaldi, 2006: 27–28).

102 Declaration on the Establishment of a New International Economic Order, UNGA Res. 3201 (S-VI), 1 May 1974, paras. 4(e) and (g); Art. 2(2) of the Charter of Economic Rights and Duties of States, UNGA Res. 3281 (XXIX), 12 December 1974.

103 Garibaldi (2006: 24); Schill (2006: 17); Shan (2008: 283). The death of the Calvo Doctrine was declared back in the 1950s (Shea, 1955: 20).

104 For some legislative action in Argentina and the US, see Garibaldi (2006: 43–55).

105 Art. 2(2)(a) of the Charter of Economic Rights and Duties of States.

106 For example, arrangements within the Commonwealth of Independent States in Central Asia (Sattorova, 2015: 1093–1095).

107 See Chen (2006: 901).

108 As was the case in Indonesia (Losari and Ewing-Chow, 2015: 999; Price, 2017: 138).

109 For example, in the Japanese Diet (Hamamoto, 2015b: 934–935).

110 Approach taken in the Indian Model BIT (Shetty and Weeramantry, 2016: 193).

111 See also comments on the 'tide of economic nationalism' in the context of Indonesian review of its BITs by Price (2017: 139–140).

112 Chi and Wang (2015: 888) state that the mainstream attitude in legal scholarship in China towards such developments has been negative.
113 See Chi and Wang (2015: 889) quoting Wei Yanru.
114 At the time of conclusion of BITs, usually little regard is paid to their future implications, and there is also evidence that many actors have simply ignored any possible risks (Poulsen and Aisbett, 2013: 279–285). Cf. Alschner (2017: 50), arguing that claims did not have such an effect on policy changes as first expected.
115 Although it signed a BIT with Syria in 2009 (Salomon and Friedrich, 2015: 808–809).
116 For East Asia and the Pacific, see Salomon and Friedrich (2015: 836).
117 The fourth being 'exceptions for the State's essential security' (Chen, 2006: 907).
118 See also for the Chinese example in particular, with the signs of change towards more acceptance of international arbitration, Qingjiang (2010).
119 See, for example, a statement by a Japanese Diet member, naming the International Court of Justice and the International Tribunal for the Law of the Sea as acceptable modes of inter-state adjudication from the Japanese constitutional perspective, compared to the unacceptable investor-state arbitration system (Hamamoto, 2015b: 935–936).
120 *Nationality Decrees Issued in Tunis and Morocco* (Advisory Opinion) (1923) PCIJ Series B – No. 4, p. 24.
121 *Interpretation of Peace Treaties with Bulgaria, Hungary and Romania (First Phase)* (Advisory Opinion) (1950) ICJ Reports 65, pp. 70–71.
122 *Renta 4 S.V.S.A. et al. v. The Russian Federation,* SCC Case No. 24/2007, Award on Preliminary Objections (20 March 2009) at para. 56; and for the suggestion that investment arbitration ensures the stability of the legal framework governing foreign investments, Schill (2010).
123 *Corn Products International, Inc. v. United Mexican States,* ICSID Case No. ARB(AF)/04/1, Separate Opinion of Andreas F. Lowenfeld (18 August 2009) at para. 1.
124 Ibid.
125 *Maffezini v. Spain* at paras. 94–98.
126 The home state of an investor does not retain any interest in the investor's dispute and arbitration with his host state (Douglas, 2003: 170).
127 For example, *Armed Activities on the Territory of the Congo (New Application: 2002) (Democratic Republic of the Congo v. Rwanda)* (Jurisdiction and Admissibility) (Judgment) (2006) ICJ Reports 6, at para. 88 (holding that every condition in a jurisdictional clause is limitation of state consent, thus deferring the definition of all the questions of access to consenting states).
128 *Millicom International Operations B.V. and Sentel GSM SA v. The Republic of Senegal,* ICSID Case No. ARB/08/20, Decision on Jurisdiction of the Arbitral Tribunal (16 July 2010) at paras. 63–66, particularly para. 65, on the protective objective achieved by standing offers to arbitrate, and then concluding that

> there is nothing extraordinary about the rule [providing consent] to the extent that it implies nothing else for the State involved except to agree to submit itself to an arbitration proceeding under the aegis of ICSID by independent arbitrators, in a proceeding during which it shall have every opportunity to defend its positions.

129 *Planet Mining v. Indonesia* at paras. 146–218.
130 Ibid. at para. 201. For the link between the loss of state control over the gateway and the objectives of international investment protection: *Millicom v. Senegal* at para. 65.

131 See, for example, reasoning in *Malaysian Historical Salvors v. Malaysia* at para. 62.
132 Questions that appeared in practice vary, for example from those of the existence and the standard of futility exceptions, to more complex issues such as the applicability of MFN clauses to dispute resolution clauses.
133 See generally D'Agnone (2013). For the futility exception standards, see Pérez Aznar (2016: 556–557). For the technique using MFN clauses, see *Maffezini v. Spain*.
134 See *Urbaser v. Argentina* at paras. 106–203.
135 *Swissbourgh Diamond Mines (Pty) Limited et al. v. Kingdom of Lesotho*, PCA Case No. 2013–29, Partial Award on Jurisdiction and Merits (18 April 2016), not public, relevant parts reported in *Kingdom of Lesotho v. Swissbourgh Diamond Mines (Pty) Limited et al.* [2017] SGHC 195, at paras. 279–282. The Tribunal held that the 'primary or direct remedy' for cancelling the SADC Tribunal would be ordering the establishment of a new tribunal to hear the claimants' claims. However, the High Court of Singapore disagreed and set aside the award.
136 For example, *CMS Gas Transmission Company v. The Republic of Argentina*, ICSID Case No. ARB/01/8, Decision of the Tribunal on Objections to Jurisdiction (17 July 2003) at para. 80 (different parties and causes of action); *Hulley Enterprises Limited (Cyprus) v. The Russian Federation*, PCA Case No. 2005–03, Final Award (18 July 2014) at paras. 1256–1272 ('triple identity' test: identity of the parties, cause of action and object of the dispute).
137 See further remarks by Peter Turner in Lew et al. (2006: 177–182).
138 It will be noted, however, that such proposals have been considered in India: Report of the High Level Committee to Review the Institutionalisation of Arbitration Mechanism in India, 30 July 2017, http://legalaffairs.gov.in/hi/sectiondivision/report-high-level-committee-review-institutionalisation-arbitration-mechanism-india, 106–107, accessed 25 July 2018.
139 It has been calculated that 81% of the TPP investment chapter was taken from previous US investment treaties, the closest example being the US-Columbia FTA (Alschner and Skougarevskiy, 2016: 341); new provisions regarding investor-state arbitration concentrated on clarifying the process, rather than the access to arbitration (Alschner and Skougarevskiy, 2016: 252–253).
140 'India to operationalize BIPA with Canada', *Live Mint*, 28 September 2016, www.livemint.com/Politics/WbAZSTb9Vf8VUjvOREghmI/India-to-operationalize-BIPA-with-Canada.html, accessed 25 July 2018.
141 For example, Australia and New Zealand excluded investor-state arbitration between themselves both from the TPP and the ASEAN-Australia-New Zealand FTA (Nottage, 2016: 17, 25). See also, for the same development regarding the CPTPP, Letter of 8 March 2018 from David Parker to Steven Ciobo, www.mfat.govt.nz/assets/CPTPP/New-Zealand-Australia-ISDS-Trade-Remedies-and-Relationship-with-Other-Agreements.pdf, accessed 25 July 2018.
142 For example, Japan (Hamamoto, 2012).
143 Prime Minister of India, 'Cabinet approves Bilateral Investment Treaty between India and Cambodia to boost investment', 27 July 2016, www.pmindia.gov.in/en/news_updates/cabinet-approves-bilateral-investment-treaty-between-india-and-cambodia-to-boost-investment/, accessed 25 July 2018; Weeramantry (2017: 950, 961).
144 It has also been suggested that the defensive attitude of India in reforming investment law can benefit third states, like those in Africa (Kidane, 2017: 475).
145 Report of the High Level Committee, India, 104.
146 *Ping An Life Insurance Company of China, Limited and Ping An Insurance (Group) Company of China, Limited v. Kingdom of Belgium*, ICSID Case No. ARB/12/29, Award (30 April 2015) at para. 230 (denying to effectively extend

a narrow jurisdictional clause by reliance on a posterior treaty between the same treaty parties); *China Heilongjiang International Economic & Technical Cooperative Corp. et al. v. Mongolia* (2017) (not public, reported in Peterson (2017b); lacking jurisdiction due to a narrow jurisdictional clause).

147 *Beijing Urban Construction Group v. Yemen* at paras. 54–109 (dismissing the objection concerning the narrow scope of the jurisdictional clause and finding jurisdiction over the issue of occurrence of expropriation).

148 For example, South Africa (Schlemmer, 2016: 188–190).

149 For example, Poland has been reported to consider the same move regarding intra-EU BITs and their incompatibility with the EU law (Orecki, 2017).

150 It has been noted that in Japan anti-investment arbitration arguments emerged only with the discussion on the conclusion of the TPP, possibly as an expression of anti-US sentiments, and remain without any real effect (Hamamoto, 2015b: 947–951).

References

Ahuja, S. (2016). Arbitration Involving India: Recent Developments. *Asian Dispute Review*, 2016, 132.

Alschner, W. (2017). The Impact of Investment Arbitration on Investment Treaty Design: Myth Versus Reality. *Yale Journal of International Law*, 42, 1.

Alschner, W. and Skougarevskiy, D. (2016). The New Gold Standard? Empirically Situating the Trans-Pacific Partnership in the Investment Treaty Universe. *Journal of World Investment & Trade*, 17, 339.

Bonnitcha, J. (2017). International Investment Arbitration in Myanmar: Bounded Rationality, But Not as We Know It. *Journal of World Investment & Trade*, 18, 974.

Caplan, L. M. and Sharpe, J. K. (2013). United States. In C. Brown, ed., *Commentaries on Selected Model Investment Treaties*, Oxford: Oxford University Press, p. 755.

Chen, A. (2006). Should the Four Great Safeguards in Sino-Foreign BITs Be Hastily Dismantled? Comments on Provisions concerning Dispute Settlement in Model U.S. and Canadian BITs. *Journal of World Investment & Trade*, 7, 899.

Chen, A. (2009). Queries to the Recent ICSID Decision on Jurisdiction Upon the Case of *Tza Yap Shum v. Republic of Peru*: Should China-Peru BIT 1994 Be Applied to Hong Kong SAR under the "One Country Two Systems" Policy? *Journal of World Investment & Trade*, 10, 829.

Chesterman, S. (2016). Asia's Ambivalence about International Law and Institutions: Past, Present and Futures. *European Journal of International Law*, 27, 945.

Chi, M. and Wang, X. (2015). The Evolution of ISA Clauses in Chinese IIAs and Its Practical Implications. The Admissibility of Disputes for Investor-State Arbitration. *Journal of World Investment & Trade*, 16, 869.

Coleman, A. and Maogoto, J. N. (2013). "Westphalian" Meets "Eastphalian" Sovereignty: China in a Globalized World. *Asian Journal of International Law*, 3, 237.

Crawford, J. R. and Grant, T. D. (2012). Local Remedies, Exhaustion of. In R. Wolfrum, ed., Vol. VI of *The Max Planck Encyclopedia of Public International Law*. Oxford: Oxford University Press, p. 895.

Crockett, A. (2015). Indonesia's Bilateral Investment Treaties: Between Generations? *ICSID Review-FILJ*, 30, 437.

Crockett, A. (2017). The Termination of Indonesia's BITs: Changing the Bathwater, But Keeping the Baby? *Journal of World Investment & Trade*, 18, 836.

D'Agnone, G. (2013). Recourse to the "Futility Exception" Within the ICSID System: Reflections on Recent Developments of the Local Remedies Rule. *Law & Practice of International Courts & Tribunals*, 12, 343.

Douglas, Z. (2003). The Hybrid Foundations of Investment Treaty Arbitration. *British Yearbook of International Law*, 74, 151.

Eliasson, N. (2012). China's Investment Treaties: A Procedural Perspective. In V. Bath and L. Nottage, eds., *Foreign Investment and Dispute Resolution Law and Practice in Asia*, Abingdon: Routledge, p. 90.

Fukunaga, Y. (2018). ISDS Under the CPTPP and Beyond: Japanese Perspectives. *Kluwer Arbitration Blog*, 30 May, http://arbitrationblog.kluwerarbitration.com/2018/05/30/isds-cptpp-beyond-japanese-perspectives/

Garibaldi, O. M. (2006). Carlos Calvo Redivivus: The Rediscovery of the Calvo Doctrine in the Era of Investment Treaties. *Transnational Dispute Management*, 3(5).

Ginsburg, T. (2011). Eastphalia and Asian Regionalism. *U.C. Davis Law Review*, 44, 859.

Haftel, Y. Z. and Thompson, A. (2018). When Do States Renegotiate Investment Agreements? The Impact of Arbitration. *Review of International Organizations*, 13, 25.

Hamamoto, S. (2012). A Passive Player in International Investment Law: Typically Japanese? In V. Bath and L. Nottage, eds., *Foreign Investment and Dispute Resolution Law and Practice in Asia*, Abingdon: Routledge, p. 53.

Hamamoto, S. (2015a). Economic Partnership Agreements Concluded by Japan. *European Yearbook of International Economic Law*, 6, 191.

Hamamoto, S. (2015b). Recent Anti-ISDS Discourse in the Japanese Diet: A Dressed-Up But Glaring Hypocrisy. *Journal of World Investment & Trade*, 16, 931.

Hanessian, G. and Duggal, K. (2017). The Final 2015 Indian Model BIT: Is This the Change the World Wishes to See? *ICSID Review-FILJ*, 32, 216.

Hepburn, J. (2017a). Indian BIT Negotiator Clarifies Country's Stance on Exhaustion of Remedies, and Offers Update on Status of Country's Revamp of Bilateral Investment Treaties. *Investment Arbitration Reporter*, 31 March, www.iareporter.com/articles/indian-bit-negotiator-clarifies-countrys-stance-on-exhaustion-of-remedies-and-offers-update-on-status-of-countrys-revamp-of-bilateral-investment-treaties/

Hepburn, J. (2017b). Unable to Unilaterally Terminate a 2011 BIT, the Government of India Persuades Counter-Party to Agree Joint Interpretive Note to Clarify BIT's Implications. *Investment Arbitration Reporter*, 17 July, www.iareporter.com/articles/unable-to-unilaterally-terminate-a-2011-bit-the-government-of-india-persuades-counter-party-to-agree-joint-interpretive-note-to-clarify-bits-implications/

Hepburn, J. (2019). India Agrees New Investment Treaty Text with Colombia, Belarus and Taiwan, Advancing Some of Its Key Concerns Such as Partial Exhaustion and Human Rights. *Investment Arbitration Reporter*, 1 January, www.iareporter.com/articles/india-agrees-new-investment-treaty-text-with-colombia-and-belarus-advancing-some-of-its-key-concerns-such-as-partial-exhaustion-and-human-rights/

Hepburn, J. and Kabra, R. (2017). India's New Model Investment Treaty: Fit for Purpose? *Indian Law Review*, 1, 95.

Heymann, M. C. (2008). International Law and the Settlement of Investment Disputes Relating to China. *Journal of International Economic Law*, 11, 507.

Jusoh, S., Razak, M. F. A. and Mazlan, M. A. (2017). Malaysia and Investor-State Dispute Settlement: Learning from Experience. *Journal of World Investment & Trade*, 18, 890.

Kang, S. (2017). Conflict of Investment-Related Provisions Under Regional Trade Agreements Between Korea and China – Navigating the "Noodle Bowl". *ICSID Review-FILJ*, 32, 418.

Kidane, W. (2017). China's and India's Differing Investment Treaty and Dispute Settlement Experiences and Implications for Africa. *Loyola University Chicago Law Journal*, 49, 405.

Kim, J. (2012). A Pivot to Asia in Investor-State Arbitration: The Coming Emergence of Asian Claimants. *ICSID Review-FILJ*, 27, 399.

Kim, S.-W. (2018). The Eastphalian Project Revisited. *Korean Journal of International & Comparative Law*, 6, 102.

Koh, T. (2011). International Law and the Peaceful Resolution of Disputes: Asian Perspectives, Contributions, and Challenges. *Asian Journal of International Law*, 1, 57.

Lévesque, C. and Newcombe, A. (2013). Canada. In C. Brown, ed., *Commentaries on Selected Model Investment Treaties*, Oxford: Oxford University Press, p. 53.

Lew, J. et al. (2006). The "Fork in the Road" Revisited. In F. Ortino, A. Sheppard and H. Warner, eds., *Investment Treaty Law. Current Issues Volume 1*, London: BIICL, p. 173.

Losari, J. J. and Ewing-Chow, M. (2015). Difficulties with Decentralization and Due Process. Indonesia's Recent Experiences with International Investment Agreements and Investor-State Disputes. *Journal of World Investment & Trade*, 16, 981.

Malintoppi, L. and Tan, C., eds. (2017). *Investment Protection in Southeast Asia. A Country-by-Country Guide on Arbitration Laws and Bilateral Investment Treaties*, Leiden: Brill.

Mangklatanakul, V. (2011). Thailand's First Treaty Arbitration: Gain from Pain. In S. D. Franck and A. Joubin-Bret, eds., *Investor-State Disputes: Prevention and Alternatives to Arbitration II. Washington and Lee University and UNCTAD Joint Symposium on International Investment and Alternative Dispute Resolution*, New York and Geneva: UN, p. 81.

Nakagawa, J. (2007). No More Negotiated Deals?: Settlement of Trade and Investment Disputes in East Asia. *Journal of International Economic Law*, 10, 837.

Nguyen, M. D. and Nguyen, T. T. T. (2017). International Investment Dispute Resolution in Vietnam: Opportunities and Challenges. *Journal of World Investment & Trade*, 18, 918.

Nottage, L. (2016). The TPP Investment Chapter and Investor-State Arbitration in Asia and Oceania: Assessing Prospects for Ratification. *Melbourne Journal of International Law*, 17, 1.

Nottage, L. and Thanitcul, S. (2017). International Investment Arbitration in Thailand: Limiting Contract-Based Claims While Maintaining Treaty-Based ISDS. *Journal of World Investment & Trade*, 18, 793.

Nottage, L. and Weeramantry, J. R. (2012). Investment Arbitration in Asia: Five Perspectives on Law and Practice. *Arbitration International*, 28, 19.

Orecki, M. (2017). Let the Show Begin: Poland Has Commenced the Process of BITs' Termination. *Kluwer Arbitration Blog*, 8 August, http://kluwerarbitrationblog.com/2017/08/08/let-show-begin-poland-commenced-process-bits-termination/

Owada, H. (2011). Asia and International Law. The Inaugural Address of the First President of the Asian Society of International Law, Singapore, 7 April 2007. *Asian Journal of International Law*, 1, 3.

Pathirana, D. (2017). An Overview of Sri Lanka's Bilateral Investment Treaties: Status Quo and Some Insights into Future Modifications. *Asian Journal of International Law*, 7, 287.

Paulsson, J. (2013). *The Idea of Arbitration*, Oxford: Oxford University Press.

Pérez Aznar, F. (2016). Local Litigation Requirements in International Investment Agreements: Their Characteristics and Potential in Times of Reform in Latin America. *Journal of World Investment & Trade*, 17, 536.

Peterson, L. E. (2017a). Investigation: In Aftermath of Investor Arbitration Against Lesotho, SADC Member-States Amend Investment Treaty so as to Remove ISDS and Limit Protections. *Investment Arbitration Reporter*, 20 February, www.iareporter. com/articles/investigation-in-aftermath-of-investor-arbitration-against-lesotho-sadc-member-states-amend-investment-treaty-so-as-to-remove-isds-and-limit-prot ections/

Peterson, L. E. (2017b). Mongolia Prevails in Long-Running Chinese BIT Arbitration, as Arbitrators Distinguish Their Reading of Constricted Jurisdiction Clause from More Generous Readings in Prior Cases. *Investment Arbitration Reporter*, 7 July, www.iareporter.com/articles/mongolia-prevails-in-long-running-chinese-bit-arbitration-as-arbitrators-distinguish-their-reading-of-constricted-jurisdiction-clause-from-more-generous-readings-in-prior-cases/

Poulsen, L. N. S. and Aisbett, E. (2013). When the Claim Hits. Bilateral Investment Treaties and Bounded Rational Learning. *World Politics*, 65, 273.

Price, D. (2017). Indonesia's Bold Strategy on Bilateral Investment Treaties: Seeking an Equitable Climate for Investment? *Asian Journal of International Law*, 7, 124.

Qingjiang, K. (2010). International Dispute Settlement: The Chinese Approach and Practice, and Their Implications. In M. Sornarajah and J. Wang, eds., *China, India and the International Economic Order*, Cambridge: Cambridge University Press, p. 314.

Ranjan, P. and Anand, P. (2017). The 2016 Model Indian Bilateral Investment Treaty: A Critical Deconstruction. *Northwestern Journal of International Law & Business*, 38, 1.

Reyes, A. (2017). Foreign Direct Investment in the Philippines and the Pitfalls of Economic Nationalism. *Journal of World Investment & Trade*, 18, 1025.

Ryngaert, C. (2015). *Jurisdiction in International Law*, 2nd edn, Oxford: Oxford University Press.

Salomon, C. T. and Friedrich, S. (2015). Investment Arbitration in East Asia and the Pacific. A Statistical Analysis of Bilateral Investment Treaties, Other International Investment Agreements and Investment Arbitrations in the Region. *Journal of World Investment & Trade*, 16, 800.

Sattorova, M. (2015). International Investment Law in Central Asia. The Making, Implementation and Change of Investment Rules from a Regionalist Perspective. *Journal of World Investment & Trade*, 16, 1089.

Sattorova, M. (2017). Reassertion of Control and Contracting Parties' Domestic Law Responses to Investment Treaty Arbitration. In A. Kulick, ed., *Reassertion of Control Over the Investment Treaty Regime*, Cambridge: Cambridge University Press, p. 53.

Schill, S. (2006). From Calvo to CMS: Burying an International Law Legacy – Argentina's Currency Reform in the Face of Investment Protection: The ICSID Case *CMS v. Argentina*. *Transnational Dispute Management*, 3(2).

Schill, S. W. (2007). Tearing Down the Great Wall: The New Generation Investment Treaties of the People's Republic of China. *Cardozo Journal of International & Comparative Law*, 15, 73.

Schill, S. W. (2009). *The Multilateralization of International Investment Law*, Cambridge: Cambridge University Press.

Schill, S. W. (2010). Private Enforcement of International Investment Law: Why We Need Investor Standing in BIT Dispute Settlement. In M. Waibel et al., eds., *The Backlash Against Investment Arbitration*, Alphen aan den Rijn: Kluwer, p. 29.

Schill, S. W. (2015). Special Issue: Dawn of an Asian Century in International Investment Law? An Introduction. *Journal of World Investment & Trade*, 16, 765.

Schlemmer, E. C. (2016). An Overview of South Africa's Bilateral Investment Treaties and Investment Policy. *ICSID Review-FILJ*, 31, 167.

Schreuer, C. (2005). Calvo's Grandchildren: The Return of Local Remedies in Investment Arbitration. *Law & Practice of International Courts & Tribunals*, 4, 1.

Shan, W. (2008). Calvo Doctrine, State Sovereignty and the Changing Landscape of International Investment Law. In W. Shan, P. Simons and D. Singh, eds., *Redefining Sovereignty in International Economic Law*, Oxford: Hart Publishing, p. 247.

Shea, D. R. (1955). *The Calvo Clause: A Problem of Inter-American and International Law and Diplomacy*, Minneapolis, MN: University of Minnesota Press.

Shen, W. (2011). The Good, the Bad or the Ugly? A Critique of the Decision on Jurisdiction and Competence in *Tza Yap Shum v. The Republic of Peru*. *Chinese Journal of International Law*, 10, 55.

Shetty, N. and Weeramantry, J. R. (2016). India's New Approach to Investment Treaties. *Asian Dispute Review*, 2016, 189.

Sornarajah, M. (2012). Review of Asian Views on Foreign Investment Law. In V. Bath and L. Nottage, eds., *Foreign Investment and Dispute Resolution Law and Practice in Asia*, Abingdon: Routledge, p. 242.

Sornarajah, M. (2015). *Resistance and Change in the International Law on Foreign Investment*, Cambridge: Cambridge University Press.

Tomuschat, C. (2011). Asia and International Law – Common Ground and Regional Diversity. *Asian Journal of International Law*, 1, 217.

Vandevelde, K. J. (2009). A Comparison of the 2004 and 1994 U.S. Model BITs: Rebalancing Investor and Host Country Interests. In K. P. Sauvant, ed., *Yearbook on International Investment Law & Policy 2008–2009*, Oxford: Oxford University Press, p. 283.

Wang, G. (2014). Consent in Investor – State Arbitration: A Critical Analysis. *Chinese Journal of International Law*, 13, 335.

Weeramantry, R. (2017). International Investment Law and Practice in the Kingdom of Cambodia: An Evolving "Rule Taker"? *Journal of World Investment & Trade*, 18, 942.

Weeramantry, R. and Mohan, M. (2017). International Investment Arbitration in Laos: Large Issues for a Small State. *Journal of World Investment & Trade*, 18, 1001.

Yeo, A. and Menon, S. (2016). Indonesia – Arbitrating with Foreign Parties: A Closer Look at Indonesia's Approach to Investor-State Dispute Settlement. *Asian Dispute Review*, 2016, 124.

5 Will Asia breathe life into a Multilateral Investment Court?

Thoughts on the feasibility and design of a new, stand-alone court

Céline Lévesque

Introduction

Let me first express my gratitude to the conference organizers and our host Xiamen University.[1] It is with some trepidation that I share with you a few preliminary thoughts on the possible establishment of a Multilateral Investment Court and this for two main reasons. First, this topic concerns government efforts that are unfolding as we speak, and as such, it is a bit of a moving target.[2] While the idea is not new, it has picked up momentum during the last year, spearheaded by the efforts of the European Union (EU) and Canada. Public statements as well as 'non papers' provide a window into recently held intergovernmental discussions, but cannot be taken as a guarantee of success (Commission and Canada, 2016a, 2016b, 2017).

Second, I tread carefully and humbly in looking at Asian perspectives on these developments, specifically asking whether Asia could breathe life into a Multilateral Investment Court. As a Canadian academic who is in no way an expert on Asia, I came to asking this question based on the following basic premise: while the EU and Canada were able to agree on a more 'court-like' system to resolve investment disputes between investors and States in the recently signed Comprehensive Economic and Trade Agreement (CETA),[3] they cannot turn this model into a truly multilateral court on their own.[4] Trade-related developments in the United States (US) (notably the withdrawal from the Trans-Pacific Partnership (TPP))[5] lead many to expect an American retrenchment from multilateral engagement along with a continued low appetite for new, supranational courts.[6] In addition, the support of many mostly capital-importing developing countries (who may be dissatisfied with the working of the current international arbitration-based investor-State dispute settlement (ISDS) system) may not be enough, while others may envision different avenues for reform. As such, important capital-exporting countries outside of Europe and the US will need to be on board if the goal of reaching a global consensus is to be realized and the court is able to attract a critical number of members to ensure its viability. Thus, my focus is on Asia and Asian leadership.

In the next few minutes, I propose to explore conditions that would allow China, Japan, South Korea, Singapore and other Asian countries that are important capital exporters (as well as important capital importers in some cases) to embrace a Multilateral Investment Court. I intend to speak on the political and practical *feasibility* of a *new, stand-alone* court. In order to assess feasibility, I will focus on the design of such a court, looking into issues of representation and size (in the first part) and asking questions such as 'who should judge' and 'how should the court function' (in the second part). In doing so, I will draw on examples and practices of international courts and bodies.

Purposively, I will *not* seek to answer *opportunity* questions, such as: is there a need for a Multilateral Investment Court? Or would it be best to create a new court as opposed to 'docking' the court into an existing institution (such as the International Centre for Settlement of Investment Disputes[7] (ICSID))? Nor will I try to answer the question of whether it is efficient to create such a court without the existence of a single multilateral investment agreement (Commission and Government of Canada, 2017: para. 5). As a starting point, I will take for granted that the decision has been made by (would be) treaty parties to a Multilateral Investment Court to (1) abandon arbitration as a model for ISDS *between themselves* and that (2) these treaty parties have confidence that they can create an *effective enforcement* mechanism for the decisions rendered by such a court.[8]

Why this single focus on the design of a Multilateral Investment Court? While I may seem to be 'jumping the gun', this approach appears justified in the sense that the best idea in the world won't materialize if it lacks *feasibility*: political and practical. As others have noted, the inability of States to agree on court composition and judges selection procedures has delayed or forestalled court initiatives in the past (Mackenzie et al., 2010: 10–17; Abi-Saab, 1996: 173–174; Wood, 2017: 5, 12–13; Three Crowns, 2015).

Before moving on, two preliminary points have to be made.

First, although the EU and Canada are careful not to dictate the outcome of the negotiations on a Multilateral Investment Court, it is clear that some of the predicates are already set. They result from the criticisms levelled at the ad hoc (as opposed to permanent) ISDS currently in place in most international investment agreements (IIAs), almost half of which EU members are party to.[9] The European Commission has repeatedly emphasized the following values or characteristics which inspire its ISDS reform efforts:

- Legitimacy (sometimes expressed in relation to concepts of accountability, independence, impartiality, objectivity and neutrality)
- Legal correctness
- Transparency
- Predictability and consistency (also legal certainty, stability)
- Efficiency (as to proceedings as well as costs)
  (Commission and Government of Canada, 2016b: 1–2, 2017: para. 13)

These values are of course intermingling and reinforcing, but they offer a useful analytical tool for this talk as they can be used as a benchmark to assess feasibility.

Second, the EU and Canada have agreed in CETA to features of the so-called 'Investment Court System' (ICS)[10] that may be hard to walk back from. Since the Commission is currently engaged in many negotiations based on this model and is wedded to its underlying values,[11] it would be politically difficult to argue that *dramatically different* features would be equally acceptable. As such, my assessment of the feasibility of the multilateral level court includes, as a starting point, the following features:

- Permanent dispute resolution structure
- Appeal instance
- Full-time adjudicators
- Fixed remuneration
- High qualifications and criteria for selecting adjudicators
- Random allocation of cases
- Transparency/full document disclosure
- High ethics standards
- Safeguard for independence (random allocation, tenure) (Commission, 2016a)

Other features flow from the fact that a multilateral court to be efficient would need to provide the flexibility and adaptability required for countries to join in time (Commission and Canada, 2016b: para. 22).

1. Conditions that could entice key Asian countries to embrace a Multilateral Investment Court

Asia, of course, is not a monolith. For the purpose of this talk I will focus on a number of countries that are mainly capital exporters (such as Japan) or that are both heavy capital exporters as well as importers (including China and Singapore). I will also mention the Association of Southeast Asian Nations (ASEAN)[12] and Vietnam, who along with Singapore, is in a peculiar situation.

1.1. *The buy-in of capital-exporting countries*

During the ministerial-level discussions on a possible Multilateral Investment Court held in Davos in January 2017, the EU and Canada emphasized that a 'fully inclusive' multilateral approach is the only way to proceed, taking 'into account the positions and experiences of all countries with a view of building a truly global consensus on the best possible regime for the resolution of international investment disputes' (Commission and Canada, 2017: para. 22). In order to reach such a consensus, negotiating countries will have to address a concern (*warranted or not*) of some important capital exporters in Asia that their voices risk being drowned out by a majority of mostly capital-importing countries in the design and composition of the court, leading to a system that systematically tilts toward States, to the detriment of investors.[13]

1.1.1. *The particular role of key Asian countries*

In order to identify key Asian countries, I rely on UNCTAD's World Investment Report (WIR) ranking of the top 20 economies for Foreign Direct Investment (FDI) outflows as well as inflows (UNCTAD, 2017a). The 2016 data ranks the following Asian countries as important capital exporters: China (no. 2), Japan (no. 4), South Korea (no. 13) and Singapore (no. 15). (UNCTAD, 2017a: 14, ch 1, table I.14.) As to capital imports, China comes at no. 3; and Singapore at no. 6 (UNCTAD, 2017a: 12, ch 1, table I.11). While the latter two countries can be expected to have more concerns for both their 'offensive' as well as 'defensive' interests, *for the purpose of this talk, I will emphasize the protection of investors abroad (i.e. offensive interests of major capital exporters).*

As demonstrated by other speakers at this conference, the experience of the listed countries with IIAs and the current, arbitration-based ISDS differs considerably.[14] As such, I will not attempt to describe each country's experience in order to evaluate their level of potential interest in a Multilateral Investment Court. I will only note that some countries, such as China and South Korea, have both signed over 100 IIAs and have been respondents in some cases, while Japan has signed fewer and has not been a respondent yet.[15] Altogether, these countries have faced relatively few ISDS claims (UNCTAD, 2017b: 33).

Political context in each country will of course also matter. A country such as Japan, which had recently been through debates on the current arbitration-based ISDS and convinced its Diet members and its population to support this model notably in the TPP, can be expected to be more reluctant to support the creation of a Multilateral Investment Court (Hamamoto, 2015: 931). In contrast, a country such as China, which looks to ascertain a leadership role in international economic law matters (President Xi Jinping, 2017), may be more willing to embrace such a proposal.

The regional and global context will also influence Asia's support for this initiative: for example, the EU has been in discussion with ASEAN members (including Singapore and Vietnam) regarding an ICS. Both of these countries have negotiated FTAs with the EU: the Singapore FTA (agreed to in 2014) included traditional ISDS, while the Vietnam FTA (agreed to in 2016) provides for the new model bilateral ICS.[16] A recent European Court of Justice (ECJ) advisory opinion will have an impact on both these agreements and their dispute settlement processes.[17] Singapore and Vietnam are in a peculiar position because they were also parties to the TPP negotiations which had led to an improved arbitration-based ISDS mechanism, which may still survive in the context of TPP-11.

1.1.2. *Court design objectives and values*

At a minimum, I will assume that key Asian countries would want to keep some of the benefits of the current regime. For my purpose, I have grouped sought-for values and characteristics in three categories.

First, as a 'means of achieving the objective of ensuring the legitimate performance of the judicial function', independence and impartiality would be sought.[18] Already in the context of CETA, critics of the new Investment Court System (ICS) have opined that the EU and Canada could 'stack' the court with pro-State appointees, disregarding the interest of their national investors, who henceforth would be excluded from the (direct) appointment of tribunal members (EFILA, 2016). In the context of a truly multilateral effort, the concern on the part of some Asian States for a potential lack of impartiality on the part of judges selected by a majority of mostly capital-importing States would need to be addressed. Of course, independence is also a foundational concept in reference to domestic judiciaries. Security of tenure is a key characteristic of independent judiciaries the world over.[19] Seeking independence and impartiality would have an impact on the qualifications sought for in judges, the role of nationality in the selection of judges, tenure and renewals as well as case-assignments.

Second, promoting efficiency in the resolution of disputes between investors and States would be a key objective. A concern of those opposed to major reforms of ISDS (including some Asian States), especially the addition of appeals, is often that increased delays and costs will follow.[20] Yet, it has also been acknowledged that the current arbitration-based ISDS system can be expensive and sometimes lengthy (UNCTAD, 2013: 4). The design and workings of a Multilateral Investment Court would need to seek timeliness and limit costs. As such, seeking efficiency would have an impact on the size of the court, the functioning of the court (ex. do judges sit in benches? of what size?) and on the design of an appeal process.

Third, means of improving the predictability and consistency of decisions would be sought-after. The current ad hoc (as opposed to permanent), arbitration-based ISDS system has produced significant uncertainty as to the interpretation of many IIA provisions and does not support the development of a predictable system of law. From the point of view of foreign investors (and their Asian home States), this situation does not provide a favourable investment climate. The predictability objective would be supported by increased transparency in the rendering of decisions as well as accessible legal documents. The promotion of the value of 'legal correctness', notably through the establishment of an appeal mechanism, would also support the goal of increased predictability and consistency in decision-making. Regrouped for my purpose under the umbrella of 'predictability and rule of law', this objective would have an impact on the size of the court, qualifications sought for in judges, tenure and the design of an appeal process.

1.2. The tension between the sought after 'global consensus' and the support of key Asian countries

Considering the potentially different interests at stake, one may wonder whether a global consensus can be reached. As noted earlier, the EU and Canada emphasized that a 'fully inclusive' multilateral approach was needed to establish a

Multilateral Investment Court (Commission and Canada, 2017: 22). One question is whether the process can be fully inclusive but its outcome not so much? In other words, how much representativeness is required to reach a global consensus?

1.2.1. *Regional courts and the required conditions for 'full representation'*

One way to ensure full representation is to have a national of each member State sit as a judge on the Court.[21] This is the case for some regional courts, such as the European Court of Human rights (ECtHR)[22] or the ECJ.[23] What distinguished these courts from many others, however, is their high volume of cases and corresponding budgets.

Let's take the example of the ECtHR. The Court was established in 1959 to hear allegations of violations of the European Convention on Human Rights. As with ISDS under most IIAs, individuals can apply directly to the court and most applications are made by individuals.[24] It currently counts 47 judges for its 47 members (ECHR: Art. 20). The court sits in benches of 1, 3, 7 and 17 judges. Every year, over 50,000 new applications are lodged, which has forced the court to adopt procedures to treat the complaints in an efficient manner.[25] Just as an illustration, in 2016, the court delivered 993 judgements. The Court's budget for 2017 is over 71 million euros, which covers judges' remuneration, staff salaries and operational expenditures (Council of Europe, 2017a).

Another example is the ECJ, which includes 28 judges for 28 member States.[26] Established in 1952, it is responsible for examining the legality of EU measures and ensuring the uniform interpretation and application of EU law. Judges of the ECJ sit in benches of 3 or 5 judges' Chambers or a Grand Chamber of 15 judges.[27] In 2016, 692 new cases were submitted to the Court (including 175 appeals) and another 704 cases were completed (CJEU, 2017a: 28–29). As of 31 December 2016, 872 cases were pending on the Court's docket (CJEU, 2017b). The 2017 budget for the Court of Justice of the European Union (CJEU) (including the ECJ and the General Court) is over 399 million euros (CJEU, 2017c: 1987).

1.2.2. *The pitfalls of 'full representation' for a Multilateral Investment Court*

In the context of a Multilateral Investment Court, the value of 'representativeness' quickly enters into conflict with the identified values of 'efficiency' and potentially of 'predictably and rule of law' as well as 'independence and impartiality'.

As to efficiency, the question of court size rears its head. Taking the most optimistic (and also unrealistic scenario!), let's imagine that the Court attracts as many members as ICSID at 153.[28] What kind of case-load would justify the maintenance of a court including over 150 full-time judges, paid full-time salaries? Even taking the average of new cases at ICSID for the last 3 years as a proxy, a volume of 50 new cases a year does not come anywhere close to justifying the costs involved (ICSID, 2017a). Assuming for now that the 150 judges sit in benches of three, it would amount to one case per judge the first year.[29] Using International Court of Justice (ICJ) judges' annual 'emoluments' (not including pensions) for 2016–2017 at US$231,766.667 as an example,[30] it would amount to costs of almost US$35 million just for the first instance judges (also not counting the cost of administrative support, logistics, etc.).[31]

Let's imagine a more realistic scenario: assume, for the sake of argument, that 60 countries are on board (including individual EU members).[32] That still makes for a very big and expensive court. It is no wonder that the EU and Canada have, in a discussion paper dated December 2016, acknowledged that 'significant challenges' would flow from a one member = one judge system (notably without listing what those challenges would be). (Commission and Canada, 2016b: para. 28) Yet elsewhere, the European Commission appears to underestimate the cost of establishing a Multilateral Investment Court. In its 'inception impact assessment' of the establishment of such a court, the Commission suggests using other courts as benchmarks and gives as examples the ITLOS (at around EUR 9 million per year) and the WTO Appellate Body (at around EUR 6.3 million per year).[33] Of course, the WTO Appellate Body is just that: an appellate level consisting of (only) seven members, who do not sit full-time and are not remunerated as such either.[34] As for ITLOS, it consists of 21 judges who (in principle) would sit together on each case (while the quorum is 11 members).[35] The judges are paid an annual allowance plus a special allowance for each day exercising his or her functions and as such do not sit full-time (ITLOS Statute: Art. 18). This makes sense, as only 25 cases have been submitted to the Tribunal since the first one was submitted in 1997.[36]

The idea of 'full representation' raises other issues. It's easy to imagine that the bigger the court, the higher the risk that the court decisions prove less cohesive and consistent, hence lacking in predictability. The existence of appeals would help, of course, and the role of the secretariat could also help ensure consistency, but a big court still presents some risks (see e.g. Kaufmann and Potestà, 2016: 65).

Also, there is a possibility that some governments select judges in-line with their interests as respondent in the system (i.e. so-called pro-State judges could be chosen to reflect the 'defensive' interests of States), leading to a less than impartial court. While the concern could apply to both capital importing as well as capital-exporting States, the concern (perhaps unwarranted) is that countries that are not important capital exporters (of which there could be a majority in the negotiations) may be more likely to do so. Presumably, States that are both capital exporters and importers would be under more pressure to put forward judges that are not seen as partial to States.

Finally, there is a *risk* (at least at the launch of the court) that not all countries would be able to offer judges of their nationality with the required knowledge, experience and skills. While the comparison is not perfect, it is notable that at least 25 ICSID Contracting States have nominated nationals of other countries on their list of four arbitrators (ICSID, 2017b). Conversely, it does occur that

ICSID Contracting States put arbitrators on their list that lack the required knowledge, experience and skills. For ICSID, the consequences are not dire, as such arbitrators may not get picked to sit on cases, but in the case of a court where all members will be called to sit, the impact could be critical.

So, where does this leave us on size? As discussed, 'full representation' is arguably not a realistic prospect. But how many judges are needed for a Multilateral Investment Court to be feasible or in other words to gather the support of a sufficient number of parties (including capital-exporting countries) to justify its establishment? There are at least two ways to determine that number: one based on use and one on representation. From the lens of efficiency, one would look at expected use and include in the analysis factors such as: expected new cases per year, time constraints for case completion that the parties would like imposed in the instrument establishing the Multilateral Investment Court,[37] size of benches, secretariat support, flexibility needed to accommodate recusals or removal for conflicts or other reasons and languages of the court. If I add the appellate level, the question gets more complex: depending on design and rules, of course, one would need to consider expected volumes of appeal. If the parties have a right to appeal in all cases, one can reasonably expect more appeals than the current rate of ICSID annulment requests (since the grounds of appeal would be broader and at a minimum cover errors of law).[38] This number would presumably decrease over time as a 'jurisprudence constante' is established.[39] Overall, it is very hard to estimate! Another way to look at this is through the lens of the necessary degree of representativeness required to find broad based support.

2. The design of a Multilateral Investment Court that could appeal to key Asian countries

In this second part, I focus on the design of the Multilateral Investment Court, looking in particular at the pursuit of the objectives and values that will make key Asian countries likely to get on board: independence and impartiality, efficiency as well as predictability and rule of law. Some design features already appear set because of EU (political) discourse, but presumably there is still room for influence.

2.1. Who should judge?

The question of 'who should judge' is key to the design of any judicial body, but it is particularly important in the current circumstances where investors stand to lose their voice in the nomination of adjudicators. If would-be claimants do not trust the Multilateral Investment Court, the risk is that they will bypass it for alternatives. This would be top of mind for key Asian capital-exporting countries. I will focus first on the decision review question (or 'appeal'). While it may seem that it should be coming at the end, decisions as to levels and scope of review have a direct impact on Court design. I will address next judges' qualifications and ethics, followed by the all-sensitive question of judges' nominations and selection.

2.1.1. *Levels of court and scope of reviews*

When the topic of appellate review in ISDS is raised, it often comes together with concerns regarding loss of efficiency, by way of increased delays and costs. For others, however, the topic raises hopes of better consistency and predictability. So, what kind of balance could be found?

The current review system for IIA awards is of course not immune to criticism. Taking ICSID annulment as an illustration, it had clear growing pains. Some cases are notorious for their length, especially when an annulled decision starts again at the tribunal level (Reisman, 1989: 739).

When pressed to improve the current ISDS system, the European Commission looked at creating an appellate level notably to assuage critics regarding inconsistency of awards and the current lack of ability to correct errors of law (Commission, 2015). In the context of the TTIP negotiations, the ICS proposal submitted to the US provided for a six-member appeal tribunal consisting of two Europeans, two Americans and two members from third countries. The third country member would act as chair of a panel of three (TTIP Proposal: Art. 9(6)). The proposal aims for a decision within 180 days of the notification of the decision to appeal and never more than 270 days (in case of delay) (TTIP Proposal: Art. 29(3)). A similar model has been accepted by Vietnam and Canada (CETA: Art. 8.39(7); EU-Vietnam FTA: Art. 28(5)), while it has been proposed to many other countries including Singapore, Japan and others (Commission, 2016b: 3). The European Commission itself acknowledges the likely heavier costs of maintaining multiple ICS, not to mention issues related to consistency across agreements (Commission, 2016b: 3 & 7).

Where does that leave us in the context of a Multilateral Investment Court? The EU and Canada have stated that they are not proposing the ICS model in CETA for this Court (while stating it may provide interesting ideas) and that negotiation are to be inclusive (Commission and Canada, 2016b: para. 3, 2017: para. 22). Which brings us to the question of whether an appellate instance is negotiable (despite the EU apparently being wedded to this idea, as mentioned in the introduction)? Could other, maybe more efficient ways of attaining the same objective be considered? Some authors suggested other methods to meet the needs of consistency and predictability, including a referral mechanism or the court sitting 'en banc' (Kaufmann and Potestà, 2016: 47–51).

Some international courts sit 'en banc' (or as a full court) to decide certain cases that pose particularly important interpretation issues or to hear certain appeals.[40] For such a system to work efficiently, the possibility of appeal should not be granted as a matter of right, but rather with permission of a smaller bench of the court (see Van Harten, 2007: 181; Kaufmann and Potestà, 2016: 48–51). As happens with other international and domestic courts, then the original bench sits with the broader court in reviewing the decision. Issues flowing from this fact in a presumably smaller court (e.g. 15 members) would need to be analysed carefully.[41]

In all, important capital-exporting countries may support a system that provides more consistency when required without leading to the multiplication of appeals (with the resulting increase in delays and costs). The use of the court 'en banc' could also avoid parties having to determine upfront the expected volume of cases justifying a full-time set of appellate judges.

2.1.2. Judges qualifications and ethics

Ensuring the court is filled with competent and experienced, as well as independent, judges would be a primary objective of court design.

In terms of judges' qualifications, statutes of international courts use very similar language, emphasizing 'appointability' to judicial office or 'recognized competence in international law'.[42] The EU sponsored ICS follows similar lines, while emphasizing relevant expertise. For example, CETA provides that:

> The Members of the Tribunal shall possess the qualifications required in their respective countries for appointment to judicial office, or be jurists of recognised competence. They shall have demonstrated expertise in public international law. It is desirable that they have expertise in particular, in international investment law, in international trade law and the resolution of disputes arising under international investment or international trade agreements.
>
> (CETA, Art. 8.27(4))

As to ethics, a further step was taken in the ICS model in order to exclude the ISDS practice of 'double hatting' (Horvath and Berzero, 2013: 1; Kalicki and Joubin-Bret, 2015: 411). This is all the more relevant as agreements such as CETA do not foresee that the investment tribunal members would be employed on a full-time basis (at the beginning at least) (CETA: Arts. 8.27(11) to (15)). The provision on independence specifically states that: 'In addition, upon appointment, they shall refrain from acting as counsel or as party-appointed expert or witness in any pending or new investment dispute under this or any other international agreement' (CETA: Art 8.30). Other court statutes also provide rules regarding the accumulation of functions. For example, the ICJ Statute provides that 'No member of the Court may exercise any political or administrative function, or engage in any other occupation of a professional nature' (ICJ Statute: Art. 16(1); see also ICC Statute: Art. 40(3); ITLOS Statute: Art. 7). While a topic of debate, thus far this has not prevented ICJ judges from sitting as arbitrators notably in traditional ISDS cases under IIAs.[43] Other courts are more explicit about the full-time and exclusive nature of the functions (see e.g. ECHR: Art. 21(3); CJEU Statute: Art. 4).

This gets us to the very practical question of who would be likely candidates to sit on a Multilateral Investment Court? Each category of potential candidates would bring relevant experience and knowledge to the task. For my purpose, I will only highlight *concerns* that have been expressed in the past,[44] again focusing on independence and impartiality, efficiency and expertise (under predictability and rule of law) of each.

- *Current arbitrators:* issues of conflict naturally come to mind as well as concerns expressed in the context of the ICS proposal (admittedly not an equivalent proposition), of whether 'top' arbitrators would be interested in leaving behind their practice for a term appointment (see EFILA, 2016: e.g. 56, 60).
- *Retired national judges:* many national judiciaries are not independent of governments, which risks lifting less than independent judges to the international plane. Domestic judges are rarely (if ever) appointed based on their knowledge of international law (Mackenzie et al., 2010: 53–54) and probably never on the basis of their knowledge of international investment law.
- *Academics:* many academics do not have experience of the practice of international investment law and may not have some of the judicial skills required (Mackenzie et al., 2010: 52–53). To be fully independent, they would have to take leave of their academic appointments.
- *Retired government officials:* a concern with government officials as international judges is their (continued) allegiance to the State. ICJ judges have often come from the ranks of former government officials with associated criticism as to independence.[45]
- *Investment law counsels:* issues of conflict naturally come to mind and they would have to leave their practice behind.

Undoubtedly, individuals could be found in each category that overcome general concerns and respond to expectations for an expert, independent court. But a specific mix of skills and experience can also be part of a new court's design. The International Criminal Court (ICC) model, providing for two categories of judges, offers an example of this. The result of a compromise amongst those who wanted 'professorial judges' and those who wanted 'real judges', the Statute provides for judges that have criminal law experience and judges that have knowledge of international human rights law. Each category is assigned different roles (Mackenzie et al., 2010: 45–46; See also ICC Statute: Art. 36(3)(b)).

2.1.3. Judges' nominations and selections

As mentioned before, the process of judges' nomination and selection can seal the fate of an international court. As also noted, when full representation is not feasible (as arguably in this case), a highly political manoeuvring process typically unfolds. In terms of the values laid out earlier, independent and impartial judges would be a key outcome of the selection and nomination process. As a matter of *principle*, this would call for judges to be chosen independent of nationality and solely based on their relevant expertise and experience. However, there is a reason why this has not been the case of international courts thus far. In order to have legitimacy, courts cannot be too far removed from the countries that constitute them. As such, most international court statutes provide for some elements of representativeness, including regional, legal systems or lately gender.[46]

Further, there is also the political reality that some countries want their 'weight' reflected in international court composition. The classical example is the ICJ which has almost always comprised, by convention, a judge for each of the members of the Security Council. Germany and Japan have also been almost continuously represented on the ICJ.[47] In practice, the ICC has followed the same pattern (Mackenzie et al., 2010: 33). As such, a key question becomes whether China or Japan would support a Multilateral Investment Court that did not ensure a judge of their nationality, even though independence and impartiality should be a key concern for them.

The ICJ also provides an example of the risk of politicization related to the nomination of ad hoc judges. When full representation is not feasible, States have recourse sometimes to a mechanism which ensures that those States who are not represented on the court can have a judge of their nationality on the bench when a case involves them.[48] In 2005, authors noted that ICJ ad hoc judges overwhelming decide in favour of their country of nationality, raising strong concerns as to independence and impartiality (Posner and Figueirdo, 2005: 599; Kaufmann and Potestà, 2016: 63–64).

Before looking at the different ways of ensuring some representativeness, without relying on given nationalities, it is interesting to note that the bilateral ICS model promoted by the EU relies in part on nationality. In the TTIP proposal, five judges would be American and five judges would come from the European Union; the other five, called to preside tribunals, would come from third-party countries (TTIP Proposal: section 3, Art. 9(2)). In the case of CETA and the EU-Vietnam FTA, the agreed texts provide that either Party can nominate members of any nationality to sit as their own.[49] In the context of CETA's signature in October 2016, concerns regarding the selection and nomination of tribunal members emanating from EU members came to the forefront, demonstrating once again how political and sensitive the issue is. I'll return to this in a minute.

So, what are ways to provide representativeness (short of relying on specific nationalities)? A common feature of international courts is to require an equitable regional representation (e.g. ICC, ITLOS, WTO Appelate Body).[50] Often, this is combined with a rule that no two members be of the same nationality (e.g. ICJ Statute: Art. 3(1); ICC Statute: Art. 36(7); ITLOS Statute: Art. 3(1)). A reference to representation of the principal legal systems of the world is also common (e.g. ICJ, ICC, ITLOS).[51] However, it has been noted that this requirement is generally held to be met through equitable geographic representation requirements (Mackenzie et al., 2010: 41). The more criteria, the more complicated the process becomes.

As to gender, 20 years ago, the ICC was a precursor in providing for 'fair representation of female and male judges' on the court.[52] This explains why the ICC has more women judges than other multilateral courts (see Grossman, 2012: 647). Gender diversity has already become an issue in the current arbitration-based ISDS due to the dearth of female arbitrators (ERA, 2017; Grossman, 2012), and the EU and Canada, in their December 2016 non-paper on a Multilateral

Investment Court, have mentioned greater diversity as a concern (Commission and Canada, 2016b: para. 33). Other courts, such as the ECtHR, have had to modify their rules to promote a fair representation of women. In principle, in the ECtHR, each member nominates three candidates, one of whom being a woman (Council of Europe, 2004a; see also Mowbray, 2008: 549). After being 'vetted', judges are then elected by the Parliamentary Assembly of the Council of Europe (Mackenzie et al., 2010: 8).

This last example reflects a two-step process, which is typical of international courts.[53] I'll now turn to such processes. The first is a **nomination process**, which often comes in two variations. One variation is for member States to put forward directly one (e.g. ICC Statute: Art. 36.4 (b)) or more candidates.[54] Another is to have a 'vetting' step of sorts before the selection is done. As to the first variation, concerns often relate to the nature of the process at the national level (formality, input, transparency, etc.).[55] Nominations will only be as good as the process leading to them.

As for the second variation (involving vetting), an approach is for candidates to be nominated by an independent commission. An example is provided by the Caribbean Court of Justice (CCJ).[56]The Regional Judicial and Legal Services Commission, constituted of the President of the Court, lawyers, lay people, academics, Bar representatives and public servants, both nominates *as well as* appoints CCJ judges (CCJ Statute: Art. V; Mackenzie et al., 2010: 9). It is hard to imagine such a model working with a Multilateral Investment Court, involving many more members and offering much less cohesion than in the Caribbean context. Also, *in theory at least*, such a model removes States completely from the selection process, which may be a step too far in the context of a Multilateral Investment Court, especially given the concerns of important capital-exporting countries.[57]

Another 'vetting' formula combines input from treaty parties with an independent evaluation of the suitability of candidates. This is the case of the ECJ. The selection of those judges, however, operates in a different context then would be the case for a Multilateral Investment Court as each EU State gets a judge on the court. Still, after judges are proposed by States, a seven member panel, made up of former judges of the CJEU, judges from national Supreme courts and lawyers of recognized competence, is responsible for giving its opinion on the prospective candidates suitability to perform the duties concerned (in a non-binding opinion).[58] If a candidate is not suitable, a State can nominate another person. The last step of the process consists of the 28-member governments appointing the judges of a common accord (TFEU: Art. 253). Similarly, the WTO AB (more relevant to our purpose), uses a committee which recommends candidates submitted by States. They are then to be decided on by the Dispute Settlement Body (DSB) by consensus.[59]

The **selection process**, as the last examples demonstrate, can be done in different ways, including through consensus or 'mutual accord' (TFEU: Art. 253), but often voting occurs (e.g. ITLOS Statute: Art. 4(4)). The voting can be done directly or through other organs, such as the UN General Assembly and the

Security Council for the ICJ (ICJ Statute: Art. 4). If voting is involved, decisions have to be made regarding the modalities of the vote: secret or public? Simple or qualified majority? And so on.

Coming back to the controversy raised in Europe regarding the risk of nomination of only 'pro-State' tribunal members in CETA, it is noteworthy that, to convince member States Assemblies to ratify CETA, the Commission and the Council agreed to the following process involving strong State involvement:

> As regards the European judges in particular, the selection process must also ensure that the richness of European legal traditions is reflected, above all over the long term. Consequently:
>
> - Candidate European judges will be nominated by the Member States, which will also participate in the assessment of candidates.
> - Without prejudice to the other conditions set out in Article 8.27.4 of the CETA agreement, the Member States will propose candidates who fulfil the criteria set out in Article 253(1) TFEU.
> - The European Commission, in consultation with the Member States and Canada, will ensure an equally rigorous assessment of the candidacies of the other judges of the Tribunal.
>
> The judges will be paid by the European Union and Canada on a permanent basis. The system should progress towards judges who are employed full-time. (Council of the European Union, 2016)

You will note that a key aspect of the process in the EU context is not addressed in this statement, which is the participation of different stakeholders and the transparency of the process. The same questions would apply to a Multilateral Investment Court. Should the investor community, or would-be claimants in front of the court, have a particular voice in the process (especially since they stand to lose their 'right' to nominate decision-makers)? (See Kaufmann and Potestà, 2016: 61.) Should NGOs[60] or labour groups have a say? Should the public at large?

In conclusion, past experience, namely with elections to the ICJ and ICC, demonstrate well the risk of politicization through horse trading or 'vote-trading' (Mackenzie et al., 2010: 122–28). Special care should be taken to ensure that merit prevails over other considerations in order to ensure the independence of the Multilateral Investment Court.

2.2. How should the court function?

Once the 'who should judge' question has been answered, one has to turn to the functioning of the Court. For my purpose, I'll focus on three aspects: judges' status and term, case-assignment and administrative support, ending with the all-important question of cost sharing.

2.2.1. *Judges' status and term*

The tenure of judges, domestic or international, is a key guarantee of their independence. But tenure, and especially length of tenure, can also serve to promote predictability and the rule of law.

Domestic court judges often serve for life or until a certain retirement age (for example 65 or 75 years old). Rules are provided to deal with incapacities and for the removal of judges in such circumstances. International courts, however, almost exclusively provide fixed terms of tenure, subject to renewal or not. For courts that do not have full representativeness, terms allow for rotation amongst member States and for more diversity on the bench (Mackenzie and Sands, 2003: 279).

Most international courts have terms of 6 or 9 years for judges.[61] Terms of 6 years tend to be renewable (see e.g. TFEU: Art. 253), while terms of 9 years are both renewable (ICJ, ITLOS)[62] and non-renewable (ECtHR, ICC).[63]

International court statutes also typically provide for 'stagger' (or rotation), for example one-third of judges every 3 years, so that not all judges leave at the same time (ICJ Statute: Art. 13(1), ITLOS Statute: Art. 5(1), ICC Statute: Art. 36(9)(b)). This helps promote predictability and rule of law, but may present issues with politicization if elections for different courts are always on and governments trade favours (at the expense of competence) (Mackenzie at al., 2010: 122–128).

In its bilateral ICS efforts, the EU has agreed to slightly shorter terms. The CETA provides terms of 5 years, renewable once, for 8 of the 15 members of the tribunal. The remaining seven members will be given an extended 6-year term (CETA: Art. 8.27(5)). The agreed text of the EU-Vietnam FTA provides for even shorter appointments, as four of the nine members of the tribunal will sit for a 4-year term, renewable once. The other five members, determined by lot, will be offered extended 6-year terms (EU-Vietnam FTA: Chapter II, section 3, Art. 12(5)). The shorter terms may reflect the need for rotation amongst EU members or reflect a willingness by States to exercise tighter control over the judges and their renewal. The latter explanation raises concerns regarding politicization. One only has to recall the recent WTO episode when the US blocked the renewal of the South Korean appellate body member to get a sense of the risk involved (see WTO, 2016; see also Shaffer, 2016).

The ECtHR provides an example of a court that has moved in 2010 to non-renewable, 9-year terms in order to preserve the independence of its judges.[64] More generally, the *Institut de droit international* has adopted in 2011 a resolution recommending that international judges be given longer, single terms (between 9 and 12 years) also in order to preserve the independence of the judges (Institut de droit international, 2011; see also Van Harten, 2007: 182).

In instances where every member State has one judge on the court, the length of term may not be much of an issue, but for a smaller court, which would be the case of the Multilateral Investment Court, more representativeness may be politically necessary and hence shorter terms, with associated downsides.

An issue for many courts, but maybe especially for a Multilateral Investment Court, is the process for adjustment to a growing membership (as the Court proves itself) and increased work load over time. For example, some courts provide for the possibility of increasing the number of judges based on volume. The Iran-US Claims Tribunal Declaration, for instance, provides for the possibility of adding judges in multiples of 3 by agreement of Parties up to 30 (which has not been done at this point in time) (see Iran-US Claims Settlement Declaration: Art. III(1); see also ICC Statute: Art. 36(2)).

2.2.2. *Case-assignment and administrative support*

Turning to the administration of the Court, something sounding as banal as case-assignment or secretariat support can actually have a significant impact on the independence and impartiality and efficiency of the court as well as predictability and the rule of law.

I've discussed the issue of nationality in relation to nomination and selection to the court, but I must return to it again as regards case-assignments. Different models exist in this regard. As a default, the ICSID Convention seeks to avoid a majority of nationals hearing cases involving either their home State or the State of the investor.[65] The bilateral ICS model promoted by the EU, on the contrary, specifically provides that a national of each of the treaty parties will sit on every case. For CETA, as an example, it means that a national of Canada and of the EU would sit in a bench of three presided by a non-national (CETA: Art. 8.27(6)).

In the same vein for international courts, some courts ensure representation of States through the institution of ad hoc judges (e.g. the ICJ) or through the right to have a judge of its nationality sit in its cases (e.g. ECtHR and ITLOS variations).[66] While for other courts, nationality is not a factor in case-assignment (ECJ and WTO AB).[67]

Beyond the question of nationality, there are different ways to assign judges to individual cases. The EU ICS model provides that the president and vice-president of the court assign cases at random ensuring that all members serve.[68] The process is similar to that of the WTO AB.[69] Some courts use ballots, while others use quite technical drawing list rules to assign cases (see e.g. CJEU Statute: Art. 16).

A question for the Multilateral Investment Court is whether disputing parties should have a role in the assignment of judges to their cases. Authors have suggested the possibility that disputing parties could choose from a roster of previously elected members (Kaufmann and Potestà, 2016: 41, 62). Even in the case of a 'semi-permanent arrangement' (Kaufmann and Potestà, 2016: 62–63) such a practice would seem to run counter to the value of independence and impartiality of the court and raise issues of workability.

In terms of efficiency but also predictability, one also has to consider the size of benches. As I mentioned earlier, courts often sit in configurations of 1, 3, 5 or 7 judges or more depending on the court and its needs.[70] Certain requests can be handled by smaller benches. In the context of a Multilateral Investment Court, one can imagine that a single judge could handle certain (simpler) claims by SMEs (Commission, 2016b: 6–7).

In the current arbitration-based ISDS, we are accustomed to benches of three arbitrators. But authors have suggested that five judges may be the best in terms of decision-making: not too big so that engagement is lost and not too small so that the judges feel exposed (Kaufmann and Potestà, 2016: 64–65). In all, different configurations should be used to meet the different needs of the court (including decisions on frivolous cases objections, decision to grant the right to appeal, decision on the merits of key cases, etc.).

Finally, the support provided by the secretariat would have an impact on the independence of the judges, efficiency and on predictability and the rule of law. A strong secretariat would support consistency over time, (Kaufmann and Potestà, 2016: 65), but it can also cross the line into decision-making. Admittedly in a different context than a full-fledged court, the example of the WTO Secretariat and its role in the drafting of panel decisions has raised eyebrows in the past (see e.g. Baetens, 2016: 306; Rogers, 2016: 296–297).

2.2.3. Cost sharing

In this talk, I can only briefly touch on issues of cost sharing. Much as judges' selection and nomination, the issue of funding can make or break an initiative such as the creation of a new international court. And in the same way, there is a risk that the main funders expect representation on the court in return for their support. Thus, funding and cost sharing touch on the efficiency of the court, but also its independence.

In the papers (and non-papers) sponsored by the EU and Canada, they already make clear that developing countries would not be expected to pay as much as developed countries (Commission and Canada, 2016b: para. 42). In CETA, the cost of the ICS is in part provided by the treaty parties and by investors on a somewhat unclear evolutionary path (Lévesque, 2016: 7–8). In an assessment of the Multilateral Investment Court, the Commission compares the cost of creation multiple ICS tribunals, under an increasing number of EU bilateral agreements, with the cost of a Multilateral Investment Court and concludes that the later would cost less (Commission, 2016b: 3 & 7). Much, however, would remain to be determined: on what scale would contributions be determined? Should the fact that EU investors are main users of the system be reflected in cost sharing? Conversely, should Asian countries that have not been involved in many cases pay less? In other words, should there exist a two tier funding formula: one for base funding and user fees for both States and investors? In the latter case, how would the share of investors be determined (see e.g. ITLOS Statute: Art. 19(2))? Should a special assistance centre modelled on the Advisory Centre on WTO Law be created? How would it be funded? Adjustments to a growing membership would also need to be provided.

Conclusion

Whether China, Japan, South Korea, Singapore and other Asian countries that are important capital exporters embrace a Multilateral Investment Court is a matter of political and practical feasibility. I submit that 'full representation' (or one treaty party = one judge) is in all likeliness not a workable or affordable proposition for a truly multilateral court. Thus arises the question of how much representativeness would be needed for a Multilateral Investment Court to take hold in Asia? Other international courts provide models in this regard, trying to balance merit choices with forms of regional, legal and diversity representation. The expected case-load of the court should also have an impact on its size.

A key challenge for a Multilateral Investment Court (maybe even more so than for other courts due to its mixed or asymmetrical nature) is the need to limit the scope for the politicization of the nomination and selection process of judges. A general trend in this matter has been identified whereby 'emphasis is being placed less on the authority of states and more on the goal of selecting independent and highly qualified judges, according to pre-determined merit-based judicial selection criteria and through a more formalized judicial selection process' (Mackenzie et al., 2010: 8). More transparency and the use of screening and selection bodies can contribute to achieving independence and impartiality, while keeping the treaty parties involved. Judges' tenure also has an impact on independence and impartiality. On balance, it would seem to be in the interest of important Asian capital-exporting countries to favour longer, non-renewable terms, with provisions for termination.

For present purposes, I have based my analysis on the promotion of independence and impartiality, efficiency and predictability and the rule of law. Attainment of these goals is more likely if consideration of the nationality of judges is secondary to consideration of their qualifications, experience and backgrounds (yet, while maintaining some elements of representativeness). At the end of the day, it may come down to whether countries such as China and Japan (or France, Germany and the UK) are willing to agree to a Multilateral Investment Court where they may not automatically have a judge. Are we there yet?

Notes

1 This is an extended version of a presentation made during the 5th Biennial Conference of the Asian International Economic Law Network (AIELN) 'Asian Perspectives on International Investment Law' delivered at Xiamen University School of Law on 17 June 2017. The author was able to participate in the conference and accomplish this research thanks to the financial support of CIGI, with which she is a Senior Fellow, and she also wishes to thank Amir Ahmad Fazel Bakhsheshi and Ana Poienaru for their research assistance. Opinions are only to be attributed to the author.

2 To this point: less than a month after my presentation, it was announced that the United Nations Commission on International Trade Law (UNCITRAL) decided 'to entrust its Working Group III with a broad mandate to work on the possible reform of investor-State dispute settlement (ISDS)' which has been said to include

a possible Multilateral Investment Court. See UNIS (2017). *UNCITRAL to Consider Possible Reform of Investor-State Dispute Settlement*, Press Release, www.unis. unvienna.org/unis/en/pressrels/2017/unisl250.html. The chapter is current as of June 2017.

3 *Comprehensive Economic and Trade Agreement Between Canada and the European Union and Its Member States*, Brussels, 30 October 2016, www.international. gc.ca/trade-commerce/trade-agreements-accords-commerciaux/agr-acc/ceta-aecg/text-texte/toc-tdm.aspx?lang=eng [CETA].

4 The Investment Court System or 'ICS' model was also adopted by Vietnam in the EU-Vietnam FTA. See *Free Trade Agreement between the European Union and the Socialist Republic of Vietnam*, agreed text – Chapter 8: Trade in Services, Investment and E-commerce, Resolution of Investment Disputes, (1 February 2016), http://trade.ec.europa.eu/doclib/docs/2016/february/tradoc_154210.pdf [EU-Vietnam FTA].

5 *Trans-Pacific Partnership*, Chapter 9: Investment (agreed text of 5 November 2015), www.international.gc.ca/trade-commerce/trade-agreements-accords-commerciaux/agr-acc/tpp-ptp/text-texte/09.aspx?lang=eng [TPP].

6 The EU formally proposed the ICS model to the US in November 2015: see *Transatlantic Trade and Investment Partnership*, Chapter II: Investment (12 November 2015 EC Proposal), http://trade.ec.europa.eu/doclib/docs/2015/november/tradoc_153955.pdf [TTIP Proposal]. In October 2015 (after a draft regarding the ICS had circulated), the US, through the United States Trade Representative (USTR), reportedly communicated its wariness of the proposal, but there appears to have been no official response. See Krista Hughes and Philip (2015). *U.S. Wary of EU Proposal for Investment Court in Trade Pact*, Reuters, www.reuters.com/article/us-trade-ttip-idUSKCN0SN2LH20151029.

7 *Convention on the Settlement of Investment Disputes between States and Nationals of Other States*, Washington, 18 March 1965, in force 14 October 1966, 575 UNTS 159 [ICSID Convention].

8 The number of member States will necessarily have an impact on the efficiency of the mechanism for enforcement of the court's decisions. On some of the difficulties related to enforcement, see Gabrielle Kaufmann-Kohler and Michele Potestà (2016). Can the Mauritius Convention serve as a model for the reform of investor-state arbitration in connection with the introduction of a permanent investment tribunal or an appeal mechanism? Analysis and roadmap, UNCITRAL, www.uncitral.org/pdf/english/CIDS_Research_Paper_Mauritius.pdf [Kaufmann-Kohler and Potestà (2016)].

9 For EU members' IIA network and ISDS use see: UNCTAD (2014). *Investor-State Dispute Settlement: an Information Note on the United States and the European Union*, IIA Issues Note, http://unctad.org/en/PublicationsLibrary/webdiaepcb2014d4_en.pdf

10 In CETA, Canada belatedly agreed to adopt the so-called 'ICS' promoted by the EU during the legal review phase of the negotiations. The word 'court' does not appear in the relevant chapter of CETA, but for the sake of simplicity, it will be referred as ICS in this chapter. The title of the relevant Section of CETA is actually 'Resolution of investment disputes between investors and states' and articles refer to the 'Tribunal' and the 'Appellate Tribunal', see CETA, *above* note 3 Art. 8.29. For details, see Céline Lévesque (2016). The European Commission Proposal for an Investment Court System: Out with the Old, in with the New? *CIGI Investor-State Series, Paper no. 10*, www.cigionline.org/sites/default/files/isa_paper_series_no.10_0.pdf

11 Commission (2016). *Inception Impact Assessment: Establishment of a Multilateral Investment Court for investment dispute resolution*, p. 3, http://ec.europa.

eu/smart-regulation/roadmaps/docs/2016_trade_024_court_on_investment_
en.pdf [Commission (2016b)]: 'The ICS also forms part of the EU negotiation
with the US, China, Myanmar, Tunisia, Morocco, Japan, Philippines and Mexico,
and planned negotiations with Indonesia, Australia, New Zealand and Chile, etc.'

12 *Charter of the Association of Southeast Asian Nations,* Singapore, 20 November 2007, in force 15 December 2008, 2624 UNTS 223.

13 See e.g. Gus Van Harten (2007). *Investment Treaty Arbitration and Public Law,*
Oxford: Oxford University Press. [Van Harten (2007)]. He states:

> The simple fact remains that the great majority of companies that own sub-
> stantial assets outside their home jurisdiction are based in a small number of
> countries which hold a minority of the world's people. To bridge the political
> gap on this issue will require the willingness of developing countries prag-
> matically to set aside many objections . . . in exchange for the commitment of
> major states to accept judicial independence as a condition for investor claims
> in international law.
>
> (p. 183)

14 See e.g. Stephan Schill, ed. (2015). Special Issue: Dawn of an Asian Century
in International Investment Law?, *The Journal of World Investment and Trade,*
16(4–5), containing articles on China, Japan, South Korea, ASEAN, etc.

15 According to UNCTAD's Investment Policy Hub, China has signed over 150
IIAs, while South Korea has signed over 110. See UNCTAD, Investment Policy
Hub, "International Investments Agreements Navigator", http://investment-
policyhub.unctad.org/IIA/IiasByCountry#iiaInnerMenu; On China, see e.g.
Cliff Manjiao and Xi Wang (2015). The Evolution of ISA Clauses in Chinese
IIAs and its Practical Implications. *The Journal of World Investment and Trade,*
16(4–5), 869; on South Korea, see Hi-Taek Shin and Liz (Kyo-Hwa) Chung
(2015). Korea's Experience with International Investment Agreements and
Investor-State Dispute Settlement. *The Journal of World Investment and Trade,*
16(4–5), 952.

16 *Free Trade Agreement Between the European Union and the Republic of Singapore*
(text of May 2015), http://trade.ec.europa.eu/doclib/press/index.cfm?id.961.

17 The ECJ held that the ISDS system envisaged in the Singapore FTA 'falls not
within the exclusive competence of the European Union, but within a competence shared between the European Union and the Member States' (paras. 290–
293) in CJEU, *Opinion 2/15 of the Court (Full Court),* ECLI:EU:C:2017:376,
(16 May 2017), http://eur-lex.europa.eu/legal-content/EN/TXT/PDF/?uri=
CELEX:62015CV0002(01)&qid=1503077668838&from=EN.

18 See James Crawford and Joe McIntyre (2011). The Independence and Impartiality of the International Judiciary. In Shimon Shetreet and Christopher Forsyth,
eds., *The Culture of Judicial Independence: Conceptual Foundations and Practical Challenges,* Leiden: Martinus Nijhoff, pp. 189–214. After analysing different
international declarations and statements, Crawford and McIntyre state that

> What emerges . . . is the connection between, and interdependence of,
> judicial independence and impartiality. Judicial independence is concerned
> with ensuring that the judge is free to perform the obligations imposed by
> the judicial function in an appropriately impartial manner. This means the
> judge should be protected from improper influences, pressures, threats or
> interference that may threaten his or her impartiality. Such threats or influ-
> ence risk rendering the judge improperly partial to one of the parties or the
> position they take.
>
> (at 196)

Much more could be said on the principles of judicial independence and impartiality and their interrelationship. But for the purpose of this chapter, I chose to rely on the use made by Crawford and McIntyre, who conclude that 'What emerges from this analysis of rationale and character is that the concepts of judicial independence and impartiality are, fundamentally, functional in character. Rather than ultimate objectives, they are means of achieving the objective of ensuring legitimate performance of the judicial function'. (at 197) [Internal notes omitted].

19 Gus Van Harten identified the lack of independence as a major flaw of the ISDS system in his PhD dissertation that promoted the creation of an international investment court, see Van Harten (2007), *above* note 13, pp. 167–175. The German Magistrates Association has also raised issues regarding the independence of the proposed TTIP ICS: see German Magistrates Association, 'Opinion on the Establishment of an Investment Tribunal in TTIP' (February 2016), No 04/16 at 2–3, http://ttip2016.eu/files/content/docs/Full%20documents/english_version_deutsche_richterbund_opinion_ics_feb2016.pdf.

20 See e.g. Karl P. Sauvant, ed. (2008). *Appeals Mechanism in International Investment Disputes*, New York: Oxford University Press. See also multiple references provided in Kaufmann and Potestà, (2016), *above* note 8, pp. 16–19.

21 'Full representation courts' are opposed to 'selective representation courts' that include fewer judges than there are parties to the Statute. See Ruth Mackenzie et al. (2010). *Selecting International Judges: Principle, Process and Politics*, Oxford: Oxford University Press, pp. 7–8 [Mackenzie et al. (2010)].

22 See *Convention for the Protection of Human Rights and Fundamental Freedoms*, Rome, 4 November 1950, in force 3 September 1953, 213 UNTS 221, Art. 22, as amended by *Protocol No. 14 to the Convention for the Protection of Human Rights and Fundamental Freedoms, Amending the Control System of the Convention*, Strasbourg, 13 May 2004, in force 1 June 2010, CETS 194, [ECHR]. This is also the case of other regional courts in the Americas and Africa. See e.g. the *American Convention on Human Rights 'Pact of San José, Costa Rica'*, San Jose, 22 November 1969, in force 18 July 1978, 1144 UNTS 143, Art. 52; *Protocol on the Statute of the African Court of Justice and Human Rights*, Annex: Statute of the African Court of Justice and Human Rights, 1 July 2008, Art. 3, http://au.int/sites/default/files/treaties/7792-treaty-0035_-_protocol_on_the_statute_of_the_african_court_of_justice_and_human_rights_e.pdf.

23 *Consolidated version of the Treaty of the European Union*, Lisbon, 13 December 2007, in force 1 December 2009, OJ C 326/13, October 2012, Art. 19(2) [TEU].

24 Unlike most ISDS cases, claimants do have to exhaust domestic remedies beforehand. See ECHR, *above* note 21, Art. 35.

25 See *Protocol No 14 to the Convention for the Protection of Human Rights and Fundamental Freedoms, Amending the Control System of the Convention*, Strasbourg, 13 May 2004, in force 1 June 2010, ETS 194, Art. 2. As an example, in 2016, over 36,000 of the 53,000 plus applications were declared inadmissible or struck out. Council of Europe (2017b) *Analysis of statistics 2016*, p. 4, www.echr.coe.int/Documents/Stats_analysis_2016_ENG.pdf.

26 For my purpose I do not cover the General Court, which will soon have two judges per member country of the EU.

27 TEU, *above* note 23, *Protocol (No. 3) on the Statute of the Court of Justice of the European Union*, OJ C 326/210, October 2012, Art. 16, http://eur-lex.europa.eu/resource.html?uri=cellar:2bf140bf-a3f8-4ab2-b506-fd71826e6da6.0023.02/DOC_3&format=PDF [CJEU Statute].

28 ICSID Convention, *above* note 7. 161 Signatory States, 153 Contracting States, see ICSID, (2017c). *Database of ICSID Member States* (consulted on 1 June 2017),

http://icsid.worldbank.org/en/Pages/about/Database-of-Member-States.aspx.

29 To keep it simple, the rate of settlement is not included, which would make the number of cases even smaller. See ICSID stats online: 36% of disputes are settled or proceedings are otherwise discontinues (at 13). See ICSID, (2017a). *The ICSID Caseload – Statistics.* Issues 2017–2, http://icsid.worldbank.org/en/Documents/resources/ICSID%20Web%20Stats%202017–1%20(English)%20Final.pdf.

30 While the ICJ internet site provides that 'Each Member of the Court receives an annual salary consisting of a base salary (which, for 2016, amounts to US$172,978) and post adjustment' (see:www.icj-cij.org/en/members), the annual report of the court provides a higher figure under 'emoluments' at US$231,766.667 a year for 2016–2017. I have not included pension liabilities as it is difficult to ascertain the amounts coverings former judges and their surviving spouses. See General Assembly, *Report of the International Court of Justice, 1 August 2016–31 July 2017*, A/72/4, UN, NY, 2017, p. 65, www.icj-cij.org/files/annual-reports/2016-2017-en.pdf. ECtHR (reportedly as of 2016) £155,000-a-year post; J. CJEU (reportedly as of 2016) have a base salary €256,000 & other benefits.

31 I do not address the question of user fees at this point and assume that States will pay.

32 This is the reported number of countries which have participated in discussions thus far. See European Commission (2016d), Summary of Discussions on a Multilateral Investment Court, Geneva, 13–14 December 2016, http://trade.ec.europa.eu/doclib/press/index.cfm?&id=1606

33 These figures appear to include the salary of judges, secretariat costs, as well as administration and 'other costs'. See Commission (2016b), *above* note 11, p. 7 under data collection.

34 See *Marrakesh Agreement Establishing the World Trade Organization*, Annex 2: Understanding on rules and procedures governing the settlement of disputes, Marrakesh, 15 April 1994, in force 1 January 1995, 1867 UNTS 154, Art. 17(3) [WTO DSU].

35 *United Nations Convention on the Law of the Sea*, Annex VI: Statute of the International Tribunal for the Law of the Sea, Montego Bay, 10 December 1982, in force 16 November 1994, 1833 UNTS 561, Art. 2 [ITLOS Statute]. Chambers of three or five members can be appointed for certain types of disputes. See e.g. *Ibid*, Arts. 14 and 15.

36 See ITLOS website for list of cases. ITLOS, *List of Cases*, www.itlos.org/cases/.

37 See CETA, *above* note 3, Art 8.39(7). If the timelines are short (e.g. 24 months), which is less than the current average timeline for ISDS cases at ICSID, the court would need more judges to work in parallel on more cases.

38 Current ICSID rate of request for annulment is about 41%. See also Kaufmann and Potestà, (2016), *above* note 8, p. 47 and Michael Wood (2017). Choosing Between Arbitration and a Permanent Court: Lessons from Inter-State Cases. *International Center for Settlement of Investment Disputes Review*, 32(1), 1, 15.

39 The WTO panels appeal rate was 100% at first, but declined over time to 66% in 2011. See WTO, *WTO Analytical Index: Dispute Settlement Understanding – for Article 17.4 (a)*, www.wto.org/english/res_e/booksp_e/analytic_index_e/dsu_07_e.htm.

40 See ECHR, *above* note 22, Art. 30; CJEU Statute, *above* note 27, Arts. 16–17. See also Iran-US Claims Tribunal, Presidential Order No. 1, 19 October 1981, para. 6, [cited in Kaufmann and Potestà, (2016), *above* note 8, p. 50 footnote 265]

41 *Rome Statute of the International Criminal Court*, Rome, 17 July 1998, in force 1 July 2002, 2187 UNTS 3, Art. 34 [ICC Statute].

42 *Statute of the International Court of Justice*, San Francisco, 26 June 1945, in force 24 October 1945, 33 UNTS 993, Art. 2 [ICJ Statute]:

> The Court shall be composed of a body of independent judges, elected regardless of their nationality from among persons of high moral character, who possess the qualifications required in their respective countries for appointment to the highest judicial offices, or are jurisconsults of recognized competence in international law.

See also ECHR *above* note 22, Art. 21(1); CJEU Statute, *above* note 27, Art. 4, See also Mackenzie et al. (2010), *above* note 21, p. 50, tracing the origin of the formulation to a compromise between 'a common law preference for international judges with national judicial experience and a civil law preference for non-judges'.

43 On outside activities, see Ruth Mackenzie and Philippe Sands (2003). International Courts and Tribunals and the Independence of the International Judge. *Harvard International Law Journal*, 44(1), 271, 282–283 [Mackenzie and Sands (2003)].

44 In the context of the ICS, see EFILA (2016). *Task Force Regarding the Proposed International Court System (ICS)*, p. 60 (at 5), http://efila.org/wp-content/uploads/2016/02/EFILA_TASK_FORCE_on_ICS_proposal_1-2-2016.pdf:

> The pool of TFI [tribunal of first instance] and AT [appeal tribunal] judges would seem to be limited to academics, (former) judges and (former) Government officials. That may not be sufficient to guarantee the practical experience and expertise needed and/or independence from the State.

45 Mackenzie et al. (2010) *above* note 21, pp. 57–58. See also (Mackenzie and Sands, 2003), *above* note 43, p. 278. In the WTO, panel members are often drawn from the ranks of current government employees. For a discussion of impacts, see Joost Pauwelyn (2015). The Rule of Law Without the Rule of Lawyers? Why Investment Arbitrators Are from Mars, Trade Adjudicators from Venus. *American Journal of International Law*, 109, 761, as well as the AJIL Unbound Symposium on this article introduced by Donald McRae, and including commentaries from, among others, Freya Baetens, Gabrielle Marceau, Robert Howse, Giorgio Sacerdoti and Catherine Rogers, as well as the Pauwelyn rejoinder. Each of the individual symposium entries listed above can be found online. See Donald McRae (2015). Introduction to Symposium on Joost Pauwelyn, 'The Rule of Law Without the Rule of Lawyers? Why Investment Arbitrators Are from Mars, Trade Adjudicators from Venus', *American Journal of International Law Unbound*, 109, 277–282. https://www.cambridge.org/core/services/aop-cambridge-core/content/view/D99083D754017AF01D020BDC534EF65F/S2398772300001598a.pdf/introduction_to_symposium_on_joost_pauwelyn_the_rule_of_law_without_the_rule_of_lawyers_why_investment_arbitrators_are_from_mars_trade_adjudicators_are_from_venus.pdf

46 This concern is reflected in Commission and Canada (2016b). *Discussion Paper: Establishment of a Multilateral Investment Dispute Settlement System*. Geneva: Expert meeting, para. 28, http://trade.ec.europa.eu/doclib/docs/2017/january/tradoc_155267.12.12%20With%20date_%20Discussion%20p:

> A possibility is that they be appointed directly by the Parties to the convention establishing the multilateral system, whereby each Party would have one or several adjudicators. Such an approach would ensure that the Parties' judicial culture and system be evenly represented at the multilateral system, but it would also present certain significant challenges.

47 Mackenzie et al. (2010), *above* note 21, pp. 27–29; 37–40; See also Georges Abi-Saab (1996). Ensuring the Best Bench: Ways of Selecting Judges. In Connie Peck and Roy S. Lee, eds., *Increasing the Effectiveness of the International Court of Justice*, Peace Palace: Martinus Nijhoff, for a history around the representation of the great powers.
48 Mackenzie et al. (2010), *above* note 21, p. 15 on the political compromise behind ad hoc judges.
49 CETA, *above* note 3, Art. 8.27(2) footnote 9 'such Members of the Tribunal shall be considered to be nationals of the Party that proposed his or her appointment for the purpose of the Article'; EU-Vietnam FTA, *above* note 4, Art. 12(2) footnote 25.
50 ICC Statute, *above* note 41, Art. 36(8)(a)(ii); ITLOS Statute, *above* note 35, Art. 2(2) & Art. 3(2); WTO DSU, *above* note 34, Art. 17(3) 'be broadly representative of membership in the WTO'.
51 ICJ Statute, *above* note 42, Art. 9:

> At every election, the electors shall bear in mind not only that the persons to be elected should individually possess the qualifications required, but also that in the body as a whole the representation of the main forms of civilization and of the principal legal systems of the world should be assured.

See also ICC Statute, *above* note 41, Art. 36(8)(a)(i); ITLOS Statute, *above* note 35, Art. 2(2).
52 ICC Statute, *above* note 41, Art. 36(8)(a)(iii). See Mackenzie et al. (2010), *above* note 21, pp. 22, 47–49. See also *Protocol to the African Charter on Human and Peoples' Rights on the Establishment of an African on Human and People's Rights*, 9 June 1998, in force 25 January 2004, OAU Doc. OAU/LEG/EXPIAFCHPRIPROT(III), Art. 12(2), www.achpr.org/files/instruments/court-establishment/achpr_instr_proto_court_eng.pdf, which stipulates that 'Due consideration shall be given to adequate gender representation in nomination process'.
53 A notable exception is the Iran-US Claims Tribunal where the two governments appoint directly three members each. The remaining three members are then chosen by the six appointed judges or by an appointing authority, see *Declaration of the Government of the Democratic and Popular Republic of Algeria Concerning the Settlement of Claims by the Government of the United States of America and the Government of the Islamic Republic of Iran* (19 January 1981) 1 *Iran-US Claims Tribunal Reports* 9, Art III(1), www.iusct.net/General%20Documents/2-Claims%20Settlement%20Declaration.pdf.
54 ITLOS Statute, *above* note 35, Art. 4(1): each State can nominate up to two candidates; ECtHR up to three, see ECHR, *above* note 22, Art. 22. In the case of the WTO AB, States can nominate candidates individually or as a group. In the case of the WTO AB, the EU puts forward candidate(s) after consulting with EU member States and after a selection panel recommends the most suitable EU candidate(s), see Commission (2016). *EU Launches Selection of Candidates for the Position of WTO Appellate Body Member*, Brussels, http://trade.ec.europa.eu/doclib/press/index.cfm?id=1565.
55 E.g. ICJ Statute, *above* note 42, Art. 6: 'Before making these nominations, each national group is recommended to consult its highest court of justice, its legal faculties and schools of law, and its national academies and national sections of international academies devoted to the study of law'.
56 See *Agreement establishing the Caribbean Court of Justice*, St. Michael, 14 February 2001, in force 23 July 2002, 2255 UNTS 319, Art. IV(1). [CCJ Statute] The agreement establishing the CCJ provides for a maximum of ten judges, including the president of the Court.

57 On the tension between independence and State sovereignty in this context, see Mackenzie et al. (2010), *above* note 21, p. 8. See also Van Harten (2007), *above* note 13, who suggested the following:

> [O]ne alternative would be a combined procedure whereby candidates were nominated by groups of capital-exporting and capital-importing states representing different regions of the world for approval by a majority vote of both the UN Security Council and the UN General Assembly.
>
> (p. 183, footnote 138)

58 See *Consolidated versions of the Treaty on the Functioning of the European Union,* Lisbon, 13 December 2007, in force 1 December 2009, OJ, L 83/02, October 2010 Art. 255 [TFEU].
59 See WTO DSU, *above* note 34, Art. 17(1) and (2). A recent selection committee consisted of the WTO Director-General, the 2016 Chairs of the General Council, the Trade in Goods Council, the Trade in Services Council and the TRIPS Council.
60 See Mackenzie et al. (2010), *above* note 21, p. 9 noting the informal involvement of NGOs in the selection processes of the ICC and ECtHR.
61 See e.g. TFEU, *above* note 58, Art. 253 (CJEU: 6 years); ICJ Statute, *above* note 42, Art. 13 (9 years); ITLOS Statute, *above* note 35, Art. 5 (9 years); ECHR, *above* note 22, Art. 23 (9 years); ICC Statute, *above* note 41, Art. 36(9) (9 years). One exception is the WTO AB with 4-year mandates (renewable once). See WTO DSU, *above* note 34, Art.17(2).
62 See ICJ Statute, *above* note 42, Art. 13 (renewable once), ITLOS Statute, *above* note 35, Art. 5 (may be re-elected).
63 See ECHR *above* note 22, Art. 23 (non-renewable; term expires when judges turn 70 years old); ICC Statute, *above* note 41, Art. 36(9) (no re-election except in specific circumstances such as serving a term under 3 years or filling the remainder of a vacancy and the remainder is under 3 years).
64 See Council of Europe, *Explanatory Report to Protocol No. 14 to the Convention for the Protection of Human Rights and Fundamental Freedoms, Amending the Control System of the Convention,* (2004b), CETS 194 [cited in Kaufmann and Potestà (2016), *above* note 21, p. 62 footnote 319], http://rm.coe.int/16800d380f.
65 ICSID Convention, *above* note 7, Art. 39 'The majority of the arbitrators shall be nationals of States other than the Contracting State party to the dispute and the Contracting State whose national is a party to the dispute; provided, however, that the foregoing provisions of this Article shall not apply if . . . each individual member of the Tribunal has been appointed by agreement of the parties'. As regards nominations by the Chairman of the Administrative Council to tribunals (under Art. 38) or to annulment committees (under Art. 52(3), the prohibition to name nationals is strict.
66 See e.g. ECHR, *above* note 22, Art. 28(3); ITLOS Statute, *above* note 35, Art. 17(1): 'Members of the Tribunal of the nationality of any of the parties to a dispute shall retain their right to participate as members of the Tribunal. (2) If the Tribunal, when hearing a dispute, includes upon the bench a member of the nationality of one of the parties, any other party may choose a person to participate as a member of the Tribunal'.
67 See e.g. CJEU Statute, *above* note 27, Art. 18(4): 'A party may not apply for a change in the composition of the Court or of one of its chambers on the grounds of either the nationality of a Judge or the absence from the Court or from the chamber of a Judge of the nationality of that party'. For WTO AB, there is no prohibition on AB members of the nationality of the appellant or appellee sitting. See Kaufmann and Potestà (2016), *above* note 21, p. 63.

68 TTIP Proposal, *above* note 6, section 3, Art. 9(7); CETA, *above* note 3, Art. 8.27(7); and EU-Vietnam FTA, *above* note 4, section 3, Art. 12(7). All three provisions provide the following: 'on a rotation basis, ensuring that the composition of the divisions is random and unpredictable, while giving equal opportunity to all Members of the Tribunal to serve'.

69 WTO, *Working Procedures for Appellate Review* (16 August 2010), WT/AB/WP/6, Art. 6(2), www.wto.org/english/tratop_e/dispu_e/ab_e.htm' while taking into account the principles of random selection, unpredictability and opportunity for all Members to serve regardless of their national origin'.

70 See *above* heading 1.2.1 on regional courts.

References

Treaties & negotiated agreements

Agreement establishing the Caribbean Court of Justice, St. Michael, 14 February 2001, in force 23 July 2002, 2255 UNTS 319.

American Convention on Human Rights "Pact of San José, Costa Rica", San Jose, 22 November 1969, in force 18 July 1978, 1144 UNTS 143.

Charter of the Association of Southeast Asian Nations, Singapore, 20 November 2007, in force 15 December 2008, 2624 UNTS 223.

Comprehensive Economic and Trade Agreement Between Canada and the European Union and its Member States, Brussels, 30 October 2016, www.international.gc.ca/trade-commerce/trade-agreements-accords-commerciaux/agr-acc/ceta-aecg/text-texte/toc-tdm.aspx?lang=eng

Consolidated Version of the Treaty of the European Union, Lisbon, 13 December 2007, in force 1 December 2009, OJ C 326/13, October 2012.

Consolidated versions of the Treaty on the Functioning of the European Union, Lisbon, 13 December 2007, in force 1 December 2009, OJ, L 83/02, October 2010.

Convention on the Settlement of Investment Disputes between States and Nationals of Other States, Washington, 18 March 1965, in force 14 October 1966, 575 UNTS 159.

Convention for the Protection of Human Rights and Fundamental Freedoms, Rome, 4 November 1950, in force 3 September 1953, 213 UNTS 221, as amended by *Protocol No. 14 to the Convention for the Protection of Human Rights and Fundamental Freedoms, Amending the Control System of the Convention*, Strasbourg, 13 May 2004, in force 1 June 2010, CETS 194.

Declaration of the Government of the Democratic and Popular Republic of Algeria Concerning the Settlement of Claims by the Government of the United States of America and the Government of the Islamic Republic of Iran, (19 January 1981), 1 *Iran-US Claims Tribunal Reports* 9, www.iusct.net/General%20Documents/2-Claims%20Settlement%20Declaration.pdf

Free Trade Agreement Between the European Union and the Republic of Singapore (Text of May 2015), trade.ec.europa.eu/doclib/press/index.cfm?id.961

Free Trade Agreement Between the European Union and the Socialist Republic of Vietnam, Agreed Text – Chapter 8: Trade in Services, Investment and E-commerce, Resolution of Investment Disputes, (1 February 2016), trade.ec.europa.eu/doclib/docs/2016/february/tradoc_154210.pdf [EU-Vietnam FTA]

Marrakesh Agreement Establishing the World Trade Organization, Annex 2: Understanding on Rules and Procedures Governing the Settlement of Disputes, Marrakesh, 15 April 1994, in force 1 January 1995, 1867 UNTS 154.

Protocol (No. 3) on the Statute of the Court of Justice of the European Union, OJ C 326/210, October 2012.

Protocol No 14 to the Convention for the Protection of Human Rights and Fundamental Freedoms, Amending the Control System of the Convention, Strasbourg, 13 May 2004, in force 1 June 2010, ETS 194.

Protocol to the African Charter on Human and Peoples' Rights on the Establishment of an African on Human and People's Rights, 9 June 1998, in force 25 January 2004, OAU Doc. OAU/LEG/EXPIAFCHPRIPROT(III), www.achpr.org/files/instruments/court-establishment/achpr_instr_proto_court_eng.pd

Protocol on the Statute of the African Court of Justice and Human Rights, Annex: Statute of the African Court of Justice and Human Rights, 1 July 2008, au.int/sites/default/files/treaties/7792-treaty-0035_-_protocol_on_the_statute_of_the_african_court_of_justice_and_human_rights_e.pdf

Rome Statute of the International Criminal Court, Rome, 17 July 1998, in force 1 July 2002, 2187 UNTS 3.

Transatlantic Trade and Investment Partnership, Chapter II: Investment, (12 November 2015 EC Proposal), trade.ec.europa.eu/doclib/docs/2015/november/tradoc_153955.pdf

Trans-Pacific Partnership, Chapter 9: Investment (agreed text of 5 November 2015), www.international.gc.ca/trade-commerce/trade-agreements-accords-commerciaux/agr-acc/tpp-ptp/text-texte/09.aspx?lang=eng

Statute of the International Court of Justice, San Francisco, 26 June 1945, in force 24 October 1945, 33 UNTS 993.

United Nations Convention on the Law of the Sea, Annex VI: Statute of the International Tribunal for the Law of the Sea, Montego Bay, 10 December 1982, in force 16 November 1994, 1833 UNTS 561.

WTO, *Working Procedures for Appellate Review*, (16 August 2010), WT/AB/WP/6, www.wto.org/english/tratop_e/dispu_e/ab_e.htm

Cases

CJEU, *Opinion 2/15 of the Court (Full Court)*, ECLI:EU:C:2017:376 (16 May 2017), eur-lex.europa.eu/legal-content/EN/TXT/PDF/?uri=CELEX:62015CV0002(01)&qid=1503077668838&from=EN

EU & government documents

CJEU (2017a). *Annual Report – 2016*, Luxembourg: Court of Justice, curia.europa.eu/jcms/upload/docs/application/pdf/2017–04/ragp-2016_final_en_web.pdf

CJEU (2017b). *Statistics Concerning Judicial Activity in 2016*, Press Release, curia.europa.eu/jcms/upload/docs/application/pdf/2017–02/cp170017en.pdf

CJEU (2017c). *General Budget of the European Union of the Financial Year 2017*. OJ, L 51/1986, eur-lex.europa.eu/budget/data/General/2017/en/SEC04.pdf

Commission (2015). *Investment in TTIP and Beyond – The Path for Reform*, Concept Paper, trade.ec.europa.eu/doclib/docs/2015/may/tradoc_153408.PDF

Commission (2016a). *The Multilateral Investment Court project*, News Release, trade.ec.europa.eu/doclib/press/index.cfm?id=1608

Commission (2016b). *Inception Impact Assessment: Establishment of a Multilateral Investment Court for Investment Dispute Resolution*, ec.europa.eu/ smart-regulation/roadmaps/docs/2016_trade_024_court_on_investment_en.pdf

Commission (2016c). *EU Launches Selection of Candidates for the Position of WTO Appellate Body Member*, Brussels, trade.ec.europa.eu/doclib/press/index. cfm?id=1565

Commission (2016d). *Summary of Discussions on a Multilateral Investment Court*, Geneva. 13–14 December 2016, http://trade.ec.europa.eu/doclib/press/index. cfm?&id=1606

Commission and Canada (2016a). *Non-Paper: Reforming Investment Dispute Settlement: Considerations on the Way Towards a Multilateral Investment Dispute Settlement Mechanism*, Paris: OECD-hosted Investment Treaty Dialogue, trade. ec.europa.eu/doclib/docs/2017/january/tradoc_155265.pdf

Commission and Canada (2016b). *Discussion Paper: Establishment of a Multilateral Investment Dispute Settlement System*, Geneva: Expert Meeting, trade.ec.europa. eu/doclib/docs/2017/january/tradoc_155267.12.12%20With%20date_%20 Discussion%20p

Commission and Canada (2017). *The Case for Creating a Multilateral Investment Dispute Settlement Mechanism*, Davos: Informal ministerial meeting, World Economic Forum, trade.ec.europa.eu/doclib/docs/2017/january/tradoc_155264.pdf

Council of Europe (2004a). *Candidates for the European Court of Human Rights*, Parliamentary Assembly, Resolution 1366 of 2004, assembly.coe.int/nw/xml/ XRef/Xref-XML2HTML-en.asp?fileid=17194&lang=en

Council of Europe (2004b). *Explanatory Report to Protocol No. 14 to the Convention for the Protection of Human Rights and Fundamental Freedoms, Amending the Control System of the Convention*, CETS 194, rm.coe.int/16800d380f

Council of Europe (2017a). *ECHR Budget*, www.echr.coe.int/Documents/Budget_ ENG.pdf

Council of Europe (2017b). *Analysis of Statistics 2016*, www.echr.coe.int/Docu ments/Stats_analysis_2016_ENG.pdf

Council of the European Union (2016). *Comprehensive Economic and Trade Agreement (CETA) Between Canada, of the One Part, and the European Union and Its Member States, of the Other Part – Statements to the Council Minutes*, Brussels, 27 October 2016, p. 26, http://data.consilium.europa.eu/doc/document/ ST-13463-2016-REV-1/en/pdf

President Xi Jinping (2017). *President Xi's Speech to Davos in Full*, Davos, www.weforum.org/ agenda/2017/01/full-text-of-xi-jinping-keynote-at-the-world-economic-forum

International organization documents

GA (2017). *Report of the International Court of Justice, 1 August 2016–31 July 2017*, 72th Session, A/72/4, p. 65, www.icj-cij.org/files/annual-reports/2016- 2017-en.pdf

ICSID (2017a). *The ICSID Caseload – Statistics*. Issues 2017–2, icsid.worldbank. org/en/Documents/resources/ICSID%20Web%20Stats%202017–1%20(English)%20Final.pdf

ICSID (2017b). *Database of ICSID Panels*. icsid.worldbank.org/en/Pages/about/ Database-of-Panel-Members.aspx#a17

ICSID (2017c). *Database of ICSID Member States*, icsid.worldbank.org/en/Pages/about/Database-of-Member-States.aspx

Institut de droit international (2011). *Sixième Commission: La situation du juge International*, 6 RES FR FINAL, Session de Rhodes, Rapporteur: M. Gilbert Guillaume, www.idi-iil.org/app/uploads/2017/06/2011_rhodes_06_fr.pdf

ITLOS. *List of Cases*, www.itlos.org/cases/

UNCTAD. Investment Policy Hub, "International Investments Agreements Navigator", investmentpolicyhub.unctad.org/IIA/IiasByCountry#iiaInnerMenu

UNCTAD (2013). *Reform of Investor-State Dispute Settlement: In Search of a Roadmap*, 2 IIA Issues Notes, http://unctad.org/en/PublicationsLibrary/webdiaepcb2013d4_en.pdf

UNCTAD (2014). *Investor-State Dispute Settlement: An Information Note on the United States and the European Union*, IIA Issues Note, unctad.org/en/PublicationsLibrary/webdiaepcb2014d4_en.pdf

UNCTAD (2017a). *World Investment Report 2017: Investment and the Digital Economy*, E.17.II.D.3, unctad.org/en/PublicationsLibrary/wir2017_en.pdf

UNCTAD (2017b). *Investor-State Dispute Settlement: Review of Developments in 2016*, IIA Issues Notes, investmentpolicyhub.unctad.org/Upload/Documents/diaepcb2017d1_en.pdf

UNIS (2017). *UNCITRAL to Consider Possible Reform of Investor-State Dispute Settlement*, Press Release, www.unis.unvienna.org/unis/en/pressrels/2017/unisl250.html

WTO. *WTO Analytical Index: Dispute Settlement Understanding – For Article 17.4 (a)*, www.wto.org/english/res_e/booksp_e/analytic_index_e/dsu_07_e.htm

WTO (2016). *WTO Members Debate Appointment/Reappointment of Appellate Body Members*, www.wto.org/english/news_e/news16_e/dsb_23may16_e.htm

Books and articles

Abi-Saab, G. (1996). Ensuring the Best Bench: Ways of Selecting Judges. In C. Peck and R. S. Lee, eds., *Increasing the Effectiveness of the International Court of Justice*, Peace Palace: Martinus Nijhoff.

Baetens, F. (2016). The Rule of Law or the Perception of the Beholder? Why Investment Arbitrators Are Under Fire and Trade Adjudicators Are Not: A Response to Joost Pauwelyn. *American Journal of International Law Unbound*, 109, 306.

Crawford, J. and McIntyre, J. (2011). The Independence and Impartiality of the International Judiciary. In Shetreet, S. and Forsyth, C., eds., *The Culture of Judicial Independence: Conceptual Foundations and Practical Challenges*, Leiden: Martinus Nijhoff, pp. 189–214.

EFILA (2016). *Task Force Regarding the Proposed International Court System (ICS)*, European Federation for Investment Law and Arbitration, efila.org/wp-content/uploads/2016/02/EFILA_TASK_FORCE_on_ICS_proposal_1-2-2016.pdf

ERA (2015). *Pledge*, www.arbitrationpledge.com

German Magistrates Association (2016). *Opinion on the Establishment of an Investment Tribunal in TTIP*, No 04/16, ttip2016.eu/files/content/docs/Full%20documents/english_version_deutsche_richterbund_opinion_ics_feb2016.pdf

Grossman, N. (2012). Sex on the Bench: Do Women Judges Matter to the Legitimacy of International Courts? *Chicago Journal of International Law*, 12(2), 647.

Hamamoto, S. (2015). Recent Anti-ISDS Discourse in the Japanese Diet: A Dressed-Up But Glaring Hypocrisy. *The Journal of World Investment and Trade*, 16(4–5), 931.

Horvath, G. J. and Berzero, R. (2013). Arbitrator & Counsel: The Double-Hat Dilemma. *Transnational Dispute Management Journal*, 10(4), 1.

Hughes, K. and Blenkinsop, P. (2015). *U.S. Wary of EU Proposal for Investment Court in Trade Pact*, Reuters, www.reuters.com/article/us-trade-ttip-idUSKCN0SN2LH20151029.

Kalicki, J. E. and Joubin-Bret, A. eds. (2015). *Reshaping the Investor-State Dispute Settlement System: Journeys for the 21st Century*, Leiden: Brill Nijhoff.

Kaufmann-Kohler, G. and Potestà, M. (2016). Can the Mauritius Convention Serve as a Model for the Reform of Investor-State Arbitration in Connection with the Introduction of a Permanent Investment Tribunal or an Appeal Mechanism? Analysis and Roadmap, UNCITRAL, www.uncitral.org/pdf/english/CIDS_Research_Paper_Mauritius.pdf

Lévesque, C. (2016). The European Commission Proposal for an Investment Court System: Out with the Old, in with the New? *CIGI Investor-State Series, Paper No. 10*, www.cigionline.org/sites/default/files/isa_paper_series_no.10_0.pdf

Mackenzie, R. et al. (2010). *Selecting International Judges: Principle, Process and Politics*, Oxford: Oxford University Press.

Mackenzie, R. and Sands, P. (2003). International Courts and Tribunals and the Independence of the International Judge. *Harvard International Law Journal*, 44(1), 271.

Manjiao, C. and Wang, X. (2015). The Evolution of ISA Clauses in Chinese IIAs and Its Practical Implications. *The Journal of World Investment and Trade*, 16(4–5), 869.

McRae, D. (2015). Introduction to Symposium on Joost Pauwelyn, "The Rule of Law Without the Rule of Lawyers? Why Investment Arbitrators Are from Mars, Trade Adjudicators from Venus". *American Journal of International Law Unbound*, 109, 277–282, https://www.cambridge.org/core/services/aop-cambridge-core/content/view/D99083D754017AF01D020BDC534EF65F/S2398772300001598a.pdf/introduction_to_symposium_on_joost_pauwelyn_the_rule_of_law_without_the_rule_of_lawyers_why_investment_arbitrators_are_from_mars_trade_adjudicators_are_from_venus.pdf

Mowbray, A. (2008). The Consideration of Gender in the Process of Appointing Judges to the European Court of Human Rights. *Human Rights Law Journal*, 8(3), 549.

Pauwelyn, P. (2015). The Rule of Law Without the Rule of Lawyers? Why Investment Arbitrators Are from Mars, Trade Adjudicators from Venus. *American Journal of International Law*, 109, 761.

Posner, E. A. and de Figueirdo, M. F. P. (2005). Is the International Court of Justice Biased? *The Journal of Legal Studies*, 34, 599.

Reisman, M. (1989). The Breakdown of the Control Mechanism in ICSID Arbitration. *Duke Law Journal*, 739.

Rogers, C. A. (2016). Apparent Dichotomies, Covert Similarities: A Response to Joost Pauwelyn. *American Journal of International Law Unbound*, 109, 294.

Sauvant, K. P., ed. (2008). *Appeals Mechanism in International Investment Disputes*, New York: Oxford University Press.

Schill, S., ed. (2015). Special Issue: Dawn of an Asian Century in International Investment Law? *The Journal of World Investment and Trade*, 16(4–5).

Shaffer, G. (2016). *Will the US Undermine the World Trade Organization?'* The *World Post*, www.huffingtonpost.com/gregory-shaffer/will-the-us-undermine-the_b_10108970.html

Shin, H.-T. and Chung, L. (2015). Korea's Experience with International Investment Agreements and Investor-State Dispute Settlement. *The Journal of World Investment and Trade*, 16(4–5), 952.

Three Crowns LLP (2015). European Commission Proposal for Permanent Investment Courts, www.threecrownsllp.com/wp-content/uploads/2015/12/OL2238_3C_Dec_Client-Briefing_013.pdf

Van Harten, G. (2007) *Investment Treaty Arbitration and Public Law*, Oxford: Oxford University Press.

Wood, M. (2017). Choosing between Arbitration and a Permanent Court: Lessons from Inter-State Cases. *International Center for Settlement of Investment Disputes Review*, 32(1), 1.

6 Rethinking the role of labour provisions under Asian international investment regime

A possible linkage with FTAAP?

*Zheng Lizhen**

1. Introduction

Compared with the heated trade-labour standard linkage debate in both academic and policy fields in 1990s, discussions on linkage of labour standard with a bilateral or plurilateral investment regime are relatively scarce before 2000. Since 2000, European countries or trade bloc, such as Austria, the Belgium-Luxembourg Economic Union (BLEU), the European Free Trade Area (EFTA), Finland, the Netherlands, the European Union (EU), have taken the lead in linking labour standard with BITs. The US and Canada practiced the investment-labour standard linkage later than their European counterparts did, although their practice of trade-labour standard linkage has already existed since the early 1990s. Some other developed countries, such as Japan and New Zealand, and developing countries or trade blocs such as the Caribbean Community (CARICOM) and the Southern African Development Community (SADC), also participate in the investment-labour standard linkage. As the largest FDI recipient region in the world, Asia has become a main target of investment-labour standard linkage.

Part I of this chapter compares the normative difference of four groups of linkage in IIAs that involve Asian countries (Asian IIAs), i.e. the linkage mode of Japan, Austria and BLEU, the linkage mode of New Zealand and EFTA, the linkage mode of the US and Canada, the linkage mode of the EU. It finds five elements that are common in all linkage practices, seven elements that exist in most linkage practices and six elements that only appear in a minor proportion of linkage practices in Asian IIAs. Analysis on how these normative elements contribute to the legalization of labour standard in Asian IIAs are further provided. Part II first provides a retrospective on three alternatives of labour standard provision discussed in MAI draft of (1995–1998). Then, based on the analysis of elements that are inherited from MAI draft, elements that are missed during the evolution, and elements are innovated in current Asian IIAs, this part sees that, on the one hand, the linkage practice in Asian IIAs will follow the same general trend of being stricter as that of the global linkage practice, and on the other hand, some unique characteristics because of the sharp contrast between rising competitive abilities of international investment and trade of Asian countries and their relatively poor situation of labour standard. Part III focuses on the social dimension that labour standard has built into the investment regime of Asia from perspectives of notion, core obligation, dispute settlement and remedy measure. It will explore both positive impacts and difficulties that labour standard have brought into the overall investment regime of Asia. Part IV evaluates the potential labour standard issue in the initiative of FTAAP and suggest how labour standard should better respond to the aims and principles of FTAAP initiative. Part V comes the conclusion.

2. Types of linkage and normative framework

As of April 10, 2017, at least 29 out of 48 Asian countries have practices of linking labour standard with at least one bilateral investment arrangement.[1] As one of the few developed countries in Asia, Japan has conducted a comparatively consistent policy of linkage under bilateral or plurilateral investment arrangements since 2008. By contrast, linkage practices of other Asian countries, especially developing Asian countries are relatively passive and partial. Nearly all parties that dominate negotiation of labour standard in Asian IIAs are from non-Asian developed countries. Besides Japan, developed countries from Europe (Austria, BLEU, EFTA and the EU); developed countries from America (US and Canada); and developed countries from Oceania (New Zealand) have applied different labour standard policies in IIAs concluded with Asian countries, leading to a variety of investment-labour standard linkage styles in Asia.

2.1. Different linkage styles

2.1.1. Linkage mode of Austria, Japan and BLEU

Austria, Japan and BLEU practice the linkage between labour standard and IIAs earlier than other countries. The uniqueness of their practice lies in their preference for the field of investment to that of trade.

Austria has no FTA in its own name. All investment-labour standard linkage practices appear in BITs. As of April 10, 2017, 18 out of 52 Austrian BITs (effective or to be effective) have labour standard provisions.[2] Among the 33 BITs concluded after 2000, 18 BITs have labour standard,[3] and 9 of them are targeted at Asian countries. Labour standard in the Austrian BIT is very brief at its initial stage. Before 2008, Austria only puts labour standard requirements in the preamble of BITs like 'Contracting Parties reaffirm their commitment to the observance of internationally recognised labour standards', without other relevant provisions in the main text. During this period, Austria models the same requirement in its BITs with six Asian countries, i.e. Bangladesh (2000), Azerbaijan (2000), Jordan (2001), Georgia (2001), Armenia (2001) and Yemen (2002). In 2008, Austria released a Model BIT, Austria, 2008 with more detailed requirements of labour standards. Besides a similar labour standard provision in the preamble to that of BITs before 2008, two more labour standard provisions are added to the main text. One is the not-lowing requirement, which recognizes it inappropriate to encourage an investment by weakening domestic labour laws[4] (Bernasconi-Osterwalder and Johnson, 2011). The other is the definition of labour laws. According to the definition, those statutes or regulations that contain six items of Model BIT, Austria, 2008 recognized labour standard are subject to the not-lowering requirement[5] (Bernasconi-Osterwalder and Johnson, 2011). Ever since the 2008 Model BIT, linkage with labour standard seems to be a stable investment policy of Austria, as all its four BITs concluded from 2008 to March 2017 are with similar linkage content. Among the four BITs, only one is concluded with non-Asian country (Nigeria, 2013), the other three are with Asian countries, i.e. Kazakhstan (2010), Tajikistan (2010) and Kyrgyzstan (2016).

Japan first links labour standard with investment in its EPA with the Philippines in 2006. As of April 10, 2017, Japan has 13 effective EPAs, all of them are concluded after 2000, and 3 of them has investment-labour standard linkage. No trade-labour standard linkages appear in these Sic. Besides the linkage practice under Sic., Japan also links labour standard with13 out of 24 effective BITs that are concluded after 2000. Among the 16 IIAs with labour standard, 8 are concluded between Japan and other Asian counties, i.e. Myanmar (2013 FTA), Philippines (2008 FTA), Uzbekistan (2008 BIT), Iraq (2012 BIT), Kuwait (2012 BIT), Kazakhstan (2014 BIT), Oman (2015 BIT) and Mongolia (2016 FTA). BLEU has no FTA in its own name. So far as of April 10, 2017, BLEU has 87 BITs (effective or to be effective), with 39 of them concluded after 2000, and at least 17 of them bear labour standard.[6] Among the 17 IIAs with labour standard, 5 are concluded between BLEU and Asian countries, i.e. the United Arab Emirates (2004), Bahrain (2006), Oman (2008), Tajikistan (2009) and Qatar (2009).

Linkage practices of Japan, Austria and BLEU are classified into the same group in that investor-state arbitration, state-state arbitration and economic sanction to disputes of labour standard are integrated with that of investment. In these IIAs, disputes arising from violation of labour standard provisions are not excluded from the dispute settlement procedures and enforcement measures of investment cases. Nevertheless, minor differences should not be omitted. As to the objective of linkage, the practice of Austria sets investment-labour standard relationship, together with investment-environment and investment-human right, into a much broader scene of global sustainable development, and practices of Japan emphasize the importance of the cooperative relationship between labour and management in promoting investment, while there is no such content in practices of BLEU. Regarding the not-lowering requirement, practices of Japan is much stricter by adding 'contracting Party should not waive or otherwise derogate from such measures and standards as an encouragement for the establishment, acquisition or expansion of investments' to what practices of Austria and BLEU have already contained as 'it is inappropriate to encourage investment by weakening or reducing the protections afforded in domestic labour laws'. Therefore, the not-lowering requirement in linkage practices of Japan applies both to labour law legislation and implementation, while it only applies to labour law legislation in cases of Austria and BLEU.

As regards the definition of domestic labour law, linkage practices of Austria are much broader than that of Japan and BLEU with four items of labour standard similar to that of ILO core labour standard, while most linkage practices of Japan and BLEU lack the item of 'elimination of discrimination in respect of employment and occupation'. Furthermore, linkage practices of BLEU are more innovative than that of Austria and Japan by including three types of clauses in most of its IIAs,[7] i.e. clauses of social regulation sovereignty in establishing, adopting or modifying its labour legislation, clause of keeping consistent with the international labour standards and striving for high level of protection, and clause of highlighting the relevance of ILO by reaffirmation of the obligation of contracting parties as members of International Labour Organisation (ILO) and their commitments under the 1998 ILO Declaration on Fundamental Principles and Rights at Work and its Follow-up, 1998.

2.1.2. Linkage mode of New Zealand and EFTA

Different from that of Austria and BLEU, all linkage practices of New Zealand and EFTA exist under the framework of an FTA rather than that of a BIT. Nevertheless, most of the labour standard provisions are applied to both trade and investment.

So far as of April 10, 2017, New Zealand has linked labour standard with 7 FTAs among all the 9 effective FTAs which are concluded after 2000. All linkage practices of New Zealand involve Asian countries or regions. Like linkage practices of New Zealand, 11 out of 25 effective FTAs of EFTA have labour standard applied to both investment and trade. The FTA with Hong Kong is the only linkage practice of New Zealand in Asia.

Linkage practices of New Zealand and EFTA are categorized as an unique mode because of their similar emphasis on effective enforcement of domestic labour law,[8] capacity building and consultation as the only resort of investment-relevant labour disputes. Contrary to that of Japan, Austria and BLEU, linkage practices of New Zealand and EFTA explicitly exclude the application of investor-state and intergovernmental dispute settlement procedure, no compensatory damages or economic sanction is allowed, either. Compared with that of Austria, Japan and BLEU, more normative elements appear in linkage practices of New Zealand and EFTA such as effective enforcement obligation in addition to the not-lowering requirement, cooperative activities, special institutional arrangement. Linkage practices of New Zealand have begun to show in the preamble multiple roles of labour standard, such as sustainable development, decent work, improvement of working condition, protection of basic workers' rights and enhancement of capacity building. Linkage practices of New Zealand even include private action and procedural guarantees[9] as well as public participation in the implementation of labour standard and public awareness.

In contrast with linkage practices of Austria, Japan and BLEU, a greater extent of relevance of ILO labour standard is emphasized. Besides the affirmation of the obligation as a member of ILO and political commitments in ILO Declaration of 1998, linkage practices of EFTA strengthen the relevance of ILO in three aspects. The first aspect, the requirement of consideration of scientific, technical and other information and relevant international standards, guidelines and recommendations in preparing and implementing measures related to labour conditions. The second aspect, the requirement of effective implementation of the ILO Conventions which they have ratified and continued and sustained efforts towards ratifying the fundamental ILO conventions as well as the other conventions that are classified as 'up-to-date' by the ILO. The third aspect, the obligation of striving to strengthen their cooperation on investment-related labour of mutual interest in relevant bilateral, regional and multilateral fora in which they participate.

Regardless of the innovations, the linkage mode of New Zealand and EFTA lack a clear definition of labour law, which makes obligations of not-lowering and effective enforcement lose much power.

2.1.3. Linkage mode of the US and Canada

Linkage practices of the US and Canada appear much later in the field of investment than that of trade. The US and Canada are the first two countries to link labour standard with regional trade regime in the world (NAFTA, 1994). However, it is not until 2006 that the US begins to put labour standard in BITs. So far, the US only links labour standard with 2 out of 42 effective BITs.[10] No BIT is concluded with Asian countries. As to Canada, no linkage appears under the BIT framework. Both the US and Canada link labour standard with recent FTAs that are partially or wholly applied to investment. The investment-labour standard linkage practice of the US covers four Asian countries of Singapore (2004), Bahrain (2006), Oman (2009) and Korea (2012), while the investment-labour standard linkage practice of Canada covers two Asian countries of Jordan (2012) and Korea (2015).

Negotiated according to 'fast track authority' of 2002 Trade Act of the US, the three FTAs between the US and Singapore, Bahrain and Oman similarly differentiate investment-labour standard linkage from trade-labour standard linkage. Obligation of effective enforcement in these three FTAs is limited to trade-related issues, therefore only default of this obligation can resort to state-state arbitration and subsequent mandatory economic remedies. For this reason, labour standard disputes relating to investment can only be solved by consultation. It is also difficult to tell that those mechanisms highly related with the obligation of effective enforcement of labour standard, such as private action, procedural guarantee, public submission (communication) and public awareness, are applied to investment. As the latest linkage practice of the US in Asia, the US-Korea FTA is concluded after the Bipartisan Trade Deal of May10, 2007, which not only fully integrates the linkage of investment-labour standard with that of trade-labour standard, but also strengthens the relevant obligations. The analysis of investment-labour standard linkage practice of the US in Asia will base on the US-Korea FTA, as labour standard policy in the Bipartisan Trade Deal has been a baseline for the US to negotiate all trade and investment agreements including those with Asian countries.

So far, as of April 10, 2017, 9 out of 12 effective FTAs of Canada have labour standard, two of them are with Asian countries of Jordan and Korea, which are concluded after 2009. Before 2009, linkage practices of Canada only appear in the field of trade. The Canada-Peru FTA (2009) is the first FTA that Canada begins to integrate the linkage practice in the field of investment with that of trade. Despite modelling that of the Canada-Peru FTA, it is difficult to construe that investment-labour standard linkage in the Canada-Jordan FTA is really meaningful, as it has no chapter of investment. Investment-labour standard linkage of the Canada-Korea FTA (2015) is similar to that of the Canada-Peru FTA, but more clear in that it explicitly allows the review panel (arbitral panel) to be applied to investment-relevant labour standard disputes. With new signs of tendency of investment-labour standard linkage, the Canada-Korea FTA will be taken as a typical example to analyse the linkage practice of Canada in Asia.

Linkage practices of the US and Canada are classified as a special mode because of more detailed obligation of effective domestic enforcement, unique complaint mechanism, state-state arbitration and economic sanction. Different from linkage practices of New Zealand and BLEU, which only include a general clause of effective domestic enforcement requirement, more factors are listed in the U.S-Korea FTA and the Canada-Korea FTA. Article 19.3.1 of the U.S-Korea FTA states 'a decision a Party makes on the distribution of enforcement resources shall not be a reason for not complying' and 'the exercise of such discretion and such decisions shall not be inconsistent with the obligations'. Article 18.4 of the Canada-Korea FTA states, 'appropriate government action, such as appointing and training inspectors, monitoring compliance and investigating suspected violations, record keeping and reporting, appropriate sanctions or remedies for violations of its labour law' should be taken to ensure effective enforcement of domestic labour law. The complaint mechanism of linkage practices of the US and Canada is unique in receiving written letters from the public, which are to be considered by the national contact point of a contracting party on inconsistency of the other contracting party with labour standard requirement in an FTA and will initiate intergovernmental consultation even arbitration. Different from the linkage mode of Austria, Japan and BLUE, which use both investor-state and state-state arbitration mechanisms to solve labour standard disputes, the linkage mode of the US and Canada only takes state-state arbitration mechanism. Compared with vague economic sanction as a result of non-compliance of state-state arbitration award in the linkage mode of Austria, Japan and BLEU, the linkage mode of the US and Canada sets substantial and procedural conditions for annual monetary assessment equivalent to the degree of adverse investment effects related to the non-compliance of labour standard. Trade sanction is even allowed to enforce the annual monetary assessment in the U.S.-Korea FTA.

Like the linkage mode of New Zealand and EFTA, linkage practices of the US and Canada empower labour standard with several roles, such as sustainable development and capacity building, but put enforcement of domestic labour law and protection of basic workers' rights as the focus. Besides similar obligations of private action, procedural guarantees, public participation and public awareness in the linkage mode of New Zealand and EFTA, linkage practices of the US and Canada include a requirement to internalize internationally recognized labour principles and rights into domestic labour law. Unlike the linkage mode of New Zealand and EFTA, linkage practices of the US and Canada have a relatively clear definition of domestic labour law, both including at least four items of core labour standard similar to that of ILO. The U.S.-Korea FTA also takes acceptable minimum employment standards as a necessary item of domestic labour law, while the Canada-Korea FTA includes in the definition of domestic labour law two additional items, i.e. the prevention of occupational injuries and illnesses, compensation in cases of occupational injuries or illnesses; and non-discrimination in respect of working conditions for migrant workers. Furthermore, with Article 8.16, the Canada-Korea FTA has become the first Asian IIA holding both host and home countries responsible to push internationally recognized corporate social responsibility (CSR) of labour standard, and also it is the first Asian IIA that investors are explicitly named to voluntarily incorporate CSR of labour standard in their practices and their internal policies.

2.1.4. Linkage mode of the EU

The EU has a relatively consistent practice in linking labour standard with regional trade regime since the agreement amending the Fourth ACP-EC Convention of Lome in 1995 (Hepple, 2005: 123), It is not until the Lisbon Treaty, 13 December 2007, in force 1 December 2009, that the EU extends its competence to foreign direct investment, and investment issues begin to be negotiated and concluded under an FTA framework. FTAs of the EU are all with investment-labour standard linkage after December 2009. Among the current 11 effective FTAs, two are with Asian countries of Korea (2011)and Georgia (2015).

The uniqueness of linkage practice of the EU lies in four aspects. First, high relevance of ILO instrument for effective domestic enforcement. Linkage practices of the EU-Korea FTA and the EU-Georgia FTA raise the relevance of ILO in four aspects. The first aspect is the obligation to respect, promote and realize four items of core labour standards of ILO in domestic law. The second aspect is contracting parties' commitment to effectively implement the ILO Conventions that both countries have ratified and make continued and sustained efforts towards ratifying more fundamental ILO Conventions as well as the other 'up-to-date' conventions. The third aspect is to recognize the importance, when preparing and implementing measures aimed at protecting social conditions, taking account of scientific and technical information and following relevant international standards, guidelines or recommendations. The fourth aspect is the obligation of contracting parties to ensure that the resolution arising from consultation reflects the activities of the ILO and require the panel of experts to seek information and advice from ILO as it deems appropriate. By highlighting the relevance of ILO and international labour standard, the EU-Korea FTA and the EU-Georgia FTA help to promote greater cooperation and coherence between unilateral, bilateral and plurilateral labour standards.

Second, obligation of CSR promotion. Linkage practices of the EU-Korea FTA and the EU-Georgia FTA are among those few linkage practices (another case is the Canada-Korea FTA) that emphasizes exchange of information and cooperation on corporate social responsibility and accountability, including the effective implementation and follow-up of internationally agreed guidelines, fair and ethical trade.

Third, supervision mechanism of joint social dialogue forum, state-state arbitration (panel of experts) and exclusion of economic sanction for non-compliance of the award (decision of the panel of experts). Different from that of the U.S.-Korea FTA and the Canada-Korea FTA, which turn to adversary dispute settlement and emphasize public submission/communication as the initiation of dispute settlement procedure, arbitral panel as the final procedure and suspension of benefits or monetary fine as remedies, the linkage practices of the EU-Korea FTA and the EU-Georgia FTA only allow the resort of non-adversary mechanism such as civil society dialogue, consultation, recommendation of panel of experts and monitoring of the decision of the panel by the Committee on Trade and Sustainable Development.

2.2. Normative framework of linkage practice in Asian IIAs

Based on this analysis, there are mainly 18 normative elements in the linkage practice of Asian IIAs, with imbalanced coverage in practices of different countries (see Table.6.1).

2.2.1. Elements of minority linkage practice

It can be seen from Table 6.1, six normative elements only exist in a minor percentage of linkage practices. Among them, private action, procedural guarantee and complaint mechanism originate from the linkage practices of the US and Canada. They are the result of the US and Canada's extending strong linkage rules that are originally applied to the field of trade to the field of investment after 2009. To seek fully domestic enforcement of labour standard, the US and Canada apply a unique dispute settlement mechanism initiated by public submission/communication, which is quite antagonist as opposed to the especially harmonious style of the EU by the avenue of joint civil society dialogue. The linkage practice of imposing CSR obligations is stemmed from the EU and Canada. Although only a few countries practice CSR clauses of labour standard currently, it is of significance that both home and host countries are obliged to ensure their multinational enterprises to conform to such rule in their business overseas. Similarly, investor-state dispute settlement mechanism is first practiced by Japan, Austria and BLEU. Different attitudes to workers' right between counties of coordinated market economy and countries of free market economy, as Peter A. Hall and David Soskice classify, (Hall and Soskice, 2001: 8–11) might explain for

Table 6.1 Normative elements of labour standard in Asian IIAs

	Japan	Austria	BLEU	New Zealand	EFTA	US	Canada	EU
1. Objective	Sustainable development	Cooperation between labour and management	Sustainable development by default[11]	Sustainable development, decent work, improvement of working condition and basic workers' right, capacity building	Sustainable development	Sustainable development, enforcement of labour laws, improvement of basic workers' rights, capacity building	Similar to that of the US	Similar to that of the US
2. The not-lowering requirement	√	√	√	√	√	√	√	√
3. Effective enforcement of domestic labour law	×	×	×	√ only New Zealand-Korea FTA	√	√ only U.S.-Korea FTA	√	√
4. Definition of domestic labour law	√ only in Japan-Philippines FTA, 5 items	√ 6 items	√ most with five items	×	×	√ most with 4items; U.S.-Korea FTA 6 items	√ 7items	√ 4 items
5. Inclusion of internationally recognized labour rights in domestic labour law	×	×	×	√ only in New Zealand-Korea FTA	×	√	√	√

Item								
6. Right to regulate and seek high-level protection	default	default	√	√	√	default	default	√
7. Reference to ILO instrument	×	√	√	√	√	√	√	√
8. Private action and procedural guarantee	×	×	×	×	× only in New Zealand-Korea FTA	√	√	×
9. Public participation	×	×	×	×	√	√	√	√ joint social dialogue forum
10. Information and public awareness	×	×	×	√	√	√	√	√
11. CSR	×	×	×	×	×	×	√	√
12. Special institutional arrangement	×	×	×	√	√	√	√	√
13. Cooperative activities	×	×	√ most BITs	√	√	√	√	√
14. Complaint mechanism	×	×	×	×	×	√	√	×
15. Consultation	default	default	√	√	√	√	√	√
16. Investor-state arbitration	√	√	√	×	×	×	×	×
17. State-state arbitration	√	√	√	√	×	√ only in the US-Korea FTA	√	√
18. Enforcement measures	√	√	√	×	×	√ only in the US-Korea FTA	√	×

this phenomena. Japan, Austria and BLEU are typical representatives of coordinated market economy, where investors are required to or voluntarily practice higher level of labour right protection both domestically and overseas. There is accordingly a possibility for investors to sue host countries for lowering/weakening labour right or not effectively enforcing domestic labour law, in order to level the playing field between investors in host countries. By contrast, the US, Canada and New Zealand are typical representatives of free market economy, where there is little incentive for their transnational corporations/enterprises to sue to raise or strengthen the labour standard in host countries, there is naturally no need to maintain such kind of clause.

2.2.2. *Elements of prevalent linkage practice*

The most common five elements in linkage practices of Asian IIAs are as follows: the objective of sustainable development, the not-lowering requirement, the obligation of striving for high-level protection, the sovereignty right of labour regulation and consultation. Additionally, more than half of linkage practices in Asian IIAs include effective enforcement of domestic labour law, definition of domestic labour law, state-state dispute settlement mechanism and enforcement measures for non-implementation of arbitration award. Most linkage practices of Asian IIAs also include the reference to ILO membership and ILO Declaration of 1998 and a special institutional arrangement. Cooperative activities also amount for a major percentage of the linkage practice.

All linkage practices in Asian IIAs explicitly or implicitly recognize the notion of sustainable development, protection of basic workers' right and its significance as the social pillar of sustainable development. Guided by this notion, three dimensions of legalization (Abbott et al., 2000: 405–406), i.e. obligation, precision and delegation, could be found in labour standards of Asian IIAs. As to the first dimension of legalization, it is possible for the combination of not lowering requirement, effective enforcement and striving for a higher level of protection to produce a real binding effect. First, the not-lowering requirement is expected to play the role of preventing 'race to the bottom' among those countries competing for investment. If supplemented with the obligation of effectively enforcing the existed labour law and striving to improve domestic labour standard in consistent with internationally recognized labour standard, it is possible for these three normative elements to produce a 'ratchet effect' in both labour protection and liberalization of trade and investment. Undeniably, explicit statement or implicit recognition of sovereignty right of labour regulation is important to ensure countries of different domestic contexts, including development, social, cultural and historical backgrounds, to have adequate policy space for bona fide decisions with regard to the allocation of resources of legislation, implementation and adjudication of labour law. Nevertheless, sovereignty right of labour regulation should not be executed in a way conflicting with the not-lowering requirement, as it is difficult to be accepted if this right is executed downward rather than upward the direction of basic workers' right protection.

Regarding the second dimension of legalization, the definition of domestic labour law adds precision to the not-lowering requirement, so does the emphasis of relevance of ILO labour standards, which has the widest international consensus of 187 members in transnational labour regulation. Additionally, cooperative activities, institutional arrangement, consultation, state-state dispute settlement mechanism and enforcement measures for non-implementation constitute the third dimension of legalization, i.e. 'delegation'. In linkage practices with third party arbitration and enforcement measures, such as that of Austria, Japan, BLEU, the US and Canada in Asia, the degree of delegation is relatively high.

Based on this analysis, a preliminary conclusion can be made that in most linkage practices of Asian IIAs, the general level of legalization of labour standard, although still lower than that of core investment obligations such as national treatment or most favoured nation treatment, is much higher than principles of merely political promises. It has to be admitted that a normative framework of investment-labour standard has come into being.

3. Evolutionary trend of Asian IIAs

Linkage practices of Asian IIAs have their roots in that of Multilateral Agreement on Investment (MAI) draft of 1995–1998, but have normative innovations during the evolutionary process. Linkage practices of Asian IIAs will follow the general trend of the global linkage practice but will take its own evolutionary track at the same time.

3.1. Normative development after MAI

Investment-labour standard linkage can be traced back to negotiation of MAI from 1995 to 1998 (Canner, 1998: 676). It was the result of pressures from transnational civil society groups but was opposed by many OECD members, such as New Zealand, Australia, Mexico and Japan at the beginning. In MAI draft of 1998, labour standard has its place in the preamble, the main text and the annex. In the preamble, it refers to the commitment of the Copenhagen Declaration of the World Summit on Social Development and to observance of internationally recognized core labour standards, and at the same time, it recognizes the ILO as the competent body to set and deal with core labour standards worldwide. Additionally, preamble of MAI affirms the support of OECD members for the OECD Guidelines for Multinational Enterprises, where labour protection is a major part to be observed on a voluntary basis.

Labour standard of MAI draft appears in the main text as the 'not-lowering standards' with three alternatives.[12]

Alternative 1 The Parties recognize that it is inappropriate to encourage investment by lowering [domestic]health, safety or environmental [standards] [measures] or relaxing [domestic] [core] labour standards. Accordingly, a Party should not waive or otherwise derogate from, or offer to waive or otherwise derogate from, such [standards] [measures] as an encouragement for the establishment, acquisition, expansion or retention in its territory of an investment of an investor. If a Party considers that another Party has offered such an encouragement, it may request consultations with the other Party and the two Parties shall consult with a view to avoiding any such encouragement.

Alternative 2 A Contracting Party [shall] [should] not waive or otherwise derogate from, or offer to waive or otherwise derogate from [domestic] health, safety or environmental [measures] [standards] or [domestic] [core] labour standards as an encouragement for the establishment, acquisition, expansion or retention of an investment of an investor.

Alternative 3

1   The Parties recognize that it is inappropriate to encourage investment by lowering domestic health, safety or environmental measures or relaxing international core labour standards.

2   A Contracting Party [shall] [should] accord to investors of another Contracting Party and their investments treatment no more favourable than it accords its own investors by waving or otherwise derogating from, or offering to waive or otherwise derogate from domestic health, safety, environmental or labour measures, with respect to the establishment, acquisition, expansion, operation, management, maintenance, use, enjoyment and sale or other disposition of an investment.

3   A Contracting Party [shall] [should] not take any measure which derogates from, or offer to derogate from, international health, safety or environmental laws or international core labour standards as an encouragement for investment on its territory.

These three alternatives speak for great difficulties in reaching a consensus on labour standard between members in MAI negotiation. However, convergence still exist in the opposition of members to lower labour standard as an encourage for investment.

Right of labour regulation is implied in the main text as two proposed provisions. One is the article of 'A Contracting Party may adopt, maintain or enforce any measure that it considers appropriate to ensure that investment activity is undertaken in a manner sensitive to health, safety or environmental concerns, provided such measures are consistent with this agreement'. The other is the article of

Provided that such measures are not applied in an arbitrary or unjustifiable manner, or do not constitute a disguised restriction on investment, nothing in paragraphs shall be construed to prevent any Contracting Party from adopting or maintaining measures, including environmental measures. . . (b) necessary to protect human, animal or plant life or health.

Labour standard in the annex comes from the OECD Guidelines for Multi-national Enterprises, where requirements of employment and industrial relations amount to a major percentage of the guidelines.

Obviously, evolution of linkage of investment-labour standard sees heavy footprints in the draft of MAI. At least four factors in current IIAs are borrowed directly from MAI. The first is the aim of sustainable development in the preamble. All linkage practices in Asian IIAs take it as the main objective. The second is the reference to ILO membership and ILO instrument especially the Copenhagen Declaration of the World Summit on Social Development or ILO declaration of 1998. All but the linkage practice of Austria model this provision. The third is the not-lowering requirement.

Among the three alternatives for the not-lowering requirement, Alternative 3 is the most detailed with an additional requirement of national treatment to foreign investors. Alternative 2 is relatively simple with only the not-lowering requirement in the stage of legislation. Alternative 1 becomes the most popular model as it includes not lowering requirement in both the stage of legislation and implementation. The fourth is the right of labour regulation. Most linkage practices of Asian IIAs take after the implicit expression of MAI. However, some linkage practices, such as that of BLEU, New Zealand, EFTA and Canada, begin to make it more detailed by explicit expression of 'recognizing the right of each Contracting Party to establish its own domestic labour standards, and to adopt or modify accordingly its labour legislation'.

Two important factors are missing during the evolution. One is the reaffirmation of ILO as the only competent authorities in developing and dealing with investment-relevant labour standards. Thus, ILO loses its dominant role in investment-relevant labour standard issues under the framework of IIAs. The other is the obligation of promoting investors to comply with the OECD Guidelines for Multinational Enterprises voluntarily. Labour standard in the OECD Guidelines for Multinational Enterprises is relatively stronger than that of other intergovernmental CSR, such as UN Global Compact and the Tripartite Declaration of Principles Concerning Multinational Enterprises and Social Policy of ILO, in that it has procedural obligations for those countries who accept it and has possible economic sanction for multinational enterprises. Although linkage practices of Canada and the EU include CSR promotion requirement, they do not focus on the application of OECD Guidelines for Multinational Enterprises. Therefore, CSR of labour standard are weakened in the process of evolution.

At least six new factors are added to the linkage practice of Asian IIAs compared with that of MAI draft. First, the obligation of striving for high level of protection, expressly or implicitly stated, in all linkage practices of Asian IIAs. This helps to balance the right of labour regulation and the prevention of downward labour protection. Second, the obligation of effective enforcement in most linkage practices of Asian IIAs. In most Asian developing countries, effective enforcement is even more critical to rectify the defects of 'law on paper'. Therefore, this new factor helps to strengthen the 'obligation' dimension of labour standard. Third, cooperative activities. Most linkage practices of Asian IIAs begin to emphasize the importance of capacity building through cooperative programs. Fourth, the scope of labour standard that might affect investment. Most linkage practices of Asian IIAs have a definition of domestic labour law which at least covers five items, i.e. 'the right of association', 'the right to organise and to bargain collectively', 'a prohibition on the use of any form of forced or compulsory labour', 'labour protections for children and young people, including a minimum age for the employment of children and the prohibition and elimination of the worst forms of child labour'. The third and fourth new factors improve the dimension of preciseness for labour standard.

Fifth, arbitration for investment-relevant labour standard disputes. Dispute settlement of investment-relevant disputes were too contentious to be included in labour standard negotiation of MAI. However, some linkage practices of Asian IIAs, such as that of Austria, Japan and BLEU, have begun to resort to state-state arbitration rather than merely turn to consultation. Linkage practices of Austria, Japan and BLEU even allow investor-state arbitration to be applied to investment-relevant labour standard disputes. Sixth, the integrated application of enforcement measures for non-implementation of the final arbitration award to labour standard with that of investment. The fifth and sixth new factors make the third dimension of legalization, i.e. 'delegation', more obvious than that of MAI draft.

In summary, legalization of investment-labour standard in Asian IIA is much elevated compared with that of MAI.

3.2. Anticipated linkage trend of Asian IIAs

Normative elements of linkage practices of Asian IIAs will develop as part of the global linkage practices, but will possibly show unique features in the process of evolution.

3.2.1. Common features with the global trend

Trend of linkage practices of Asian IIAs are similar to that of the global in participants, framework, strictness and responsible body.

First, owing to its double attributes as human right and economic factor, especially the rising emphasis of its economic attribute, labour standard will be accepted by more developed and developing countries globally, so is in Asia. Economic attribute of labour standard is recognized by ILO ever since its establishment. ILO regards it important for labour standard to prevent vicious competition between members since its establishment. In the preamble of ILO Charter of 1919, it states 'the failure of any nation to adopt humane conditions of labour is an obstacle in the way of other nations which desire to improve the conditions in their own countries'. The economic role of labour standard has been more emphasized by ILO in recent years. In response to social challenges of economic globalization, ILO stresses on the one hand that labour standard should not be used for protectionist trade purposes in its ILO Declaration on Fundamental, and on the other hand, 'violation of fundamental principles and rights at work cannot be invoked or otherwise used as a legitimate comparative advantage' in its Declaration of 2008. It is also the fact that the economic attribute of 'leveling the playing field for domestic workers and enterprises' is recognized by more developed countries, as can be seen from the more consistent labour standard in FTAs or BITs that the EU, the US and Canada have concluded with both developing and other developed countries. Therefore, it is possible for developed countries who invest in Asia to link labour standard with investment more frequently so as to create fair competition environment for investors and workers both in host and home countries.

Compared with the situation of developed countries, it is mainly the attribute of human right that makes labour standard more acceptable for developing countries in order to avoid a lower moral position in negotiations of economic agreements. In addition, as more developing countries, especially emerging Asian economies such as China and Korea, become the source of outward capital as well as inward capital, they will have to consider labour standard in economic agreements so as to make their outward investment more acceptable by civil society groups in developed host countries.

Second, from a global vision, while traditional linkage of investment-labour standard appears in BITs, future practices of linkage will appear more frequently under the framework of FTAs where there is an integrated application of labour standard to both trade and investment, the same is in Asia. In recent years, with appearance of more cross-cutting issues and innovation of one-single package negotiation, investment provisions are negotiated and concluded more often under FTA frameworks. Trade relevant labour standard and investment-relevant labour standard are so closely interrelated that trade policies of some countries, such as the US Bipartisan Agreement of May10, 2007 and Trade Promotion Act of 2015, require labour standard to be applied to investment in the same way as it is applied to trade. Similar integration practice appear in the new trade and investment strategy of the EU,[13] where labour standard is regarded as one of key values sustaining both trade and investment liberalization.

Similarly, Trade Agenda 2030 of New Zealand emphasizes that trade and investment agreements are playing an increasingly important role in shaping labour and will contribute to address relevant challenges. Considering the fact that investment-related labour standard and trade-related labour standard are intertwined with each other, some latest FTAs, such as labour cooperation agreements of the Canada-Panama FTA and the Canada-Honduras FTA, even define 'trade-related' as 'related to trade or investment covered by the trade agreement'. However, to what extent investment-related labour standard will be merged with trade-related labour standard, and to what extent they will be distinctively separated, still remains to be observed in Asian IIAs, as different developed countries competes with each other to construct or reconstruct their linkage style in Asia.

Third, investment-labour standard linkage will become stricter globally, so is in Asia. There are currently two main mechanisms for international cooperation of labour standard. The first exists under the framework of multilateral labour convention which is dominated by ILO, the second appears under the frame-work of bilateral or plurilateral economic agreements. The former international cooperation is a typical case of 'coordinated game' which need not be coercive measures for cooperation because of no obvious conflict of interests. The lat-ter international cooperation is a typical case of 'game of prisoner's dilemma' which needs enforcement for cooperation, or otherwise each contracting party will choose betrayal to benefit herself at the cost of the others. In the former international cooperation of labour standard, members of ILO is only required to recognize the necessity of improvement and enforcement of domestic labour right, thus, they are allowed much flexibility in options as regards obligation undertaken, the content of obligation and methods of application (Valticos and Potobsky, 1995: 57–59). Consequently, there is no need to take coercive meas-ures to enforce cooperation as there is little incentive for a contracting party to betray his commitments in an international labour convention.

On the contrary, in the case of the latter form of international cooperation, since violation of labour standard obligation is better for the betraying party, benefits of another contracting party and the whole will be deteriorated unless greater enforcement mechanism for cooperation is imposed. As can be seen in TPP labour chapter, full enforcement of domestic implementation and trade sanction are imposed to level the playing fields for workers and enterprises of contracting parties. The proposed TTIP labour chapter might be even stricter than that of TPP, as it is reported that ETUC and AFL-CIO have urged nego-tiating parties to agree with 'ratification and effective implementation of core labour conventions' and 'right of consultation and information disclosure for works council of multinational enterprises',[14] which are not included in TPP. Therefore, with increasing competition in trade and investment between devel-oped countries with linkage practice and Asian emerging economies, investment-labour standard linkage in Asian IIAs might become more rigorous.

Fourth, globally the significant role of multinational enterprises in transna-tional labour regulation will be more emphasized than before, so is in Asia. It has been widely recognized that roots of transnational labour problems lie in the self-benefiting expansion of the capital, where multinational enterprises are the main beneficiary. Thus, the main task of transnational labour regulation is to make the external pressures work towards guiding the self-regulation of mul-tinational enterprises. Multinational enterprises have great potentials to be the most important transnational labour regulator through its vertical and horizontal leverage of supplying and contracting network. It cannot be expected that mul-tinational enterprises will effectively solve transnational labour problems unless the external pressure is adequately powerful. Although CSR of labour standard only makes multinational enterprises bear an indirect obligation in IIAs, it does provide international trade unions with a stronger discourse for labour protection and will produce external pressures for governments of host and home countries to take measures to ensure compliance of multilateral enterprises.

Currently external pressures for multinational enterprises to self-regulate transnational labour problems in the global supply chain are much greater than before; the same is in Asia. Because of low positions in the global value chain, most supplier companies in Asian developing countries are already subject to the influence of CSR and global framework agreement (GFA) between international trade unions and multinational enterprises. It cannot be denied that international labour unions have played a critical role in supervising the implementation of CSR and GFA in Asia and other continents through internal grievance procedure, social dialogue, media mobilization and consumer boycott. In addition, labour standard problems in Asia have become a major focus of intergovernmental initiatives for labour standard such as the OECD Guidelines for Multinational Enterprises, ILO Tripartite Declaration of Principles Concerning Multinational Enterprises and Social Policy, UN Global Compact and UN Guiding Principles on Business and Human Rights. So far as April 21, 2017, complaints under OECD Guidelines for Multinational Enterprises have covered quite a number of Asian host countries, such as Japan, Korea, Bangladesh, China, Hong Kong of China, India, Indonesia, Iraqi, Laos, Malaysia, Maldives, Myanmar, Nepal, Pakistan, Philippines, Sri Lanka, Thailand, Uzbekistan, Vietnam and Yemen.

Although being soft rules, through subsequent amendments or reforms, i.e. the 2000, OECD Guidelines for Multinational Enterprises, 2011 Amendment, the ILO Tripartite Declaration of Principles Concerning Multinational Enterprises and Social Policy, 2000 amendment, the 2000 Guidelines on Cooperation and UN Global Compact, 2003 Communication on Progress, clarity, precision and delegation dimensions of these intergovernmental labour standard CSR initiatives have been increased. The Guiding Principles on Business and Human Rights endorsed by UN Human Rights Council in 2011 is expected to strengthen transnational labour regulation and other human rights in Asia and other continents by building three pillars, i.e. duty of the state to protect human rights against infringements of human rights by third parties, including business enterprises; the corporate responsibility to respect human rights; and access to effective remedy for victims of business-related human rights abuses. As can be seen that a complex web of transnational regulation woven by labour standard CSR requirements in Asian IIAs, private mechanism and intergovernmental initiatives, has emerged. In this regulation web, multinational enterprises become the fundamental and main responsive body, while intergovernmental organizations, governments of both host and home countries, NGOs especially international labour unions, are acting as the external pressing power.

3.2.2. Special characteristics in the evolutionary process

Most Asian developing countries has a history of being colonized, during which period labour protection was so excluded or discriminated that labour protection between the colonial and the colonized are called 'two separate world' during 1919–1939 (Maul, 2012: 17–27). This situation was not changed radically until these Asian countries gained independence after World War II (Maul, 2012: 111–114). Driven by their policy of priority for development, improvement of

Table 6.2 Ratification of fundamental labour conventions by region

Country	Freedom of association		Forced labour		Discrimination		Child labour	
	C087	C098	C029	C105	C100	C111	C138	C182
Total: 187	154	164	178	175	172	173	169	180
Africa (54)	49	54	54	54	52	54	52	53
Americas (35)	33	32	34	35	33	33	32	35
Arab States (11)	3	6	11	11	7	10	11	11
Asia and the Pacific (35)	18	21	28	25	29	25	23	30
Europe (51)	51	51	51	51	51	51	51	51

Source: ILO NORMLEX database updated as of May 17, 2017.

fundamental labour right has been relatively slow compared with that of America and Africa (Table 6.2).

Quite a number of developing countries in Latin America and Africa, such as Peru, Columbia, Costa Rica, Guatemala, Haiti and Honduras, Cameroon, Congo, Egypt, Ghana, Mozambique, Namibia, Nigeria, Rwanda, Swaziland, Tanzania, Zambia and Zimbabwe, have progressed in ratification of all eight fundamental labour conventions by becoming contracting parties of FTAs or beneficiaries of Generalized System of Preference of the US or the EU. By contrast, those Asian countries that are pursuing active strategies of FTAs and BITs, such as Korea, Singapore, Jordan, Malaysia, only ratify part of eight fundamental labour conventions. There are still fifteen Asian countries among the total 23 countries that have not ratified C87 which protects freedom of association, and 11 Asian countries among the total 22 countries that have not ratified C98 which protects right to organize and collective bargaining.[15] As countries of the largest and the second largest population as well as two fast-growing economies, China and India respectively only ratifies 4 and 6 of all eight fundamental labour conventions.

The sharp contrast between rising competitive abilities of international investment and trade and the relatively poor situation of labour standard of Asian countries, especially Asian developing countries, will lead to their counterparts, especially developed countries among them to strengthen labour standard in Asian IIAs. A case in point is labour standard in the TPP which is applied to both trade and investment. Negotiation of labour standard in the TPP is conducted between countries of two extremes in labour standard. One extreme is the US and Canada who put currently the strictest requirement on labour standard in FTAs. The other extreme is Vietnam, Brunei and Malaysia, who are new or weak players of economic globalization and are thought to face great difficulties to improve domestic labour standard.

Originally the negotiation of the TPP's labour standard was dominated by the US based on its labour standard requirement of trade policy and legislation.[16] Labour standard in the TPP transcends all other linkage practices that the US has ever concluded, providing a new benchmark for the linkage practice in Asia and other parts of the world. At least four articles are tailored to current circumstances of Asian developing countries.

First, Article 19.6 of the TPP sets up commitments of contracting parties to discourage importation of goods that are produced by forced labour or that contain inputs produced by forced labour, including forced child labour, regardless of whether the source country is a TPP country. This provision is a direct response to the widely criticized forced labour including forced child labour by transnational civil society groups such as AFL-CIO, and concerns of ILO on the relatively severe situation of forced labour in Asia.[17] Second, Article 19.4 of the TPP emphasizes the uniform application of labour standard to foreign trade zones/export processing zones in the territory of contracting parties. This is to draw lessons from the adverse labour standard effects in free trade zones resulting from the selective promotion of foreign trade and investment policies of some Asian countries, such as Bangladesh, Malaysia and Pakistan (ILO, 1998: 26–27). The ILO reported in 1998 that Pakistan excluded its export processing zones from the scope of the Industrial Relations Ordinance, Pakistan and prohibited all forms of industrial action by Export Processing Zones Authority Ordinance (1980), Pakistan and Export Processing Control of Employment Rules (1982), Pakistan. Third, for the first time, labour standard in the TPP includes annexes of bilateral implementation plans between the US and Asian contracting parties of Vietnam, Brunei and Malaysia, focusing respectively on freedom of association, child and forced labour, minimum wage and collective bargaining. These labour problems are not isolated cases among a few Asian developing countries, and they are widely concerned by other developed countries.

The choice of the US to exit from the TPP is not to devalue the role of its labour standard. Strict and domestically enforceable labour standard has been the consistent trade policy from Obama Government to Trump Government. As stated in the Memorandum For The United State Trade Representative of January 23, 2017, trade agreement negotiations, although shifted from regional arena (such as the TPP) to bilateral basis, will not change the core aim of fair and free trade deals that serve the interests of American people especially America workers. In its 2017 Trade Policy Agenda, Trump Government also reaffirms to continue to promote labour rights as one of the topics relevant to the effort to strengthen economic integration and to continue to support inclusion by APEC economies of labour and social issues in next generation trade agreements. As a consequence, it is reasonable to predict that labour protection in the TPP will be transplanted or even be further strengthened in future FTA or BIT labour standard negotiation in Asian IIAs that the US joins.

Based on the potential impact of the TPP labour standard and the current effective linkage practice from Japan, Austria, BLEU, New Zealand, EFTA, the US, Canada and the EU, five preliminary judgements can be made to future linkage practices of Asian IIAs.

First, dilemma between sovereignty right of labour regulation and cooperation for fair competition and protection of basic workers' right will be more obvious. Owing to the miserable history of being colonized and the priority for development after political independence, developing Asian countries will tend to make more explicit the sovereign right of labour legislation, administration and adjudication. In case of those strict obligations of domestic implementation, such as the not-lowering requirement, effective enforcement of domestic labour law, private action and procedural guarantee, if have to be accepted, these countries might try to argue for more discretion. In the same logic, developing Asian countries will insist no linkage with ratification of un-ratified fundamental labour conventions and other updated labour conventions of ILO.

Second, normative elements of labour standard will be expanded. In face of pressures for stricter linkage from developed countries out of the motive of levelling the playing field, developing Asian countries might try to avoid normative elements of great challenge such as state-state arbitration and economic sanction. Nevertheless, they might choose to accept more obligations of less challenge, such as striving for high level of protection, transparency, public awareness, cooperative activities, inter-governmental institutional arrangements, etc., in order to show political willingness for cooperation. Therefore, more soft normative components of labour standard will appear in future Asian IIAs.

Third, it is possible for developing Asian counties to exclude as much as possible public submission and joint social dialogue mechanism that are initiated by transnational civil society groups including trade unions, because of low ratification rate or criticized implementation ineffectiveness of C87 and C98 of ILO.

Fourth, it is possible for rule of no protectionism to extend to be applied to investment alongside with trade, as developing Asian countries try to seek as much investment competitive advantage over developed countries as possible. This means, rule of no investment protectionism by way of labour standard will be more emphasized than before in future Asian IIAs.

Fifth, intergovernmental arbitration and trade sanction will be the most challenging elements for developing Asian countries, because of a mix of reasons including sovereignty right of social regulation, economic competitiveness, cultural acceptance and so on. If developing Asian countries have to accept such provisions, like what Vietnam, Brunei and Malaysia did in the negotiation of the TPP, they will definitely bargain for additional investment market access or trade concession to balance the possible economic loss in case of non-compliance of labour standard.

4. Influence on Asian investment rules

As the core issue of social policy, labour standard plays a critical role in balancing investment liberalization and social protection. It can be seen from the very first linkage effort in MAI draft, labour standard in IIAs is to respond to concerns of negative effects of investment liberalization on labour protection. Social redistribution through labour protection and social welfare policies has long been considered an issue of domestic jurisdiction since the end of WW II. However, investment liberalization alone does not lead to the improvement of social protection. Conversely, the inborn character of maximizing profits of the capital usually drives investment liberalization at the expense of domestic social protection. In this sense, it is necessary for state governments to improve labour standard and other social policies in exchange for social support for further investment liberalization, as what ILO called, 'to give a humane face to globalization'. Briefly, deficits of national labour protection lead to the desire for labour protection on the international level. Reasons why trade unions of developed countries urge their home countries to link labour standard with IIAs lie not only in levelling the playing field to resume comparative advantage for domestic workers, but also in forcing home countries to effectively enforce domestic labour law. The evolution of investment-labour standard linkage reflects such kind of investment liberalization that workers really expect, and therefore these new normative elements will definitely affect the traditional international investment regime in different aspects.

4.1. Innovation of notion

Compared with IIAs without linkage practice, labour standard in Asian IIAs regards improvement of labour protection as an important social aim of investment liberalization. This broadens the objective of traditional IIAs that only seek to promote investment and protection of investors. In linkage practices of Japan, Austria, the EU, New Zealand and EFTA in Asia, labour standard is regarded by contracting parties as a core part of social pillar of sustainable development, which needs to be supported by the other two pillars of economic development and environment protection. There is nearly no exception that all linkage practices of Asian IIAs regard it an important objective to promote foreign direct investment without lowering or reducing domestic labour standards of contracting parties. In addition, some linkage practices of Asian IIA, such as the EU-Korea FTA, have expressly emphasized to seek investment that favours labour standard. Article13.6 of the EU-Korea FTA recognizes the beneficial role that core labour standards and decent work can have on economic efficiency, innovation and productivity and highlight the value of greater policy coherence between relevant economic policies and employment and labour policies.

4.2. New dimension of fair competition

Traditional IIAs emphasize fair competition mainly from the economic perspective, such as investors' treatment of non-discrimination. By contrast, labour standard in Asian IIAs strengthens fair competition from the social dimension. Labour standard in Asian IIAs has an economic attribute in addition to that of human right. Its economic role is to ensure fair competition. Take core obligations of the not-lowering requirement and effective enforcement as examples. There are two dimensions as to the not-lowering requirement. One is for legislation, which is recognized by all linkage practices of Asian IIAs as inappropriate to encourage investment by lowering the levels of protection afforded in domestic labour law. The other is for implementation, which is required by contracting parties not to waive or derogate from, or offer to waive or derogate from its labour law as an encouragement for the acquisition, the expansion or the retention of an investment of an investor in its territory. In addition to the not-lowering obligation, in some linkage practices such as that of the US, Canada, the EU, New Zealand and EFTA, contracting parties are required not to fail to effectively enforce its labour laws through a sustained or recurring course of action or inaction, in a manner affecting investment between the contracting parties.

Both the not-lowering requirement and effective enforcement obligation in labour standard are expected to ensure four aspects of fair competition. The first aspect is to guarantee fair competition in labour regulation cost as to ensure fair opportunities for inward investment between contracting parties, especially developing contracting parties in IIAs, plurilateral. The second aspect is to ensure national treatment in labour regulation between foreign investors and domestic investors of contracting countries. The third aspect is to ensure the most favoured nation treatment in labour regulation between foreign investors in plurilateral IIAs. The fourth aspect is to level the playing field for workers of contracting parties, especially those who suffer unemployment and weakened labour protection because of domestic enterprises moving to the other contracting parties of lower labour standard.

4.3. New category of investment dispute and remedy mechanism

Traditional investment disputes arising from implementation of IIAs are seldom relevant with labour standard. Among the few cases that involve labour standard, such as *Piero Foresti, Laura de Carli and others v. Republic of South Africa*,[18] the investors claimed against improved labour standard. However, with linkage practices of Asian IIAs, more investment-relevant labour standard disputes will be claimed against lowered labour standard or ineffective enforcement rather than against improved labour standard. A second difference between investment-related labour standard disputes arising from Asian IIAs and traditional investment disputes lies in public participation in the dispute settlement procedure. Traditional investment disputes are mainly investor-initiated, while investment-related labour standard disputes in quite a number of linkage practices of Asian IIAs are initiated by civil society groups.

Dispute settlement procedure under linkage practices of the US and Canada in Asia is initiated by the public submission, mainly by transnational civil society groups that are concerned with labour standard issues. By comparison, under linkage practices of the EU in Asia, investment-relevant labour standard disputes are first resorted to the joint civil society forum. The joint civil society dialogue forum is also empowered to assist the Trade and Sustainable Development Sub-Committees to monitor the implementation of report and recommendations awarded by the expert panel in linkage practices of the EU.

As to linkage practices of Japan, Austria, BLEU, the US and Canada in Asia, economic compensation is the last resort of the complainant country to ensure compliance of the respondent country. In linkage practices of Japan, Austria and BLEU in Asia, the respondent country will also be enforced to pay economic compensation to complainant investors in case of non-compliance of the final award. Obviously in most linkage practices of Asian IIAs, labour standard issues are solved in the logic of economics rather than sociology. By linking labour standard with Asian IIAs, an economic path for transnational labour regulation has been created outside the traditional path of human right protection provided by multilateral labour conventions.

4.4. Impact on the whole investment regime

In general, inclusion of labour standard helps to improve Asian IIAs, but difficulties in subsequent implementation should not be omitted.

4.4.1. Positive impacts

Globally labour standard plays an important role to correct the imbalance problem of international investment regime as a whole, so is in Asia.

First, labour standard plays a vital role to balance rights and obligations between investors and host countries. On the one hand, those countries who are both contracting parties of a particular BIT and the International Covenant on Economic, Social and Cultural Rights have an obligation to respect, promote and realize labour rights and other social rights. On the other hand, investors are given so comprehensive protection that there are possibilities for them to sue against illegal indirect expropriation or unfair and unequal treatment by reason of enhanced labour standard in the host country. Lack of explicit labour standard often drives host countries into a passive defence position in traditional Asian IIAs. Things are expected to change with inclusion of labour standard in Asian IIAs. In linkage practices of Asian IIAs, raising labour standard for domestic workers are not only rights but also obligations of host countries. This will empower host countries to defend or even counterclaim in investor-state disputes.

Second, labour standard helps to balance rights and obligations between host countries and home countries. Protection of investors are the focus obligation of contracting parties in traditional Asian IIAs. As the flow of investment are mainly from the developed to the developing countries, there are few substantial requirements for home countries in traditional Asian IIAs. This imbalance is expected to be corrected gradually as socially responsive investment are emphasized in more and more IIAs. Some linkage practices of Asian IIAs, such as that of Canada and the EU, have included such provision that home countries are obliged to promote their investors to comply with internationally recognized social responsibility initiatives of labour standard. In addition, liberalization of investment not only results in worries with 'race to the bottom' in labour standard between different host countries, but also the downgraded labour protection in home countries because of emigration of multinational companies from home countries of higher labour standard to host countries of lower labour standard. Therefore, raised labour standard in recent Asian IIAs reflect the call of trade unions and other civil society groups for home countries to strengthen their domestic labour standards, where the not-lowering requirement, effective enforcement are the same core obligations as that of host countries.

Third, labour standard is of significance to reconstruct the balance between market, government and society. Investor-state relationships have dominated international investment regime for over half a century since the world's first West Germany-Pakistan BIT, 1959. This belongs to market-government relationship. In linkage practices of Asian IIAs, workers' rights are protected in parallel to that of investors. To ensure the effective performance of labour standard, quite some linkage practices of Asian IIAs, like that of the US, Canada, the EU and New Zealand, have empowered civil society groups, especially representatives of workers or enterprises from contracting parties, to advise domestic labour legislation and relevant policies of contracting parties and to supervise the implementation of labour standard in the agreements. With linkage of labour standard, a social dimension has been built into Asian IIAs. In this new dimension, investment liberalization is embedded in a society where protection of workers' right and effective enforcement of domestic labour law are regarded as one of its basic objectives, and qualified civil society groups have a say in the making and implementation of social policies. In this way, a new balance between market, government and society has been reconstructed in linkage practices of Asian IIAs.

To sum up, labour standard is contributed to rectifying the legality deficit by balancing investment liberalization and social protection, thus making it possible for Asian IIAs to become more balanced and more sustainable.

4.4.2. Difficulties of implementation

Labour standard in Asian IIAs will suffer quite a number of dilemmas because of inevitable defects as normative elements in their initial stage of evolution.

4.4.2.1. VAGUENESS OF OBLIGATION

As to the two core obligations of not lowering requirement and effective enforcement, linkage practices of Austria and most practices of New Zealand (all but the New Zealand-Korea FTA) in Asia only claim that it is inappropriate to encourage an investment by weakening domestic labour laws, without requirement of effective enforcement. It is difficult for such provision to be considered as a full legal obligation, much less its enforceability.

Most other obligations are diluted with phrases like 'strive to', 'promote' and 'encourage' in linkage practices of Asian IIAs. As to linkage practices of New Zealand, the US, Canada and the EU in Asia that are with requirement of including internationally recognized labour rights in domestic labour law, contracting parties are only required to 'strive to include' rather than 'shall include'.

Regarding linkage practices of Canada and the EU that contain social responsibility of labour standard, contracting parties only shoulder obligation of 'promote' rather than 'enforce'. Concerning linkage practices of BLEU, New Zealand, the US, Canada and the EU in Asia that includes cooperative activities, contracting parties only need to 'facilitate' or take it as a right that 'may' conduct or choose not to conduct.

4.4.2.2. INADEQUATE PRECISION

With regard to linkage practices of Japan, BLEU, EFTA, the US and Canada in Asia that contain mandatory obligation of the not-lowering or effective enforcement, only that of Canada contains detailed items as to what belongs to effective enforcement. No linkage practice of Asian IIAs clarifies what essential elements are needed to judge 'effective enforcement'. Linkage practices of the US in Asia try to make it clear what constitute 'effective enforcement' by setting conditions of 'through a sustained or recurring course of action or inaction, in a manner affecting trade or investment between the Parties' and 'the distribution of enforcement resources shall not be a reason for not complying with the provisions of this Chapter',[19] but new problems arise as to what is 'sustained or recurring', how many times or period can be taken as 'course', what means 'in a manner affecting investment', etc.

Definition of domestic labour law is critical to increase the precision of core obligations of the not-lowering requirement and effective enforcement. No definition is provided in linkage practices of New Zealand and EFTA in Asia. Japan only provides the definition of domestic labour law in its FTA with the Philippines. Only three out of five linkage practices of BLEU in Asia provide the definition of domestic labour law.

Furthermore, different definitions exist in different styles of linkage practice, ranging from four labour standards similar to that of ILO core labour standard like the practice of the EU, to 'ILO core labour standard plus' like the practices of Austria, the US and Canada and to standards that overlap with ILO core labour standard like the practice of Japan and BLEU. Implication of each item of labour standard is not identical since its explanation depends on domestic labour law of individual contracting party, without uniform criteria.

4.4.2.3. DILEMMAS OF REMEDY

There will be a dilemma of remedy as to whether violation of labour standard should resort to economic sanction or not and how to measure it in subsequent implementation of labour standard in Asian IIAs. Some linkage practices of Asian IIAs, such as that of Austria, Japan, BLEU, the US and Canada, have integrated the remedy of investment-related labour standard disputes between contracting parties or between investors and host states with that of traditional investment disputes. How can a scientific, monetary assessment of the violation be made? Will it be based on deficiency of enforcement resources or the loss suffered by the non-violating contracting party because of the unfair competition advantage gained by the violating contracting party? Should monetary assessment be used to cover the loss of the winning party or to make up the deficiency of labour protection of the losing party? It is really a challenge to draw a reasonable balance as there seem to be internal conflicts between protection of basic workers' right and fair competition of investment.

In short, labour standard in Asian IIAs is fragmented because of no uniform criteria of interpretation, different extent of clarity of obligation and dilemma of remedy measures. These fragmented social elements make the international investment regime that is already so complicated by a composite of 3,328 IIAs,[20] more fragmented. Similarly, it is easy to foresee implementation difficulties from fragmentation of both economic and social elements in Asian IIAs.

5. Possibility of linkage in the future FTAAP investment regime

5.1. *Potential labour standard issues in FTAAP*

The initiative of the Free Trade Area of the Asia-Pacific (FTAAP) is aimed to promote regional economic integration of Asian and the Pacific, who is home to 40% of the world's population, produces 48% of international trade and 57% of global GDP. If realized, FTAAP is expected to provide the largest economic liberalization in Asian history. Supported by the US, FTAAP was first built formally into APEC Leaders' Declaration as a vision in the 18th APEC Ministerial Meeting in Hanoi in 2006. The initiative has gained much wider support ever since then and progresses steadily. In 2010, APEC leaders issued 'Pathways to FTAAP' and instructed APEC to make contributions as an incubator toward the realization of FTAAP. In 2014, the vision of FTAAP is translated into concrete steps as the landmark 'Beijing Roadmap' establishes common views for APEC members to follow. Initiative of FTAAP is supported by the US and China, two largest economies in the world, Chinese President Xi Jinping even announces to ratify 'Beijing Roadmap' in 2014. With a solid basis of the political will of members, APEC 2016 Leaders' Declaration moves further by endorsing the 'Collective Strategic Study' on issues Related to FTAAP. Despite its preliminary and vague status, some normative elements on labour standard can be observed based on commitments and current linkage practices of APEC members.

First, investment-relevant labour standard issues will come into consideration, as FTAAP seeks to do more than achieving liberalization in its narrow sense. APEC members agree in 'Beijing Roadmap' to head for a comprehensive, high quality and incorporate integration and to address 'next generation' trade and investment issues. Linkage between investment and labour standard has been an obvious trend,[21] and is widely recognized as a significant component of 'next generation' trade and investment agreements. Furthermore, investment-relevant labour standard has reached its peak in strictness in the TPP, which is recognized by APEC members to be a possible pathway to FTAAP in Lima Declaration on

Free Trade Area of the Asia-Pacific of 2016. It is seldom denied that rules of the TPP including labour standard will have an important influence on the reconstruction of trade and investment rules of 21st century, regardless of the choice of the US to leave or to return. In this sense, it is difficult for investment-labour standard linkage to be evaded in the evolution of FTAAP.

Second, APEC members has committed in Leaders' Declaration of 2016 to strengthen efforts to ensure decent work and work life quality for all, especially socially vulnerable groups. APEC members commit to achieve these social goals by providing access to quality inclusive education and vocational training; boosting entrepreneurship; improving social protection; and enhancing regional cooperation. These common views directly or incorrectly relating to labour protection have laid necessary foundation for future labour standard provisions.

Third, it is necessary for FTAAP to learn lessons from the negotiation of MAI and experiences from the negotiation of FTAA (the Free Trade Area of the Americas) in investment-labour standard linkage. The abortion of MAI was mainly resulted from the opposition of stakeholders, especially the civil society, who blame governments for not reimbursing the social and environmental disruption created by the increasing mobility of capital. Although labour standard was added to the draft MAI in 1998, the vague and loose social promises were finally proved to dissatisfy the civil society.

On the contrary, across the Pacific, active attitude towards the linkage of investment-labour standard is critical to social acceptance of FTAA negotiation. In the first draft of 2001, there is no linkage in FTAA either. Under the pressure of the civil society, contracting parties begin to include two elements for linkage in the second draft of 2002. The first element is a commitment not to relax domestic labour laws to attract investment. The second element is a precondition of compensating access to the Regional Integration Fund for the training of workers on the promise not to relax domestic labour laws by small economies. The linkage of investment and labour standard is strengthened greatly in the third draft of FTAA, which not only reserves in its investment chapter the two elements of the 2002 draft, but also includes a special chapter. This special chapter of labour in FTAA draft of 2003 was based on labour standard requirement of 2002 Trade Act of the US and therefore is similar to the linkage practice of FTAs that the US has concluded with Chile, Singapore, Australia, Morocco, Bahrain, Oman and Central American countries, which have been negotiated according to this Act. Dominance of the linkage style of the US in FTAA is a reflection of concerns that this kind of linkage had better consider the concerns of the civil society, especially those of the key contracting parties that have great impact on the ratification of an economic agreement in domestic congress. The same logic is applied to the ultimate realization of FTAAP.

5.2. Possible linkage style

Substantial negotiation of FTAAP is yet to start. Despite this situation, some preliminary and anticipatory observations can be made based on the general trend of investment-labour standard linkage in Asian IIAs and the progress of FTAAP initiative. All linkage styles existing in Asia IIAs except that of Austria, BLEU and the EU are going to compete with each other in the negotiation of labour standard in FTAAP, as the original contracting parties of FTAAP are confined as members of APEC including these countries. The relatively consistent and stable linkage policy of the US, Canada, Japan and New Zealand and domestic civil society groups in these countries will have a great impact on negotiation of labour standard in FTAAP. However, driven by the principle of sovereign right and policy of priority for development, most developing Asian and Pacific countries including China and India, will possibly be reluctant to accept strict linkage practice such as that of the US and Canada. In this case, three preliminary observations can be drawn as follows.

First, based on the negotiation principle of 'by consensus' and the principal objective of 'removing investment and trade barrier' in 'Beijing Roadmap' of FTAAP, concerns of developing countries, such as no usage of labour standard for investment and trade protectionism, sovereign right of labour regulation, adequate policy space for effective enforcement and implementation capacity building, shall not be omitted.

Second, it is both a challenge and an opportunity to find how to avoid the problem of fragmentation in the negotiation of labour standard in FTAAP. As is stated in 'Beijing Roadmap', FTAAP should aim to minimize any negative effects resulting from the proliferation of regional and bilateral RTAs/FTAs and will be pursued by building on current and developing regional architectures. Challenges exist in integration of diversified linkage styles of Asian IIAs, as different extent of clarity of obligation, precision and delegation are usually the result of the bargaining among negotiating parties. Nevertheless, there is an opportunity for FTAAP to agglomerate the greatest consensus between countries of the strictest linkage practice (such as the US) and countries with most opposed attitude (such as India). Currently India is actively engaging in the FTA negotiation with Canada, who has consistent linkage practice nearly as strict as that of the US. There is a possibility for India to step forward to accept the labour standard negotiation of FTAAP.

Third, based on the second observation, if FTAAP is to bridge the divergence between negotiating parties of different level of development, three critical questions should be first discussed. One is 'whether the dominant function of labour standard should be moral or economic'. Different answers to the question will lead to different extent of obligation and precision. If labour standard is considered to be dominantly moral in order to be consistent with multilateral labour conventions, then contracting parties only need to shoulder the obligation of respect, promotion and gradual realization. In such case, low extent of clarity and precision of obligation might be needed to reserve enough flexibility for contracting parties. However, if labour standard is regarded as of prevailing economic character, then greater external pressure will be needed to ensure compliance, and greater extent of clarity and precision of obligation will be required accordingly.

The other is 'what is the aim of remedy for violation'. Answers to the question will affect the extent of delegation. In case a remedy is taken to strengthen the capacity of the violating contracting party, then there is no need for contracting parties to resort to a third party arbitration or expert panel to solve disputes. If a remedy is aimed to effective enforcement of domestic labour law so as to ensure fair competition between contracting parties, then a neutral third party dispute settlement body is necessary to ensure the violation to be ascertained and corrected. Still another is 'What role ILO can play in treaty interpretation and dispute settlement?'. This is a question of whether integration of international labour standard under both the framework of multilateral labour conventions and the framework of Asian IIAs could help to solve the problem of fragmentation or not.

6. Conclusion

All linkage styles existing in Asian IIAs except that of Austria, BLEU and the EU are going to compete with each other in the negotiation of labour standard in FTAAP. Before the ultimate realization of FTAAP, four main styles of linkage from Japan, Austria and BLEU; New Zealand and the EFTA; the US and Canada; and the EU will continue to compete with each other to construct or reconstruct the linkage style of Asian IIAs. The linkage practice of Asian IIAs are valuable efforts to correct deficits of legality in the global investment regime, but more work have to be done to respond to difficulties arising from vagueness of obligation, inadequate precision and dilemmas of remedy.

Notes

* This chapter is supported by the National Social Science Foundation of China (Grant No. 17BFX217). My gratitude goes to the State Scholarship Fund of China for the opportunity to survey in Cornell University Industrial and Labor Relationship School of USA for this chapter.
1 This figure of linkage does not cover a few BITs that are concluded in non-English language. Countries or separate customs unions with linkage practice are East Asian countries or regions (China, Hong Kong, Mongolia, Korea, Japan); Southeast Asian countries (the Philippines, Vietnam, Myanmar, Thailand, Malaysia, Brunei, Singapore); South Asian countries (Bangladesh); Central Asian (Kazakhstan, Kyrgyzstan, Tajikistan, Uzbekistan); and West Asian countries (Iraq, Iran, Jordan, Bahrain, Qatar, Kuwait, The United Arab Emirates, Oman, Yemen, Georgia, Armenia, Azerbaijan, Turkey).
2 The figure is from UNCTAD database of international investment agreements, excluding those terminated.
3 Among the 18 Austrian BITs, the other contracting parties are 9 Asian Countries (Bangladesh, Kazakhstan, Kyrgyzstan, Tajikistan, Jordan, Yemen, Georgia, Armenia, Azerbaijan) and 9 non-Asian Countries (Bosnia and Herzegovina, Belize, Macedonia, Slovenia, Malta, Namibia, Nigeria, Cuba, Guatemala).
4 Art. 5(2) of the 2008 Austrian Model BIT.
5 According to Art. 5(2) of the 2008 Austrian Model BIT, those that can be defined as labour law are statutes or regulations directly relating to six items of labour standard:

a. the right of association;
b. the right to organize and to bargain collectively;

144 *Zheng Lizhen*

    c. a prohibition on the use of any form of forced or compulsory labour;

    d. labour protections for children and young people, including a minimum age for the employment of children and the prohibition and elimination of the worst forms of child labour[;]

    e. acceptable conditions of work with respect to minimum wages, hours of work, and occupational safety and health[; and]

    f. elimination of discrimination in employment and occupation.

6 This figure of linkage does not include a few BITs that are concluded in non-English languages.

7 The exceptions are three BITs between BLEU and the United Arab Emirates, Panama and Oman.

8 All linkage practices of the EFTA have the requirement of effective domestic enforcement. Most linkage practice of New Zealand has no such requirement, but the latest effective New Zealand-Korea FTA has strengthened this point by requiring contracting parties not to fail to effectively enforce their labour laws through a sustained or recurrent action or inaction, in a manner affecting trade or investment between the parties.

9 For example, the linkage practice of the New Zealand-Korea FTA states that the operation and enforcement of its labour laws, regulations, policies and practices, including administrative, quasi-judicial or judicial tribunals, are appropriately accessible by persons with a recognized interest under its law, transparent, fair and equitable.

10 US-Uruguay BIT (2006) and USA-Rwanda BIT(2012).

11 As UN members, all the countries with linkage practice in Asian IIAs recognize the mutually supported of three dimensions of sustainable development, i.e. social development, environmental development and economic development, see UN, The Future We Want: Final Document of the Rio+20 Conference, 2012, A/CONF.216/L.1.

12 The content in the brackets of the draft provisions shows where consensus has not been reached by contracting parties.

13 European Commission, Trade for All: Towards a More Responsible Trade and Investment Policy, 2015.

14 AFL-CIO, ETUC Urge Exclusion of Public Services in Joint TTIP Declaration, Inside USA. Trade, July 11, 2014.

15 The 15 Asian countries that have not ratified C87 are Afghanistan, Bahrain, Brunei, China, India, Iran, Korea, Laos, Myanmar, Oman, Qatar, Saudi Arabia, Thailand, United Arab Emirates, Vietnam; the 11 Asian countries that have not ratify C98 are India, Iran, Korea, Laos, Myanmar, Oman, Qatar, Saudi Arabia, Thailand, United Arab Emirates and Vietnam.

16 Bipartisan Agreement of May10, 2007, and Trade Promotion Act of 2015.

17 Among the nine countries that have not ratified C29 (abolition of forced labour), four are from Asia, i.e. Afghanistan, Brunei, China and Korea. Among the ten countries that have not ratified C105, six are from Asia, i.e. Brunei, China, Korea, Japan, Laos and Myanmar.

18 ICSID Case No. ARB(AF)/07/1. The issue in dispute concerning labour standard is whether the new legislations (the Mineral and Petroleum Resources Development Act and the Mining Charter)which improve social protection for historically disadvantaged South Africans, have breached the prohibitions on expropriation in the Italy-South Africa BIT.

19 Art.19.3.1 of the US-Korea FTA.

20 Based on UNCTAD data as of 22 May 2017.

21 Linkage between investment and labour standard is on the rise as more developed countries apply linkage policies universally and more developing countries

join the linkage team. Under the framework of BITs alone, the rate of linkage between 2010 and 2014 is already 40%.The ratio will be much higher since more investment-labour standard linkage appears under the framework of FTAs. International Labour Office, Assessment of labour provisions in trade and investment arrangements, ILO Publication, 2016.

References

Abbott, K. W., Keohane, R. O., Moravcsik, A., et al. (2000). The Concept of Legalization. *International Organization*, 54(3), 405–406.

Bernasconi-Osterwalder, N. and Johnson, L. (2011). *Commentary to the Austrian Model Investment Treaty*, IISD Report.

Canada-Korea FTA (2015). https://international.gc.ca/trade-commerce/trade-agreements-accords-commerciaux/agr-acc/korea-coree/index.aspx?lang=eng

Canada-Peru FTA (2009). https://international.gc.ca/trade-commerce/trade-agreements-accords-commerciaux/agr-acc/peru-perou/fta-ale/background-contexte.aspx?lang=eng

Canner, S. J. (1998). The Multilateral Agreement on Investment. *Cornell International Law Journal*, 31, 676.

Export Processing Zones Authority Ordinance (1980) and Export Processing Zones Control of Employment Rules (1982). https://www.ilo.org/dyn/natlex/natlex4.detail?p_lang=en&p_isn=50073&p_country=PAK&p_count=490&p_classification=01&p_classcount=138

Hall, P. and Soskice, D. (2001). *Varieties of Capitalism: The Institutional Foundations of Comparative Advantage*, Oxford: Oxford University Press.

Hepple, B. (2005). *Labour Laws and Global Trade*, Oxford: Hart Publishing.

ILO (1998). Labour and Social Issues Relating to Export Processing Zones (Report for Discussion at the Tripartite Meeting of Export Processing Zones – Operating Countries),TMEPZ/1998: 26–27.

ILO Tripartite Declaration of Principles Concerning Multinational Enterprises and Social Policy. https://www.ilo.org/empent/areas/mne-declaration/lang--en/index.htm.

Maul, D. (2012). *Human Rights, Development and Decolonization: The International Labour Organization, 1940–70*, Hampshire: Palgrave Macmillan.

NAFTA (1994). https://ustr.gov/trade-agreements/free-trade-agreements/north-american-free-trade-agreement-nafta.

OECD Guidelines for Multinational Enterprises. http://mneguidelines.oecd.org/guidelines/.

Valticos, N. and Potobsky, G. W. (1995). *International Labour Law*, Geventer: Kluwer Law and Taxation Publisher.

UN Global Compact Full Principle. https://www.unglobalcompact.org/.

UN Guiding Principles on Business and Human Rights. https://www.unglobalcompact.org/library/2.

7 In the habit of giants

Fair and equitable treatment and structural risk factors in conglomerate-led newly industrialized countries

Soo-Hyun Lee

1. Introduction

Abrupt changes in the world, whether they be technological innovation or socio-political upheaval, can find themselves ensnared by an inelastic regulatory system – for better or for worse. This chapter deals with the same issue but with reversed roles: a legal system in metamorphosis stymied by an economy that is structurally obstinate towards change. The central role that conglomerates played in the newly industrialized countries (NICs) of Asia were built on fraternal ties with a paternal State. In economies such as those of South Korea with the *chaebol* and Japan with the *zaibatsu*, the centrality of conglomerates continues to this day, both economically and socioeconomically.

Conglomerates are thoroughly engrained in these economies, representing a large portion of national income, employment and even national identity. The governments of such economies are then left facing a fundamental conflict. Intervening on behalf of these conglomerates using public policy interventions not only encourages them to engage in further risk-taking behaviour, but also shall have rising costs on the rule of law and the public finance needed for such interventions. These costs become even more exacting if these risk factors are left unaddressed amidst trends of growing economic integration, such as through international investment agreements (IIAs). Conversely, should governments no longer intervene on behalf of these economic giants, the socioeconomic impacts of their fall are harrowing. This chapter elaborates on that conflict by identifying risk factors in connection to: (1) attributes intrinsic to these conglomerates, such as risk-taking behaviour and (2) policy interventions made on their behalf. Yet with greater integration into global value chains, this chapter identifies risk factors arising from characteristic features of such economies as they relate to fair and equitable treatment (FET) and legitimate expectations. The urgency involved in resolving this conflict can best be identified in the continued rise of investor-State disputes (ISD) in Asia.

2. FET

When admitting a foreign investment, the recipient State is obligated to follow a minimum standard of treatment (MST) towards the foreign nationals and their assets. Underlying this due diligence to such MST are the guarantees agreed upon in IIAs such as inter alia bilateral investment treaties (BITs) or a binding contract between the parties involved. These obligations are construed through good faith interpretation and object and purpose of those agreements as enshrined in the Vienna Convention on the Law of Treaties (VCLT). MST protects foreign investors from directly or indirectly adversarial treatment by the State as a matter of international law. One concept associated to MST has been FET, which protects foreign investors from direct, indirect expropriation and/or creeping expropriation and also serves to protect legitimate expectations. Should the investor have reasonable cause to believe that the State has not been acting in accordance with those obligations, then they may choose to pursue legal action through international dispute settlement, such as investor-State dispute settlement (ISDS). While the types of obligations vary based on the specific IIA, the State is obliged to provide certain assurances, or standards of protection, to the investor to the extent that the treaty, agreement or other instrument of international law so dictates or is interpreted as provisioning by object or purpose (Van Harten, 2010). Of the three standards of protection common to international law – FET, the national treatment principle and full protection and security – this chapter deals with FET.

The concept of FET in relation to investment first appeared in the middle of the 20th Century, which was a time that gave rise to many key international legal mechanisms that comprise today's international trade and investment regulatory system, such as the North American Free Trade Agreement (1992) and the Energy Charter Treaty (1994). NAFTA Article 1105 illustrates standard inclusion of the clause: *Each party shall accord investments of investors of another Party treatment in accordance with international law, including fair and equitable treatment and full protection and security.* In spite of its wide inclusion in many international investment agreements including bilateral investment treaties, the FET clause remains broad in its interpretation: does the FET put in place a minimum standard of treatment that that is universal and inviolable? Alternatively, does FET depend on the circumstances of the case, avoiding any internationally standardized threshold?

Opinions even within the practice of law remain split. A decision made in 2009 by the World Bank Group's International Centre on the Settlement of Investment Disputes (ICSID), *Azurix Corp v. The Argentine Republic,* viewed FET as setting a "floor" in terms of a minimum standard of treatment as a means to prevent interpretation from falling below a certain standard. This was of the opinion that such a minimum standard is identifiable in terms of international law. Meanwhile, a separate ruling made in 2004, *Waste Management, Inc. v. United Mexican States ("Number 2"),* described FET as being an open-ended standard that must be interpreted in light of the circumstances of each individual case since the range of possibilities were too many, rendering broad generalizations inapplicable. Furthermore, in *Merrill & Ring Forestry L.P. v. Government of Canada,* the Tribunal introduced a FET, dynamic interpretation on the basis of past rulings. They meant that FET as a standard of customary international law would change over time as more IIAs are ratified. States change their practices involving foreign investments and as different arbitral tribunals deliberate disputed matters in different ways. This dynamic interpretation of, or additive approach to, FET over decades of being considered and implemented by legal professionals and scholars has become not only more accepted as a principle of international law, but also as a cause for contestation in the courtroom.

At the heart of this debate is whether there should be set expectations that an investor can hold in relation to a recipient State as well as whether those expectations are adaptable to different circumstances. Furthermore, how do obligations within other agreements between the host and recipient States interact with IIAs and ultimately on regulating the due diligence of the State as well as protections for the foreign investor – a widely debated topic involving umbrella clauses?

Such questions are especially timely in Asia, not only because of the increase of interest in IIA dispute settlement within Asian countries, but also because countries like China, Japan and Korea as well as the other first generation Asian NICs have a similar economic legacy that involve close ties between the government and national corporations. The free reign given to such corporations have indubitably left a lasting structural impact in these countries, in part due to the fact their respective governments employed policy measures to, in many ways, sustain their rapid growth. Yet as these economies more openly embrace international investment superstructures and governance regimes, they also join into a fraternity of States that seek to prevent such a deep involvement of the State. The question then becomes how prepared are these States to join the neoliberal cohort? In exploring these topics, this chapter examines by way of example the implications of disputes in Korea as well as suggests potential policy countermeasures for these countries as they further engage in the ISDS regime.

3. Owner risk

Newly industrialized countries (NICs), especially early generation NICs like South Korea, have shown to bear comparatively larger risks attributable to *dirigiste* relationships between the State and business. A coherent and holistic policy approach towards international investment law ensures that the growth of a legal market that is compatible with that relationship while nurturing the rule of law. Taking after arbitration booms in Singapore and Hong Kong, the general approach in Korea has been to try to make the country into an "international arbitration hub" due to its geographical centrality (Lee, 2016) and more frequent involvement in ISDS. One way to achieve this end has been to increasingly open the country's legal market in order to attract foreign IIA experts. The *Foreign Legal Consultant Act, Korea*, pursuant to free trade agreements with the European Union and the United States, removes restrictions placed on foreign law firms and attorneys to practice in Korea. As a result, foreign firms specializing in ISDS can then more easily leverage their considerable financial and human capital advantages over domestic firms, potentially crowding out Korean law firms. This has been the trend for mergers and acquisitions with six out of every ten cases represented by a foreign firm (Kim, 2016).

In that context, the first risk factor addressed in this work is "owner risk", which is representative towards general risk factors associated to the intrinsic qualities of NIC conglomerates, particularly in South Korea. Before converging into larger systems of investment regulation and dispute settlement, Korea must take into consideration such potential risk factors. Failure to do so can mean that the type of liberalization currently underway in Korea can in fact constrain the government's manoeuvrability in pursuing existing public policy goals as well as responding to new challenges.

3.1. Owner risk: accountability

Accountability continues to be one of the most persistent challenges in Korea. While the heyday of Korean conglomerates heads sitting down with government ministers to design the economy behind closed doors may have passed, corporations continue to maintain close ties with the State. Both the existence and scale of such ties have been reaffirmed by such recent debacles as Samsung and Choi Soon-sil, resulting in the impeachment and imprisonment of former President Park Geun-hye, as well as the persistence of government lifelines to zombie companies. The latter of these has been a recurring problem for the country since its early years of rapid growth from the 1960s. The YTN news agency reported that between 2014 and 2016, 68 companies listed on the Korean Stock Price Index (KOSPI), or 10.7% of all listed companies, qualified as zombie companies. This includes major units within Korean conglomerates such as Daewoo Shipbuilding & Marine Engineering, which has the largest debt-to-income ratio; Hyundai Merchant Marine; and Samsung Biologics (Hahm, 2017). According to a statement by the minister of SMEs and startups in 2015, there were 557 support programmes available to small- to medium-sized enterprises. This was despite the fact that there was a rapid increase in corporate debt starting in 2012 as well as reports of abuse (Son and Song, 2015; Kim and Lee, 2010).

Lacking transparency and accountability have shown to cultivate crisis in Korea. When these crises mature in full-blown disasters, their impacts magnify at a geometric scale, threatening shareholder assets. An ISDS initiation by the US hedge fund Elliot Associates in 2018 for losses arising out of a succession of power from Samsung head Lee Kun-hee to his son Lee Jae-yong that took the form of a merger between two Samsung business units testifies to such risks. The *ratione materiae* of the Elliot appeal to ISDS was based on the involvement of the South Korean government through the National Pension Service, Korea, which used its shareholder rights to vote in favour of the merger. Unsuccessful negotiations concerning losses to Elliot Associates regarding compensation bloomed into the initiation of ISDS procedures in 2018 July (Park, 2018).

As is, ISDS and the conglomerates of Korea are propped up together on a foundation that is made tenuous by their cohabitation. The rapid development of ISDS systems and a conservative base of conglomerates are two features that shall inevitably clash. One such potential conflict resulting from a lack of accountability is "owner risk". A recent study by *CEOSCORE*, a management appraisal system based on data analysis, helps shed some light on this issue. Their study showed that employees working in the top fifty companies of Korea with some sort of familial tie with the founding generation of the company enjoyed rapid promotions to executive roles (Jung, 2017). Called the "golden spoon" generation, they are the third to fifth generation descendants of first or second generation founders and heads of these firms. While a regular employee took an average of 24 years to reach the wuthering heights of a company, the golden spoon generation took an average of 4 years and 2 months to attain an executive position. The data showed a trend of this generation reaching an executive position by 29 to 33 years-of-age and then reaching a director or CEO position by 42.

Nepotistic hiring and vertical movement structures fan the flames of accountability risk by placing the golden spoon generation into executive positions despite their higher propensity for risk-taking behaviour (Lee, 2017). This often involves personal or familial scandals ranging from illicit activities like tax evasion and graft to feuds over inheritance (with "nuttier" variations here and again). In more widely recognized terms, accountability risk is a form of reputational risk to firms. In its *2014 Global Risk Survey, Reputation@Risk*, Deloitte assessed that a negative reputation event resulted in considerable losses in company earnings and brand value and frequently results in regulatory investigations for companies in the Asia-Pacific with one of the largest stakeholders being investors (Deloitte, 2014: 12). Such regulatory investigations may provide *ratione materiae* for a foreign investor to raise violations of FET under the protections entitled under a relevant bilateral or multilateral treaty, as was the case in *LSF-KEB v. Korea*. The poor performance of a company with foreign shareholders as a result of actions of the host State does not permit the shareholder to pursue claims against the host State, though this depends on the wording of the presiding international investment agreement as was ruled in the *Barcelona Traction* case. However, as demonstrated in *GAMI v. Mexico*, explicit interference by the State that affects the value of shareholding in the company can be interpreted as an expropriation.

Lacking transparency and accountability have shown to cultivate crisis in Korea. When these crises mature in full-blown disasters, their impacts magnify at a geometric scale, threatening shareholder assets. An ISDS initiation by the US hedge fund Elliot Associates in 2018 for losses arising out of a succession of power from Samsung head Lee Kun-hee to his son Lee Jae-yong that took the form of a merger between two Samsung business units testifies to this such risk. The *ratione materiae* of the Elliot appeal to ISDS was based on the involvement of the South Korean government through the National Pension Service, which used its shareholder rights to vote in favour of the merger. Unsuccessful negotiations concerning losses to Elliot Associates regarding compensation bloomed into the initiation of ISDS procedures in July 2018 (Park, 2018).

Owner risk is intensifying in Korea and very well may hit catastrophic heights in coming years. As the average age of the executives (first to second generation) of Korea's largest conglomerates reached 76 (Dong, 2014), passing the mantle to the next generation is unlikely to occur without upset. As a result of the on-going

Lotte Group family feud, for instance, conflict over control of the conglomerate-led to a loss of KRW 1.5tn (USD 1.3bn) in stock value over 20 days after the fight for ownership was first announced, with a KRW 1.74tn (USD 1.51bn) loss in stock value for Lotte Chemicals (Japan) alone (Lee, 2015).

The State will have to assess and prepare for the impacts of many more such cases on not only the economy, but also in relation to FET and legitimate expectations for investors. For instance, if Korea does not permit the transfer of Lotte Group units in Korea to Japan due to its macroeconomic impacts under the pretext of a regulatory investigation, Lotte Group Japan may then prepare to appeal that decision through ISDS should its efforts be frustrated by domestic legal institutions. Given the vast geographical diversity of operations for a Korean conglomerate, an especially hostile family feud may easily play host to transfers of power over even wider distances and across many more borders.

Accountability risk cannot be approached *post-facto*, when the crisis has already bloomed and cripples the company's operations and performance. Unfortunately, this has often been the case (Roh, 2017). In such circumstances, foreign investors who feel their assets are at risk may experience delays or even holds on making decisions concerning their investments for matters like on-going investigations or other matters mandated by executive order.

In relation to international investment law, accountability risk begs the question of the extent of the State's good faith observation of its treaty obligations. In circumstances where the State is directly involved in the loss of shareholder value or a foreign investor is denied the protections and rights guaranteed to them by treaty, the investor may raise claim for indirect or creeping expropriation by the State. Alternatively, if the government is proven to extend favourable treatment to a domestic corporation in violation of the national treatment principle as defined in the General Agreements on Tariffs and Trade (GATT) Article 3 as well as in bilateral treaties between States (Article 11.3 of KORUS).

3.2. Owner risk: conglomerates acting on public interest

In the first-known ISDS case mentioned earlier in this chapter, involving a shrimp farm destroyed by Tamil Tigers, the tribunal overseeing proceedings observed that Sri Lankan security forces had taken all possible measures to prevent damages to the shrimp farm. The idea of a minimum standard of treatment (MST) for investments, which include full protection and security (FPS), continues to be a common feature of bilateral and multilateral investment treaties. Korea is no exception to such standards: China-Japan-Korea trilateral Investment Agreement, Art. 5(1)[1] and KORUS FTA, Art. 11.5[2] of KORUS. While there is little precedence to provide clear guidance on this issue, the International Institute for Sustainable Development observed (Malik, 2011) that the interpretation of this standard as either being purely related to physical security or taking on more expansive interpretations, such as was decided in *Biwater Gauff v. Tanzania*

2008, para. 729: "a State's guarantee of stability in a secure environment, both physical, commercial and legal".

One development seen in Korea has been a conglomerate acting on behalf of the State for matters related to the public interest (national security) that resulted in material injury. One illustrative example includes a decision by the Lotte Group to allow the government to deploy the Terminal High Altitude Area Defence (THAAD) missile system on its Seongju golf course in a land swap amidst objection by China (Reuters, 2017a). The fallout of the decision was so pronounced that it became known as "THAAD retribution", with Lotte seeing halts on construction projects in China and the closure of retail stores in China, both due to fire safety violations (Kim, Chang and Chan, 2018). The impacts of THAAD retribution were not limited to Lotte, reaching the point where South Korea began initiations for trade-restrictive measures to be investigated by the WTO, though ultimately no action was taken (Won, 2017).

Depending on the interpretation of full protection and security, one basis on which a foreign investor may seek compensation for a loss of assets can be a lack of due diligence on the part of the Korean government to protect foreign investors and their assets. As geopolitics continue to fluctuate and uncertainty presents itself, the question of proportionality shall inevitably play an important role in assessing the balance between the measure taken and their impacts on the threshold of due diligence that the country is prepared to guarantee, especially as investment inflows grow larger in scale. One way to pursue this examination of proportionality may be political risk ratings. While most ratings agencies typically cite the recurrence of boom-and-bust cycles in North-South tensions as well as South Korea's alliance with China and the United States as stabilizing geopolitical risk (Lee, 2016), unpredictability in all of those factors cannot be overlooked. Major trade and credit insurance agencies like Charles Schwab (Kleintop, 2016) and Euler Hermes (Euler Hermes, 2016) have already been deepening the weights of geopolitical risk on ratings since 2016, diverging from more common assessments including the World Bank's *Doing Business* evaluation.

4. State intervention and FET in Korea

In relation to Korea, its position in international investment regimes has been a topic of great concern from the start of its first investor-State dispute settlement (ISDS), *Lone Star Funds-Korea Exchange Bank (LSF-KEB) Holdings SCA and others v. Republic of Korea* dispute (hereinafter, "*LSF-KEB v. Korea*"). The *LSF-KEB v. Korea* case involves an investment in and an eventual acquisition of the Korean Exchange Bank (KEB) by the American private equity firm Lone Star Funds through a subsidiary firm LSF-KEB Holdings SCA, a company registered in Belgium as partnership limited by shares representing a group of investors. While Banking Act, Korea, Art. 15 limited a single entity from holding an excess of 10/100 of the total number of issued voting stocks of a financial institution, LSF-KEB Holdings SCA was exempt from this restriction by the Financial Supervisory Commission (FSC) of Korea in September 2003. This decision was based on an assessment by the FSC that permitting the acquisition of KEB would "contribute to the efficiency and soundness of the banking business" in accordance to *Banking Act* Article 15(5). The FSC further assessed that KEB was an "insolvent financial institute" as defined by Act on the Structural Improvement of the Financial Industry, Korea, Art. 3(2). Yet the basis on which the FSC made this assessment was based on data that was later suspected of falsification, which set the Bank of International Settlements (BIS) capital adequacy ratio (CAR) of KEB at 6.2%, falling short of the internationally accepted minimum of 8% of assets to cover potential losses. Korean State intervention became as notorious as to christen the so-called "Korea discount" (Economist, 2012).

LSF-KEB SCA began its attempts to sell its shares in January 2006, though its efforts were frustrated in every attempt until 2012. When it was permitted to unload its shares to the Hana Financial Group (Korea) for KRW 3.9tn (3.43bn in current USD), it was at a steep contrast to the KRW 6.3tn (8.18bn in current USD) offered by Kookmin Bank (Korea) in 2006 or the KRW 5.9tn (5.2bn in current USD) offered by HSBC in 2007. The FSC delayed approval of the sale under claims of on-going prudential and tax investigations until HSBC eventually rescinded its offer in 2008 given the increasingly bleak conditions of the world financial system. A group of six Belgian investors including LSF-KEB Holdings SCA submitted its request for arbitration to the International Centre for the Settlement of Investment Disputes (ICSID) in December 2012 under claims that it was subject to "repeated acts of harassment" as well as "arbitrary and contradictory tax assessments" that resulted in "billions of euros in damages" (Thomson, 2012).

These regulatory delays were argued to have violated FET pursuant to Article 2(2) of the Belgium Luxembourg European Union–Korea bilateral investment treaty (BLEU-Korea BIT). Notable here is that LSF-KEB Holdings SCA is a paper company, or a conduit company, that was established to "treaty-shop", which is an abusive practice used by firms to either enjoy the benefits of a tax haven or have a disputed matter fall into the remit of an international agreement that they believe will be favourable to their side. In this case, that was the BLEU-Korea BIT. The second claim raised by LSF-KEB Holdings SCA fully exploited this standard of protection, which was that it was impermissible under the BLEU-Korea BIT for Korea to apply a transfer tax in the sale of KEB. LSF-KEB Holdings SCA claimed that there was an unfair acquisition of its assets by the Korean government or an expropriation, which then demanded prompt, adequate and effective compensation (Kim, 2012). Since the acquisition was not a direct nationalization of foreign assets, the actions taken by Korea are being assessed as qualifying as an indirect expropriation. One of the main points of contention in assessing an indirect expropriation is whether the actions by the State resulted in a substantial deprivation, which is when interference by the State causes "total impairment" (Sauvant, 2013). This test of substantial deprivation was executed in *Pope & Talbot Inc v. Government of Canada* (2000), which evaluated whether the investor was able to continue its main operations after accounting for losses connected to interventions by the State. On the basis of this test, it may be determined that while on-going prudential investigations barred LSF-KEB Holdings SCA from making a more profitable sale of KEB, the main operations of the bank and of LSF-KEB Holdings SCA were not impaired in their totality.

The Korean government exercised its sovereign right to regulate in what it perceived to be in the public interest. Divestment through the sale to a foreign firm or liquidation of a domestic financial institution as large as KEB would result in not only considerable noncyclical impacts to employment, but also the financial sector as a whole. In fully assessing the State's capacity to make good faith arrangements on its due diligence, one must also consider the circumstances of the State at the time of the accession, or when the investment was first approved. In the case of South Korea, the LSF-KEB Holdings SCA investment was permitted during a period of considerable financial restructuring following the Asian Financial Crisis of 1997. LSF-KEB Holdings SCA then attempted to sell its KEB holdings during a period of economic recovery, which, if permitted, would have very clear economic ramifications, perhaps best expressed by the vociferous public outcry against the sale.

When contemplating whether this constitutes a breach of FET, one may look to Argentina in *LG&E v. Argentine Republic*, which appealed for public interest exceptions to its IIA obligations under the claim of sovereign debt restructuring. While the disputes raised against Argentina involved the State undergoing a default, thereby necessitating sovereign debt restructuring, there are many lessons that can be drawn and applied to *LSF-KEB v. Korea*. One is the extent to which the actions of the State were necessary and proportionate in achieving its public interest objectives by withholding the sale of KEB. The necessity and proportionality of a measure taken by a State, in this case Korea, to accomplish an objective in the public interest essentially asks whether delaying the sale of KEB was a necessary step in accomplishing such objectives. Furthermore, if any contingent losses were proportional, or balanced, to the extent to which those objectives were accomplished and impactful within their scope of their intended goals. If Korea's intervention is deemed both necessary and proportionate, or balanced, then LSF-KEB Holdings SCA will not have the grounds to request compensation from the government.

5. State intervention and FET in Japan

The implications of the attempted sale of the Toshiba Corporation's memory arm, Toshiba Memory Corporation (TMC), in mid-2017 and the subsequent legal dispute with Western Digital have raised the topic of FET in Japan. While the sale attracted competitive offers from foreign bidders including Hon Hai Precision Industry (Foxconn), which Toshiba considered earlier in the bidding process, a State-backed consortium led by Bain Capital (US) was tapped as the preferred bidder. Representing 90% of this consortium at the time of the offer was the Innovation Network Corporation of Japan (INCJ), a State fund that provides capital investment in areas of "green energy, electronics, IT, and biotechnology"

(INCJ, 2017). As of September 2017, the INCJ and Development Bank of Japan (DBJ) temporarily withdrew their involvement in the consortium, which became represented by a special purpose acquisition company (SPAC) located in Hokkaido, Japan, led by Bain Capital. This newly created SPAC is composed of not only global leaders in semiconductor development and production, but also Toshiba as a reinvestment and other Japanese corporations and financial institutions to retain the 50% majority share within Japanese control.

Before Pangea, the roles of the INCJ and DBJ were much more pronounced, leading the consortium with a JPY 2trn offer. The attempted sale of Toshiba memory to the State-led consortium was expedited without prior notice to Western Digital, which through its subsidiary, SanDisk, had a joint venture agreement with Toshiba. On the basis of what it believes to be its rights as an investor, Western Digital filed for international arbitration at the International Chamber of Commerce (ICC) International Court of Arbitration on the basis that the attempted sale without consent represented a contractual violation of the agreed terms between Toshiba and SanDisk (Reuters, 2017b). In order to prevent the sale from taking place until the international arbitration process is complete, Western Digital stalled the sale through processes via the Court of California for the County of San Francisco (Western Digital, 2017b) in accordance to the dispute settlement clause of the joint venture agreement with Toshiba through SanDisk as laid out in Article 12.4 of the *Equipment Purchase Agreement* (2009).

The Japanese government has been firm in its resolve to keep Toshiba's memory technology and business inside Japan. A government spokesperson explained that the decision to push the consortium acquisition forward was made in the public interest, namely to protect jobs and Toshiba technology (Ezaki and Shinozaki, 2017). The role of the INCJ and DBJ in KK Pangea has been deemphasized, though the Toshiba Corporation stated in a press release that it "plans to leave the decision-making in respect of the exercise of a portion of its voting rights held in Pangea to INCJ and DBJ". Furthermore, the INCJ and DBJ expressed that it would invest into KK Pangea after the conclusion of the Western Digital arbitration (Toshiba, 2017).

Toshiba (and KK Pangea) is eager to expedite the sale so that it may rebalance its accounts after devastating losses in its other enterprises, namely the Westinghouse Electric Company, a nuclear power company in the United States. Should Toshiba be unable to bring its assets greater than its liabilities, in other words come out of insolvency, by March of 2018, then it will be required to delist from the Tokyo Stock Exchange as per the delisting criteria of Japan Exchange Regulation (JPX, 2017). Delisting stocks is oftentimes a step toward bankruptcy as shareholders prepare to unload their assets before prices dwindle and financial institutions seek loan repayments.

The economic repercussions of such an outcome would not be isolated to Toshiba or even its memory subsidiary alone. The *keiretsu* business structure of Japanese conglomerates like Toshiba means that the impacts would travel across a wide network of interlinked subsidiary and affiliated businesses. The company's website identified 50 affiliated domestic business and at least 99 additional affiliated domestic businesses that Toshiba heads. The deeply rooted socioeconomic role of Toshiba Memory, not to mention Toshiba as a whole, means that its interests are interwoven into the very fabric of the society, economy and thus the public interest. This relationship is recognized by the conglomerates themselves, as is the role of the State in protecting those interests. This was recently shown in a survey conducted by Reuters involving 220 medium- to large-sized enterprises, to which 87% responded that the sale to a State-backed fund and not allowing acquisitions by Chinese companies were appropriate measures in stopping the leakage of technology as well as protecting the interests of Japan as a whole (Reuters, 2017b).

Ultimately, the outcomes of the Western Digital dispute are not as important as the implications of the case itself: the larger conflict between standards of protections like FET and a State's capacity to rule in favour of what it perceives to serve the public interest or its right to regulate. While the original dispute arose from what Western Digital perceived to be a contractual violation of the joint venture with its subsidiary SanDisk, the involvement of the Japanese government through the State-backed consortium may be sufficient grounds to raise issues within the scope of international investment law depending on the level of the State's involvement. Though speculative, this may explain the decision by INCJ and DBJ to disengage from the acquisition. *Siemens A.G. v. The Argentine Republic*, for instance, showed that a fairly broad range of government intervention influencing the performance of a contract can fall into the remit of international law. This means that, while the original dispute may have arisen from a private contract, a certain degree of involvement by the State with provable influence on one of the contracting parties is then eligible to be taken to international dispute settlement under an FET claim. In application to Toshiba, the role of the State in the potential acquisition may lead Western Digital to take such a path on the basis of allegedly violating Article XVII(2) of the *Treaty of Friendship, Commerce and Navigation between the United States of America and Japan* (1953), which provides "nationals, companies and commerce of the other Party fair and equitable treatment".

Japan is inclined to obstruct the acquisition of Toshiba Memory as an effort to protect the public interest objectives identified earlier in this section. In such a case, the State will have to confront head-on the question of FET and the limitations to its right to regulate in the public interest. This scenario, though based on conjecture, presents noteworthy implications. That is, how will Japan attempt to justify the obstruction of an acquisition in reference to international standards? In other words, how does Japan's justification of stopping the acquisition of TMC to China or Western Digital, which also made a separate consortium bid, hold up against general standards in international economic law, which have established principles disallowing preferential treatment of one foreign entity to another (most-favoured nation treatment principle) or a domestic entity (national treatment principle)?

Given the financial circumstances of Toshiba and its considerable socioeconomic position in Japan, as explored earlier in this section, the question may very well become whether an attempt by the Japanese government to intervene in such an acquisition would qualify as being based on a legitimate objective, thereby testing the threshold applicability of FET. More broadly, as contemplated earlier in this chapter, the question becomes whether there is an international standard in place. Cases like *International Thunderbird Gaming Corporation v. The United Mexican States* (2006) show that exceedingly high thresholds in interpreting minimum standards of treatment like FET did not define international standards. The position of Toshiba within the Japanese economy as well as its relationship with the State remain unique enough that the applicability of any sort of threshold or international standard will have to be carefully examined and justified.

6. Discussion

Finding ways to mitigate the risk factors identified in this chapter will require a comprehensive policy approach that attempts to strengthen the rule of law by addressing socioeconomic and geopolitical concerns that have yet to have found a clear legal solution. Yet rather than transplanting systems from foreign jurisdictions where the use of a wide range of legal *fora* matured over time, Korea must take to adopting systems gradually and only after careful assessment of the risks involved. While the risks identified in this work have distinct impacts on the investment climate and ISDS, the solution can be seen as a single suite of measures to strengthen relevant aspects of the rule of law through two policy objectives.

6.1. Encourage diverse participation, open the enclave

Empowering civil society to ensure that public and private sector actors are accountable for their actions can be an effective measure in mitigating associated risks. Governments would benefit from involving nonpartisan and nongovernmental institutions in providing independent review of policy, especially in relation to ISDS. Minority shareholders for instance can play an important role in preventing corporations from heightening accountability risk. Furthermore, as involvement in ISDS grows, ensuring that these procedures and their results are transparent is certain to not only improve public perception towards ISDS, but also the conglomerates that become involved in these processes and show a willingness to resolve their disputes in an open manner. To do this, there should be a greater push forward efforts to increase ratification of the United Nations Convention on Transparency in Treaty-based Investor-State Arbitration (or the "Mauritius Convention"), making ISDS a transparent process rather than a cunning means to circumvent national courts.

Ensuring that ISDS procedures and their results are transparent is certain to not only improve public perception towards ISDS, but also encourage the conglomerates involved in these processes to resolve their disputes in an open and transparent manner. Pushing for this to happen during the earlier stages ISDS in both countries would help mitigate some of the negative public perception surrounding these issues as well as help these governments and involved private sector actors align themselves with global practices through efforts by the UN. Unfortunately, *LSF-KEB v. Korea* has been shrouded in mystery as none of the proceedings have been made public (Jang, 2016). Given its considerable impact on the public interest, Korea should move to ensure that future processes are transparent.

The continued centrality of transparency was recently again confirmed by the adverse decision concerning *Dayani v. Korea*. The first loss in ISDS for Korea, the decision was revealed to have hinged on adverse interference. Irresponsive to a request to produce additional materials by the arbitral tribunal, the FSC later claimed that the requested materials, which were documents by the Public Fund Oversight Committee between December 2010 and March 2011, did not exist (Ahn, 2018b).

In addition to bolstering transparency in proceedings, another approach may be to reduce the enclave effect surrounding ISDS. One way to do this is examine how national court systems can be empowered (Henckels, 2013) and in which circumstances their judicial discretion better services mitigating risk. Investors seeking to employ ISDS with a mind to elude national court systems ultimately eclipse those and other institutions in ways that are ultimately harmful for the future of domestic legal system (Rogers, 2015). Taking too many liberties in an international regulatory system that is already well established, however, can threaten investor confidence in dealing with a State that likes to bend the rules. Balancing these interests shall prove to become one of the greatest policy challenges yet.

One recent dispute that bears relevance to national courts involves the Schindler Group, which filed a notice of intent to submit for arbitration on 2018 July 11 (Lee, 2018). The Schindler complaint involves the recapitalization of Hyundai Elevators, effectively securing its control within the Hyundai Group. Schindler, which began its investment into Hyundai Elevator (HE) in 2004 and by 2014 had up to 34% equity in the company, began making demands based on its shareholder rights in 2011 and even attempted at acquisition. These moves pushed HE into recapitalizing twice, halving the Schindler claim to 15.87%, which it argues was a violation of its investor rights as a shareholder. Its filing for ISDS follows unsuccessful attempts to settle the dispute in Korean court, which rendered the matter as permissive under Korean law. With this move, Schindler changed its approach by submitting a claim against the Korean government on the fact that the Financial Supervisory Service (FSS) permitted the recapitalization, which enabled the alleged infraction to take place (Ahn, 2018a).

6.2. Update treaty obligations

Greater materiality should be placed on political risk and its potential impacts on treaty obligations related to investment. Korea, specifically, should set out clear guidelines in the instance of loss or damage to foreign assets or property resulting from any manner of North Korean provocation, South Korean countermeasures against such provocation, and/or the threat of such thereunto. Proportionality in the protection of foreign investors and their assets is difficult to define when facing exogenous political conditions that have little precedence. After setting out clear national guidelines, South Korea must also re-examine the text of its bilateral investment treaties to provide more specific guidelines on measuring for proportionality in exercising general regulatory measures for national security.

One way that these countries may choose to do this is by participating in efforts by the UN Conference on Trade and Development (UNCTAD) to reform IIAs. Now in the second phase of this project (UNCTAD, 2017), the UNCTAD has been encouraging States to revisit old treaties and ensure that such IIAs do not contradict with their national agendas. Japan and Korea would benefit from engaging in this process by, for instance, reforming MFN and full protection and security standards of protections through jointly interpreted provisions. This would entail Japan and Korea clarifying provisions within relevant international agreements in ways that are more in line with their respective public interests. Some of the unique characteristics of those interests were mentioned earlier in this chapter. This process shall become exponentially more important with UNCITRAL designating ISDS reform as a matter for Working Group deliberation.

In addition to updating existing treaty obligations, States may choose to better reflect these specific concerns in admission processes. For instance, in comparing the original text of the Republic of Korea–United States free trade agreement (KORUS FTA) and the text of the Comprehensive and Progressive Agreement for Trans-Pacific Partnership (CPTPP), one can identify promising differences that may act as a powerful tool in addressing some of the challenges and risks identified in this chapter. For instance, Article 11.10 of the KORUS FTA presents safeguard exceptions relevant to environmental concerns as qualifying for public interest exceptions. In contrast, Articles 9.16 and 9.17 of the CPTPP/TPP chapter on investment presents a more advanced version of this provision, which one may argue reflects the particular circumstances of the CPTPP Signatory States. Article 9.16[3] adds to the wording of KORUS FTA Article 11.10[4] additional matters of legitimate concern, namely health and "other regulatory objectives", which may emphasizes the text's broader approach to public interest exceptions (CPTPP, Art. 9.8). Especially relevant to the normative risks presented in this chapter is the corporate social responsibility provision of the CPTPP presented in Article 9.17, which identifies the need for national entities to observe "internationally recognized standards".[5]

While the CPTPP does not specify the creation of an appellate review mechanism, the avail of the UNCITRAL Arbitration Rules and Korea's recently demonstrated proclivity to challenge arbitral awards (*Mohammad Reza Dayyani and others v. Republic of Korea*) can imply that Korea may be more open to CPTPP should it provide a means to such a mechanism.

7. Conclusion

From the first-known ISD incident involving a partly British-owned shrimp farm in Sri Lanka destroyed by Tamil rebels, both the interest in and scale of investor-State dispute settlement (ISDS) in Asia have been on the rise. From 1994 to 2000, the caseload reached 248 incidents. Reactive to this trend, China, Japan and Korea have been proactively strengthening their ISDS infrastructure. Such preparations can be seen as efforts to hedge the unforeseeable impacts of political and economic upheavals within global economic landscape with the rise and fall of regional economic blocs and trade agreements.

These efforts are well-founded: international regulatory systems are especially important for conglomerate-led, export-oriented economies like that of South Korea. In spite of the smaller relative size of its economy in comparison to its neighbours, South Korea has significantly more BITs and TIPs than Japan and is shy of only 1/5 of those of China. The total per cent of GDP from the export of goods and services from Korea is significantly higher than that of China and Japan.

Regulatory systems that observe international standards can provide alternative means of legal recourse to the national courts of the host State, which may be influenced by domestic political, social and/or economic considerations. Yet when investor-State dispute settlement result in adversarial rulings against the host State, especially those with burgeoning ISDS regimes like in Korea and Japan, governments will face transition pains. Adversarial rulings will inevitably elicit a strong response from the public and impact perception towards ISDS as well as IIAs as a whole. If the perception toward ISDS turns sour, then the respective governments will have to wade through palpable public outcry at the use of public finance to retain top-shelf firms and pay lofty arbitral awards. As

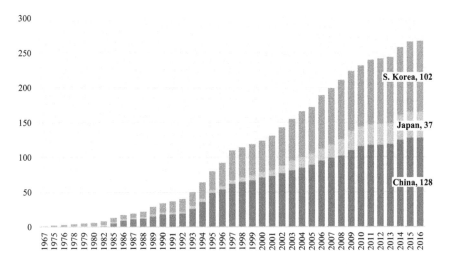

Figure 7.1 BITs and TIPs entered into force in China, Japan and Korea
Source: UNCTAD IIA Database

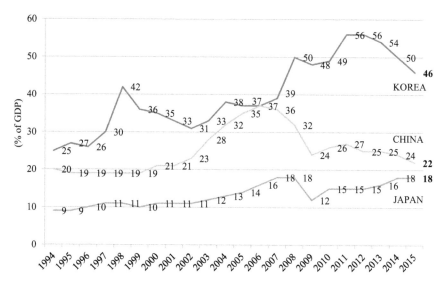

Figure 7.2 Export of goods and services (% of GDP) for the Republic of Korea, China and Japan from 1994 to 2015

Source: World Bank Databanks

described in this chapter, the beginnings of such a response are observable in South Korea. The only alternative is to refuse to enforce arbitral awards, though this was seen with India following the decision of *White Industries Australia Limited v. The Republic of India* (2009), which took approximately a decade to conclude and was subject to extensive criticism.

The task is to find that rather difficult equilibrium between strengthening the rule of law, maintaining an attractive investment climate and reserving the right to regulate in the public interest. However, perhaps a far more thoughtful question one may ask en route, as the UN Commission on International Trade Law is now asking itself, is whether the difficulty is in the travails of a State attempting to achieve such a task or in the *travaux préparatoires* of the systems in which the State is attempting to achieve it.

Notes

1 Article 5(1) reads,

> Each Contracting Party shall accord to investments of investors of another Contracting Party fair and equitable treatment and full protection and security. The concepts of "fair and equitable treatment" and "full protection and security" do not require treatment in addition to or beyond any reasonable and appropriate standard of treatment accorded in accordance with generally accepted rules of international law.

2 Article 11.5 reads, "Each Party shall accord to covered investments treatment in accordance with customary international law, including fair and equitable

treatment and full protection and security. [F]ull protection and security" requires each Party to provide the level of police protection required under customary international law.

3 Article 9.16 reads,

> Nothing in this Chapter shall be construed to prevent a Party from adopting, maintaining or enforcing any measure otherwise consistent with this Chapter that it considers appropriate to ensure that investment activity in its territory is undertaken in a manner sensitive to environmental, health or other regulatory objectives.

4 Article 11.10 reads,

> Nothing in this Chapter shall be construed to prevent a Party from adopting, maintaining, or enforcing any measure otherwise consistent with this Chapter that it considers appropriate to ensure that investment activity in its territory is undertaken in a manner sensitive to environmental concerns.

5 Article 9.17 reads,

> Parties reaffirm the importance of each Party encouraging enterprises operating within its territory or subject to its jurisdiction to voluntarily incorporate into their internal policies those internationally recognised standards, guidelines and principles of corporate social responsibility that have been endorsed or are supported by that Party.

References

International treaties

Accord entre l'Union économique belgo-luxembourgeoise et le Gouvernement de la République de Corée concernant l'encouragement et la protection réciproques des investissements (Belgium-Luxembourg-Korea BIT). 24 March 2011, www.italaw.com/sites/default/files/laws/italaw6036.pdf

Treaty of Friendship, Commerce and Navigation between the United States of America and Japan (1953), http://tcc.export.gov/Trade_Agreements/All_Trade_Agreements/exp_005539.asp

Vienna Convention on the Law of Treaties, Vienna, 23 May 1969, in force 27 January 1980, 115 UNTS 331; (1969) 8 ILM 679; UKTS (1980) 58.

Investment contracts

Equipment Purchase Agreement, Article 12.4 (29 January 2009), http://corporate.findlaw.com/contracts/operations/equipment-purchase-agreement-sandisk-corp-and-toshiba-corp.html//

Judgments of international courts and arbitral awards

Azurix *Corp. v. The Argentine Republic*, ICSID Case No. ARB/01/12, www.italaw.com/cases/118

Barcelona *Traction, Light and Power Co., Ltd. (Belgium v. Spain)*, Judgment, 5 February 1970, ICJ reports 1970.

Biwater *Gauff (Tanzania) Ltd. v. United Republic of Tanzania*, ICSID Case No. ARB/05/22.

Daniels, R. J. (2004). *Defecting on Development: Bilateral Investment Treaties and the Subversion of the Rule of Law in the Developing World*, University of Toronto, Faculty of Law.

GAMI *v. Mexico*, Award, 15 November 20014, 44 ILM (2005).

International Thunderbird Gaming Corporation v. The United Mexican States, UNCITRAL Rules (NAFTA), Award, 26 January 2006.

LG&E Energy Corp., LG&E Capital Corp., and LG&E International, Inc. v. Argentine Republic, Decision on Liability, ICSID Case No. ARB/02/1, www.italaw.com/cases/documents/623

Pope & Talbot Inc. v. The Government of Canada, UNCITRAL Rules (NAFTA), Award, 26 June 2000, www.italaw.com/cases/863

Siemens *A.G. v. The Argentine Republic*, ICSID Case No. ARB/02/8.

Waste *Management, Inc. v. United Mexican States* ("Number 2"), ICSID Case No. ARB(AF)/00/3, www.italaw.com/cases/1158

White *Industries Australia Limited v. The Republic of India*, UNCITRAL Rules 2009 (Australia-India BIT), Final Award, 30 November 2011, www.italaw.com/cases/1169

Books and articles

Ahn, D. G. (2018a). Schindler Shakes Up Hyundai Elevator, Initiatives ISD Case Against Korean Government (in Korean). *Korea Economy.* 20 July 2018, http://plus.hankyung.com/apps/newsinside.view?aid=2018071994891&category=NEWSPAPER&sns=y

Ahn, H. R. (2018b). [Editorial] Unbelievable Response by FSS to ISD Claim . . . Did Not Produce Materials Resulting in 73 Billion Loss (in Korean). *JoongAng Daily.* 16 July 2018, https://news.joins.com/article/22834800

Deloitte (2014). *2014 Global Survey on Reputation Risk, Reputation@Risk*, Deloitte Touche Tohmatsu.

Dong, S. H. (2014). The Chaebol's Total Life Expectancy Is 76 Years . . . Who Is Choi Jang Soo? (in Korean). *ChosunBiz.* 20 May 2014, http://biz.chosun.com/site/data/html_dir/2014/05/20/2014052000955.html

Economist (2012). Minority Report: The Korea Discount. *The Economist.* 11 February 2012, www.economist.com/finance-and-economics/2012/02/11/minority-report

Energy Charter Treaty (1995). 2080 UNTS 95; 34 ILM 360.

Euler Hermes (2016). South Korea. *Economic Research.* 22 June 2016, www.eulerhermes.com/economic-research/country-reports/Pages/South-Korea.aspx

Ezaki, D. and Shinozaki, N. (2017). Will public support work for Toshiba? (in Japanese). *Special Report, NHK.* 28 June 2017, http://www3.nhk.or.jp/news/business_tokushu/2017_0628.html?utm_int=news_contents_tokushu_004

Henckels, C. (2013). Balancing Investment Protection and the Public Interest: The Role of the Standard of Review and the Importance of Deference in Investor-State Arbitration. *Journal of International Dispute Resolution*, 4(1), 197–215.

Hahm, H. G. (2017). One Out of 10 Listed Companies Is a "zombie company" . . . the Need to Increase Interest Rates (in Korean). *YTN News.* 5 April 2017, www.ytn.co.kr/_ln/0102_201704051629152977

Innovation Network Corporation of Japan (INCJ) (No Date). Introduction, www.incj.co.jp/english/

Jang, H. J. (2016). Government-Lone Star ISD, Final Hearing Concluded . . . If Recognized, Decision This Year (in Korean). *Law Times.* 7 June 2016, www.lawtimes.co.kr/Legal-News/Legal-News-View?Serial=101005

Japan Exchange Group (JPX) (2017). "Criteria for Delisting" Equities, Listing (Domestic Stocks). 17 May 2017, www.jpx.co.jp/english/equities/listing/delisting/

Jung, I. H. (2017). Only 4.9 Years After Entering Company Before Family Members of Top 5 Conglomerates Become Promoted to Executive Positions (in Korean). *CEOSCORE.* 8 February 2017, www.ceoscore.co.kr/bbs/board.php?bo_table=S00L04&wr_id=350

Kim, A. S. (2016). Six Out of Ten Merger and Acquisitions Are Handled by Foreign Firms (in Korean). *Chosun Ilbo.* 27 April 2016, http://news.chosun.com/site/data/html_dir/2016/04/26/2016042602319.html

Kim, H. J. (2012). A Study of Core Issues in Investor-State Dispute (*Lone Star Funds vs. the Republic of Korea*) (in Korean). *Dankook University Law Review,* 36, 2, http://kiss.kstudy.com/journal/thesis_name.asp?key=3120696

Kim, S. H., Chang, R. and Chan, V. (2018). Hit by Political Crossfire, Lotte's China Exit Stalls. *Bloomberg News.* 13 February 2018, www.bloomberg.com/news/articles/2018-02-12/hit-by-political-crossfire-lotte-s-china-exit-said-to-stall

Kim, Y. S. and Lee, H. D. (2010). [Monday Interview] Director Han Jeong-hwa, 557 Support Policies . . . We Look to Consolidate Redundant Projects (in Korean). *Hankyung.* 3 May 2015, http://news.hankyung.com/article/2015050371071.

Kleintop, J. (2016). Geopolitical Risks in 2016: Is Your Portfolio Prepared? *Charles Schwab.* 11 January 2016, www.schwab.com/public/schwab/nn/articles/Geopolitical-risks-in-2016-Is-your-portfolio-prepared

Lee, H. W. (2016). Making Korea Into an "international arbitration hub" (in Korean). *Hankyung.* 6 June 2016, www.hankyung.com/news/app/newsview.php?aid=2016060609901

Lee, J. Y. (2016). Korea Geopolitical Risks Rise with Gaeseong Closer: Moody's. *Bloomberg Markets.* 2 February 2016, https://www.bloomberg.com/news/articles/2016-02-12/korea-geopolitical-risks-rise-with-gaeseong-closure-moody-s

Lee, T. H. (2015). Lotte Group Companies Lost 1.6 Tril. Won in Stock Value Since Family Feud Surfaced (in Korean). *Hankyung.* 4 August 2015, http://english.hankyung.com/all/2015/08/04/1405451/lotte-group-companies-lost-17-tril-won-in-stock-value-since-family-feud-surfaced

Lee, Y. E. (2018). "Schindler" launches ISD Lawsuit Against Korean Government (in Korean). *Dong-A Ilbo.* 20 July 2018, http://news.donga.com/BestClick/3/all/20180719/91137362/1

Lee, W. (2017). The Chaebol Golden Spoon Generation and Their Super High Speed Rise to Executive Positions (in Korean). *Hankyoreh.* 8 February 2017, www.hani.co.kr/arti/economy/marketing/781818.html?_fr=mt2

Malik, M. (2011). The Full Protection and Security Standards Comes of Age: Yet Another Challenge for States in Investment Treaty Arbitration? *Best Practices Series,* International Institute for Sustainable Development.

McCurry, J. and Safi, L. (2016). North Korea Claims Successful Hydrogen Bomb Test in "'self defence against US". *The Guardian.* 6 January 2016, www.theguardian.com/world/2016/jan/06/north-korean-nuclear-test-suspected-as-artificial-earthquake-detected

Ministry of Statistics, Republic of Korea (2016). Foreign Direct Investment (in Korean). 2 February 2016, www.index.go.kr/potal/main/EachDtlPageDetail. do?idx_cd=1065

North American Free Trade Agreement (1993). 32 I.L.M. 289 and 605.

Park, G. Y. (2018). US Hedge Fund Mason Capital Seeks US$175m in Damages from Samsung Merger. *The Investor.* 4 July 2018, www.theinvestor.co.kr/view. php?ud=20180704000542

Reuters Staff (2017a). South Korea's Lotte Approves Land Swap for Missile Defence: Ministry. *Retuers.* 27 February 2017, www.reuters.com/article/us-southkorea-usa-thaad-lotte/south-koreas-lotte-approves-land-swap-for-missile-defence-minis try-idUSKBN1660P6

Reuters Staff (2017b). Reuters Company Survey: Toshiba Delisting "abolished" 37%, "cautiously" 58% (in Japanese). *Reuters.* 25 May 2017, http://jp.reuters.com/ article/reuters-poll-toshiba-idJPKBN18K36G

Rogers, C. A. (2015). International Arbitration, Judicial Education, and Legal Elites. *Journal of Dispute Resolution*, 2015(1), 71–77.

Roh, G. M. (2017). Global Corporate Management Gap . . . Special Investigation Bent on "putting it in gear" (in Korean). *Hankyung.* 15 February 2017, www. hankyung.com/news/app/newsview.php?aid=2017021490361

Sauvant, K. P., ed. (2013). *Yearbook on International Investment Law & Policy 2011– 2012*, Oxford: Oxford University Press.

Son, Y. I. and Song, C. H. (2015). Money to Support SMEs Goes to Zombie Companies . . . an Endless Poison to Economic Support (in Korean). *Dong-A News.* 18 May 2015, http://news.donga.com/Economy/3/01/20150518/71317622/1

Thomson, M. D. (2012). Memorandum Required by Article 8.1 of the Agreement Between the Government of the Republic of Korea and the Belgium-Luxembourg Economic Union for the Reciprocal Promotion and Protection of Investments with Respect to the Dispute Between Lone Star and the Republic of Korea. 21 May 2012.

Toshiba Corporation (2017). Notice on the Signing of a Share Purchase Agreement with Bain Capital-led Consortium for the Sale of Toshiba Memory Corporation. *Investor Relations.* 28 September 2017, www.toshiba.co.jp/about/ir/en/ news/20170928_1.pdf

United Nations Commission on Trade and Development (UNCTAD) (2017). Phase 2 of IIA Reform: Modernizing the Existing Stock of Old-Generation Treaties. *IIA Issues Note* Issue 2, http://unctad.org/en/PublicationsLibrary/ diaepcb2017d3_en.pdf

Van Harten, G. (2010). Investment Treaty Arbitration, Procedural Fairness, and the Rule of Law. In S. Schill, ed., *International Investment Law and Comparative Public Law*, Oxford: Oxford University Press, pp. 627–657.

Western Digital Resubmits Bid with KKR for Toshiba Chip Unit. *Mainichi Japan.* 27 June 2017, https://mainichi.jp/english/articles/20170627/ p2g/00m/0bu/076000c

Western Digital's SanDisk Subsidiaries Obtain Court Protection against Toshiba in Preliminary Injunction Hearing. *Western Digital Press Room.* 14 July 2017, www. wdc.com/about-wd/newsroom/press-room/2017-07-14-western-digitals-sand isk-subsidiaries-obtain-court-protection.html

Won, H. J. (2017). Seoul Mulls Taking China to WTO Over THAAD Retribution. *Korea Herald.* 7 March 2017, www.koreaherald.com/view.php?ud=20170307000806

8 Objective criteria and *ratione legis* condition in the definition of investment

Global trends and the Chinese practice

G. Matteo Vaccaro-Incisa[1]

Details make perfection, and perfection is not a detail.
– (Leonardo da Vinci, 1452–1519)

1. Introduction

The definition of investment is a key provision of all international investment agreements (IIAs, including both bilateral and multilateral investment agreements and investment chapters of free trade agreements), as it essentially delimits their scope of application, provided that only qualified investments enjoy the guarantees therein offered (UNCTAD, 2011; WTO, 2002). From the embryonic open-list pivoting on 'capital' enshrined in the 1959 Germany-Pakistan Bilateral Investment Treaty (BIT),[2] and passing through the broad notion of 'property' featured in the 1967 Draft Convention on the Protection of Foreign Property,[3] the definition of investment over the time has gone through a process of standardization. However, while all major model BITs build on a common open-ended structure and notion comprised of a chapeau and a list of instances,[4] no universally binding definition or concept of investment has been yet agreed upon.

Since the beginning of its foreign investment protection program, with the signing of the China-Sweden BIT in 1982, and until recently, the People's Republic of China (China, Mainland China or PRC) followed the principal European States – i.e. the most active in stipulating such agreements – shaping its models[5] and practice[6] on the basis of theirs, all the while developing some distinctive traits. These reflect China's traditionally cautious and 'conservative' understanding of international law, where alterations of traditional policy patterns are rare and, anyway, gradual (Xue, 2011).

With regard to the notion of investment, this chapter focuses on two specific elements: the investment's so-called 'objective criteria' and what is herein defined as the '*ratione legis*' condition. The former consists of those characteristics that States provide in the definition, in addition to the list of instances, aimed at supporting the interpreter in determining what constitutes an investment;[7] the latter, also known as 'legality requirement', is the condition for which only investments made 'in accordance with the laws' of the host State are covered by the relevant IIA. China's policy with regard to these two elements is distinctive – recently changing, in the first case, and remaining steadfast to its traditional paradigm with almost no exceptions, in the second.

Both aspects are the subject of considerable debate. On the one side, the absence of objective criteria in the definition of investment in most IIAs, coupled with the lack of an express definition of investment in the 1965 Convention for the Settlement of Investment Disputes (ICSID Convention), has generated significant discussion, within and without ICSID arbitration, regarding what constitutes an investment. On the other, some arbitral decisions have appeared to extend the reach of the review of the legality requirement to matters that, from the perspective of States, fall within the *domaine réservé* of domestic criminal jurisdiction.

Therefore, in light of *i)* the importance of these characteristics in arbitral decisions (and considering the tribunals' frequent reliance on the 'treaty practice' of States); *ii)* the extent of the Chinese investment treaty network and its relative uniformity; and *iii)* the flow of investment China commands and receives, second only to the US (UNCTAD, 2014), this analysis aims at offering, along an overview of the evolution of both case-law and international treaty practice, a specific focus on China.

As such, this chapter first reviews the Chinese BIT program (Section 2) and outlines the definition of investment in general, highlighting key interpretive issues (Section 3). It then focuses first on the objective criteria (Section 4) and then on the *ratione legis* clause (Section 5), contrasting general trends and the Chinese practice. Finally, some thoughts on the points developed are offered with regard to the negotiations currently being pursued by China with the US and the EU (Section 6).

In carrying out the analysis, reliance is primarily placed on those modifications gradually introduced in China's IIAs, in light of the relevant case law.

2. The Chinese BIT program

Since it seized power, in 1949, the Chinese communist ruling establishment, under the leadership of Mao Zedong, refused to pursue a policy aimed at the protection of foreign direct investment (FDI). This was, instead, gradually yet effectively excluded from Mainland China, with the exception of some joint ventures with Soviet Union entities (Thompson, 1979). The meagre fruits this approach carried over the two decades that followed, however, ultimately prompted its reversal and the launch, in 1978, under the leadership of Den Xiaoping, of China's 'Open Door policy'. Throughout the decade that followed, a number of political choices demonstrated China's will to resume and normalize the FDI flow in the country. In 1982, China inaugurated its investment protection program (with Sweden); by 1985, it had signed 13 agreements, more than most States at the time (even if with several limitations), with capital exporters such as Germany (1983), France (1984), Italy (1985), the Netherlands (1985) and

Singapore (1985). China would readily accept arbitral clauses (even though limited to disputes relating to the amount of compensation following expropriation) and, soon afterwards, enhanced protection standards (even if, at first, only on a 'best effort' basis).[8] By the end of the following decade (1998), China had signed 89 BITs, for the most part developed along the lines of its first two model investment treaties of 1984 and 1989. Such a highly significant path dependence is also due to the fact that Chinese negotiators, until 1997, did not enjoy the power to autonomously consider amendments[9]; instead, amendments had to be each time approved by the State Council (thus dramatically slowing down negotiations or halting them altogether).[10] Consequently, the Chinese policy, coupled with its negotiators' constraints, ultimately produced an investment treaty network characterized by limited substantive variances. Nonetheless, Chinese investment standards needed to be adapted to the evolving economic backdrop (domestic and international) as well as the interpretive trends (or inconsistencies) emerging from investment arbitration.[11] In 1997 (four years after its accession to the ICSID Convention), China adopted a new model BIT, bringing its practice, already modelled on the major European capital exporters (especially, Germany and the UK) in line with these. Notably, on this basis and from 2000 on, China began systematically granting unrestricted access to Investor-State Dispute Settlement (ISDS).[12] Both moves were consistent with the 1999 launch of the 'Go-Global' strategy and the focus on outbound investment: in the subsequent years, China concluded over 30 new agreements (mostly, with African and South American States), renegotiated at least 17 (mostly with European States) and acceded to the WTO in 2001. After some 'spot' experimentations with trusted partners (e.g. 2003 BIT renegotiation with Germany, 2006 FTA with Pakistan), in the second half of the past decade, China began shifting its program from the synthetic models and practice of European States (which condense investment promotion, admission and protection in no more than 15 provisions) to the more analytical version of the US and Canada (several sections featuring up to 50 articles, plus annexes – hereinafter jointly referred to, where appropriate, as the North American model or practice. Also, it began including the investment protection regime into wider free trade arrangements (i.e. FTAs with New Zealand and South Korea; supplementary investment agreements to FTAs with ASEAN and Chile).

China's overall IIA practice comprises 154 IIAs, of which 146 BITs and 8 investment chapters of FTAs (or FTA-related agreements).[13] Of these, 119 are the IIAs which, signed or in force (thus, excluding the BITs expressly terminated), offer at least partial access to ISDS,[14] whose text is public available and are not superseded by subsequent renegotiations, investment chapters in FTAs or FTA-related agreements or regional FTA or investment regimes (Vaccaro-Incisa, forthcoming). The Chinese network, as such, is second only to that of Germany. A detailed study of the available Chinese IIAs, however, reveals that only 60 IIAs grant unrestricted *a priori* access to ISDS (among the excluded e.g. are the UK and Italy, whose BITs with China are outdated, and the US, with which BIT negotiations have been on and off since 1983). Of these, only 55 to ICSID arbitration.[15] The study of these agreements shows that while several provisions have undergone gradual yet major transformations over the time (e.g. NT, ISDS), others were either left untouched or altered only on specific accounts. In light of the foregoing, the evolution of China's definition of investment (in particular, in those IIAs that grant full ISDS access) is worth a dedicated analysis. The alterations therein contained arguably reflect discernible policy choices that affect the Chinese conception of the investment protection regime, especially in the context of certain interpretive developments in the arbitral case-law.

3. Definition of investment

3.1. *Definition, treaty practice and the intertwining between ICSID and IIAs*

According to the Oxford Dictionary, 'investment' means 'the action or process of investing money for profit', 'a thing that is worth buying because it may be profitable or useful in the future', or 'an act of devoting time, effort or energy to a particular undertaking with the expectation of a worthwhile result'. According to the Merriam Webster Collegiate Encyclopedia, 'investment' means:

> *Process of exchanging income for an asset that is expected to produce earnings at a later time.* An investor refrains from consumption in the present in hopes of a greater return in the future. . . . Investment cannot occur without saving, which provides funding. *Because investment increases an economy's capacity to produce, it is a factor contributing to economic growth.*
>
> (Merriam-Webster, 2000)

As mentioned earlier, in the field of international investment law, the definition of investment vests critical importance, especially in the case of ICSID arbitration (to which China has granted *a priori* consent in 60 IIAs, 45 only of which in force). The numerous disputes that pivot on the very matter of the relationship between the definitions of investment respectively featured in the ICSID Convention and the relevant IIA demonstrate its significance. Indeed, the former (at Art. 25) does not contain an express definition of investment (Mr Broches in ICSID, 1968: 54, 566). The latter, in contrast, always contains a detailed definition. In German, British, Dutch, French and Italian practice (hereinafter, jointly referred to, where appropriate, as the European model or practice), as well as in Chinese practice, the definition is:

• Introduced by a chapeau that provides for some delineating elements (such as the *ratione personae*[16] and *ratione loci*[17] of the notion; often also the *ratione temporis*[18] and *ratione legis*),[19]
• Followed by an open-ended, asset-based series of instances exemplified in a list of five or six categories (e.g. property rights, contractual rights, intellectual property rights, concession rights), and
• Closed with the extension of protection to any alteration to the form in which assets are invested.

Since 2004, in the North American practice, the definition of investment is most often preceded by that of 'covered investment', which subsumes the *ratione loci and ratione temporis.* While Canada does not maintain a chapeau to the definition of investment, the US does, thereby adding further specifications to the *ratione personae*[20] *and, most importantly, the three objective criteria of i)* commitment of capital or other resources, *ii)* expectation or gain of profit and *iii)* assumption of risk. Even though framed in a different fashion, both US and Canadian models and practice incorporate a more comprehensive list of investment instances than European agreements, notably expanding the definition to expressly include company participation and concessions categories.[21] North American models and most practice, though, do not feature the *ratione legis* requirement in the definition of investment.

Taking into account that, so far, European-styled BITs have been the legal ground of all known investment disputes, it is noteworthy that both the first texts finalized or still being negotiated and made public by the EU, as well as those of ASEAN, and most of China since 2008, are all shifting towards the North American model. This is of particular significance with regard to the definition of investment, in light of the greater detail it is therein dealt with. This may be considered also a common response coming from four diverse areas (US and Canada, the EU, ASEAN, China) that, combined, currently command the vast majority of inward and outbound global FDI worldwide. In this respect, it could be considered that States have begun providing an answer to the interpretive issues pivoting around the definition of investment.

3.2. The Chinese definition of investment

Notwithstanding the innovations over the time introduced in its program, the definition of investment remains an instance of overall uniformity throughout Chinese investment treaty practice, especially with respect to specific characteristics deemed of strategic importance. Specifically, the definition contained in China's 1997 model BIT essentially reproduces the wording employed since the Model BIT, China, 1984, which in turn merged, for the most part, elements either common or distinctive of the British and German model BITs. Regarding the investment chapeau, Art. 1.1 of the 1997 Chinese model (unchanged since 1984) provides that:

> The term investment means every kind of asset invested by investors of one Contracting Party in accordance with the laws and regulations of the other Contracting Party in the territory of the Latter, and in particular, though not exclusively, includes: . . .
>
> (1997 Chinese model BIT, Art. 1)

The articulated phrasing of the chapeau is featured since China-Sweden BIT, 1982. As such, however, it does not appear in any preceding agreement of Germany, the UK, the Netherlands, France, Italy, Sweden, Switzerland or Japan. In addition, until the renegotiation of the China-Germany BIT, 2003, China never altered this wording. Such a uniform practice highlights the importance China attaches to this text (and, overall, to stability and uniformity of its own practice). While the opening ('every kind of assets') derives from both the British and German models and the closing ('and in particular, though not exclusively, includes') is literally drawn from the British model, the Chinese chapeau features three additional and original elements, seemingly intended to introduce clear limits to the scope of the BIT coverage:[22]

- the *ratione personae*
- the *ratione legis*
- the *ratione loci*

Before focusing on the *ratione legis*, the following analysis turns, first, on the objective criteria.

4. The objective criteria

4.1. Definition, treaty practice and interpretive trends

As noted, the 'objective criteria' are those elements spelled out in a IIA in connection with the definition of investment, aimed at supporting the interpreter in ascertaining whether a given operation falls within the definition as intended by the contracting parties. The usefulness of the objective criteria emerges not much in the case of traditional investment (e.g. concession contracts with foreign operators for the setting up of infrastructure, energy or mining projects)[23] – rather, in less immediate cases (e.g. promissory notes, participation contracts, sovereign bonds) and with reference to the context that brought to the establishment of the ICSID Convention in 1965. In the absence of a definition of investment in that treaty (Art. 25), interpretation becomes necessary.

Again, all publicly known ICSID investment disputes that have dealt with the issue of what constitute an investment are grounded on European synthetic BITs – which, in contrast to North American models and practice since 2004, does not enrich the definition of investment with objective criteria. The arbitral jurisprudence has yet to settle on whether the lack of an express definition of investment in the ICSID Convention delegates the defining issue entirely to the relevant IIA or if the term, as present in the Convention, should be given a meaning of its own (whether drawn from a dictionary or construed out of a 'reasonable interpretation' of what an investment should constitute, *in abstracto* or *in casu*). This issue has in turn ignited another i.e. which could be and how to weigh in the objective criteria each time individuated. Two lines of thought have developed. In brief, the first school, originating with the *Fedax N.V . v. The Republic of Venezuela* and *Salini Costruttori S.p.A. and Italstrade S.p.A. v. Kingdom of Morocco* cases,[24] tests to varying degrees the alleged investment against a number of criteria, four (investor's commitment and investment duration, risk and contribution to the host State development) or more (with the addition of returns and/or legality and/or good faith).[25] In some cases, however, these criteria have each been treated as a jurisdictional requirement, the lack thereof resulting in exclusion from ICSID arbitration. The second school rejects,[26] to varying extent, one or more criteria (as not expressly mentioned in the ICSID Convention, especially given the absence of a definition of investment in the treaty) and, in particular, the assumption that any such criterion may be assumed as a jurisdictional bar. On occasion, however, this position has come close to disregard the very dictionary meaning of the term investment.[27]

Although *in casu* most readings may be justified, the interpretive rebounds have contributed to an appearance of uncertainty that is ultimately detrimental to the foreign investment protection system as a whole. Indeed, the presence of objective criteria in the IIA does not directly solve potential jurisdictional issues arising out of the lack of a definition of investment in the ICSID Convention. However, in case of doubt (and at least formally bowing to the interpretive criteria enshrined in the 1980 Vienna Convention on the Law of Treaties), arbitrators often look at the treaty practice of States to corroborate their interpretation of the various clauses. Given the virtual impossibility of amending the ICSID Convention, for a State (or group of States) to consistently steer or maintain its treaty practice with respect to certain clauses, especially after certain arbitral decisions, is deemed significant.

4.2. *The Chinese practice*

In contrast to the US, China, along with the European States, offered scarce reaction to the jurisprudential debate on the definition of investment, at least until recently. Thus, Chinese models – and almost all actual treaties – do not list objective criteria to qualify the notion of investment.

However, in connection with the process of updating its investment treaty network by renegotiating BITs, which China embarked in since 2001, the definition of investment has progressively been articulated in greater detail. The first time occurred with the China-Germany BIT, 2003, addendum 1.a to Art. 1 clarifies:

> For the avoidance of doubt, the Contracting Parties agree that investments as defined in Article 1 are those made for the *purpose* of establishing *lasting economic relations in connection with an enterprise, especially* those which allow to *exercise effective influence* in its management.
>
> (emphases added)

It has to be preliminarily noted that the wording the parties agreed upon is exceptional, for both of them. Never was it previously employed, nor will either Party resort to it subsequently.[28] It is, hence, a significant innovation that the 2003 China-Germany BIT uniquely features, arguably justified by the consistent (and increasing) two-way investment flow (Hanemann and Huotari, 2017). The text appears to be, nevertheless, carefully crafted, apparently elaborating upon the

2001 *Salini* award. Compared to the Model BIT, US, 2004, and with reference to the above-mentioned doctrinal debate, the text of the *addendum* appears to offer more some cumulative guidelines than actual objective criteria, fashioning a compromise solution: out of the four *Salini* criteria, the treaty assumes as *preconditions* the elements of 'contribution' and 'risk' (as the investment 'purpose' is 'in connection with an enterprise'), but 'duration' (i.e. 'lasting economic relations') appears *controlling* (thus potentially excluding forms of venture capitalism or holdout exchanges). This nestling of elements appears in line with the plain dictionary meaning of investment. As regards to the 'effective influence' the investor may exercise, through the investment, on the management of the enterprise, it appears that the use of the preceding word 'especially' implies for such an 'influence' to be understood as an *inclusive* criterion (i.e. to support the qualification of investment as such, when from the analysis of the previous elements a clear-cut answer may not be ascertained), rather than a self-standing one (cf. Gallagher and Shan, 2009). This reading is also consistent with the 25% minimum shareholding stake required by Chinese law for joint ventures to properly qualify as 'foreign invested enterprise' (thus enjoying the related benefits).[29]

As mentioned, the wording of the 2003 China-Germany BIT is exceptional. The first time China actually included the objective criteria in the definition of investment has been in the 2008 BIT with Colombia, where the typical three US model characteristics are contained in a dedicated paragraph and listed in a cumulative fashion (2008 China-Colombia BIT, Art. 1.3). However, this was not yet established practice for China, as the other IIAs concluded in 2008 (with Mexico and New Zealand) and in 2009 (with Mali, Malta, Switzerland, Peru, and, most notably, ASEAN) do not feature any. It is in the 2011 BIT with Uzbekistan that the objective criteria appeared again, this time placed right after the definition of investment, but again framed cumulatively (2011 China-Uzbekistan BIT, Art. 1). From that moment on, it seems that the objective criteria became established Chinese practice. However, it should be noted that, in the BIT with Chile and the China-Japan-Korea trilateral Investment Agreement, 2012 (both of 2012), as well as in the FTAs with South Korea and Australia (both of 2015), the criteria lose their exclusive and cumulative characters and are fashioned as mere instances as in the US practice (the three listed elements are only 'such as' and separated by an 'or'). The 2012 BIT with Canada, perhaps due to its 18-year-long negotiation (Carter, 2009),[30] features instead what appears to be a transitional solution, as the list is closed, like in the earlier agreements with Colombia and Uzbekistan (i.e. it does not mention 'such as'), but the listed characteristics are alternatives (thanks to the 'or' between them). In interpretive terms, it thus seems that:

• In the two earlier agreements with Colombia and Uzbekistan the investment is required to possess all three mentioned characteristics;
• In the transition agreement with Canada any of the three; and
• In the more recent agreements with Chile, Japan and South Korea, Australia and South Korea, any characteristics 'such as' those listed.

The transitional definition in the BIT with Canada deserves a closer look, as with the shift toward the North American model, the provision is *in casu* based on the Canadian model. Consequently, the definition of investment does not feature the chapeau preceding the list of instances and the additional elements (i.e. *ratione personae* and *ratione loci*) are brought under the definition of 'covered investment'. Only the first part of this definition, however, reflects the Canadian custom; the second, as noted earlier, reproduces the US model objective criteria – albeit making them as a 'closed list' (as per Canada's practice on the list of investment instances). It may be inferred that China insisted on such an addition: on the one hand, Canada does not contemplate it in any other stipulation to which it is a Party; on the other, the simultaneously negotiated China-Chile Supplementary Agreement on Investment (SAI) features those criteria too (as all agreements concluded by Chile,[31] except that with Canada), as well as the China-Japan-Korea trilateral Investment Agreement. It seems that China, in its shift to the North American model and relying on Chile's extensive experience, chose to conform not only to the practice of Chile and the US,[32] but to a quite uniform trend in the Pacific (including the TPP).[33] The agreement with Chile, nevertheless, lacks the notion of covered investment and maintains the chapeau in the definition of investment (China-Chile SAI, Art. 1).

Paraphrasing the language in a recent award:[34] 'these provisions, whether or not introduced *ex abundanti cautela*, reflect the position under general international law' (para. 301). It seems that the intention of the contracting States, in light of the doctrinal debate detailed earlier, is that to provide some guidance in the interpretation of the elements expressly listed (and consented to), thus reducing (even if not prohibiting) resort to other means of interpretation and enhancing the predictability of the interpretive outcome.

5. 'In accordance with the laws': the *ratione legis* requirement

5.1. *Definition, treaty practice and interpretive trends*

The 'in accordance with the law' clause (less frequently formulated as 'pursuant to the law', here *ratione legis*) is a fairly typical IIA feature for most States and can be found in the majority of models (with the exception of Canada). The clause can take various forms,[35] and State practice differs on its position and frequency of repetition within the overall text. The Dutch and British models deprive it of its potential pre-merit character (whether of jurisdiction or admissibility, as discussed in the following text): in the latter, the clause appears, phrased differently, only as an exceptional condition *against* admission (each Party 'shall admit' the investment 'subject to its right to exercise powers conferred by its laws': Model BIT, UK, Art. 2.1). Together with the US, the three models resort to the wording of the clause only with reference to the concession category (as a specific instance in the definition of investment).[36] In the German model, instead, it is featured both in the 'promotion and protection' (i.e. each Party shall 'admit such investments in accordance with its legislation': German model BIT, Art. 2.1) and the 'application' provisions (i.e. the treaty applies to investments made 'consistent with the [host State] legislation': German model BIT, Art. 8). In the French, Italian and Chinese models, the clause is also reserved a highlighted status within the definition of investment.[37] It is on the rationale of this latter instance that the following focuses, without discarding however the other practices.

Preliminarily, it is to be observed that the wording is often referred in doctrine as the 'legality requirement' (e.g. *Saba Fakes*: 37 *et seq.*). Such a label, however, is a bit misleading: framing the clause in terms of 'legality', and the investor's alleged contrary conduct as 'illegal' (*Salini*, para. 46), brings the legal reasoning nearer to the criminal domain – which may not properly reflect the intention of the contracting parties. According to the Oxford Dictionary:

- 'illegal' means 'contrary to or forbidden by law, especially criminal law';
- 'unlawful' means 'not conforming to, permitted by or recognized by law or rules'.

Therefore, something that is illegal is against the law, whereas an unlawful act merely contravenes the rules that apply in a particular context. To frame the issue in terms of lawfulness/unlawfulness is arguably more appropriate, as the latters' meaning is closer to the text actually employed in investment agreements resorting to such clause. It follows the indication of the issue as *ratione legis* requirement (or condition), as clearly identifying the scope of the clause within the context in which it is used (along e.g. *ratione loci* and *ratione personae*).

Perhaps also because of the not uniform State practice, the implications of this clause have proved controversial. An overview of the relevant case-law is instructive in order to understand the rationale behind the various perspectives adopted.

The first case to have touched upon the issue seems to be the 2001 *Salini* award.[38] There, Art. 1.1 of the Italy-Morocco BIT featured the *ratione legis* clause in the definition of investment.[39] Contrary to Morocco's submission, the Tribunal convincingly held that reference to a host State's domestic law concerns not the domestic definition of the term investment, but solely its legality. In the words of the Tribunal, the clause:

> En visant 'les catégories de biens investis . . . conformément aux lois et règlements de la dite partie', la disposition en cause se réfère à la régularité de l'investissement et non à sa définition. Elle tend notamment à éviter que l'Accord bilatéral protège des investissements qui ne devraient pas l'être, notamment parce qu'ils seraient illicites.
>
> (*Salini*, para. 46)[40]

The locution 'la disposition se réfère à la *régularité* de l'investissement' has been translated differently into English on two occasions. The English translation of Gaillard and Banifatemi correctly provides 'this provision refers to the *validity* of the investment'. However, in the later *Inceysa Vallisoletana*,[41] where the quote above is relied upon in its entirety, the word 'regularité' has been translated into Spanish as 'legalidad' and in English as 'legality', which causes the sentence to acquire a different meaning than that intended by the *Salini* Tribunal. It is true that the last word in the second sentence of the quoted passage in *Salini* is 'illicite' and that such choice of word may be considered *a posteriori* not the most felicitous, as leading the reasoning toward the criminal law domain, which was something not in question at the time. That the *Salini* Tribunal was not considering the facts under a criminal perspective appears also from the rest of the paragraph from which the above quote is extracted (and often overlooked). The Tribunal, in fact, added:

> Yet, in the present case, the Claimants *took part in the tender process in conformity with the legal rules applicable to invitations to tender*. At the end of this procedure, they also won the bid and concluded the corresponding contract for services in conformity with the laws in force at that time.
>
> Thus, whether one looks to the *pre-contractual stage* or that corresponding to the *performance of the contract* for services, it has never been shown that the Italian companies infringed the laws and regulations of the Kingdom of Morocco.
>
> (*Salini*, para. 46; emphases added)

The Tribunal's reasoning appears thus concerned with conformity to tender rules and pre-contractual stage obligations, the breach of which may result into an 'illegal' (*rectius*, unlawful or uncovered) investment. For this reason, reference to the *ratione legis* clause or condition as the 'legality requirement' seems not to be entirely correct (as worded in *Saba Fakes*).

The *ratione legis* requirement has subsequently fallen under the scrutiny of various ICSID tribunals, including *Inceysa, Fraport*,[42] *Desert Line*,[43] and *Saba Fakes*.

In *Inceysa*, the dispute was grounded on the Spain-El Salvador BIT. There, the definition of investment does not feature the *ratione legis* requirement; however, Art. 2 ('promotion and admission') ties investment admission to such a condition.[44] After a careful analysis of the will of the State parties to the BIT as emerging form the *travaux preparatoires*, the Tribunal autonomously 'restored' the *ratione legis* requirement in the notion of investment.[45] However, it also went on to determine which violations of the *ratione legis* condition should be subject to its jurisdiction. There, somewhat surprisingly, it found that:

> [A]ny resolutions or decisions made by the State parties to the Agreement concerning the legality or illegality of the investment *are not valid or important* for the determination of whether they meet the requirements of ICSID Convention, Art. 25 and of the BIT, in order to decide whether or not the Arbitral Tribunal is competent to hear the dispute brought before it.
>
> (para. 210; emphasis added)

To hold otherwise, the Tribunal added,

> [W]ould imply giving signatory States of agreements for reciprocal pro-
> tection of investments that include the 'in accordance with law' clause the
> power to withdraw their consent unilaterally (because they would have the
> power to determine whether an investment was made in accordance with
> their legislation), once a dispute arises in connection with an investment.
>
> (para. 211)

Moreover, the Tribunal read the 'in accordance with the host State law'
requirement as a reference to general principles of law. Thus, it weighed the
investor's conduct against a number of such principles[46] (rather than the law
of the host State, as the *ratione legis* clause would have perhaps more plainly
required), one of them identified as 'international public policy'. The Tribunal
hence relied on such 'meta-positive provision that prohibits attributing effects to
an act done illegally' (para. 248) and concluded that 'not to exclude Inceysa's
investment from the protection of the BIT would be a violation of international
public policy, which this Tribunal cannot allow' (para. 252). Meta-reasoning
and public policy excursus notwithstanding, the Tribunal *in concreto* ultimately
weighed in the multiple procedural violations the investor performed in order to
secure the tender (paras. 104–127).

In *Fraport*, the dispute was grounded on the Germany-Philippines BIT, whose
definition of investment features the *ratione legis* requirement, reflecting the consistent practice of the Philippines (Germany-Philippines BIT, Art. 1.1).[47] There,
the respondent successfully pleaded that the investor 'consciously, intentionally
and covertly' structured its investment in a way that it knew was in violation of
the State's law on foreign participation and control in public utility companies
(para. 323) (i.e. not a criminal violation). In this respect, no question of estoppel
was held against the State (i.e. from raising violations of its own law as a jurisdictional defence), as there was 'no indication in the record that the Republic of the
Philippines knew, should have known or could have known of the covert arrangements which were not in accordance with Philippine law' (para. 347).

In *Desert Line*, the 1998 Yemen-Oman BIT featured, in the chapeau of the
definition of investment, a quite specific *ratione legis* condition: 'The term investment shall mean . . . accepted by the host party, as investment according to its
laws and regulations, and for which an investment certificate is issued' (1998
Yemen-Oman BIT, Art. 1.1). In the case, Yemen's claim that the investment
was in violation of such a tight *ratione legis* clause was self-defeating, as its highest authorities were the first to act *per facta concludentia*;[48] elementary considerations of *bona fide* and estoppel could have perhaps sufficed in countering the
argument.[49] The Tribunal, instead, while ultimately reached a similar conclusion,
offered first an analysis of the previous case-law in *L.E.S.I.*,[50] *Inceysa*, and *Fraport*,
concluding that the *ratione legis* clause is 'intended to ensure the legality of the
investment by excluding investments made in breach of *fundamental principles*
of the host State's law' (paras. 104–105; emphasis added). Also with regard to

the stringent 'acceptance' and 'certificate' requirements of the BIT, the Tribunal, relying e.g. on *Tokio Tokeles*[51] and *Salini*, found that the appropriate interpretation of the clause should not render an investment excluded from BIT protection due to 'minor errors' (paras. 113–117). Still, the decision left a vast grey area between 'fundamental principles' (*Inceysa*) and 'minor errors' (*Desert Line*) undefined.

Lastly, in *Saba Fakes*, the Netherlands-Turkey BIT expressly mentioned the *ratione legis* requirement only with regard to admission (as in *Inceysa*). The Tribunal held that

> violation [of legislation relating to the encouragement of foreign investment], if demonstrated, might be covered by the legality requirement of Article 2(2) of the Netherlands-Turkey BIT and – as a consequence – might lead the present Tribunal to conclude that the conditions set forth by the BIT for an investment to be protected were not met.
>
> (para. 120).

In deciding the case, however, the Tribunal ultimately found that the claimant did not hold an investment in Turkey, therefore it did not entertain any further analysis on the *ratione legis* criterion.

It cannot escape that all aforementioned decisions were rendered in the form of decisions on jurisdiction (*Salini*), jurisdictional awards (*Inceysa, Fraport, LESI, Saba Fakes*), or awards on both jurisdiction and merit where the *ratione legis* criterion would nevertheless be dealt with in the jurisdictional section (*Desert Line*). Consequently, it seems clear that the issue is understood as one of jurisdiction.

Some scholars have expressed concerns as to the way the issue was dealt with e.g. in *Fraport* (Bottini, 2010).[52] On the contrary, it appears that, by including in the text of the BIT the *ratione legis* clause, the intention of States is that to insist on respect for domestic civil and administrative laws and regulations on investments, with particular attention to those on admission (Pollan, 2006, as cited in Dolzer and Schreuer, 2012: 89; Carreau and Juillard, 2010).[53] It seems uncontroversial that it is up to the tribunal to determine the existence of such violations (as one of the key purposes of the investment protection system, even today, is to avoid the host State's civil courts – with the limit of findings pertaining to criminal jurisdiction, because *domain réservé* of States). It is, however, debated whether the issue vests an exclusively jurisdictional character, or it may also be one of admissibility or simply contribute to the assessment of facts (cf. Cremades dissenting opinion attached to the *Fraport* decision, paras. 37–38). In this author's opinion, the answer to this question depends on the location of the *ratione legis* clause: if inserted in the treaty provision of scope or application (alongside e.g. the *ratione temporis* and *ratione materiae*, as per the German model), the issue accordingly assumes a jurisdictional character. Conversely, in the context of the definition of investment, the *ratione legis* requirement appears more fit to pertain to admissibility.

5.2. *The uniform Chinese treaty practice*

It has been observed that China supports the principle that 'foreign investment does promote national development very much *on the condition* that it can be effectively regulated' (Cai, 2012: 281). It is therefore unsurprising that the opening statement of Model BIT, China, 1997, Art. 1 model requires the investment, in order to properly qualify as such, to be an asset 'invested . . . in accordance with the laws and regulations of the other Contracting Party'.

Analysing the Chinese practice reveals that, out of the 119 IIAs that are *i)* publicly available *ii)* in force, *iii)* not superseded by subsequent stipulations and *iii)* feature at least some form of ISDS,[54] the definition of investment features the *ratione legis* condition in 109 cases. In five of the nine instances where it is not expressly mentioned (BITs with the Netherlands, Germany, Uganda, Portugal and Switzerland), it is nevertheless featured in both the admission and application provisions; in one case (BIT with Canada), it is featured in the definition of 'covered investment' and in the admission provision; in another (BIT with Seychelles, not in force) it is mentioned with reference to 'indirect investment'; in two cases, identically worded and with partly identical parties (Japan and Korea TIA, and FTA with Korea), it is limited to the British formulation on admission; and, in only one case (FTA with New Zealand), it is entirely absent.

Notwithstanding the question of the jurisdictional or admissibility character of the clause, the consistency of the Chinese practice on the point appears highly significant, the condition being expressly tied to the definition of investment in over 91% of the treaties and anyway featured in other key provisions in over 96% of the cases.[55] Indeed, it has been a constant without exception for China up to the 2001 BIT renegotiations with the Netherlands and, more clearly, to the 2003 renegotiation with Germany[56] – where China adjusted to the German practice of including it in the admission and application provisions.

That China's concern is the uniform application of and respect for its domestic civil and administrative laws is also confirmed not only by the fact that, in most agreements where the *ratione legis* clause is not expressly tied to the definition of investment, it is nonetheless reaffirmed elsewhere, but also by the understanding reached with Cuba in the 2007 amendment to the 1995 China-Cuba BIT, where the Parties expressly agreed that 'in accordance with the laws and regulations':

> [S]hall mean that for any kind of invested assets to be considered as investment protected in this Agreement, it shall be *in accordance with any of the investment modalities defined by the legislation* of the Contracting Party receiving the investment *and registered as such in the corresponding registry.*
> (2007 China-Cuba BIT, 2007 renegotiation, point 1; emphasis added)

The concern appears procedural (rather than substantive) and of a civil and administrative (rather than criminal) nature. As illustrated in the previous section, by including the *ratione legis* requirement in the definition of investment, States seem thus to establish a ground for an objection on admissibility, as 'investment' comes to include the investor's compliance with the requirements dictated by domestic law regarding operating a business, and the administrative *iter* for admission (Dolzer and Stevens, 1995). Such a reading of the *ratione legis* clause is significant for the People's Republic, as it still operates a systematic case-by-case admission screening on each foreign investment.[57] In that sense, this practice is shared by regional neighbour ASEAN, which is concerned with the respect for domestic civil and administrative laws and regulations among its Member States as regards admittance and approval of foreign investments.[58] Designed (and understood) as such, the provision stresses the relevance of the party's administrative regulations – as only assets invested accordingly can be considered investments covered by the IIA guarantees. Operating at the admissibility level, the investment's *ratione legis* clause would thus refer to cases of (alleged) breaches of civil and administrative norms.

As noted earlier, in three recent IIAs China agreed to exclude the *ratione legis* clause not only in the definition of investment, but in the agreement as a whole: the 2008 FTA with New Zealand (China-NZ FTA), the 2012 Japan and South Korea TIA and the 2015 FTA with South Korea (the last two identically worded on the point).[59]

The China-NZ FTA reproduces most of the wording of the 2003 China-Germany BIT renegotiation (thus, not featuring the *ratione legis* clause). In this respect, the agreement is noteworthy, as the wording 'in accordance with the law' is not mentioned at all in the text of the FTA (however, numerous generic references to general international law – otherwise entirely absent in China's practice – are found).[60]

A much different result was reached just the following year, within the 2009 China-ASEAN Investment Agreement (CAIA). Sharing ASEAN with China the same concern and mind set at the basis of the *ratione legis* criterion, it is not surprising that, leveraging on the old BITs between China and each ASEAN Member State, in the CAIA the definition of investment features the wording of the first Chinese model of 1984, expressly mentioning 'in accordance with the relevant laws and regulations of the other Party' at the heart of the provision (CAIA, Art. 1.1.d). Actually, the requirement is strengthened with the addition of the ASEAN-derived 'policies'.

By employing the Canadian model BIT as template,[61] the 2012 China-Canada BIT features the definition of 'covered investment' (a first, for China). The first part of this definition is a repetition of the wording featured in the 2004 Canadian model for the *ratione loci* and *temporis*.[62] Subsequently, an alternative 'or' introduces the second part of the sentence, which covers 'an investment of an investor *admitted* in accordance with its laws and regulations thereafter' (emphasis added). The typical Chinese *ratione legis* requirement is here phrased in the past tense 'admitted' (*in lieu* of the usual 'made').[63] As such, the Parties have been unequivocal in their intention that the clause covers only laws relating to the admission of investments – as opposed to a generalized review of the investment's legality. As a result, this part of the provision replicates the 'application' provision of the Chinese model (not considering *de minimis* departures) (1997 China model BIT,

Art. 11). The definition of covered investment in the China-Canada BIT consti- tutes thus a 'separated yet living together' state of affairs, with the coexistence of two self-standing notions, separated by an 'or': the first, reproducing the Cana- dian standard; the second, originally – and, so far, uniquely – combining the tra- ditional Chinese *ratione legis* requirement to the typical objective criteria featured in the US chapeau of the notion of investment (actually, *in lieu* of the chapeau).

In the China-Chile Supplementary Agreement on Investment (SAI), which maintains the Canadian model template and was signed on the very same day than the China-Canada BIT,[64] the definition of covered investment is neverthe- less discarded, and a more typical Chinese definition of investment restored, including the *ratione legis* condition.

6. Objective criteria and *ratione legis* condition in the future BITs with the US and the EU

China is currently negotiating separate BITs with the US and the EU, and these latter are, in turn, negotiating the Transatlantic Trade and Investment Partner- ship (TTIP). The parallel negotiations between the world's three largest eco- nomic players undoubtedly create expectations – especially taking into account that a uniform result on any aspect of these treaties would *motu proprio* tend to create an international standard. Nevertheless, none of the three agreements is likely to see the light of day soon. China's negotiations for a BIT with the US commenced in 1983: paused and restarted on several occasions, despite recent announcements of major breakthroughs (cf. US Department of Treasury, 2013) the process seems to have slowed down again (by reason of the US presiden- tial elections first and its outcome). Negotiations for the China-EU BIT were launched in November 2013, but quick results are not likely to be forthcoming in light of several roadblocks on the part of the EU (Vaccaro-Incisa, 2016) cou- pled with what seems to be China's lack of interest in negotiating an investment regime with the EU devoid of a more comprehensive FTA framework.[65] Some considerations may nonetheless be offered as regards the definition of investment based on the investment treaty policy and practice of the actors involved.

With regard to the objective criteria, it seems that China has embraced the US formulation – and this not only as a matter of 'policy mirroring', but also because the very presence of criteria reflects an attempt to bridle the interpreter, thus responding to Chinese policy concerns. As regards the EU, the texts finalized (agreements with Singapore, Canada and Vietnam) and drafts publicly known (TTIP) reveal that the EU has embraced the US model as well. In addition, all EU texts feature the criterion of 'a certain duration' (in the agreement with Can- ada and in the TTIP proposal, placed first and framed in a mandatory fashion), which echoes the China-Germany BIT renegotiation of 2003. In this sense, it is believed China will welcome this addition.

The inclusion of the *ratione legis* condition tied to the definition of investment, however, is more uncertain. While the condition is featured in the vast majority of Chinese treaties, in some recent stipulations – even with a key partner like

Japan – China has been open enough to strike it from the entire treaty. As noted earlier, the US does not consider it in its model or practice. The EU, in contrast, retains such a condition: in the agreement with Canada and the draft TTIP proposal, it is featured in in the definition of 'covered investment'; in the agreements with Singapore and Vietnam, it has been merged in the 'scope' provision (echoing the German practice).

For these reasons, it is possible to infer that the objective criteria will make their way into all three treaties (the additional element of 'duration' being however more plausible at this stage in the China-EU BIT); it remains to be seen whether the combined template negotiating position of China and the EU will induce the US to accept the *ratione legis* condition, whether tied to the definition of investment or elsewhere in the treaty.

7. Conclusion

The foregoing, alongside a general review of two key characteristics of the definition of investment – namely, the objective criteria and the *ratione legis* clause – outlined China's treaty-making policy and practice in these particular areas.

Regarding the objective criteria, it appears that China has recently evolved its policy. Until 2008 and the conclusion of the comprehensive FTA with New Zealand, the Chinese investment program consisted only of BITs,[66] largely based on a Chinese model text. Consequently, the exceptional BIT renegotiation with Germany of 2003 aside, no agreement featured additional qualifying elements to the notion of investment. Subsequently, in 2008 with Colombia and in 2011 with Uzbekistan, the typical US criteria were included, albeit in a narrower and cumulative fashion. With the gradual turn towards the North American model of investment protection and the stipulation, in 2012, of the agreements with Canada, Chile and Japan and South Korea, this seems to have become common practice for China (i.e. the 2015 FTAs with Australia and China-Korea FTA, 2015, but not the 2015 BIT with Turkey). Along other policy developments, China's openness to include the objective criteria appears dictated principally by three factors. The first is the People's Republic shift, from a predominantly recipient State to one of the most significant sources of FDI worldwide: as such, China was pushed to consider granting more advanced standards of protection to its own interests abroad (considering that *i)* mostly are primarily conducted through State owned enterprises; *ii)* Chinese FDI is expected to rise to over 1 trillion USD by 2020 (Hanemann and Rosen, 2012); and *iii)* Chinese investors have started exploiting China's BIT network to protect their investments).[67] The second reason flows from the first, as it is not at all surprising that China modulates its growing economic power internationally by emulating US standards in the same field (as it traditionally relied on the German and British experience before, given their significant BIT networks and investment outflows). The third is the jurisprudential debate that continues to take place with regard to the definition of investment: a question that the presence of the objective criteria may contribute to settle (responding to the concern for securing a stable and predictable system).

It therefore appears that China is prepared to accept the progressive enrichment of the definition of investment, *inter alia* with the introduction of the objective criteria.

With regard to the *ratione legis* condition, China displayed remarkable path dependence, without significant exceptions until 2003. Then, the clause began being occasionally removed from the definition of investment, but remained in the admission and application provisions (BITs with Germany, Switzerland, Portugal and Uganda), thus leaving a clear jurisdictional *ratione legis* threshold. In the BIT with Canada, the condition is solely framed with reference to admission. Yet, it is only with the China-NZ FTA, the Japan and South Korea TIA and the subsequent FTA with South Korea that the clause is left out of the text of the treaty altogether. In light of China's very broad investment treaty network, these are, however, exceptions, but Chinese policy on this issue reveals a high degree of uniformity, seemingly aimed at underscoring the fundamental character of investor compliance with domestic civil laws and regulations on admission and management of foreign investment in the host State.

Analysing the Chinese investment treaty practice – not only with exclusive reference to the definition of investment – reveals constant and consistent attention to shielding policy and sovereign concerns (analogous to those of ASEAN) and an attempt to set definitions capable of conveying predictable interpretive outcomes, namely what constitutes an investment.[68] Indeed, albeit from a different perspective, concerns over the protection of sovereign prerogatives are now common also in most Western States. It may be concluded that alterations to the Chinese template are taken in *cum grano salis*,[69] in light of the concrete necessities of China, at home and abroad, without policy overturns. Convenience appears to be the leading criterion at the basis of the current partial and gradual reshaping of China's investment treaty policy, though always carried out within a general conservative framework and with the desire to maintain a uniform investment treaty regime. The current negotiations to establish an investment protection regime with the US, on the one side, and the EU, on the other, if ever concluded, are expected to ultimately achieve a relatively uniform result, which may in turn set the international standard in international investment law well beyond the two key issues analysed in this chapter.

Notes

1 The chapter develops an issue tangentially touched upon in the course of the Ph.D. research on China's policy rationale and treaty-making on the protection of foreign investment: a comparative perspective, from the model BITs to the latest stipulations. I wish to thank Jurgen Kurtz (Melbourne) and Julien Chaisse (CUHK) for their comments to earlier draft of this work. I also wish to thank Ms. Alessandra Moroni for her editing assistance. Any errors are the author's sole responsibility.
2 Art. 8.1: '(a) The term "investment" shall comprise capital brought into the territory of the other Party for investments in various forms in the shape of assets such as foreign exchange, goods, property rights, patents and technical knowledge.

The term "investment" shall also include the returns derived from and ploughed back into such "investment". (b) Any partnership, companies or assets of similar kind, created by the utilization of the above-mentioned assets shall be regarded as "investment"'.

3 Art. 9.c: '"Property" means all property, rights and interests, whether held directly or indirectly, including the interest which a member of a company is deemed to have in the property of the company'; the comment attached to the text of the Draft Convention stresses, at p. 43, that the use of the term 'property' was 'meant to be used in its widest sense which includes, but it not limited to, investments'.

4 e.g. German, British, Dutch, French, Italian, US models; in the Canadian model, the list of instances is closed.

5 Over the time China has adopted three model BITs: in 1984, 1989 and 1997 (Gallagher and Shan, 2009).

6 According to the UNCTAD online database, China is currently party to 139 IIAs in force (http://investmentpolicyhub.unctad.org/IIA); however, see Section 1, below.

7 Among the principal model BITs, only the US, since 2004, expressly lists some of them; cf., Art. 1 US model BIT: *i)* commitment of capital or other resources, *ii)* expectation of gain or profit and *iii)* assumption of risk.

8 e.g. the first 'best effort' NT clause was featured in the 1986 PRC-UK BIT.

9 In 1997, in occasion of the negotiations for the China-Barbados BIT, 'The [Request for Authorization of negotiation] suggested the State Council giving a general or standing authorization on such negotiations with other States based on [the 1997 model BIT], so that the [Ministry of Foreign Trade and Economic Cooperation] and the [Ministry of Foreign Affairs] did not need to seek specific authorization on such negotiations, unless there were "major changes" in the treaty text' (Gallagher and Shan, 2009: 40).

10 This is the case e.g. of the negotiations for the China-US BIT and the China-Canada BIT: the former begun in 1983, repeatedly halted and re-launched and still on-going; the latter lasted for 18 years, from 1994 to 2012.

11 E.g. adjusting the wording of national treatment (NT), MFN, expropriation and investor-State arbitration clauses.

12 Unrestricted *a priori* consent was granted the first time in the 1997 BIT with South Africa; it is however only with the 1998 BIT with Barbados that the same was granted in the context of ICISD arbitration.

13 The data contained in UNCTAD's Investment Policy Hub has been scrutinized in order to focus only on the agreements actually establishing a foreign investment protection regime. In combination with the data contained on the MOF-COM website, as well as the treaty texts not publicly available yet kindly disclosed by the Ministry to the author for this research, the data shown here is believed to be the most accurate and up to date on the Chinese IIA network.

14 i.e. feature ISDS at least for the amount of compensation due to expropriation (58 IIAs out of 119).

15 ICSID arbitration is not mentioned in the BITs with South Africa (1997), Iran (2000), Nigeria (2001), North Korea (2005) and Cuba (1995, overhauled in 2007).

16 i.e. that the investment must be made by a properly qualifying investor.

17 i.e. that the investment must be made in the territory of the host State.

18 i.e. that the investment must be made after the entry into force of the agreement.

19 i.e. that the investment must be made in accordance with the law of the host State.

20 The definition in the US model indicates as well that the investor must own or control, directly or indirectly, the investment.

21 As the list of investment instances is therein closed, the Canadian model is particularly detailed.

22 Regarding the wording specific of the Chinese model, it shall be noted that the *ratione personae, legis* and *loci* criteria made their way in the subsequent German practice, at times all of them (e.g. BITs with USSR and Poland, of 1989; Brazil, 1995; Iran, 2002), at times only *personae* and *loci* (e.g. China, 2003; Libya, 2004), at times only *legis* (e.g. India, 1995; Indonesia, 2003; Yemen, 2005; Oman, 2007). Nevertheless, most times Germany kept the simple 1991 model approach (e.g. BITs with Guyana, 1994; Croatia, 1997; Gabon, 1998; Lebanon, 1999; Nigeria, 2000; Timor-Leste, 2005; Guinea, 2006). It appears, in this respect, that more articulated stipulations were reserved to counterparts with either a stronger negotiating position or investment potential. With the 2008 model BIT, Germany ultimately adopted both *ratione personae* and *loci* in the chapeau of the definition of investment.

23 Despite being elaborated for the first time in *Salini Costruttori S.p.A. and Italstrade S.p.A. v. Kingdom of Morocco*, ICSID Case No. ARB/00/4, Decision on Jurisdiction, 23 July 2001, an infrastructure project.

24 e.g. *Fedax N.V. v. The Republic of Venezuela*, ICSID Case No. ARB/96/3, Decision on Objections to Jurisdiction, 11 July 1997; *Salini*, fn. 22 above; *Joy Mining Machinery Limited v. Arab Republic of Egypt*, ICSID Case No. ARB/03/11, Award on Jurisdiction, 6 August 2004; *Mr. Patrick Mitchell v. Democratic Republic of the Congo*, ICSID Case No. ARB/99/7, Decision on the Application for Annulment of the Award, 1 November 2006; *Saipem S.p.A. v. The People's Republic of Bangladesh*, ICSID Case No. ARB/05/07, Decision on Jurisdiction and Recommendation on Provisional Measures, 21 March 2007; *Malaysian Historical Salvors, SDN, BHD v. The Government of Malaysia*, ICSID Case No. ARB/05/10, Award on Jurisdiction, 17 March 2007.

25 e.g. *Phoenix Action v. The Czech Republic*, ICSID Case No. ARB/06/5, Award, 15 April 2009, paras. 100–113.

26 e.g. *M.C.I. Power Group L.C. and New Turbine, Inc. v. Republic of Ecuador*, ICSID Case No. ARB/03/6, Award, 31 July 2007; *Biwater Gauff (Tanzania) Ltd. v. United Republic of Tanzania*, ICSID Case No. ARB/05/22, Award, 24 July 2008; *Malaysian Historical Salvors, SDN, BHD v. The Government of Malaysia*, ICSID Case No. ARB/05/10, Decision on the Application for Annulment, 16 April 2009 (note however, the dissenting opinion of Judge Mr Shahabuddeen); *Saba Fakes v. Turkey*, ICSID Case No. ARB/07/20, Award, 14 July 2010; *Abaclat and Others v. Argentine Republic*, ICSID Case No. ARB/07/5, Decision on Jurisdiction, 4 August 2011; *Deutsche Bank AG v. Democratic Socialist Republic of Sri Lanka*, ICSID Case No. ARB/09/2, Award, 31 October 2012. It is significant that in *Saba Fakes* the criteria were reduced to three: *i)* a contribution, *ii)* a certain duration and *iii)* an element of risk. The taking is significant, as in 2001 the Tribunal in *Salini*, fn. 22 above, made an express reference to the three criteria individuated by Professor Gaillard (president of the 2010 Tribunal in *Saba Fakes*) in 1999, to which it added the 'contribution to the host State development' in light of the ICSID preamble (cf. *Salini*, para. 100). The fact that in *Saba Fakes* such fourth criterion was nevertheless discarded is believed to mark a strong doctrinal response in the context of the debate over the characteristics of foreign investments.

27 e.g. *Biwater*, fn. 25 above, para. 321, and the possibility to consider investment a 'loss leader' project (see fn. above).

28 Germany has not made use of such wording in the agreements with Iran (2002), Libya (2004), Afghanistan (2005), Timor-Leste (2005), Guinea (2006), Madagascar (2006). Out of such BITs, those with Afghanistan, Madagascar and Timor-Leste feature an *Addendum* to Art. 1 which, however, provides as follows:

(a) Returns from the investment and, in the event of their reinvestment, the returns therefrom shall enjoy the same protection as the investment. (b) Without prejudice to any other method of determining nationality, in particular any person in possession of a national passport issued by the competent authorities of the Contracting State concerned shall be deemed to be a national of that Contracting State.

29 From 1979 (adoption of the Law of Sino-Foreign Equity Joint Ventures, China, 1979 was passed) until 1986 (adoption of the Law of Wholly Foreign Owned Enterprises, China, 1986), equity joint ventures were the only form of foreign investment possible in China. In 1988, with the adoption of the Law of Sino-Foreign Contractual Joint Ventures, this form of investment was ultimately opened to foreigners. According to the OECD, joint ventures are still the most popular form of foreign investment in China (cf. Davies, 2013).

30 The first attempts to negotiate the China-Canada BIT date back to 1994. Difficulties in reconciling the Parties' positions on a number of issues, however, stalled off negotiations. Part of the difficulty in reaching an agreement has been attributed to divergences in the respective BIT programs (e.g. China's early refusal to negotiate for investor-State dispute settlement mechanisms; China's accession to the WTO, in 2001, contributed to mitigate the parties' respective positions). The China-Canada BIT has had a strong impact also on structure and content of the China-Chile SAI.

31 i.e. Chile's IIAs with the US, Australia, Japan and Korea; the wording is always the same, drawn from the US model BIT.

32 e.g. the recent Korea-US FTA, Art. 11.28.

33 e.g. the ASEAN Comprehensive Agreement on Investment (ACIA), at footnote 2 of the definition of investment (Art. 4), establishes an explicit binding condition: 'Where an asset lacks the characteristics of an investment, that asset is not an investment regardless of the form it may take. The characteristics of an investment include the commitment of capital, the expectation of gain or profit, or the assumption of risk'.

34 *Philip Morris Brands Sàrl, Philip Morris Products S.A. and Abal Hermanos S.A. v. Oriental Republic of Uruguay*, ICSID Case No. ARB/10/7, Award, 8 July 2016.

35 In this sense, also *Saba Fakes*, fn. 25 above, para. 186: 'among the mechanisms used to include this limitation is to add it into the definition of investment itself, making it clear that for the purposes of that reciprocal protection agreement only those made in accordance with the laws of the host State will be deemed investments'.

36 i.e. in the US model 'licenses, authorizations, permits, and similar rights conferred pursuant to domestic law'; in the UK model: 'business concessions conferred by law'.

37 In the Chinese and Italian models, in the chapeau; in the French model, in a dedicated paragraph after the list of investment instances.

38 Even though under a different perspective; see *Salini*, fn. 22 above.

39 Art. 1.1 Italy-Morocco BIT (the French text being authoritative):

> Le terme "investissement" désigne toutes les catégories de biens investis après l'entrée en vigueur du présent Accord par une personne physique ou morale, y compris le Gouvernement d'une Partie Contractante, dans le territoire de l'autre Partie Contractante, conformément aux lois et règlements de ladite Partie.

40 According to the translation of Gaillard and Banifatemi (counsels for the claimant in the case):

> In focusing on 'the categories of invested assets . . . in accordance with the laws and regulations of the aforementioned party' this provision refers to the

validity of the investment and not to its definition. More specifically, it seeks to prevent the Bilateral Investment Treaty from protecting investments that should not be protected because they would be illegal.

English text available at <www.italaw.com/cases/documents/959>.

41 *Inceysa Vallisoletana S.L. v. Republic of El Salvador*, ICSID Case No. ARB/03/26, Award, 2 August 2006.

42 *Fraport AG Frankfurt Airport Services Worldwide v. Republic of the Philippines*, ICSID Case No. ARB/03/25, Award, 16 August 2007 (decision annulled, on grounds unrelated to the present analysis, on 23 December 2010).

43 *Desert Line Projects LLC v. The Republic of Yemen*, ICSID Case No. ARB/05/17, Award, 6 February 2008.

44 Art. 2.1 Spain-El Salvador BIT: 'Cada Parte Contratante promoverá la realización de inversiones en su territorio por inversores de la otra Parte Contratante y admitirá estas inversiones conforme a sus disposiciones legales'.

45 Where there was clear evidence that El Salvador insisted for the *ratione legis* condition to be inserted in the notion of investment, and Spain's reply that it was already understood as being part of it, without express mention. Cf. *Inceysa*, fn. 40 above, paras. 190–196.

46 i.e. *i) bona fide, ii) nemo auditor propriam turpitudinem allegans, iii)* international public order, *iv)* general prohibition of unlawful enrichment; id., fn. 40, para. 230 *et seq.*

47 Art. 1.1 Germany-Philippines BIT: 'The term "investment" shall mean any kind of asset accepted in accordance with the respective laws and regulations of either Contracting State, and more particularly, though not exclusively.' The Philippines, even more than China or ASEAN, and even within the ASEAN framework, traditionally display a very cautious approach towards the protection of foreign investment, with specific attention on admission.

48 i.e. by implicit consent.

49 The Tribunal addresses the estoppel argument at para. 120.

50 Which shared the same president of the tribunal of *Desert Line* (i.e. Mr. Tercier); cf. *L.E.S.I. S.p.A. and ASTALDI S.p.A. v. République Algérienne Démocratique et Populaire*, ICSID Case No. ARB/05/3, Decision on Jurisdiction, 12 July 2006.

51 *Tokios Tokelés v. Ukraine*, ICSID Case No. ARB/02/18, Decision on Jurisdiction, 29 April 2014; paras. 83–86.

52 Bottini, expresses concerns with regard to the application of a criterion as such in the case of corruption. The problem, however, appears not correctly posited.

53 See especially Pollan, 2006 (as cited in Dolzer and Schreuer, 2012: 89), where it is synthetically illustrated the difference between admission and establishment, in that 'the right of "admission" concerns the right of entry of the investment in principle, whereas the right of "establishment" pertains to the conditions under which the investor is allowed to carry out its business during the period of investment'.

54 i.e. including IIAs that allow for ISDS solely on the amount of compensation due to expropriation.

55 i.e. excluding the IIAs with Seychelles, Japan and Korea, Korea and New Zealand.

56 In the case of the China-Netherland renegotiation, while the *ratione legis* condition is not expressly mentioned in the definition of investment, the Addendum to Art. 1 features it with regard to indirect investment. Taking into account that the clause is also featured in the admission and application provisions, an argument *a minore ad maius* seems plausible (if indirect investment are covered, why direct investment should not be).

57 China has undertaken some international obligations to open up certain service sectors in accordance with GATS commitments; nevertheless, the entry of foreign

investment is dealt with in China's domestic laws and regulations. According to the 'Regulation on Guiding Foreign Investment, China' and the 'Industrial Catalogue for Guiding Foreign Investments, China' (both available online in their latest versions) industries and sectors (*i.e.* manufacturing, services and agriculture) related to foreign investment are classified into four categories: encouraged, permitted, restricted and forbidden; the number of conditions and permits required by each of them varies greatly; for a detailed description of those and for an overview of China's FDI approval system (Shan, 2005).

58 For instance, the *ratione legis* requirement can be found in the ASEAN Comprehensive Agreement on Investment, the China-ASEAN Investment Agreement and the ASEAN-Australia-New Zealand FTA. In the AANZFTA, the condition is made only eventual ('where applicable'); in the ACIA, to the contrary, the admission phase (and the investor's compliance with it) appears mandatory, while the eventual supplemental condition ('where applicable') refers to the requirement for the investment to be 'specifically approved in writing by the competent authority of a Member State'.

59 The investment regime featured in the China-Australia FTA, 2015 contains the *ratione legis* clause in the definition of covered investment, even though with reference to admission only. The FTA is not here considered as *i)* its access to ISDS is approximately immaterial (being allowed only for violations of the NT standard) and *iii)* its text is expected to be comprehensively reviewed within the next 3 years.

60 e.g. Art. 3.2 (Relation to Other Agreements); Art. 143.1 (FET standard); Art. 190.3 (Functions of Arbitral Tribunals).

61 See fn. 7.

62 'Covered investment means, with respect to a Contracting Party, an investment in its territory of an investor of the other Contracting Party existing on the date of entry into force of this Agreement'; Canada's 2006 draft model adds in the definition the notion of ownership or control, absent in the 2004 model.

63 The verb 'admitted' is also used in ACIA's definition of covered investment (Art. 4.a).

64 Both the China-Chile SAI and the China-Canada BIT feature and follow the order of the first three sections typical of the Canadian template (Section A – 'Definitions'; Section B – 'Substantive obligations'; Section C – 'Investor-State dispute settlement'); both feature, also, a fourth section (Section D) listing, however, provisions on exceptions and exclusions (rather than State-to-State dispute settlement procedure, as per the Canadian Models). Curiously, it is not China's agreement with Canada the one featuring also the fifth section (i.e. Section E – 'Final provisions'), but that with Chile Section D of the China-Canada BIT features both exceptions and final provisions.

65 The EU-China trade is in excess of 480 billion euros; conversely, only 2.1% of EU FDI lands in China and 6% of Chinese FDI is destined to the EU area (the European Commission, available at <http://ec.europa.eu/trade/policy/countries-and-regions/countries/china/>). On China's preference for an FTA, see Godement and Stanzel (2015: 5–8).

66 With the exception of the 2006 FTA with Pakistan, whose investment protection regime, nonetheless, reproduced literally the Chinese model BIT of 1997.

67 With mixed success (partly so because of the various limits older Chinese BIT feature, at the time thought to shield China from foreign claims): e.g. *Señor Tza Yap Shum v. The Republic of Peru*, ICSID Case No. ARB/07/6, Decision on Jurisdiction and Competence, 19 June 2009; *Sanum Investments v. Laos*, UNCITRAL, PCA Case No. 2013–13, Decision on Jurisdiction, 13 December 2013; *China Heilongjiang v. Mongolia*, UNCITRAL, PCA (initiated in 2010, pending);

Ping-An Life Insurance Company of China Ltd. v. Kingdom of Belgium, ICSID Case No. ARB/12/29, Award on Jurisdiction, 30 April 2015; *Beijing Urban Construction v. Yemen,* ICSID Case No. ARB/14/30, Decision on Jurisdiction, 31 May 2017.

68 On the other hand, market economies prefer a more liberal approach, where the definition of investment is as open as possible (possibly including additional references to 'ownership and control' or 'direct and indirect' investment).

69 *i.e.* with a grain of salt.

References

Bottini, G. (2010). Legality of Investments Under ICSID Jurisprudence. In M. Waibel et al., eds., *The Backlash Against Investment Arbitration,* Wolters Kluwer, pp. 297–314.

Cai, C. (2012). China. In W. Shan, ed., *The Legal Protection of Foreign Investment – A Comparative Study,* Oxford: Hart Publishing, pp. 243–286.

Carreau, D. and Juillard, P. (2010). *Droit International Économique.* Dalloz.

Carter, J. (2009). The Protracted Bargain: Negotiating the Canada-China Foreign Investment Promotion and Protection Agreement. *Canadian Yearbook of International Law,* 47, 197–260.

Davies, K. (2013). *China Investment Policy: An Update,* OECD Working Papers on International Investment 2013/01.

Dolzer, R. and Schreuer, C. (2012). *Principles of International Investment Law,* Oxford: Oxford University Press.

Dolzer, R. and Stevens, M. (1995). *Bilateral Investment Treaties,* Leiden: Martinus Nijhoff Publishers.

Gallagher, N. and Shan, W. (2009). *Chinese Investment Treaties – Policies and Practice,* Oxford: Oxford University Press.

Godement, F. and Stanzel, A. (2015). The European interest in an investment treaty with China, www.ecfr.eu/publications/summary/the_european_interest_in_an_investment_treaty_with_china332

Hanemann, T. and Huotari, M. (2017). *Chinese Investment in Europe: Record Flows and Growing Imbalances.* Joint Report by Mercator Institute for China Studies and Rhodium Group, www.merics.org/sites/default/files/2017-09/MPOC_3_COFDI_2017.pdf

Hanemann, T. and Rosen, D. (2012). *China Invests in Europe – Patterns, Impacts and Policy Implications.* Report by Rhodium Group, https://rhg.com/wp-content/uploads/2012/06/RHG_ChinaInvestsInEurope_June2012.pdf

ICSID (1968). *History of the ICSID Convention: Documents Concerning the Origin and the Formulation of the Convention on the Settlement of Investment Disputes Between States and Nationals of Other States.* ICSID Publication, Volume II-1.

Merriam-Webster (2000). *Merriam-Webster's Collegiate Encyclopedia.* Springfield.

Pollan, T. (2006). *Legal Framework for the Admission of FDI.* Eleven International Publishing. Oxford Dictionaries, www.oxforddictionaries.com

Shan, W. (2005). *The Legal Framework of EU-China Investment Relations – A Critical Appraisal,* Oxford: Hart Publishing.

Thompson, T. N. (1979). China's Nationalization of Foreign Firms: The Politics of Hostage Capitalism – 1949–1957. *University of Maryland Law School, Occasional Papers/Reprints Series in Contemporary Asian Studies,* 27(6), 1–69.

UNCTAD (2011). *Scope and Definition.* UNCTAD Series on Issues in International Investment Agreements, http://unctad.org/en/pages/PublicationArchive.aspx?publicationid=354

UNCTAD (2014). UNCTAD in the World Investment Report 2014 – Investing in the SDGs: An Action Plan, http://unctad.org/en/pages/PublicationWebflyer.aspx?publicationid=937

US Department of Treasury (2013). *Note of 15 July 2013.* US and China Breakthrough Announcement on the Bilateral Investment Treaty Negotiations, www.treasury.gov/connect/blog/Pages/U.S.-and-China-Breakthrough-Announcement-.aspx

Vaccaro-Incisa, G. M. (2016). Protection of Foreign Investment and the EU: Framework, Legal Risks, and First Fruits. In E. Mišcenic and A. Raccah, eds., *Legal Risks in EU Law.* Springer, pp. 111–133.

Vaccaro-Incisa, G. M. (forthcoming). *China's Treaty Policy and Practice on the Protection of Foreign Investment: A Comparative Perspective, from the Model BITs to the Latest Stipulations and Current Negotiations,* Brill.

WTO (2002). *Report of the Working Group on the Relationship Between Trade and Investment to the General Council.* WT/WGTI/6.

Xue, H. (2011). Chinese Contemporary Perspectives on International Law: History, Culture and International Law. *Recueil Des Cours,* 355, 41–234.

9 The ASEAN comprehensive investment agreement approach to due process

Does arbitral case law matter?

Fulvio Maria Palombino and Giovanni Zarra[**]

1. Introduction

Since the late 1980s, investment arbitration has become the most popular method for solving disputes between States and foreign investors (so-called investment disputes).[1] This is because the existence of a forum for the settlement of investment disputes which is not perceived by foreign investors as biased in favour of host States (as, instead, domestic courts might be) has been a strong incentive for commencing foreign investments.[2] Unsurprisingly, most States have negotiated Bilateral Investment Treaties (BITs) with the view, *inter alia*, to ensuring certain standards of treatment to foreign investors and to granting them the possibility to solve disputes related to their violation before arbitral tribunals.[3]

Among those standards, the obligation to provide fair and equitable treatment (FET) proves to be the most invoked one,[4] going so far as to be described as the basic norm of international investment law.[5] However, it is quite difficult to give a precise meaning to such a general label, and it is not by chance that both FET's meaning and normative basis continue to be shrouded in ambiguity and to inspire, as a consequence, a considerable number of interpretations in case law.[6]

In this regard, the lack of certainty as to the FET's content led a number of tribunals to assume investor-oriented approaches, thus generating several doubts concerning the legitimacy of this kind of arbitration and inducing host States to perceive it as a serious threat to their power to regulate on public matters.[7] Unsurprisingly, several calls for reform are taking place in the debate surrounding investor-State dispute settlement (ISDS).

These calls move from the drastic proposal of entirely replacing investment arbitration with a multilateral investment court,[8] to the possibility of re-drafting treaty standards in a narrower way (so as to reduce the abstract possibility of interpreting standards of treatment in favour of investors),[9] passing through the establishment of an appellate body[10] or of a mechanism of preliminary rulings similar to the one existing in EU law.[11] It is worth pointing out that several authoritative scholars have already demonstrated that the solutions which involve a structural reform of investment arbitration (either by replacing it with a new Court or by establishing additional bodies such as an Appellate Body) do not ensure the achievement of the goal of limiting pro-investor interpretations of treaty standards and also risk reducing the confidence of foreign investors in the dispute settlement mechanism and, as a consequence, in the possibility of starting foreign investments.[12] Quite the opposite, the re-drafting of treaty clauses can be a balanced compromise between the host States' necessity of safeguarding a certain degree of freedom in regulating public matters and the need of ensuring investors' trust in the possibility of safely making foreign investments. It is, indeed, possible to identify a trend which is common to countries all over the world (see for example the 2016 Morocco-Nigeria BIT, Art. 23),[13] which consists of moving away from the traditional FET wording, with a view to accommodating the State power to regulate in the public interest.[14]

In this regard, it is very interesting to note the approach which has been endorsed so far by certain Asian countries in re-drafting their FET obligations.[15] Such an approach is exemplified by Art. 11 of the Association of Southeast Asian Nations (ASEAN) Comprehensive Investment Agreement (ACIA), stating that 'each Member State shall accord to covered investments of investors of any other Member State fair and equitable treatment' (para. 1), and, for greater certainty, pinpointing that this same standard 'requires each Member State not to deny justice in any legal or administrative proceedings in accordance with the principle of due process'.[16]

Now, within the realm of international investment law, the wording of the provision here scrutinized seems to be quite innovative. First of all, it seems to entirely exclude that the FET may involve also violations of legitimate expectations or of proportionality, as instead happens within the framework of the 2012 US Model Bilateral Investment Treaty, where at Art. 5 it is said that 'fair and equitable treatment *includes* the obligation not to deny justice . . . in according to the principle of due process', thus not excluding that other kinds of violations of investors' rights might fall under the spectrum of the FET. Moreover, differently from other treaties affecting the same geographical area, it does not identify the FET content either by means of a reference to the customary international law minimum standard (as in the case of the China-Japan-Korea Trilateral Investment Agreement, Article 5)[17] or by relying on the generally accepted rules of international law (as in the case of the Trans-Pacific Partnership, Article 9.6).

While it is obviously possible that, with the aim of maintaining a wide regulatory space, a group of States make the *political* choice to limit the range of obligations which may fall into the spectrum of FET violations to the sole concept of due process (involving, as we will see in detail in Section 3, both denial of justice and lack of fair administrative proceedings),[18] the ACIA formulation makes us wonder whether there exists any 'ASEAN way' of perceiving due process clauses at treaty law level. Such a solution could be inferred if one thinks, as it has been done e.g. by Diane Desierto, that the reference to 'due process' in Art. 11 of the ACIA is not to such a standard as developed in international law but to the principle as it is recognized by the ASEAN Member States in their domestic laws.[19] The goal of the present chapter is to understand to what extent the ACIA's standard of due process may be considered as isolated from existent investment case law relating to the principle of due process. First, we will discuss the relevance of arbitral case law in investment arbitration and demonstrate that it is not possible for arbitral tribunals, including the ones established under the ACIA, to completely disregard what has been done by previous tribunals, especially where this is symptomatic of the existence of a rule of general international law (Section 2). Having said the above, we will briefly trace the contours of the due process standard as emerged in the international legal order (Section 3). We will then outline the essential role of arbitrators in ensuring coherence in the application of the due process standard in international investment law (Section 4). Section 5 will be devoted to some concluding remarks.

2. The relevance of arbitral case law of non-ASEAN tribunals in the interpretation of the ACIA

It is well established that international investment arbitration (at least when it is based on a treaty claim)[20] is integrated within public international law and that sources of general international law may be applied in ISDS.[21] Art. 42 of the ICSID Convention, providing that, in the absence of an agreement on applicable law, the Tribunal shall apply the law of the Contracting State party to the dispute *and* such rules of international law as may be applicable, is a clear example of this. BITs usually make reference to principles of international law in their provisions of applicable law.[22] The ACIA is not different in this regard; Art. 40 sets forth that arbitral tribunals shall decide the issues in dispute in accordance with the same ACIA, any other applicable treaty between the Member States *and* the applicable rules of international law. It is therefore possible to say that general international law may find a place in the ACIA context both as a direct source of applicable law and as an interpretative aid for reading the treaty's provisions.[23] It is worth noting, in this regard, that a reference to general international law involves, in these authors' view, custom,[24] general principles common to domestic legal systems (set forth by Art. 38(1)(c) of the ICJ Statute)[25] and general principles of international law, i.e. principles which have developed and are applied in international law. The reference applies, in this regard, to those legal sources, usually with a very broad meaning, which – by themselves or by means of a more specific principle or rule gathered by them – express the key goals and values of international law.[26]

The above implies an additional consideration. Arbitral tribunals applying sources of general international law may not simply ignore the existing case law concerning such sources, which is essential to understand how general principles behave in specific and concrete situations.

Similarly, arbitrators dealing with broadly drafted treaty clauses such as the fair and equitable treatment will necessarily turn to existing case law which already gave a meaning to such clauses. Indeed, as noted by Hervé Ascensio, the meaning of FET 'has emerged thanks to the synthesis carried out by the arbitral jurisprudence, leading to a legal source with a complex but stabilized content'.[27]

It is therefore possible to say that tribunals have a functional duty to *take into account* what has been done by previous tribunals, even if they may obviously depart from their conclusions by offering a valid motivation for such a departure.[28] Several reasons bring us to this conclusion: (i) the parties' expectations to be treated in accordance with the principle of equality before the law; (ii) the belief that precedents are a repository of legal experience; (iii) the idea that to follow precedent is a way to avoid the appearance of any excess of judicial discretion; and (iv) the circumstance whereby judges are reluctant to admit that they were wrong.[29] Hence, from a practical perspective, arbitrators, first of all, identify prior relevant decisions for the case at hand and then compare the costs of departure from prior decisions with the consequences of following prior decisions, taking into account whether the policies underlying those prior decisions remain relevant under contemporary conditions. On that basis, tribunals decide which prior decisions to follow or depart from, and, finally, articulate reasons for their decision.[30]

In these authors' opinion, arbitrators working in the ACIA framework may not abandon the abovementioned approach, otherwise they would risk losing their legitimacy (in particular from the investors' point of view). Starting from the contours of the fair and equitable treatment as defined by the treaty, which limits the standard's scope of application to the principle of due process, tribunals will in any case have to take into account both general international law and existing arbitral case law as interpretative tools necessary to give an acceptable meaning to Art. 11 of the ACIA.[31]

3. The role of arbitral case law in shaping the due process principle

Having demonstrated, in general terms, the relevance of arbitral case law for the sake of interpreting Art. 11 of the ACIA, we will now specifically turn to the concept of due process. We will, first of all, give evidence of the fact that due process is a general principle of international law which arbitrators (including those acting in the ACIA framework) shall take into consideration as it developed in international investment law. Second, we will briefly outline the content of this principle in accordance with existing arbitral case law.

Some sources seem to equalize the concepts of due process and denial of justice, regarding them as a rule of general international law – in the form of a principle common to domestic systems or of a custom – with a clear-cut content. This would define, at least in part, the FET content. This argument seems to be reflected in the preparatory works to the 2013 Institute of International Law (Institut de Droit International) Resolution ('Legal Aspects of Recourse to Arbitration by an Investor Against the Authorities of the Host State under Inter-State Treaties')[32] and more recently in the 2015 Indian Model Investment Treaty (Article 3).[33]

However, the argument is unconvincing in terms of both the content and the legal nature of due process of law as a FET element.

In terms of its content, not only has due process taken on a meaning so broad as to include also the right to procedural fairness in administrative proceedings – as

Article 11 of the 2009 ASEAN Comprehensive Investment Agreement clearly confirms – but the very notion of denial of justice remains fairly uncertain[34]; the only aspect to appear clear-cut in arbitral practice is that the occurrence of this wrongful act may be established only where the investor has exhausted all internal remedies to challenge the allegedly unlawful decision (or has proved that such remedies would be futile).[35]

In terms of legal nature of due process, reliance by legal writers on both general principles common to domestic systems[36] and custom[37] is questionable. On the one hand, the concept here referred to may expand and contract from State to State and is tied to the idiosyncrasies of each legal system; hence the inadequacy of the above principles. On the other hand, a number of awards increasingly advance the opinion whereby a distinction must be drawn between a denial of justice claim based on customary law and one based on the FET clause: should a claim for denial of justice fail under custom, the competent arbitral tribunal would not be exonerated 'from carefully appraising the alleged facts and deciding whether they amount to a breach of the fair and equitable treatment standard'.[38]

For the whole matter to be rightly assessed, the assumption from which one must move is the following one: due process broadly understood embodies a general principle of international law which, as such, can be inferred by way of induction and generalization from a number of customary and conventional rules.[39] As a general principle of international law, due process primarily plays a 'directive' role.[40] Accordingly, its application in the field of foreign investments is not automatic, but demands a complex interpretative activity by the judge concerned. Thus, with specific regard to international investment law, due process has found (by way of deduction) concrete applications which have delineated its specific application as a principle concerning this particular area of international law. By this activity, due process has been conceived in terms of both denial of justice and of procedural fairness in administrative proceedings.

3.1. Denial of justice

The first constituent element of due process is denial of justice, viz. the traditional international wrong concerning the treatment of aliens which a State can incur for the breach of the principle. Support for this proposition may be found in a number of arbitral decisions whereby the concepts of due process and denial of justice are closely linked; accordingly, a failure to guarantee the former will often result in the occurrence of the latter.[41] Indeed, it seems that arbitrators' reasoning usually assumed the existence of a general principle providing for due process of law;[42] on the basis of this principle, and in the wake of the features peculiar to the matter of foreign investments, they have formulated the rule of denial of justice; finally, by way of a constant and uniform case law, this rule has then become 'stable' going so far as to be subsumed under FET.

In order to try to give a precise meaning to denial of justice in ISDS, it may be helpful to start from an analysis of the traditional distinction of German origin between denial of justice (Justizverweigerung) and denial of law

(Rechgsverweiverung), i.e. the different type of activities (judicial or legislative) that may result in a violation of the State obligation to protect an alien.[43] A strict interpretation of this distinction, indeed, allows two hypotheses to be identified: (i) the situation where State responsibility stems from a judicial misapplication of national law which proves manifestly unjust (*denial of justice*) and (ii) the situation where State responsibility stems from the (substantive and procedural) rules in force domestically, namely rules that the judge concerned cannot do anything but apply (*denial of law*). Now, a careful appraisal of case law sheds light on the fact that denial of justice, as a FET element, is anchored in the German model of *Justizverweigerung* only and does not include the different concept of denial of law. Whoever decides to invest part of his capital in a foreign country (especially in the case of multinational enterprises), does so in the wake of the *whole regulatory framework* existing in that country, therefore having regard not only to the rules making the investment convenient, but also to those governing the judicial system, and which may be relevant when a dispute between this investor and the host State arises.

All business transactions involve some degree of risk. When business transactions occur across international borders, they carry additional risks not present in domestic transactions. These additional risks, called country risk, typically include risks arising from a variety of national differences in economic structures, policies, socio-political institutions, geography, and currencies.[44]

Significantly enough, Andrea Giardina, serving as rapporteur of the already cited 2013 IIL Resolution in matter of investments, made the point clear that the breach of due process of law 'might be attributed to the host State judiciary', but not to the legislator.

In other words, the business risk that an investor takes on covers also the possible deficiencies of the local justice system, i.e. a system which he 'should reasonably have known at the time of the investment',[45] and the effects that this circumstance may produce in the lawsuits involving him. This idea is not new to international case law, and a significant precedent can be found in the PCIJ judicial practice first.[46] On the other hand, the two leading decisions in the matter, namely *Mondev International Ltd. v. United States* and *Loewen v. United States*, support such a conclusion: in *Mondev* the existence of a national rule conferring immunity from jurisdiction to public agencies was not regarded as contrary to FET[47]; in *Loewen* the provision of a *cautio iudicatum solvi* did not frustrate – in terms of the decision – the right of access to justice and so on.[48]

Contrariwise, a failure by a national judge to apply (or to correctly apply) its national law may constitute a denial of justice which is to be considered as a FET violation. A clear and recent example of the above may be found in *Dan Cake v. Hungary*.[49] The Claimant was a Portuguese company supplying biscuits in Hungary through its Hungarian subsidiary Danesita. This latter company did not pay certain debts and was consequently involved in insolvency proceedings in Hungary. During such proceedings, the insolvent entity reached certain agreements with creditors to settle its debts and therefore requested that the Metropolitan Court of Budapest convene a 'composition hearing' in which hopefully creditors would vote in its favour (with the consequence that Danesita would not be declared bankrupt). Danesita's request for a composition hearing was filed in accordance with the applicable provisions of domestic law. As a consequence, *it was Danesita's right* to be convened by the judge in order to formally discuss with its creditors. The Court, however, discretionally established several additional requirements (which were not set forth on the law) for the filing of the request by the insolvent entity, refused to convey the composition hearing and forced the liquidator to sell the company's assets. This *de facto* impeded Danesita in exercising its right to a composition hearing and condemned the company to bankruptcy. In the opinion of the arbitral tribunal, it was of course uncertain whether the composition hearing would have led to Danesita's survival, but the decision of the Court of Budapest surely deprived the company of a chance of continuing its business. This constituted a misapplication of the law and was an evident denial of justice which involved a FET violation.

3.2. *Procedural fairness in administrative proceedings (Audi Alteram Partem)*

We will now turn to the second due process component, i.e. procedural fairness in administrative proceedings. Given the express reference contained in Art. 11 of the ASEAN Comprehensive Investment Agreement to the necessity of respecting due process in administrative proceedings, this element is extremely interesting for the present discussion.

That fairness in administrative proceedings, especially conceived as the right to be heard (*audi alteram partem*), falls under the due process principle is unsurprising and echoes the circumstance whereby due process (and the guarantees related thereto) has gone much further than the limits of the judicial function and has become the typical way by which to exercise the administrative function as well.[50]

Historically speaking, support for this proposition may be traced back to several domestic legal systems. In the US, the Supreme Court has traditionally interpreted the Fifth and Fourteenth Amendments of the American Constitution, requiring that neither the federal government nor the States deprive any person of life, liberty or property without *due process of law*, as a clause dealing not only with the administration of justice but also applying to administrative proceedings.[51] Similar decisions may be found in English case law in relation to the principle of natural justice, i.e. a concept that is very similar to due process and represents the basis of procedural protection in the English legal system. Starting from *Ridge v. Boldwin*, natural justice has been considered to be a principle of *universal application* equally valid with reference to any proceedings leading to a discretionary decision.[52] Although with delay, the same result has also been reached in civil law countries, like the Italian legal system. Reference has to be made to the Administrative Procedure Act, Italy which does nothing but extend to administrative procedures one of the main rules governing adjudication, namely the *audi alteram partem* principle.[53]

Finally, this rule belongs to the general principles of EU law and may be applied in any proceedings, regardless of their judicial or administrative nature. In *Transocean Marin Paint Association*, the Court of Justice of the EU (CJEU) stated that, generally speaking, 'a person whose interests are perceptibly affected by a decision taken by a public authority must be given the opportunity to make his point of view known'.[54] Last, but not least, the same principle has been recognized in Art. 41 of the Charter of Fundamental Rights of the European Union ('Right to good administration'); in terms of its para. 2, indeed, every person has the right to be heard, before any individual measure which would affect him or her adversely is taken.[55]

Apparently, the above remarks seem to sustain the existence of a general principle common to domestic systems, which guarantees the *audi alteram partem* principle in the relationship between individuals and the administrative power. Such a view, however, proves unconvincing. Indeed, depending on the legal order where it is invoked, the principle here scrutinized tends to undertake a different content. One divergence, for example, concerns the fact that while in some countries (such as the United States, Sweden and Japan) administrative procedural acts 'provide for a hearing, in some civil law countries only a possibility to make written submissions is required'.[56] On the other hand, the circumstances under which the principle may be applied vary significantly from case to case; thus, where in some cases what counts is the 'nature' of the activities performed by the administration, in other cases one has to establish whether a person has a reasonable expectation to be heard in a given proceeding. Unsurprisingly, also within the context of the EU legal order (i.e. a context where the *audi alteram partem* rule belongs to the category of general principles of law), the way this rule is applied by the Court of Justice is shrouded in ambiguity: despite the fact it is regarded as a general principle, it only applies 'to certain categories of procedure (particularly those producing adverse effects) but not all of them (even if an unfavourable effect was indeed produced)'.[57]

Similarly, the existence of a customary international law provision in the matter should be excluded; beyond some specific treaty regimes[58] and a narrow number of judgements,[59] the rule in question has been broadly and consistently applied precisely within the area of foreign investments; needless to say, its features have to be determined with reference to this area only.

Once again, the reasoning followed by arbitral tribunals turns out to be the same. The *audi alteram partem* rule has been inferred, by way of induction, from due process, regarded as a general principle, and adapted to the features peculiar to the international law of foreign investments; subsequently, thanks to a constant and uniform case law, this rule has become a 'stable' FET element.

In administrative proceedings involving foreign investors, a violation of the *audi alteram partem* principle, conceived as a FET element, may be claimed under the presence of two cumulative conditions. For the first condition to occur, the host State's legal order is required to expressly or tacitly provide for the principle. Otherwise, the same argument advanced with reference to denial of justice should be relied on: it is assumed that the investor is and must be aware of the State's normative framework and takes the risks that are connected to it.

The fact that the *audi alteram partem* rule is provided for in some way in the host State's legal order, but is not guaranteed in a given administrative proceeding involving a foreign investor, does not necessarily entail a FET violation. To this end, arbitral case law requires an additional requirement: the decision passed *in absentia* must be able, at least potentially, to cause a serious economic loss to the investment. The decision in *Middle East Cement Shipping* corroborates this line of thought.[60] In this case, the investor's ship (Poseidon) was seized and auctioned without due notification; indeed, both the attachment order and notice for an auction were applied by the competent authority on board of Poseidon (having found neither the debtor nor his representative), notified to the chief of the Suez port's Police, and published in a local newspaper. Bearing in mind that such a serious sanction should have been notified to the claimant by a direct communication, the Tribunal found the auction procedure as contrary to due process of law and therefore to the FET principle.[61]

A recent example of lack of fairness in administrative proceedings leading to a violation of the fair and equitable treatment may be found in *Urbaser v. Argentina*.[62] One of the claims in this case was related to the fact that the Argentinean Province of the Greater Buenos Aires suddenly interrupted the negotiations with the Claimant for an increase of the tariffs for the supply of water services without giving a meaningful explanation for such an interruption. This amounted, in Urbaser's view, to a violation of FET. Argentina, contrariwise, contended that the negotiations failed because of the very high increase of tariffs requested by the Claimant. The Tribunal, however, agreed with Urbaser and found that such a tariff increase might not have been as extraordinary as having the effect of an immediate closing of the negotiation. It would have been more reasonable that the Province continued the negotiations by inviting the Claimant to lower its requests significantly. The Tribunals also noted that Argentina interrupted the negotiations due to a political choice, without giving to the Claimant the possibility of starting a meaningful discussion on the tariff increase with the Province:

> even if the proposals were excessive, there was no serious reason to react by an abrupt end of discussions with a Concessionaire with whom negotiations had been conducted in correct terms over more than a year and who still showed its interest in continuing the service under the Concession.[63]

It was therefore surprising for the Claimant to be suddenly confronted with the effects of this evolution in February 2005 without any earlier and appropriate warning from the Province. The Tribunal therefore considered unfair and inequitable that the Province conducted administrative proceedings first inviting the Claimant to submit proposals for a renegotiation and to entertain intensive discussions and then bringing such discussions to an end abruptly in reliance on federal policies unrelated to the concession under negotiation of which the Province should have informed the Claimant appropriately.

4. The role of arbitrators in the interpretation of treaty clauses and the necessity to safeguard coherence

This discussion demonstrates that it is not possible to look at standards of treatment encapsulated in BITs as single entities, the interpretation of which may take place completely disregarding general international law and the interpretation that other tribunals have given of the same standards. Efraim Chalamish has spoken, in this regard, of the 'multilateral dimension of bilateralism', in accordance to which arbitrators may turn to comparable BITs as interpretative tools[64] and to give coherence to the application of standards of treatment.[65]

This, in turn, lets the essential role of arbitrators emerge. Tribunals should act as more than simple judges of a single dispute and as operators of a bigger legal framework in which they cannot simply ignore each other. Despite the fact that they are not obliged to follow precedents and that their authority descends from a manifestation of party autonomy only in relation to the dispute at hand, they cannot avoid confronting themselves with the outside world.

It is indeed undeniable that, in lack of detailed treaty provisions setting forth clear-cut substantive standards of treatment of foreign investments, arbitrators are the real balancing factor between the necessity to issue an award that is the appropriate one for the case at hand and the need to grant that such an award is integrated within the legal framework in which it operates. The recourse to general principles of international law and existing arbitral case law 'make it possible to avoid fragmentation, to bring diversity back to a certain degree of unity and, in other words, to erect arbitration and international investment law in a system'.[66]

Arbitrators' role, therefore, should be that of *guarantors* of the issuance of a fair award in relation to the dispute at hand and the expectations of the parties on the one hand and of *intermediaries* between the single dispute and the surrounding legal framework on the other hand.[67]

It seems therefore possible to say that arbitrators are responsible for finding a point of optimality between commitment and flexibility, by way of satisfying the needs of the parties according to the wording of the relevant treaty or contract (flexibility) without disregarding the necessity of ensuring coherence (commitment), which is considered to be a form of safeguard for the stakeholders and the respect of which is, finally, essential in order to grant the legitimacy of the method of dispute settlement.

In the ACIA framework, therefore, arbitrators shall respect the treaty wording and the will of Member States to reduce the spectrum of obligations included in concept of FET to the sole principle of due process. Yet they are also required to avoid disregarding general international law and the existing investment case law relating to the principle of due process.

5. Conclusion

In a nutshell, this chapter argues that due process (which encapsulates both denial of justice and fairness in administrative proceedings) is a general principle of international law, with its own foundations in the international legal order itself. As a FET element, on the other hand, this principle has been shaped by arbitral tribunals according to the features typical of international investment law: due process is 'contextual' and, as such, its content depends on the normative field, rather than on the national legal order, where it is supposed to operate (which is even more so, considering that due process does not include, for example, the figure of denial of law).

From this angle, an Asian approach to due process may not actually exist nor is it desirable as a matter of principle: Article 11 of the ASEAN Comprehensive Investment Agreement, despite its ground-breaking wording limiting the FET obligation of ASEAN States only to the prohibition of violating due process, does not embody a self-standing treaty clause and its application requires that both general international law and the relevant case law in matter of due process to be taken into account. As a result, arbitrators end up representing the real balancing factor between the will of ASEAN States as expressed in the ACIA and the necessity to ensure the coherence of international investment law.

Notes

** This chapter is the result of the joint work of the two Authors. However, in detail, Prof. Palombino wrote Sections III and V and Dr. Zarra wrote Sections I, II and IV.
1 Reisman, 2017: 6 ff.
2 See, in general terms, Schaufelberger, 1993.
3 Savarese, 2012: 19 ff.
4 Palombino, 2018: 20 ff.
5 This has been already sustained in *Suez and AWG v. Argentina*, ICSID Case No. ARB/03/19, Decision on Liability of 30 July 2010, para 181, where the Tribunal said: 'Indeed, to borrow the terminology of Hans Kelsen, it is no exaggeration to say that the obligation of a host State to accord fair and equitable treatment to foreign investors is the *Grundnorm* or basic norm of international investment law'.
6 The FET standard and its interpretations in the case law are analysed in depth, inter alia, by Paparinskis, 2013; and Tudor, 2008.
7 Giardina, 2008: 337–9. Tanzi, 2012: 48–52.
8 Henke, 2017; Zarra, 2018. See in this regard to European Commission *Recommendation for a Council Decision authorising the opening of negotiations for a Convention establishing a multilateral court for the settlement of investment disputes*, COM(2017) 493 final, adopted on 13 September 2017.
9 Hanessian and Duggal, 2017: 220 ff.
10 See Bottini, 2016, and Smith, 2013.
11 Schreuer, 2008.
12 See, inter alia, Bernardini, 2017; Jansen Calamita, 2017; and Henke, 2017. Moreover, it is to be noted that investment arbitration tribunals are putting in place certain self-adjustments aimed at balancing both parties' interests and offering a perception of acceptability of the adjudication mechanism. See Alvarez, 2011, and Schreuer and Kriebaum, 2011. For an analysis of the deferential approach of tribunals towards regulatory powers of host States see Schill, 2012.

13 Para. 1 of such Article states that:

> The Host State has the right to take regulatory or other measures to ensure that development in its territory is consistent with the goals and principles of sustainable development, and with other legitimate social and economic policy objectives.

14 See Reisman, 2017, 12 ff., who puts this phenomenon in relation with the circumstance that those countries which were traditionally only capital exporting are now becoming also capital importing. Such countries (e.g. the US) are therefore using their bargaining power in order to negotiate treaty clauses which highly safeguard their regulatory power.

15 The ASEAN approach to standards of treatment of foreign investment, aimed at preserving a large regulatory power to host States, has been analysed in Wongkaew, 2014: 3 ff.; Schill, 2016a; Schill, 2016b; Desierto, 2015; Cho and Kurtz, 2016; Nottage and Thanitcul, 2016; Chaisse, 2013; Magiera, 2017. For a general analysis of Chinese practice, see Shan and Gallagher, 2009: 126 ff.; Cappiello and Vanino, 2015; see also: Berger, A. (2008). China's new bilateral investment treaty programme: Substance, rational and implications for international investment law making. Paper prepared for the American Society of International Law International Economic Law Interest Group 2008 Biennal Conference \"The Politics of International Economic Law: The Next Four Years\", Washington D. C., November 14–15, 2008, www.die-gdi.de/uploads/media/Berger_ChineseBITs.pdf, last accessed 16 September 2017, 1–18.

16 For an analysis of this provision see Chaisse and Jusoh, 2016: 116 ff.

17 Similarly, with regard to the sole due process clause, Art. 3 of the 2015 Model Text for the Indian Bilateral Investment Treaty without even mentioning the label 'fair and equitable treatment' stipulates that investors shall not be subject to denials of justice under customary international law and un-remedied and egregious violations of due process. In this regard see also Art. 5 of the 2009 Agreement on Investment Among ASEAN and the Republic of Korea and Art. 6 of the 2009 Agreement Establishing the ASEAN-Australia-New Zealand Free Trade Area.

18 Palombino, 2018: 57 ff.

19 Desierto, 2015: 1031–2.

20 On the difference between contracts and treaty claims see Zarra, 2017 b: 3 ff.

21 Gaillard and Banifatemi, 2003.

22 See e.g. Art. 30 of the US Model BIT. See also, inter alia, Art. 10, para 6, of the 2001 BIT between Denmark and Uganda.

23 Ascensio, 2016: 119 ff.

24 Characterized by the two elements of *diuturnitas* and *opinio juris sive necessitatis*. See Conforti, 2015: 40 ff.

25 For a meaningful analysis of these principles and their differences with other sources of general international law see Magnani, 1997: 71 ff.

26 Palombino, 2012: 56–58; Zarra, 2017 b: 115; Iovane, 2008: 103 ff. A meaningful analysis of this source is also carried out by Strozzi, 1992: 164 ff.

27 Ascensio, 2016: 125 (own translation). See also Iovane, 2018: 2. In this regard, it is to be noted that various authors talked about international investment tribunals as a network (Savarese, 2012: 26 and 231 ff.) or as *ad hoc* tribunals, which in any case behave as if they are a system (Palombino, 2012: 195). The orderliness of international investment law and arbitration is analysed in depth in Zarra, 2017 a; and Zarra, 2017 b: 25 ff.

28 Palombino, 2018: 154 ff. Zarra, 2017 a: 669–672.

29 Rigo Sureda, 2009: 832–833.

30 Cheng, 2006: 1031.

31 The same conclusion seems to have been reached by Chaisse and Jusoh, 2016: 121–122.
32 Para. 130 states as follows:

> The violation of [due process] determines an international wrongful act of denial of justice. The denial of justice can be interpreted on the basis of customary international law. . . . This requirement is considered to be so fundamental that in the practice of US BIT and FTA is specifically indicated.

33 This Article, quoted at fn. 17 above, clearly speaks of denial of justice under customary international law.
34 Paulsson, 2005: 13 ff.
35 Sattorova, 2012: 226 ff. Goldhaber, 2013: 383 ff.
36 This opinion has been sustained inter alia by Borchard, 1940: 445 ff.
37 See Diehl, 2012: 455 ff.
38 *See*, for instance, *Franck Charles Arif v. Moldova*, ICSID Case No. ARB/11/23, Award of 8 April 2013, para. 423 et seq. In same vein, one may mention *Flughafen Zürich A.G. and Gestión e Ingeniería IDC S.A. v. Venezuela*, ICSID Case No. ARB/10/19, Award of 18 November 2014, para. 378: 'Y aunque la denegación de justicia no estuviera contenida en el estándar de TJE [fair and equitable treatment], adicionalmente, la denegación de justicia representa en todo caso un ilícito sancionado por el Derecho internacional consuetudinario'.
39 The existence of a notion of international due process has been advanced, for example, by Kotuby 2013: 411 ff.
40 In effect due process in international law does not involve only denial of justice and may be classified under three major groups. A first set of provisions, which are provided for in most human rights treaties (both universal and regional), seeks to ensure the individual's right to a fair trial and embody, in the view of some authors, a veritable custom in criminal matters. Further relevant norms of general international law refer to some fundamental canons of international adjudication, like that protecting the juridical equality between parties in their capacity as litigants as well as that of *audi alteram partem*. Last but not least, international norms reflecting concerns of due process are those providing for the right to fairness in administrative/law-making proceedings, the scope of which extends to both individuals (at national and international levels), and States insofar as they are part of international organizations (of which both the EU and the WTO are good examples) acting as law-makers.
41 *Waguih Elie George Siag and Clorinda Vecchi v. Egypt*, ICSID Case No. ARB/05/15, Award of 1 June 2009, para. 452. In the same vein, Article 5, para. 2 (a), of the 2012 US Model BIT should be considered: ' "fair and equitable treatment" includes the obligation not to deny justice in criminal, civil, or administrative adjudicatory proceedings in accordance with the principle of due process embodied in the principal legal systems of the world'.
42 This way of reasoning may be generalized, considering that it is commonly applied by international judges. See Iovane, 2018: 8–21.
43 See Hatshek, 1923: 397; Strupp, 1925. In the past, this distinction had been drawn, with the view to claiming that denial of justice always entails State responsibility, whereas denial of law does so under exceptional circumstances only. For a critique of this distinction see Quadri, 1936: 220 ff., in the footnotes.
44 Meldrum, 2000: 33.
45 *Electrabel S.A. v. Hungary*, ICSID No. ARB/07/19, Decision on Jurisdiction, Applicable Law and Liability of 30 November 2012, para. 7.78.

46 Reference has to be made to the case *Oscar Chinn* (*United Kingdom v. Belgium*), Judgment of 12 December 1934, p. 84:

> Mr. Chinn, a British subject, when, in 1929, he entered the river transport business, could not have been ignorant of the existence of the competition which he would encounter on the part of Unatra, which had been established since 1925, of the magnitude of the capital invested in that Company, of the connection it had with the Colonial and Belgian Governments, and of the pre-dominant role reserved to the latter with regard to the fixing and application for transport rates.

47 *Mondev International Ltd. v. United States*, ICSID Case No. ARB (AF)/99/2, Award of 11 October 2002, para. 101 ff.
48 *Loewen v. United States*, ICSID Case No. ARB/98/3, Award of 26 June 2003, paras. 168–169.
49 *Dan Cake (Portugal) S.A. v. Hungary*, ICSID Case No. ARB/12/9, Decision on Jurisdiction and Liability of 24 August 2015, para. 100 ff.
50 Buffoni, 2009: 297.
51 Evidence of such a broad application of the rule is reflected in a number of decisions whereby actions requiring some right to be heard include, *inter alia*, deprivation of welfare benefits and dismissal of a government employee. 397 U.S. 254 (1970). In this case, in particular, the Supreme Court held that the Fourteenth Amendment due process clause required a state agency to provide an evidentiary hearing before terminating a person's welfare benefits after the agency determined that the individual was no longer eligible for such benefits.
52 *Ridge v. Boldwin* [1964] AC 40.
53 *See* Law No. 241, 7 August 1990 and subsequent amendments. A number of national decisions further support such a conclusion. One may mention Italian Court of Cassation, first civil section, 20 May 2002, No. 7341.
54 Judgment of 23 October 1974, para. 15. Likewise, one may mention the decision passed by the Court of First Instance in *Lisrestal*:

> it is settled law that respect for the rights of the defence in all proceedings which are initiated against a person and are liable to culminate in a measure adversely affecting that person is a fundamental principle of Community law which must be guaranteed, even in the absence of any specific rules concerning the proceedings in question.
>
> (Judgment of 6 December 1994, para. 42)

55 Bifulco, 2001.
56 Della Cananea, 2010: 71.
57 Della Cananea, 2011: 100.
58 One example in this regard lies in Articles 6 et seq. of the Aarhus Convention on Access to Information, Public Participation in Decision-Making and Access to Justice in Environmental Matters. These Articles actually state that the public concerned shall be adequately informed in an environmental decision-making procedure and benefits from a number of guarantees, such as that guaranteeing the participation in the procedure and the submission of comments and questions. The Agreement on Implementation of Article VI of 1994 GATT is equally revealing. Art. 6, par. 1, of this agreement ('Evidence') states as follows: 'All interested parties in an anti-dumping investigation shall be given notice of the information which the authorities require and ample opportunity to present in writing all evidence which they consider relevant in respect of the investigation in question'.

59 Reference can be made to the judgment passed by the International Tribunal for the Law of the Sea in *Juno Trader* (*San Vincent and the Grenadines v. Guinea-Bissau*), Judgment of 18 December 2004. Its para. 77 states as follows:

> The obligation of prompt release of vessels and crews includes elementary considerations of humanity and *due process of law*. The requirement that the bond or other financial security must be reasonable indicates that a concern for fairness is one of the purposes of this provision.
>
> (emphasis added).

The separate opinion of judge Treves confirms the impression that due process, in this case, was understood in terms of fairness in administrative proceedings:

> In the present case, the essential fact seems to me to be that between the time of the arrest of the ship and the time of the application to the Tribunal (and also up to the hearing before the Tribunal) all domestic procedures held in the case (whatever other possibilities might have been open under the local law) have been *inaudita altera parte* (namely, without giving the accused party the possibility of being heard)'.
>
> In this regard see Cassese, 2006: 120 ff.

60 *Middle East Cement Shipping and Handling Co.S.A. v. Egypt*, ICSID Case No. ARB/99/6, Award of 12 April 2002, para. 143.
61 'The Tribunal has found . . . the auction procedure applied here to have not been "under due process of law" (Art. 4a of the BIT) and specifically the notification procedure to have not been sufficient': idem, para. 147.
62 *Urbaser S.A. and Consorcio de Aguas Bilbao Bizkaia, Bilbao Biskaia Ur Partzuergoa v. The Argentine Republic*, ICSID Case No. ARB/07/26, Award of 8 December 2016, para. 818 ff.
63 See para. 840.
64 Chalamish, 2009: 317.
65 *Id.*, 342.
66 Ascensio, 2016: 118 (own translation).
67 Zarra, 2017 a: 676–677.

References

Alvarez, J. E. (2011). The Return of the State. *Minnesota Journal of International Law*, 20(2), 223–264.

Ascensio, H. (2016). Le droit non-écrit dans la jurisprudence des tribunaux d'investissement. In P. Palchetti, ed., *L'incidenza del diritto non scritto sul diritto internazionale ed europeo*. Naples: Editoriale Scientifica, pp. 115–130.

Berger, A. (2008). China's New Bilateral Investment Treaty Programme: Substance, Rational and Implications for International Investment Law Making. *Paper Prepared for the American Society of International Law International Economic Law Interest Group 2008 Biennial Conference "The Politics of International Economic Law: The Next Four Years"*, Washington, DC. 4–15 November 2008, pp. 1–181, www.die-gdi.de/uploads/media/Berger_ChineseBITs.pdf.

Bernardini, P. (2017). Reforming Investor-State Dispute Settlement: The Need to Balance Both Parties' Interests. *ICSID Review – Foreign Investment Law Journal*, 32(1), 38–57.

Bifulco, R. (2001). Articolo 41. In R. Bifulco, M. Cartabia and A. Celotto, eds., *L'Europa dei diritti. Commento alla Carta dei diritti fondamentali dell'Unione europea*. Bologna: Il Mulino, pp. 284–293.

Borchard, E. (1940). The "Minimum Standard" of the Treatment of Aliens. *Michigan Law Review*, 38(4), 445–461.

Bottini, G. (2016). Present and Future of ICSID Annulment: The Path to an Appellate Body?. *ICSID Review – Foreign Investment Law Journal*, 31(3), 712–727.

Buffoni, L. (2009). Il rango costituzionale del "giusto procedimento" e l'archetipo del "processo". *Quaderni costituzionali*, 2(1), 277–302.

Cappiello, B. and Vanino, E. (2015). The New Silk Road: Achievements and Perspectives of EU-China Investment Relations. *Diritto del commercio internazionale*, 29(2), 509–529.

Cassese, S. (2006). *Oltre lo Stato*, Rome-Bari: Laterza.

Chaisse, J. (2013). Investment Claims against Asian States – A Legal Analysis of the Statistics, Trends and Prospects. *Centre for Financial Regulation and Economic Development – The Chinese University of Hong Kong, Working Paper No. 14/2013*, 1–26.

Chaisse, J. and Jusoh, S. (2016). *The ASEAN Comprehensive Investment Agreement*, Cheltenham: Edward Elgar Publishing.

Chalamish, E. (2009). The Future of Bilateral Investment Treaties: A De Facto Multilateral Agreement. *Brooklyn Journal of International Law*, 34(2), 304–354.

Cheng, T. H. (2006). Precedent and Control in Investment Treaty Arbitration. *Fordham International Law Journal*, 30(4), 1014–1049.

Cho, S. and Kurtz, J. (2016). Legalizing the ASEAN Way: Adapting and Reimagining the ASEAN Investment Regime, pp. 1–51, https://papers.ssrn.com/sol3/papers.cfm?abstract_id=2878817

Conforti, B. (2015). *Diritto internazionale*, Naples: Editoriale Scientifica.

Della Cananea, G. (2010). Minimum Standards of Procedural Justice in Administrative Adjudication. In S. Schill, ed., *International Investment Law and Comparative Public Law*, Oxford: Oxford University Press, pp. 39–74.

Della Cananea G (2011) The Genesis and Structure of General Principles of Global Public Law. In E. Chiti and B. G. Mattarella, eds., *Global Administrative Law and EU Administrative Law. Relationships, Legal Issues and Comparison*, Heidelberg: Springer, pp. 89–110.

Desierto, D. A. (2015). Regulatory Freedom and Control in the New ASEAN Regional Investment Treaties. *The Journal of World Investment & Trade*, 16(5–6), 1018–1057.

Diehl, A. (2012). *The Core Standard of International Investment Protection: Fair and Equitable Treatment*, The Hague: Kluwer Law International.

Gaillard, E. and Banifatemi, Y. (2003). The Meaning of "and" in Article 42(1), Second Sentence, of the Washington Convention: The Role of International Law in the ICSID Choice of Law Process. *ICSID Review – Foreign Investment Law Journal*, 18(3), 375–411.

Giardina, A. (2008). L'arbitrato internazionale in materia di investimenti: impetuosi sviluppi e qualche problema. In N. Boschiero and R. Luzzatto, eds., I rapporti economici internazionali e l'evoluzione del loro regime giuridico. Naples: Editoriale Scientifica, pp. 319–339.

Goldhaber, M. D. (2013). The Rise of Arbitral Power Over Domestic Courts. *Stanford Journal of Complex Litigation*, 1(2), 374–416.

Hanessian, G. and Duggal, K. (2017). The Final 2015 Indian Model BIT: Is This the Change the World Wishes to See? *ICSID Review – Foreign Investment Law Journal*, 32(1), 216–226.

Hatshek, J. (1923). *Völkerrecht als System rechtlich bedeutsamer Staatsakte*, Leipzig: Deichert.

Henke, A. (2017). La crisi del sistema ISDS e il progetto di una nuova corte internazionale permanente, ovvero della fine dell'arbitrato in materia di investimenti. *Diritto del commercio internazionale*, 33(1), 133–170.

Iovane, M. (2008). Metodo costituzionalistico e ruolo dei giudici nella formulazione dei principi generali del dirittointernazionale. *Ars Interpretandi* 13(1), 103–129.

Iovane, M. (2018). Some Reflections on Identifying Custom in Contemporary International Law, pp. 1–23, www.federalismi.it/nv14/articolo-documento.cfm?Artid=36198

Jansen Calamita, N. (2017), The (In)Compatibility of Appellate Mechanisms with Existing Instruments of the Investment Treaty Regime, pp. 1–14, https://papers.ssrn.com/sol3/papers.cfm?abstract_id=2945881

Kotuby, Jr. C. T. (2013). General Principles of Law, International Due Process, and the Modern Role of Private International Law. *Duke Journal of Comparative & International Law*, 23 (2), 411–443.

Magiera, S. L. (2017). International Investment Agreements and Investor-State Disputes: A Review and Evaluation for Indonesia. *ERIA Discussion Paper Series*, pp. 1–31, www.eria.org/ERIA-DP-2016-30.pdf

Magnani, R. (1997). *Nuove prospettive sui principi generali nel sistema delle fonti nel diritto internazionale*, Bologna: Mursia.

Meldrum, D. H. (2000). Country Risk and Foreign Direct Investment. *Business Economic*, 35(1), 33–40.

Nottage, L. and Thanitcul, S. (2016). International Investment Arbitration in Southeast Asia: Guest Editorial. Sydney Law School – Legal Studies Research Paper No. 16/95, pp. 1–40.

Palombino, F. M. (2012). *Il trattamento giusto ed equo degli investimenti stranieri*, Bologna: Il Mulino.

Palombino, F. M. (2018). *Fair and Equitable Treatment and the Fabric of General Principles*, Heidelberg: Asser-Springer.

Paparinskis, M. (2013). *The International Minimum Standard and Fair and Equitable Treatment*, Oxford: Oxford University Press.

Paulsson, J. (2005). *Denial of Justice in International Law*, Cambridge: Cambridge University Press.

Quadri, R. (1936). *La sudditanza nel diritto internazionale*, Padua: Cedam.

Reisman, W. M. (2017). The Empire Strikes Back: The Struggle to Reshape ISDS, pp. 1–23, https://papers.ssrn.com/sol3/papers.cfm?abstract_id=2943514

Rigo Sureda, A. (2009). Precedent in Investment Treaty Arbitration. In C. Binder, et al., eds., *International Investment Law for the 21st Century: Essays in Honour of Christoph Schreuer*, Oxford: Oxford University Press, pp. 830–850.

Sattorova, M. (2012). Denial of Justice Disguised – Investment Arbitration and the Protection of Foreign Investors from Judicial Misconduct. *International & Comparative Law Quarterly*, 61(1), 223–246.

Savarese, E. (2012). *La nozione di giurisdizione nel sistema ICSID*, Naples: Editoriale Scientifica.

Schaufelberger, P. (1993). *La protection juridique des investissements internationaux dans les pays en développement: Étude de la garantie contre les risques de l'investissement et en particulier de l'Agence multilatérale de garantie des investissements*, Zurich: Schulthess Polygraphischer.

Schill, S. W. (2012). Deference in Investment Treaty Arbitration: Re-conceptualizing the Standard of Review. *Journal of International Dispute Settlement*, 3(2), 577–607.

Schill, S. W. (2016a). Can Asia Transform International Investment Law?, www.easta siaforum.org

Schill, S. W. (2016b). Changing Geography: Prospects for Asian Actors as Global Rule-Makers in International Investment Law. *Columbia FDI Perspectives n. 177*, https://academiccommons.columbia.edu/catalog/ac:201617

Schreuer, C. (2008). Preliminary Rulings in Investment Arbitration. In K. P. Sauvant, ed., *Appeals Mechanisms in International Investment Disputes*, Oxford: Oxford University Press, pp. 207–12.

Schreuer, C. and Kriebaum, U. (2011). From Individual to Community Interest in International Investment Law. In Fastenrath, U. et al., eds., *From Bilateralism to Community Interest: Essays in Honour of Judge Bruno Simma*, Oxford: Oxford University Press, pp. 1079–1096.

Shan, W. and Gallagher, N. (2009). *Chinese Investment Treaties*, Oxford: Oxford University Press.

Smith, C. (2013). The Appeal of ICSID Awards: How the AMINZ Appellate Mechanism Can Guide Reform of ICSID Procedure. *Georgia Journal of International and Comparative Law*, 41(2), 567–593.

Strozzi, G. (1992). I "Principi" dell'ordinamento internazionale. *La comunità internazionale*, 47(1), 162–179.

Strupp, K. (1925). Rechts- und Justizverweigerung, Rechtsverzögerung. In J. Hatschek and K. Strupp, eds., *Wörterbuch des Völkerrechts und der Diplomatie, Vol. II.*, Berlin: De Gruyter, pp. 340–341.

Tanzi, A. (2012). On Balancing Foreign Investment Interests with Public Interests in Recent Arbitration Case Law in the Public Utilities Sector. *The Law and Practice of International Courts and Tribunals*, 11(1), 47–76.

Tudor, I. (2008). *The Fair and Equitable Treatment Standard in the International Law of Foreign Investment*, Oxford: Oxford University Press.

Wongkaew, T. (2014). A Resilient Boat Sailing in Stormy Seas: ASEAN Investment Agreements and the Current Investor-State Dispute Settlement Regime. *Transnational Dispute Management*, 11(1), 1–36.

Zarra, G. (2017a). Orderliness and Coherence in International Investment Law: An Analysis Through the Lens of State of Necessity. *Journal of International Arbitration*, 34(4), 653–678.

Zarra, G. (2017b). *Parallel Proceedings in Investment Arbitration*, The Hague: Eleven International Publishing – Turin: G. Giappichelli Editore.

Zarra, G. (2018). The New Investor-State Dispute Settlement Mechanisms Proposed by the EU and the Geneva Centre for International Dispute Settlement. A Step forward or a Hasty Reform? *Studi sull'integrazione europea*, 13(2), 389–412.

10 The role of non-disputing contracting party's expression of intention in investment arbitration

Observations on the PRC letters in the Saga of *Sanum v. Laos*

Tianshu Zhang

1. Introduction

Sanum Investments Limited ('Sanum') is a company incorporated in Macao Special Administrative Region ('Macao' or 'Macao SAR') of People's Republic of China ('PRC' or 'China') in 2005. It has invested in the gaming and hospitality industry in Lao People's Democratic Republic ('Laos') since 2007. Due to the allegedly unfair and discriminatory taxes imposed by the government of Laos, Sanum lodged a UNCITRAL arbitration proceeding under the Agreement Between the Government of the People's Republic of China and the Government of the Lao People's Democratic Republic Concerning the Encouragement and Reciprocal Protection of Investments (the 'China/PRC-Laos BIT' or the 'Treaty') on 14 August 2012. Singapore was the place of arbitration.

On 13 December 2013, the Tribunal rendered the Award on Jurisdiction (the '2013 Award'), finding that, among other things, the PRC-Laos BIT applied to Macao. Shortly after, the Laotian Ministry of Foreign Affairs (the 'Laos MFA') sent a letter to the PRC Embassy in Vientiane (the '2014 Laos Letter'), stating Laos' view that the treaty did not apply to Macao and seeking the view of China on the same. The PRC Embassy replied and agreed that the Treaty did not extend to Macao unless both states make separate arrangements in the future (the '2014 PRC Letter').

Immediately, Laos commenced the challenge proceedings before the High Court of Singapore (the 'HC') and later applied for the two 2014 Letters being admitted into evidence. On 25 January 2015, the HC rendered a judgment (the '2015 Judgment'), granting the Laos's application and vacating the 2013 Award. Unsurprisingly, Sanum appealed the judgment.

In November 2015, the Laos MFA sent another letter to the PRC Embassy in Vientiane (the '2015 Laos Letter'), requesting the Chinese Ministry of Foreign Affairs (the 'MFA of China' or the 'PRC MFA') to confirm the authenticity of the 2014 PRC Letter. The MFA of China later responded by letter that the 2014 PRC Letter was issued under its authorization (the '2015 PRC Letter').

On 30 September 2016, the CA reversed the 2015 Judgment, upholding the 2013 Award. This dramatic outcome drove *Sanum v. Laos* back to where the Tribunal used to stand.

The factual situation as of today, however, is different from that at the time when the Tribunal reached its conclusion in 2013: China has made several statements through different channels, declaring that, in line with the 'one country, two systems' policy and the Basic Law in Macao SAR, Chinese bilateral investment treaties (the 'BITs') in principle do not automatically apply to Macao SAR, unless the Chinese central government decides so after consulting with the government of Macao SAR. This position was reflected in the letter issued by the 2014 PRC Letter and the 2015 PRC Letter (collectively, the 'PRC Letters'), which fell within the period of the set-aside proceedings initiated by Laos in Singapore. One way or another, the PRC Letters have been taken into account in the deliberation of the judges of Singaporean courts.

The sharply divergent results of the CA and HC reflect their different approaches to weigh the value of PRC Letters. Such difference also insinuates the contrasting views towards the role of the expression of opinions by a Non-Disputing Contracting Party (the 'NDCP') during the investment arbitration.

The primary aim of this chapter is to outline the approaches of the Tribunal, the HC and CA and to evaluate the role of the expressions of opinion by China with regard to the territorial application of the PRC-Laos BIT so as to investigate how the forms and timing of an NDCP's expression of opinion could become significant variables to the outcome of an investment dispute. Therefore, it is beyond the scope of this chapter to cover other thought-provoking issues in *Sanum v. Laos*, such as the substantive debates of the moving treaty frontier rule (MTF rule), State succession and so on.

With that in mind, the chapter is composed of four sections. The first section gives a brief overview of the 2013 Award and two judicial decisions delivered by the Singaporean HC and CA respectively. The second section then goes on to closely examine the approaches the Tribunal and two Singaporean courts took on China's position of the PRC-Laos BIT's territorial application. The third section presents the observations on the forms and timing of the NDCP's expression of opinion and how these factors may affect the interpretation of the disputed treaty in investment disputes. The final section makes a brief conclusion.

2. Overview of *Sanum v. Laos* on the territorial application of the PRC-Laos BIT

During the arbitration proceeding, one of the central questions of the Tribunal's jurisdiction is whether the PRC-Laos BIT applies to Macao. In the end, different answers have been given by the Tribunal, the HC and the CA as elaborated in detail in Sections 2.1, 2.2 and 2.3, with the parties having mounted arguments surrounding Article 29 of Vienna Convention on the Law of Treaties (the 'VCLT') and Article 15 of Vienna Convention on the Succession of States in Respect of Treaties (the 'VCST'). Given the importance of these two articles, they bear repeating here:

Article 29 of the VCLT reads:

> Unless a different intention appears from the treaty or is otherwise estab-
> lished, a treaty is binding upon each party in respect of its entire territory.

Article 15 of the VCST reads:

> When part of the territory of a State, or when any territory for the interna-
> tional relations of which a State is responsible, not being part of the territory
> of that State, becomes part of the territory of another State:
>
> (a) treaties of the predecessor State cease to be in force in respect of the
>   territory to which the succession of States relates from the date of the
>   succession of States; and
> (b) treaties of the successor State are in force in respect of the territory to
>   which the succession of States relates from the date of the succession of
>   States, unless it appears from the treaty or is otherwise established that
>   the application of the treaty to that territory would be incompatible
>   with the object and purpose of the treaty or would radically change the
>   conditions for its operation.

2.1. *The 2013 Award*

To determine the question of whether the Treaty should apply to Macao, the Tribunal applied the rules of treaty interpretation under international law (Award,
2013: 58) as well as customary international law on State succession (Award,
2013: 62).

The Tribunal's analysis began by finding Laos's heavy reliance on the 1999
Notification filed by the PRC to the UN Secretary-General (the '1999 Notification') irrelevant to the present case because, in its view, the 1999 Notification
concerned multilateral treaties instead of bilateral treaties (Award, 2013: 60).

Then, the Tribunal turned to assess the applicable rules in the present case, i.e.
Article 29 of the VCLT and Article 15 of the VCST as well as their exceptions
therewith (Award, 2013: 62–65).

Before delving into the concrete situation of the PRC-Laos BIT, the Tribunal
remarked that it had difficulty with ascertaining the application of the Treaty
because there were no affidavits or negotiation materials from China, Laos or
the Macao SAR. Although the Tribunal conjectured that such affidavit could
have been obtained from the respective authorities, Sanum and Laos did not
track down any evidence in the record regarding any negotiation materials of
the Treaty in any form from the Chinese side. As a result, the Tribunal was left
with no actual information on the status of the Treaty on territorial application
(Award, 2013: 65–66).

Since the central question was whether the application of the Treaty fell within
the general rule or the exceptions of Article 15 of the VCST and Article 29 of the
VCLT, the Tribunal underscored that the different consequences would follow

in applying the different rules: if the general rule applies, the Treaty will apply to Macao since the moment of China resuming the sovereignty over Macao; if the exceptions apply, the Treaty will not be applicable to Macao (Award, 2013: 66).

To answer this question, the Tribunal adopted a 'negative approach'. It first verified if any of the exceptions under Article 15 of VCST or Article 29 of VCLT applied. If it does not apply, the Tribunal went on to examine whether the general rules should automatically apply (Award, 2013: 66). Remarkably, the Tribunal accentuated that it did not intend not to contradict the PRC's position when applying the rules of State succession (Award, 2013: 66).

Eventually, the Tribunal concluded that no exceptions were established for four reasons: (1) the application of the Treaty to Macao was not incompatible with its objective and purpose (Award, 2013: 66–67); (2) such application would not radically change the conditions for its operation since it would not jeopardise the capitalist system and the liberal way of life there (Award, 2013: 67–73); (3) the Treaty itself was silent on whether it supports the extension or not and therefore no definite conclusion can be drawn from the treaty language (Award, 2013: 73–75); and (4) it is not otherwise established the PRC-Laos BIT was inapplicable to the entire territory of China (Award, 2013: 75–79). As such, the Tribunal found that the PRC-Laos BIT did extend to Macao (Award, 2013: 97).

2.2. The 2015 Judgment

Following the 2013 Award, Laos referred the jurisdictional issue to the HC of Singapore, the place of arbitration, under Section 10 of the International Arbitration Act (the 'IAA') of Singapore (IAA, 2002: Art. 10) in January 2014. At the same time, Laos applied for the admission of two diplomatic letters exchanged between Laos and China in 2014.

The first letter is the 2014 Laos Letter, which was sent from the MFA of Laos to the PRC Embassy in Vientiane on 7 January 2014. It stated that Laos believed the PRC-Laos BIT does not apply to Macao and seeks for the view of China (Judgment, 2015: 5). The second letter, i.e. the 2014 PRC Letter, was the response from the PRC Embassy in Vientiane. It concurred with Lao's position that the Treaty did not apply to Macao 'unless both China and Laos make separate arrangements in the future' (Judgment, 2015: 5).

The HC admitted the 2014 Letters as evidence, subject to Sanum's right to objection to the admissibility of the evidence at the hearing (Judgment, 2015: 5).

As one preliminary issue of jurisdiction, the HC addressed why Laos was entitled to rely on the IAA to seek a review of the Tribunal's positive ruling on jurisdiction (Judgment, 2015: 8). In the view of the HC, this issue concerned Lao's right to challenge the Tribunal's jurisdiction, which related to the interpretation of the PRC-Laos BIT (Judgment, 2015: 10). While the HC recognised the eminence of the Tribunal members, it rejected the alternative argument of Sanum that the standard of review was limited due to the deference and respect for the Tribunal and applied the *de novo* standard of judicial review in Laos' application (Judgment, 2015: 10–11).

2.2.1. *Admissibility of the 2014 Letters*

Sanum contended that Laos did not satisfy any of the conditions set out in *Ladd v. Marshall* under Singaporean law. In particular, Sanum contended that Laos could have but did not obtain the 2014 Letters with reasonable diligence and that there was no evidence of any communication between Laos and China even though Laos claimed that it was reaching out to the PRC government in April 2013 during the arbitration proceeding (Judgment, 2015: 14–15). Additionally, Sanum challenged the authenticity and credibility of the 2014 PRC Letter for lacking to the author's department or designation and for the PRC national emblem affixed to the translation (Judgment, 2015: 15).

In determining whether further evidence should be accepted, the HC referred to *Ladd v. Marshall* and *Lassiter Ann Masters* that set out the conditions for admitting fresh evidence (Judgment, 2015: 15–16):

(1) the party seeking to admit the evidence demonstrates sufficiently strong reasons why the evidence was not adduced at the arbitration hearing;

(2) the evidence if admitted would probably have an important influence on the result of the case though it need not be decisive; and

(3) the evidence must be apparently credible though it need not be incontrovertible.

The HC opined that the 2014 Letters satisfied all three conditions. For the first condition, the HC reviewed all circumstances leading up to the 2014 Letters and accepted Laos' explanation that diplomatic communications and discussion between two States needed times and efforts. The HC noted that no evidence suggested that the 2014 Letter would have been obtained earlier even if Laos had tried to obtain them earlier (Judgment, 2015: 18). For the second requirement, the HC found no difficulty to decide that the 2014 Letters would probably have an important influence on the result of the case, because they indicated the intention of the Contracting Parties of drafting the Treaty, especially for the central question of whether the Treaty applies to Macao. In this regard, the 2014 Letters were relevant to whether the exceptions to Article 29 of VCLT and Article 15 of VCST were established and hence whether the PRC-Laos BIT applies to Macao (Judgment, 2015: 18–19). On the last requirement regarding the credibility, the HC took a view that no evidence to support Sanum's contention that no consultation with any PRC governmental authority was undertaken (Judgment, 2015: 19). Specifically, the HC did not accept the assertion from Sanum's counsel about China's diplomatic practice was not supported by any factual or expert evidence (Judgment, 2015: 19–20). More importantly, the HC received an affidavit from Laos' Vice-Minister for Foreign Affairs attesting to the authenticity of the 2014 Letters and found no reason to doubt the authenticity or veracity of this testimony (Judgment, 2015: 20).Accordingly, the HC decided to admit the 2014 Letters as evidence.

2.2.2. The HC's approach to the MTF rule

Contrary to the Tribunal's 'negative approach', the HC first presumed the Treaty was *prima facie* applicable to the entire territories of the Contracting Parties, which include Macao. Next, it assessed the two exceptions to the MTF rule, i.e. whether the Treaty appears, or the Contracting Parties had intended otherwise (Judgment, 2015: 21–22).

With this different approach, the HC succinctly stated that the parties did not dispute the general rule of the MTF rule applied and contemplated that the first exception was difficult to prove because the Treaty itself was silent on whether it applies to Macao (Judgment, 2015: 22). As a consequence, the HC agreed with the Tribunal that 'no definite conclusion' could be drawn from the silence in the Treaty (Judgment, 2015: 22). Attempting to establish the first exception, Laos argued that the 2014 Letters constituted a subsequent agreement within the meaning of Article 31(3)(a) of the VCLT. However, the HC characterised this submission as an argument for the second exception, i.e. the Contracting Parties to the Treaty *intended* otherwise (Judgment, 2015: 22–23).

To ascertain whether the common intention of the Treaty's Contracting Parties indicates otherwise, in addition to the opinions of the parties' experts as well as relevant scholarly works, the HC determined to examine several documents in a sequential manner (Judgment, 2015: 23):

1   the 2014 Letters;
2   other BITs to which PRC or Macao SAR is a contracting party;
3   the 1987 PRC-Portugal Joint Declaration;
4   the 1999 Notification;
5   the analogy to be drawn with Hong Kong; and
6   the World Trade Organisation Trade Policy Report.

It went without saying that the HC devoted great lengths to address the objections from Sanum and analyse the nature of the 2014 Letters and the effect thereof.

Again, the HC emphasised that the 2014 Letters came up after the 2013 Award and recalled that the Tribunal's finding on the Treaty's territorial application was made in the absence of such express indication of the Contracting Parties' intention (Judgment, 2015: 24).

Notably, Sanum put forward the 'critical date' argument that the two Letters and whatever intention shown therein were irrelevant because they were produced after the commencement of the arbitration proceeding on 14 August 2012 (the 'Critical Date'). Sanum submitted that the intention that matters should be that formed at the time when PRC resumed the sovereignty over Macao (Judgment, 2015: 24). The HC held this contention failed to take into account the possibility of subsequent agreement (Judgment, 2015: 24–25).

Sanum also disputed Laos' characterisation of the 2014 Letters as 'subsequent agreement' in terms of the VCLT. It contended that the 2014 PRC Letter was at best an interpretive statement of Article 138 of Macao Basic Law (domestic law) and hence extraneous to the interpretation of the PRC-Laos BIT under international law (Judgment, 2015: 25–26). The HC opined this argument meritless on the ground that Sanum conflated the subsequent agreement reached between the Contracting Parties with the reason supporting such agreement (Judgment, 2015: 26): the 2014 Letters did not even mention Article 138 of Macao Basic Law, and the reference to Macao Basic Law in the 2014 Laos Letter served as one of the reasons (Judgment, 2015: 26).

Further, Sanum submitted that fairness and due process prevented the HC from considering the 2014 Letters. It argued that if the HC concluded that the Treaty does not apply to Macao based on the 2014 Letters, such finding would deprive the investor of Macao of investment protection under a significant number of PRC-related BITs (Judgment, 2015: 26). The HC, however, was not of the opinion that it would be unfair or lacking due process to take into account a subsequent agreement in terms of Article 31(3)(a) of the VCLT, since it believed that the PRC government would have been fully aware of the implications of their opinion stated in the 2014 PRC Letter (Judgment, 2015: 27). Adopting this 'categorical approach', the HC concluded that the general wording of the 2014 PRC Letter represented a position of confirming the status quo rather than a 'dramatic upheaval' of the current expectations held by States entering treaties with China. In this regard, the HC further noted that the 2014 Letters did not retroactively alter the position and expectation of third parties such as an investor like Sanum. As such, the HC found the 2014 Letters strongly supported Laos' proposition that the Treaty does not apply to Macao (Judgment, 2015: 27).

For other evidence that has been considered by the Tribunal as listed earlier, the HC's view can be summarized in two categories: (1) evidence suggesting, to a limited extent, that the PRC-Laos BIT does not apply to Macao: the other BITs (the PRC-Portugal BIT, the PRC-Netherland BIT, the Macao-Portugal BIT and the Macao-Netherlands BIT) (Judgment, 2015: 31), the analogy to be drawn with Hong Kong, i.e. the 1984 PRC-HK Joint Declaration (Judgment, 2015: 37), and the 2001 WTO Trade Policy Report (Judgment, 2015: 39); and (2) evidence of no relevance and to which no weight should be given: the 1999 Notification (Judgment, 2015: 24).

Having weighed all evidence, the HC held that Laos has established the second exception 'on a balance of probabilities'. Accordingly, it found that the PRC-Laos BIT does not apply to Macao. It recalled that the Tribunal's application of the default MTF rule as stipulated in Article 29 of the VCLT and Article 15 of VCST was based on contemporaneous evidence at a time when the 2014 Letters had not been adduced. The situation faced with the HC is thus distinguished from that with the Tribunal since the 2014 Letters were produced after the 2013 Award issued. Reading the 2014 Letters together with the 2001 WTO report which, in the HC's opinion, indicated clearer intention of China, the HC concluded that the PRC-Laos BIT does not apply to Macao (Judgment, 2015: 39).

2.3. The 2016 Judgment

Unsatisfied with the HC's finding on the jurisdiction of the Tribunal, it should come as no surprise that Sanum appealed against the HC's decision by way of a Notice of Appeal dated 20 July 2015 (Judgment, 2016: 5). Sanum submitted three propositions: (1) the HC should have accorded deference to the Tribunal's finding on interpreting a treaty to which Singapore was not a party and on the application of public international law (Judgment, 2016: 9); (2) the HC erred in finding the PRC-Laos BIT inapplicable to Macao because the default rule of Article 29 of the VCLT and Article 15 of VCST was not replaced by Laos' evidence whatsoever (Judgment, 2016: 9–10); and (3) the HC also erred in admitting the 2014 Letters under the applicable evidentiary rules (Judgment, 2016: 10). Laos rejected each of the submissions (Judgment, 2016: 10).

The CA summarised two issues to be dealt with: first, whether the 2015 Letters should be admitted into evidence; and second, whether the HC correctly found that the Tribunal did not have jurisdiction to hear the claims brought by Sanum under the PRC-Laos BIT (Judgment, 2016: 11).

2.3.1. Admissibility of the 2015 Letters

Before the appeal hearing, Laos sought for admission of another two diplomatic letters: the 2015 Laos Letter from the MFA of Laos to the PRC Embassy in Vientiane dated 18 November 2015, requesting the MFA of China to confirm the authenticity of the 2014 PRC Letter; and the 2015 PRC Letter which confirmed that the 2014 PRC Letter had been sent under its authorisation (collectively the '2015 Letters') (Judgment, 2016: 5).

Since the parties did not dispute about the rules of admitting new evidence set out in *Ladd v. Marshall* (Judgment, 2016: 12), the strongest objection that Sanum advanced against the admission of the 2015 Letters was the first condition in *Ladd Marshall* (Judgment, 2016: 12), i.e. the party seeking to admit the evidence demonstrates sufficiently strong reasons why the evidence was not adduced at the arbitration hearing. It followed Sanum's further challenge of the authenticity of the 2014 Letters because after the HC's judgment Laos sought confirmation of the authenticity of the 2014 PRC Letter from the MFA of China (Judgment, 2016: 12).

In response, Laos identified five reasons: (1) the 2015 Letters did not exist at the time of the hearing at the HC and thus could not be produced (Judgment, 2016: 12); (2) China, as the NDCP of this case, was not obliged to respond to Laos' request for confirmation of the authenticity of the 2014 PRC Letter (Judgment, 2016: 13); (3) Laos has provided an affidavit of its MFA Vice-minister who had personally involved in the diplomatic process that generated the 2014 Letters and who confirmed that the 2014 PRC Letter represented the official position of China (Judgment, 2016: 13); (4) Sanum did not rebut the affidavit above and merely objected to it during the HC hearing (Judgment, 2016: 13); and (5) China only showed its willingness to provide the 2015 PRC

Letter after Sanum was granted the leave to appeal the HC's judgment (Judgment, 2016: 13).

The CA found the first two points were determinative. First, the CA considered that the documents that had not come to exist before the hearing could not be produced at that stage and consequently this point should not be held against the party seeking to adduce the evidence (Judgment, 2016: 13). Second, the HC underscored that the real issue was whether such documents could have been brought into existence earlier in a rare circumstance here where the evidence sought to be admitted originated from an NDCP that had no legal obligation to provide such documents; it concluded that in such circumstance the court would be inclined to admit such new evidence (Judgment, 2016: 13–14).

Turing to the factual assessment, the CA acknowledged that Laos depended on the PRC MFA's willingness to respond to its request for confirmation of the authenticity of the 2014 PRC Letter. Sanum argued that the interval between the 2015 Letters was relatively short, which suggested that if Laos had requested earlier, it would have received the response earlier. The CA, however, considered that this argument fell short of considering the likelihood of informal discussion and consultation between Laos and China before issuing a formal request, which would explain the time span between the 2015 Letters. It also noted the type and content of the 2015 PRC Letter, i.e. 'an official statement' by China on the application of an international investment treaty, possibly required formal diplomatic consultation and communication that justified the substantial amount of time spent (Judgment, 2016: 14). As regards Sanum's emphasis on the timing of Laos approaching the PRC MFA, the CA considered it immaterial (Judgment, 2016: 15). Accordingly, the CA held that the first condition of *Ladd v. Marshall* test was satisfied.

Given the 2015 Letters substantiated the authenticity of the 2014 Letter and their nature as formal diplomatic correspondence between States, the CA had no difficulty in finding the second and third *Ladd v. Marshall* condition fulfilled. As such, the CA allowed Laos' application and admitted the 2015 Letters into evidence (Judgment, 2016: 15).

2.3.2. *The CA's approach to the MTF rule*

To start with, the CA confined its assessment to a relatively narrow scope, i.e. what the Contracting Parties to the PRC-Laos BIT have done to establish whether this particular treaty applies to Macao. In so doing, it decided not to contemplate what other parties may have done in relation to other treaties or what the PRC and Laos may have done with respect to other treaties concluded between them (Judgment, 2016: 19).

In terms of the MTF rule, the CA opined that it was a presumptive rule that may be displaced by proof of exceptions (Judgment, 2016: 21). In other words, the CA presumed that the PRC-Laos BIT automatically applies to Macao upon recovery of sovereignty by China on 22 December 1999, unless any of the exceptions to Article 15 of the VCST and Article 29 of the VCLT could be established

(Judgment, 2016: 21–22). As noted by the CA, the experts in this case agreed to this approach (Judgment, 2016: 22).

The CA characterised the exceptions to the MTF rule under Article 15 of the VCST and Article 29 of the VCLT into three groups: (1) the Treaty appears or it is otherwise established that the application of the Treaty would be incompatible with the objective and purpose of the BIT; (2) the Treaty appears or it is otherwise established that the application of the Treaty would radically change the conditions of its operation; and (3) an intention appears from the Treaty or is otherwise established that the Treaty does not apply to the entire territory of China (Judgment, 2016: 22).

The CA aligned with the Tribunal's finding that the first two exceptions did not apply to the present case. On the one hand, the CA contemplated that the expanding application of the Treaty would enlarge the scope of protection of foreign investors and further economic cooperation over a larger territory, which, as a result, would not be incompatible with the object and purpose of the PRC-Laos BIT (Judgment, 2016: 22–23). On the other hand, the extension as such would not radically alter the conditions for its operation (Judgment, 2016: 23). As such, the CA believed the only available exception for Laos to prove was the third. That being said, Laos must prove that either the Treaty 'appears' an intention that it was not designed to apply to Macao, or the evidence must 'otherwise establish' that the Treaty was not intended to apply to Macao (Judgment, 2016: 23).

For what the Treaty appears, as a first step, the CA's approach was to focus solely on the text of the Treaty as well as its context, objective and purpose, without taking the 2014 Letters into account. In the CA's view, the evidence like the 2014 Letters should be examined separately when assessing whether it was otherwise established that the Treaty was not intended to apply to Macao (Judgment, 2016: 24). Applying this approach, the CA easily concluded that nothing in the text, objective and purpose, or in the circumstance of concluding the Treaty suggested the Contracting Parties intended to exclude the Treaty's application to Macao (Judgment, 2016: 24). The CA then analysed the provision of the PRC-Laos BIT and underscored that the Treaty itself was silent on its territorial applicability. The language of the Treaty provisions neither expressed it applies to Macao nor excluded such application. The CA surmised that the absence of any express provisions may be attributed to the fact that the conclusion of the PRC-Laos BIT in 1993 predated China's recovery of exercising sovereignty over Macao in 1999 and, to that extent, it could not draw any definite conclusion from the Treaty provisions (Judgment, 2016: 24).

Nevertheless, the CA discovered two factual points which it believed supported the extensive application of the Treaty to Macao (Judgment, 2016: 24).

First is the chronological sequence of events. As the 1987 PRC-Portugal Joint Declaration predated the PRC-Laos BIT of 1993, the CA opined that it could not be unforeseeable for the Contracting Parties to contemplate China's future recovery of sovereignty over Macao and accordingly the extension of the territorial applicability of the PRC-related treaties to Macao (Judgment, 2016: 25). In the CA's opinion, the Contracting Parties must have been aware of the default position of the MTF rule which dictated the automatic extension of the Treaty to Macao upon China's recovery of sovereignty. As such, the CA held that the PRC-Laos BIT need not articulate any express provision saying so; the non-exclusion expression of the Treaty language pointed towards the applicability of the Treaty to Macao. Even taking one step back, the CA found the silence of the Treaty could not displace the presumptive position of the MTF rule (Judgment 2016: 25).

Second, the CA conceded that even if the Contracting Parties did not contemplate Macao's reversion to China when concluding the Treaty, they would have undertaken a review of the PRC-Laos BIT shortly after the handover in 1999. Based on this premise, the CA observed that the Contracting Parties did not include any specific provision excluding the applicability of the Treaty to Macao after the reversion. It emphasised that the ten-year validity period of the Treaty and the Contracting Parties could give the notice to terminate the Treaty one year before the expiration; in this regard, the Contracting Parties would have had sufficient time to review the applicability of the Treaty when they had to decide whether the Treaty would remain in force. However, the CA saw no evidence, e.g. the exchange of letters between the Contracting Parties, to show their intention to replace the default position of the MTF rule (Judgment, 2016: 26). Accordingly, the CA concluded that the Treaty did not appear to exclude its application to Macao (Judgement, 2016: 27).

After reaching the conclusion, the CA turned back to examine the standard of proof under international law so as to determine whether a different intention has been otherwise established under Article 29 of the VCLT (Judgement, 2016: 27). It recognised that the standard of proof under international law was simpler and less specific than those under domestic systems and that international tribunals were not bound by technical or judicial rules of evidence (Judgement, 2016: 27). On a balance consideration, the CA decided to apply 'the standard of satisfaction on a balance of probabilities' to examine whether the evidence established an intention that the Treaty was not applicable to Macao (Judgement, 2016: 27–28).

At this juncture, the CA brought in the 'Critical Date' doctrine raised by Sanum, finding it particularly relevant to the 2014 Letters. Clearly, the CA was not satisfied with either Lao's arguments or the HC's reasoning grounded on the subsequent agreement or subsequent practice under the VCLT (Judgement, 2016: 29). The Critical Date, as the CA underlined, was the date on which the dispute had been crystallised, i.e. 14 August 2012 when Sanum initiated the UNCITRAL arbitration proceedings. In the CA's view, the HC seemed to confuse the Critical Date with the date on which China's recovery of exercising sovereignty over Macao or the date of concluding the Treaty (Judgement, 2016: 30). To that extent, the CA clarified that Sanum's objection only targeted at the evidence that had been produced after the Critical Date (Judgement, 2016: 31). Notwithstanding this, the CA stated that it did not mean that any evidence after the Critical Date would be automatically inadmissible but special care would have to be taken in assessing the weight or relevance of such evidence (Judgement, 2016: 31).

By chronological order, the CA categorised the evidence which the HC took into account into three groups (Judgment, 2016: 31): (1) the pre-handover evidence, i.e. the 1987 PRC-Portugal Joint Declaration and China's analogous practice with Hong Kong and the UK; (2) evidence emerged during the period between the handover date and the Critical Date, i.e. the 1999 Notification, the 2001 WTO Report; and (3) the post-Critical Date evidence, i.e. the 2014 Letters and the 2015 Letters.

The overall assessment of the pre-Critical Date evidence was not in support of the non-application of the Treaty to Macao (Judgment, 2016: 45). On the evidence falling within category (1), the CA disagreed with the HC's finding that the 1987 PRC-Portugal Joint Declaration required a positive act in order to extend the PRC-Laos BIT to Macao, which was absent in this case (Judgment, 2016: 32). The CA highlighted that the real question was whether China's position reflected in the 1987 Joint Declaration could and did replace the default operation of the MTF rule (Judgment, 2016: 33). According to the CA's reasoning, the answer was negative because the 1987 Joint Declaration constituted a treaty between China and Portugal which could not override the presumptive effect of the MTF rule having a customary nature (Judgment, 2016: 33). For the PRC's practice dealing with the UK regarding Hong Kong, the CA held a similar view that the PRC's internal constitutional arrangement in relation to extending the PRC-signed treaties to Hong Kong or Macao could not unilaterally replace the customary MTF rule (Judgment, 2016: 37–41). Therefore, the CA concluded that there was no sufficient evidence in the pre-handover date to 'otherwise establish' the Contracting Parties' intention to exclude the Treaty's application to Macao (Judgment, 2016: 42). For the category (2) evidence, the CA agreed with the HC's finding on the 1999 Notification which was irrelevant to the applicability of the bilateral treaty at the present case (Judgment, 2016: 43). With respect to the 2001 WTO Report, the CA did not accept that it had any bearing on supporting Laos' contention (Judgment, 2016: 43–45). Similarly, the CA did not find the evidence in the period between the handover date and the Critical Date relevant, persuasive or sufficient to 'otherwise establish' that the Treaty was not intended to apply to Macao (Judgment, 2016: 45).

Lastly, the CA approached the 2014 Letters which not only came into being after the Critical Date but even after the 2013 Award. Contrary to the HC's finding, the CA found that the 2014 Letters could not be seen as mere confirmation to the Contracting Parties' intention when signing the Treaty (Judgment, 2016: 45). The CA accounted that although the rules of admitting new evidence, relevance and credibility, as set out in *Ladd v. Marshall*, were helpful, the principles in relation to evidence admissibility and weight under international law, such as the 'Critical Date' doctrine, should also be considered in the present case (Judgment, 2016: 46). In this regard, the CA held that this doctrine rendered the post-Critical Date evidence of little or even no weight if such evidence was self-serving and intended by the disputing party putting forward to improve its position (Judgment, 2016: 46).

Following the 'Critical Date' doctrine, Sanum argued that the 2014 Letters were irrelevant due to their post-Critical Date nature (Judgment, 2016: 46–47). The CA noted that Laos seemed to accept that the post-Critical Date evidence should not be admitted or at least be given less weight if it modified the *status quo* of the Contracting Parties to the Treaty; Laos' real contention was to adduce post-Critical Date evidence that confirmed the *status quo* prior to the Critical Date (Judgment, 2016: 48).

For the CA, the difficulty was that the existing pre-Critical Date evidence was not sufficient to establish a clear position (Judgment, 2016: 48–49). Since the exception to the 'Critical Date' doctrine was when the evidence merely confirms what has been established by the pre-Critical Date evidence, the CA determined to attach greater weight to the 2014 Letters if the content of which demonstrated evidentiary continuity and consistency with pre-Critical Date evidence (Judgment, 2016: 49).

First, the CA reiterated that it did not consider the 2014 Letters confirming the pre-Critical Date *status quo* of the Contracting Parties because, in its opinion, they reflected a position contradictory to the pre-existing position governed by the presumptive position of the MTF rule. To be specific, the CA deemed that Laos failed to use the pre-Critical Date evidence to otherwise establish the MTF default rule had been displaced and consequently the post-Critical Date evidence put forward by Laos would contradict the position prevailing at the time when the arbitration (Judgment, 2016: 50). As such, the CA held that the 2014 Letters bore no weight (Judgment, 2016: 51).

For the sake of completeness, the CA went on to presume that even if the 2014 Letters were admissible, they could not bear any material weight for several reasons: (1) the 2014 PRC Letter was grounded on PRC domestic law and thus was irrelevant and inadmissible as a consideration in international law under Article 27 of VCLT (Judgment, 2016: 51); (2) Laos could not rely on the operation of the PRC's domestic law to justify its position of not being bound to arbitrate Sanum's claim (Judgment, 2016: 51); and (3) the 2014 Letters could not qualify as a 'subsequent agreement' or 'subsequent practice' under Article 31(3) of VCLT, because nothing in the 2014 Letters showed any pre-Critical Date accord between the Contracting Parties for the Treaty not to apply to Macao. Thus, the CA considered it impermissible to give any effect to the 2014 Letters so that they would have retroactive effects on amending the Treaty (Judgment, 2016: 51–54).

In this sense, the CA found the HC erred in placing any evidentiary weight on the 2014 Letters and accordingly ruled that no sufficient evidence to otherwise establish the Contracting Parties' intention to exclude the Treaty's applicability to Macao at the time of conclusion (Judgment, 2016: 51–54). Nor did the CA find the 2015 Letters had any bearing as it had not even touched upon the authenticity of the 2014 Letters (Judgment, 2016: 56). In conclusion, the CA reversed the HC's judgment on the Treaty's applicability, found that it indeed extends to Macao and restored the Tribunal's award on this point (Judgment, 2016: 57).

2.4. PRC's expression of opinion after the 2016 Judgment

In a regular press conference on 21 October 2016, Ms. Hua Chunying, spokesperson of the PRC MFA, mentioned the CA's judgment on the PRC-Laos BIT's application to Macao (Hua Chunying, 2016). She stated that the CA's judgment had been noted but the territorial scope of application of the PRC-Laos BIT was a question of fact concerning acts of State, which was 'up to the contracting parties to decide' (Hua Chunying, 2016). She underlined that China had confirmed twice in diplomatic notes that the PRC-Laos BIT did not apply to Macao and stressed that the CA's ruling on this 'question of fact' was incorrect (Hua Chunying, 2016). She also commented in general that China's treaty practice has been guided by 'one country, two systems' policy and the Basic Laws in Hong Kong and Macao; specifically, the Chinese central government made the final decisions on 'whether the international treaties to which the PRC is or becomes a party apply to the SARs based on the circumstances and their needs after seeking the views of the governments of the SARs' (Hua Chunying, 2016).

On the following day, Mr. Xu Hong, Director of the Treaty and Law Department of the PRC MFA, published a comment to clarify China's treaty practice in relation to the applicability to Hong Kong and Macao (Xu Hong, 2016). In this note, Mr. Xu reaffirmed that China's recovery of exercising sovereignty over Hong Kong and Macao does not concern the change of territory, thus irrelevant to State succession nor treaty succession (Xu Hong, 2016). As he explained, the bilateral treaties concluded by the central government in the fields other than defence and foreign affairs, in principle, are not applicable to Hong Kong and Macao, unless it decided otherwise after consulting with the SAR governments, while, in practice, the central government would not expressly indicate that the bilateral treaties in this kind are non-applicable to Hong Kong and Macao, and the contracting parties share the same understanding (Xu Hong, 2016). However, he noted, during the negotiation process, if any counterparty did not have a clear understanding regarding the non-application practice, China would clarify the relevant provisions of the Basic Laws and previous Chinese treaty practice and the counterparty would understand and agreed to the non-application. In exceptional circumstances, upon the request of the counterparty, China would agree to reaffirm in writing its consistent position of the non-application of the treaty to Hong Kong and Macao. Besides, the said practice does not exclude the possibility that, if necessary, the central government would consult with the SAR government and reach the agreement with the counterparty so as to enable the relevant bilateral treaty to apply to Hong Kong or Macao. Only in this circumstance, the contracting parties should expressly state the special arrangement for such application. However, Mr. Xu added, no precedent has ever taken place so far (Xu Hong, 2016).

On 7 July 2017, Mr. Xu delivered a speech in Hong Kong, addressing China's treaty practice relating to Hong Kong (Xu Hong, 2017). He mentioned that China's treaty practice breaks through the rules of territorial application in the traditional law of treaties in a way that the bilateral treaties concluded by the PRC central government do not apply to Hong Kong in principle, unless after consultation with the government of Hong Kong SAR and being accepted by the other contracting party (Xu Hong, 2017). Again, Mr. Xu restated that except for certain extremely rare circumstance, China-related treaties would not expressly provide that a treaty does not apply to SARs, and all the counterparties understand and accept such practice. While acknowledging that such practice is different from traditional international law as reflected in Article 29 of the VCLT, Mr. Xu indicated that China's practice has become a new practice could be seen as 'otherwise established' as provided for in Article 29 of the VCLT. Interestingly, Mr. Xu specifically pointed to CA's judgment, taking it as an example of foreign judicial organs' lack of understanding of China's treaty practice (Xu Hong, 2017).

3. The role of the PRC letters as the NDCP's expression of intention: two-step assessment

What role has the PRC Letters played in *Sanum v. Laos*? The answers vary depending on the perspectives from and the approaches taken by the Tribunal and the Singaporean courts. Lacking evidence indicating the Contracting Parties' intention, the Tribunal found that the general rule of MTF rule applied since no exceptions were established. However, with the PRC Letters at hand, the HC and the CA differed in how to weigh in these Letters in ascertaining whether the general rule or exceptions of MTF shall be applied.

Nevertheless, the two judgments are comparable even though the CA was provided with the 2015 PRC Letter which did not exist in the HC's proceeding since the HC and the CA relied on the similar rules to admit the PRC Letters but reached an entirely different conclusion. Their disagreement is rooted in the approaches to applying the evidentiary rules and the law of treaties.

The Singaporean courts took a two-step approach in examining the PRC Letters. First, the PRC Letters must pass the procedural threshold to be admitted in the proceedings. The admission of the new evidence like the PRC Letters hinges on the evidentiary rules adopted by the courts. It follows the questions regarding different standards of admitting evidence, especially new evidence produced after the dispute was submitted to arbitration. Theoretically, had the PRC Letters failed to meet the evidentiary threshold, no further consideration would have taken place as they were procedurally barred, regardless of their contents or potential effects. Second, if the evidentiary threshold has been satisfied, the courts will move to assess the evidential value of the PRC Letters for facilitating the decision on the Treaty's territorial application.

3.1. First step: admissibility

Since the disputing parties did not raise any objections regarding the admissibility of evidence or produce any new evidence after the commencement of the arbitration during the arbitration proceeding, the Tribunal need not address the issue of applicable evidentiary rules. Nonetheless, it placed a mark on the difficulty of determining the territorial application of the Treaty in the absence of any affidavits or negotiation materials from China, Laos or the Macao SAR (Award, 2013: 65).

The HC and the CA applied the same rules as set out in *Ladd v. Marshall* for admitting fresh evidence under national law (Judgment, 2015: 15–16; Judgment, 2016: 12), whereas they also took into account the 'Critical Date' doctrine under international law due to the nature of the arbitration at a later stage (Judgment, 2015: 24; Judgment, 2016: 29–31).

Applying the *Ladd v. Marshall* test to the PRC Letters, the HC and the CA both understood that the diplomatic communication between two States needs time and efforts (Judgment, 2015: 17–18; Judgment, 2016: 13–14), especially when the new evidence came from an NDCP which has no legal obligation to provide such documents (Judgment, 2016: 14). As such, the late application of admitting new evidence could not be an obstacle to be taken against Laos (Judgment, 2016: 13). The satisfaction of the second and third conditions of *Ladd v. Marshall* is self-explanatory: the PRC Letters, as an unequivocal expression of PRC's intention, would significantly impact the result of the case; the credibility of the 2014 PRC Letter issued by the Chinese Embassy in Vientiane (Judgment, 2015: 5) was reinforced by the 2015 PRC Letter from the MFA of China (Judgment, 2016: 5) and the affidavit from the Vice-Minister for Foreign Affairs of Laos which the CA found no reason to doubt the authenticity or veracity of this testimony (Judgment, 2015: 20).

3.2. Second step: evidentiary value

3.2.1. The 2013 Award

The Tribunal adopted a reverse approach when applying the MTF rule and its exceptions to the facts. It started with verifying whether any of the MTF exceptions was proven; if not, it applied the general rule (Judgment, 2015: 21–22). In line with this approach, the Tribunal primarily looked into the evidence in support of the exceptions of the MTF rule, which, in this case, meant the proposition that the Treaty was not applicable to Macao. Since this proposition went beyond what the terms of the Treaty appear, it thus called for the clarification of the Contracting Parties' intention when concluding the Treaty, especially the intention of the NDCP. Having noted that neither Laos nor China had produced any documents evidencing the Contracting Parties' common intention regarding the territorial application of the Treaty, the Tribunal cautiously suggested that it wished not to contradict the PRC's position on State succession concerning the recovery of sovereignty over Macao (Award, 2013: 66).

The drawback of lacking manifestation of the Contracting Parties' common intention to the Treaty is apparent. The Tribunal had to decide with 'paucity of factual elements presented by the parties' to confirm the intention of the Contracting States when the treaty was concluded (Award, 2013: 65). Without sufficient evidence to show that the Contracting Parties' intention otherwise established to support Lao's contention of excluding Macao from the Treaty's application, the Tribunal found no exceptions to the MTF rule proven and the factual situation leads to no definite conclusion from the Treaty (Award, 2013: 75). After a comparative analysis of relevant treaty practice, the Tribunal reached a conclusion in favour of an expanding application of the Treaty to Macao (Award, 2013: 79).

Bearing in mind the caveat that came up with the Tribunal that no actual information from the Contracting Parties' common intention was acquired during the proceedings, had the 2014 Letters been produced earlier and were available to the Tribunal before or even during the arbitral proceeding, would the Tribunal reach a different conclusion?

It is safe to say that the answer may not be a firm no. The Tribunal underlined the silence of the Treaty and that it was not aware of any expression of intention by China or Laos to exclude the application (Award, 2013: 74). Following the Tribunal's reverse approach, if any document from the PRC side to show the NDCP's intention was produced and submitted in the proceedings, it is highly plausible that such evidence (if admitted) could break the silence of the Treaty, add more weight on the 'otherwise established' intention to the MTF rule, or at least offer a perspective of the NDCP regarding the application status of the Treaty. This will inevitably add variants to the decision-making process of the Tribunal.

3.2.2. *The 2015 Judgment*

In terms of the 2014 PRC Letter's evidentiary value, the HC's approach appears relatively straightforward in three folds: (1) it recollected that the Tribunal's conclusion regarding the application of the Treaty to Macao was made in the absence of the 2014 Letters; (2) it then analysed the Treaty's language and again found that no indication could be drawn from the silence in the text; and (3) it concluded that the 2014 Letters constituted a 'subsequent agreement' between the Contracting Parties to the PRC-Laos BIT, which clarified the status of non-application of the Treaty to Macao (Judgment, 2015: 25), and consequently prevail over the 'Critical Date' doctrine (Judgment, 2015: 24–25).

In addition to the 2014 PRC Letter's critical role, the HC's finding on other evidence should also be considered as paramount and vital in confirming the 'otherwise established' intention of the Contracting Parties to the MTF rule. Because the HC viewed the other evidence either, to a limited extent, in support of the Treaty's non-application to Macao (Judgment, 2015: 31, 37, 39), or of no relevance and to which no weight (Judgment, 2015: 24), the 2014 Letters, signified by the HC as 'subsequent agreement' in terms of the VCLT, seem not to contradict with the position reflected in the evidence produced prior to the Critical Date. This has become the source of the fundamental difference between the HC and the CA's findings on this issue.

3.2.3. The 2016 Judgment

The CA's approach is different. At the outset, the CA proclaimed that Article 15 of the VCST and Article 29 of the VCLT indicated a presumptive rule that may be displaced by proof of certain exceptions (Judgment, 2016: 21). On this premise, the CA presumed that the Treaty automatically extends to Macao, which means Laos must establish at least one of the exceptions to remove the 'default position' of the MTF rule (Judgment, 2016: 21).

The sharpest divergence between the approaches of the CA and the HC occurs when they considered the key question regarding whether the 2014 Letters constituted a 'subsequent agreement' and superseded the 'Critical Date' doctrine.

Although the 2014 Letters stand for the common ground of the Contracting Parties on the Treaty's territorial application, the CA held the 2014 PRC Letter contradicted the pre-existing position presented by other evidence and therefore cannot constitute a 'subsequent agreement' or 'subsequent practice' with retroactive effect under the VCLT (Judgment, 2016: 51–52). In other words, the CA used the 'Critical Date' doctrine to characterise the 2014 Letters as contradictory with the status quo shown by the pre-Critical Date evidence (Judgment, 2016: 45) and accordingly excluded the 2014 Letters in spite of admitting them in the first place (Judgment, 2016: 15).

Yet, it is impossible to ignore that this approach suffers from the illogical reasoning during the process of assessing the evidence in the context of the MTF rule and exceptions thereto in the following aspects.

First and foremost, the CA conflated the indication of the Treaty's silence on the territorial application and the so-called 'presumptive rule' or 'default position' of the MTF rule. While admitting that the Treaty itself shows no clear indication of the Contracting Parties' intention of excluding the application to Macao (Judgment, 2016: 24), which means no definite conclusion could be drawn, the CA nevertheless interpreted the absence of the intention to the contrary as the Contracting States did not exclude the Treaty's application to Macao under the default position of the MTF rule (Judgment, 2016: 25). Since the default rule denotes an automatic extension of the Treaty's territorial application, the silence of the Treaty cannot displace such default position (Judgment, 2016: 25).

The problem here, however, is that the silence of the Treaty on the territorial application cannot be seen as equivalent to a vacuum where the MTF default rule can fill in anytime. By no means can the CA's presumption of automatic extension be regarded as a mature rule establishing such expansive application of the Treaty. The silence in the Treaty calls for a further examination of other evidence conceivably reflecting the common intention of the Contracting Parties, especially when such evidence in this kind is available and admitted in the case.

Second, it is arguable that the automatic extension of a treaty to the entire territory is a 'default' position in treaty law, given that the International Law Commission (the 'ILC') stated that 'the territorial scope of a treaty depends on the intention of the parties and that it is only necessary in the present article to formulate the general rule which should apply in the absence of any specific provision or indication in the treaty as to its territorial application' when drafting the VCLT (ILC Report, 1966b: 213). According to the ILC's comment, a proper analysis of the territorial application of a treaty should embark on verifying the intention of the contracting parties, and by no means presuppose a 'default' rule to assume the automatic extension of the treaty.

Further, with respect to the application of the 'Critical Date' doctrine, the CA characterised the evidence submitted by Laos into three categories, by which the 2014 Letters and the 2015 Letters amounted to the post-Critical Date evidence (Judgment, 2016: 31). The CA decided that only 'if the content of such evidence demonstrates evidentiary continuity and consistency with pre-critical date evidence', it would place a greater evidentiary weight on them (Judgment, 2016: 48). Following this logic, the only way for the post-Critical Date evidence being deemed relevant is to confirm that it does not alter the status quo reflected by the pre-Critical Date evidence (Judgment, 2016: 48). As the CA's overall assessment on the pre-Critical Date evidence disfavouring the non-application of the Treaty to Macao (Judgment, 2016: 45), the 2014 Letters were regarded as having no material weight because they contradict the status quo (Judgment, 2016: 50–51).

The CA's analysis is defective because, as stated earlier, no presumptive rule should be taken for granted before all admitted evidence has been examined. As the CA acknowledged, neither the Treaty language nor the pre-Critical Date evidence demonstrates the Contracting Parties' intention favouring application or non-application to Macao (Judgment, 2016: 33–45). This means the so-called 'status quo' is a vacuum as a matter of fact and cannot be automatically taken over by the 'default position' of the MTF rule. As such, the 2014 PRC Letter is impossible to 'contradict' the pre-existing position because the latter remains to be vacant. And should the 2014 PRC Letter not contradict but clarify the intention of the Contracting Parties, the 'Critical Date' doctrine would not render it irrelevant or of no weight in determining the territorial application of the Treaty. In short, the CA's approach merely contemplates the scenario that the pre-Critical Date evidence shows a definite position and cannot apply to a scenario where the pre-Critical Date evidence lacks information to establish anything. As such, no post-Critical Date evidence would be considered as relevant unless it indicates vagueness similar to pre-Critical Date evidence to guarantee the 'continuity and consistency' in this case.

4. Observations on the NDCP's expression of opinion: timing, admissibility and deference

Even though the interpretation of the 2013 Award and the 2015 Judgment regarding the Treaty's application status are different, their approaches may not have been that far apart (Tams, 2016: 339). While the main reason caused the divergence between the Tribunal and the HC can be accounted to the availability of the 2014 Letters, the difference between the HC and the CA emerges from the approaches with regard to treaty interpretation and the understanding of the MTF rule and the exceptions thereto.

Also, it is not surprising to see the CA's finding on the expanding application of the Treaty to Macao attracts sharp criticism from the PRC side. The PRC government now clearly signifies its position on the territorial application of the China-related treaties with regard to Macao and Hong Kong.

For the case of *Sanum v. Laos* under the UNCITRAL proceedings at this stage, the conclusion on the Treaty's application status is settled. Looking back to the moves of China as the NDCP in this case, lessons can be learned in many ways, such as the timing and the forms to express or clarify the NDCP's intention regarding treaty interpretation, the admissibility of the NDCP's expression of intention during an investment dispute, and the deference among the Tribunal, the national courts and the contracting parties in respect to treaty interpretation.

4.1. Timing and forms

For a BIT being applied in a way not departing from the intention of the contracting parties at the time of concluding it, timing is crucial for an NDCP to react. The NDCP can do in relation to a BIT interpretation at different stages in different forms (UNCTAD, 2011: 6–12).

In treaty drafting process, the negotiators and drafters from the contracting States need to anticipate future interpretations with farsighted and precise treaty language so as to avoid the potential interpretation departing from the shared understanding of the contracting parties.

Once the treaty is concluded, the contracting parties could issue a joint interpretive statement, conclude a subsequent agreement, exchange of notes or letters to elucidate the meaning of the treaty (International Law Commission, 1966a: 161). *Sanum v. Laos* is not the only case involving the NDCP's diplomatic letter regarding treaty interpretation. For instance, in *Gruslin v. Malaysia*, Belgium sent a *note verbale* to Malaysia on 28 August 1992 regarding the meaning of the term 'approved project' under the inter-governmental agreement, Malaysia answered the inquiry in a formal manner on 28 September 1992. With regard to this exchange of notes, the sole arbitrator, Gavan Griffith QC, pointed out that the exchange of notes does not directly amend the terms of the inter-government agreement and must be regarded as an enduring and authoritative expression of the Treaty (*Gruslin v. Malaysia* Award, 2000: 503).

When the investment arbitration has been triggered, the NDCP may intervene in the proceedings, such as submitting *amicus curiae*, subject to the applicable arbitral rules and instruments, such as the US's submission on Article 1128 of NAFTA in *Eli Lilly v. Canada*.

Even after the dispute has been decided by the Tribunal, the opportunities are still open to the NDCP to respond to the findings of the award. It can scrutinise the reasoning awards, comment on the interpretation approach and make public statements in this respect. These actions may not retroactively affect the concluded adjudications but will definitely provide guidance for future cases.

4.2. Admissibility standard

In *Sanum v. Laos*, the admissibility test of fresh evidence under national law has been applied by the Singaporean courts. The 'Critical Date' doctrine under international law has also been taken into account in assessing the weight of evidence. Given the nature of investment arbitration, and particularly when the case concerns a sensitive sovereign issue like the territorial application of a treaty, the Tribunal and the national courts (if the issue falls within their purview) should adopt the admissibility standard to allow all evidence that has been put forward should be assessed in consideration of all circumstance (Tams, 2016: 334).

4.3. Deference

After the 2016 Judgment upholding the Treaty's extension to Macao, one must admit that there is not much can be done for an NDCP after the jurisdictional issue being settled, except for strong criticism and statements reaffirming its position. It is certainly not easy for the NDCP to accept the fact that a domestic court of a third party interprets a treaty to which it is not even a party, especially when such provision relates to issues that are more sensitive to sovereign States, such as China's territorial application of treaties to Hong Kong and Macao SARs.

As one major criticism of the legitimacy of investment arbitration is the interpretation and application of investment law (Waibel et al., 2010: 3), it is worth contemplating that how much deference the investment treaty tribunal or the national court that has power review the investment arbitration award should accord to the expression of intention by the NDCP. China obviously learned a lesson from the Singaporean courts' judgments, as it realised that it is paramount to take measure (e.g. official statements, public speeches, published articles or comments from government officials) to ensure the public as well as foreign judicial organs or arbitral tribunals to know China's treaty practice in relation to territorial application. More transparency in this regard can avoid further misinterpretation of China-related treaties by foreign courts or tribunals (Xu Hong, 2016).

5. Concluding remarks

In *Sanum v. Laos*, one cannot overlook the theoretical value of the approaches taken by the Tribunal and the Singaporean courts regarding treaty interpretation, as they indeed shed lights upon the applicability issue of a China-related investment treaty to Macao under China's 'one country, two system' policy, from the perspectives of the international and foreign decision-makers.

However, it is not necessary to overestimate the so-called 'precedential' value of the 2016 Judgment of the CA, as it should only be binding upon the disputing parties. The subsequent responses from China suggest that the 2016 Judgment's finding on the extension application of the PRC-Laos BIT would become an exceptional case. Therefore, for future investment disputes involved the PRC-related BITs, it would be difficult to ignore the PRC's unequivocal intention expressed in its two letters in conjunction with a series of statements. These actions form China's State practice on treaty law and clarify its position regarding the territorial application of the PRC-related BIT. As such, one can hardly imagine that the CA's approach and its finding would have much 'preferential value' in interpreting the PRC-related BITs in further cases. In the end, the power and authority of the judicial decision in respect of pronouncing and interpreting international law lies in the influence of the cogent and persuasive reasoning, not in the terms of the statute (Lauterpacht, 1982: 22).

The views articulated in this chapter are the personal views of the author and do not necessarily reflect those of the law firm with which she is associated.

References

International treaties

Vienna Convention on the Law of Treaties (Concluded 23 May 1969, Entered Into Force 27 January 1980) 1155 UNTS 331.
Vienna Convention on the Succession of States in Respect of Treaties (Concluded 23 August 1978, Entered Into Force 6 November 1996) 1946 UNTS 3.

Domestic laws

International Arbitration Act of Singapore (Chapter 143A), Singapore, Original Enactment: Act 23 of 1994, revised edition 2002, 31 December 2002

Arbitral awards and judgments of international courts and domestic courts

Eli Lilly and Company v. The Government of Canada, UNCITRAL, ICSID Case No. UNCT/14/2, NAFTA Article 1128 Submission of United States of America, 18 March 2016.
Government of the Lao People's Democratic Republic v. Sanum Investments Ltd [2015] SGHC 15.
Ladd v. Marshall [1954] 1 W.L.R. 1489 (25 November 1954).
Philippe Gruslin v. Malaysia, ICSID Case No. ARB/99/3, Award, 27 November 2000.
Sanum Investments Limited v. Lao People's Democratic Republic, PCA Case No. 2013–13, Award on Jurisdiction, 13 December 2013.
Sanum Investments Ltd v. Government of the Lao People's Democratic Republic [2016] SGCA 57.

Books and articles

Hua, Chunying (2016). *Foreign Ministry Spokesperson Hua Chunying's Regular Press Conference on October 21, 2016*, www.fmprc.gov.cn/mfa_eng/xwfw_665399/s2510_665401/t1407743.shtml

International Law Commission (1966a). *Yearbook of the International Law Commission*, 1966 Vol. I, Part II, A/CN.4/SER.A/1966, http://legal.un.org/ilc/publications/yearbooks/english/ilc_1966_v1_p2.pdf

International Law Commission (1966b). *Report of the International Law Commission on the Second Part of Its Seventeenth Session and on Its Eighteenth Session* (UN Doc. A/6309/Rev.l) in *Yearbook of the International Law Commission* 1966, vol. II. New York: UN. (A/CN.4/SER. A/1966/Add. 1)

Sir Hersch Lauterpacht (1982). *The Development of International Law by the International Court*, Cambridge: Cambridge University Press.

Tams, C. J. (2016). State Succession to Investment Treaties: Mapping the Issues. *ICSID Review*, 31, 314–343.

United Nations Conference on Trade and Development (UNCTAD) (2011). Interpretation of IIAs: What States Can Do. *IIA Issues Note*, 3, 6–12.

Waibel, M., A. Kaushal, K-H Chung, and C. Balchin. (2010). The Backlash Against Investment Arbitration: Perceptions and Reality. In M. Waibel, A. Kaushal, K-H Chung and C. Balchin, eds., *The Backlash Against Investment Arbitration*, Kluwer Law International, p. 3ff, https://ssrn.com/abstract=1733346

Waldock, Sir Humphrey (1962). Twenty-Three Draft Articles on the Conclusion, Entry into Force and Registration of Treaties Together with Commentaries, Article 1, Subparagraph 1(b). *Yearbook of International Law Commission*, Vol. II, pp. 161–162.

Xu Hong (2016). *Practice of the Application of International Treaties to Hong Kong and Macao Special Administration Regions*, http://epaper.legaldaily.com.cn/fzrb/content/20161022/Articel04004GN.htm

Xu Hong (2017). *The Implementation of the 'One Country, Two Systems' Policy and Its Contribution to the Development of International Law – From the Perspective of Application of International Agreements and Treaties to the Hong Kong Special Administrative Region*, http://mp.weixin.qq.com/s/Pq2ZKGtcIEPHQVDTOXDXiQ

Subject index

Index of cases

Index of treaties

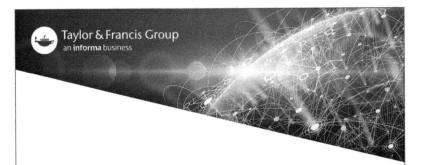

For Product Safety Concerns and Information please contact our EU
representative GPSR@taylorandfrancis.com
Taylor & Francis Verlag GmbH, Kaufingerstraße 24, 80331 München, Germany

www.ingramcontent.com/pod-product-compliance
Ingram Content Group UK Ltd.
Pitfield, Milton Keynes, MK11 3LW, UK
UKHW021004180425
457613UK00019B/807